ALSO A

THE HOWARD

The

M

The Immigrants

Bunker Hill: The Prequel to The Crossing

2nd Generation

Helmet for My Pillow
By Robert Leckie

The Way of the Gladiator
By Daniel P. Mannix

Horizon: Ancient Rome
By Robert Payne

Horizon: Ancient Greece
By William Harlan Hale

Samurai!
By Saburo Sakai with Martin Caidin
and Fred Saito

Fork-Tailed Devil: The P-38
By Martin Caidin

The B-17 The Flying Forts
By Martin Caidin

Thunderbolt
By Robert S. Johnson with Martin Caidin

When Hell Froze Over
By E.M. Halliday

The American Heritage New History of the Civil War
By Bruce Catton
Edited by James M. McPherson

The World War II Reader
By the Editors of *World War II* magazine

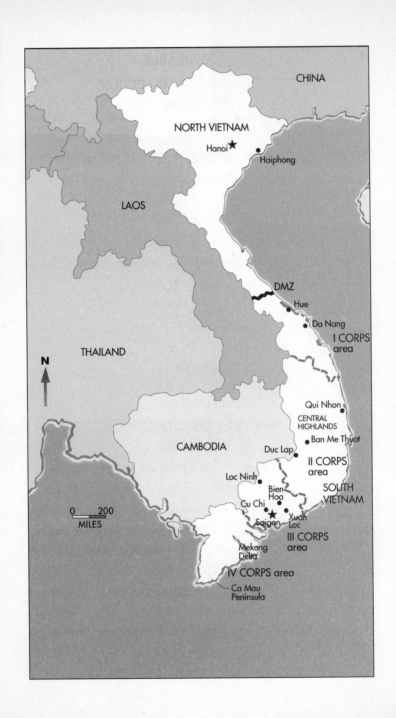

CHINA

NORTH VIETNAM

Hanoi ★ • Haiphong

LAOS

DMZ
• Hue
• Da Nang

I CORPS
area

THAILAND

N

• Qui Nhon

CENTRAL
HIGHLANDS

• Ban Me Thuot

CAMBODIA

Duc Lap •

II CORPS
area

Loc Ninh •

Bien
Hoa

Cu Chi •

★
Saigon

Xuan
Loc

III CORPS
area

Mekong
Delta

IV CORPS area

Ca Mau
Peninsula

SOUTH
VIETNAM

0   200
MILES

VIETNAM
A READER

Brigadier General David Zabecki,
U.S. Army Reserve
Editor

FROM THE PAGES OF

VIETNAM MAGAZINE

ibooks
new york
www.ibooksinc.com

DISTRIBUTED BY SIMON & SCHUSTER, INC

This book is dedicated to Vietnam *magazine's founding editor,*
Colonel Harry G. Summers, Jr.

An Original Publication of ibooks, inc.

An ibooks, inc. Book

Ibooks, inc.
24 West 25th Street
New York, NY 10010

The ibooks World Wide Web Site address is:
http://www.ibooksinc. com

Material originally appeared in *Vietnam* magazine.

To subscribe to *Vietnam* magazine or any of the other Primedia History
Group publications, call
1-800-829-3340 or 1-386-447-6318 (foreign) or visit the website
www.thehistorynet.com.

Editor: Dwight Jon Zimmerman
Cover Design: J. Vita
Map: Rick Brownlee

ISBN: 0-7434-3504-4
First ibooks printing March 2002
10 9 8 7 6 5 4 3 2 1

Share your thoughts about *Vietnam A Reader* and other ibooks titles in
the new ibooks virtual reading group at www.ibooksinc.com

Contents

CONTENTS

CONTENTS

PART FOUR FORGETTING AND REMEMBERING

Introduction

By Brigadier General David Zabecki,
U.S. Army Reserve

In many ways America's war in Vietnam was like any other of history's countless wars—a nasty and brutal business at best. On both sides young soldiers (and some not so young) died for their countries, often with only the vaguest understanding of the larger geo-political issues that put them in harm's way in the first place. As in any other war, both sides recorded countless acts of battlefield heroism and cowardice; both sides committed war crimes; and the civilians on whose home-ground the war was fought were often caught in the middle and suffered accordingly. These have been the enduring characteristics of all wars from antiquity to Bosnia.

There were, however, some unique aspects about Vietnam. For one thing, it was one of the few wars in which the side that won all the battles still lost the war. This happened because there was a total disconnect between America's battlefield tactics and its overarching war fighting strategy—or more accurately, the total absence of such strategy. While many analysts and military historians today remain divided on the efficacy of American tactics in Vietnam, there is almost universal agreement that the basic strategy was bankrupt. There was never a precise objective; never a clearly articulated end-state. Colonel Harry G. Summers, Jr., the founding editor of *Vietnam* magazine, laid this all out in his book, *On Strategy: The Vietnam War in Context,* an insightful analysis of America's strategic failure. It remains one of the most important books about Vietnam ever written.

Vietnam also was the first television war, the first "prime-time war." For the first time in history raw combat footage was beamed directly into the living rooms of Americans (and the rest of the world) within hours of the event. Television, however, proved to be a great tool for recording sensational actions, but very limited in its ability to explain those events and place them in the broader context. Thus, the Viet Cong attack on the American Embassy during the Tet Offensive became in the American public's mind a military disaster second only to the attack on Pearl Harbor, when in reality it was "a piddling little platoon action," of almost no military significance. Regardless of the real underlying issues, the distortion of the perceptions on a daily basis contributed significantly to the undermining of public support for the war. The North Vietnamese recognized this American vulnerability, and they exploited it brilliantly.

One of the longer-term effects of the Vietnam War was a sense of distrust and even hostility between the military and the media. Many journalists felt the military lied to them and tried to manipulate them. Many in the military believed the media's unfair and inaccurate reporting cost them the support of the public. It's not as simple as all that, of course, but there are indicators that the reporting was selective. My Lai and Hue are probably the best examples. My Lai today is regarded as *the* defining atrocity of the Vietnam War. And it was a war crime. There can be no question of that. Yet, while the media covered the My Lai story from every conceivable angle, they virtually ignored the massacre of more than 6,000 civilians by Communist troops at Hue during the Tet Offensive. Almost every American high school student today has heard about My Lai. How many know about Hue?

The American people too came to distrust their own military, even to the point of blaming the war on the common soldiers who fought it. That general feeling was reinforced by the bloody rescue attempt on the *Mayaguez* and the failed rescue attempt of the hostages in Teheran. The actions in Grenada and Panama and the bombing of the Marine barracks in Beirut did little to improve public opinion about the military. It was only the Gulf War that finally started to change attitudes and allowed the American military to escape the long shadow of Vietnam. But virtually all the military's senior leaders in the Gulf War, from Generals Colin Powell and Norman Schwarzkopf down to the brigade command level, were Vietnam veterans. And as this is being written, shortly after the deadly terrorist attacks of September 11, 2001, the American people have learned once again why they have a military.

The great irony about Vietnam is that even though it was the most thoroughly documented war in history to that time, it remained at the time and still remains shrouded in a cloud of misconceptions, bogus myths, and distorted facts. Although many people believe Vietnam was America's longest war, the Philippine Insurrection was at least as long, and the Indian Wars were much longer. Nor was Vietnam necessarily America's most unpopular and socially divisive war. It was the Civil War that tore apart American society like no other war in our history. And during the American Revolution roughly one third of the population supported the British, and another third didn't care one way or the other. Nor were the combat conditions really any worse or more intense in Vietnam than in most other wars. For horrible and protracted combat almost no other war can match the Western Front in World War I or the Eastern Front in World War II. One popular book published in the late 1980s actually claimed that more Americans died in Vietnam than in World War II—which of course is utter nonsense.

Perhaps the worst myths and misconceptions about Vietnam are the ones that surround the soldiers, sailors, airmen, Coast Guardsmen, and Marines who served there. Many of those myths will not go away, despite the fact that author B.G. Burkett de-bunked most of them in his widely acclaimed—and widely criticized—book, *Stolen Valor: How the Vietnam Generation was Robbed of its Heroes and its History*. Contrary to the deeply-held popular beliefs, the majority of those Americans who served in Vietnam and the majority of those on The Wall were not draftees. Nor were minorities disproportionately represented or unfairly assigned. Vietnam, however, was the first war in American history in which a significant number of minorities served in higher level combat leadership positions. As a direct result, minorities today hold a greater proportion of positions at the highest levels in the U.S. military than in almost any other segment of American society.

Perhaps the most damaging and unfair of all the Vietnam myths is the enduring one of the Vietnam veteran as a drug-addicted loser who can't keep a job or hold a marriage together. Many studies have shown that the drug addiction, suicide, joblessness, and divorce rates among Vietnam veterans are no higher than for the population as a whole, and some studies have even shown them to be slightly lower. As Burkett points out, many of those "Vietnam veterans" decked out in ratty jungle fatigues and medals, telling their wild stories of killing babies and secret Special Forces assassination missions are complete phonies. Many never set foot in Vietnam, and some never even served a day in the military. For them, Vietnam provides a cover, a plausible excuse for an otherwise failed life. But it is not just the failures of Baby Boomer Generation who conjure up phony Vietnam War records for themselves. In recent years doctors, politicians, judges, and college professors have been unmasked as phony Vietnam veterans.

The following collection of essays and first-person accounts from the pages of *Vietnam* magazine offers the reader a series of snapshots from the Vietnam War. Founded by Colonel Harry Summers in 1988, *Vietnam* magazine is dedicated to documenting, recording, and analyzing the history of the Vietnam War—"warts and all." The magazine's mission is not to re-fight the war, nor is it to serve as an advocate or an apologist for any particular cause or group. It does not have an ax to grind. As Colonel Summers noted in his editorial in the premier issue, "The Vietnam War was time and space dependent. The 'truth' of an American Army advisor in the Mekong Delta in 1958 was not the 'truth' of a Marine rifleman on the DMZ in 1968. And neither of these 'truths' were that of the river rats of the brown-water Navy, the pilots dodging SAMs in the skies over Hanoi, or of the nurses struggling to save lives in an evacuation hospital. There were literally millions of 'truths' about the Vietnam War."

No single book could ever hope to solve the puzzle of Vietnam. As with most large and complex human events, the Vietnam War will only come into proper historical focus long after it has passed from living memory. In the meantime, all we can do is examine each of the pieces of that puzzle as objectively as possible. In the pages of this book we offer the reader a small but what we believe to be a representative sampling of the pieces to that puzzle— some of "the many truths about Vietnam."

Foreword

AS I SAW IT AND NOW SEE IT

By General William C. Westmoreland, U.S. Army (ret.)

The war in Vietnam was a traumatic experience for our country. It was a war so complex that few understood it. It is still a confused issue, but is becoming less so. Based on my knowledge as COMUSMACV (Commander, United States Military Assistance Command Vietnam) from early 1964 to mid-1968 and as Army Chief of Staff and member of the Joint Chiefs of Staff (JCS) from 1968 to 1972, as well as my subsequent reflections and analyses, I will try to untangle that knot of confusion and misunderstanding.

First, one must understand that the Vietnam War, like all wars, was first and foremost a political act. Its genesis was the 1947 "Truman Doctrine," where President Harry S Truman pledged us to the unconditional support of "free people who are resisting attempted subjugation by minorities or by outside pressure." The Congress, representing the people of the United States, approved this doctrine by an overwhelming majority.

In 1950, in accordance with that doctrine, President Truman sent a military mission to Saigon. Later, President Dwight D. Eisenhower reaffirmed Truman's actions and emphasized a policy of "containment" of Communist expansion. In 1956, then Senator John F. Kennedy stated that "the cornerstone of the Free World is Southeast Asia." ASEAN, the Association of Southeast Asian Nations—the Philippines, Brunei, Indonesia, Malaysia, Singapore and Thailand—is an area rich in resources and in control of vital sea routes. Also part of Southeast Asia is Indochina— Cambodia, Laos and Vietnam—which is a "buffer" region between Southeast Asia and China.

Elected to the presidency in 1960, Kennedy set the tone

of his administration in his inaugural address when he pledged our nation "to bear any burden, meet any hardship, support any friend, and oppose any foe to assure the survival and success of liberty."

And these were more than mere words. After his verbal confrontation with the Soviet Union's Chairman Nikita Khrushchev in 1961, Kennedy reportedly emphasized, "We have a problem in making our power credible, and Vietnam looks like the place."

During the Kennedy administration, American presence in Vietnam was dramatically increased from a total of some 900 U.S. military personnel in November 1960 to some 16,000 by 1963. Not only did President Kennedy substantially increase the number of U.S. advisers, he also dispatched to South Vietnam U.S. Army "Green Beret" Special Forces, American-manned helicopters and U.S. tactical aircraft.

In his zeal, the young president made a grievous mistake in assenting to the overthrow of South Vietnamese President Ngo Dinh Diem in 1963. In my view that action morally locked us in Vietnam. If it had not been for our involvement in the overthrow of President Diem, we could perhaps have gracefully withdrawn our support when South Vietnam's lack of unity and leadership became apparent. But that was not to be. Twenty days after President Diem was overthrown and assassinated, President Kennedy himself was assassinated, and President Lyndon Baines Johnson inherited the problem.

Mr. Johnson was obsessed with his "Great Society" programs and, in the hope that the war would somehow go away, expanded our military efforts in South Vietnam. But there was no attempt to mobilize public support or to sacrifice for the war effort. No one "bore a burden, met a hardship" except those on the battlefield.

In the spring of 1964, I had a private talk in Saigon with Secretary of Defense Robert S. McNamara. I warned him that it would probably be a long war that would challenge public support. The secretary did not reply. Unfortunately, my prediction proved to be all too correct, for in the long run public support proved to be our Achilles' heel.

There was no question about our overall objective—a free and independent South Vietnam. That was bipartisan. But the strategy that emerged was based on wishful thinking and faulty assumptions, particularly as to the nature of the threat and the character of the leadership in Hanoi.

The conventional wisdom in Washington, which unwittingly mirrored the deceptive Communist propaganda line on the nature of the war, was that the threat was a home-grown Communist insurgency supported by guerrillas. The counter to that threat was pacification. Indeed, the Viet Cong internal threat was a very important element, but it was not the overriding consideration.

South Vietnam was not to be conquered by the guerrilla. It was to be conquered by the North Vietnamese Army. But our policies and strategies formulated in Washington never focused on that threat. The objective of both of our political parties here at home was to defeat aggression in the South and to bring the enemy to the conference table, not to conquer North Vietnam. President Johnson's first official policy statement was that we would not geographically expand the war. Militarily, that boxed us in.

The will and toughness of the leadership in Hanoi was greater than expected. The bombing campaign, directed from Honolulu by my military boss, the able Admiral U. S. Grant Sharp, the Commander-in-Chief, Pacific Command, was intended to break that will, but political restraint on the exercise of our capacity was too great, and was only lifted in 1972—four years too late.

These political constraints on the exercise of military power were based on several considerations. First was the fear of bringing the Chinese army to the battlefield. Influenced by our Korean War experience, our political leaders recalled General Douglas MacArthur's move to the Yalu River along the Chinese border. The resulting massive intervention of the Chinese Communist armies forced us back south of the 38th parallel with great losses.

In the Korean War, the enemy was reportedly forced to agree to the Korean Armistice Agreement of 1953 by President Eisenhower's alleged diplomatically delivered threat to use nuclear weapons. At that time, the enemy had no counter to that threat. In Vietnam, facing a nuclear-armed China and Russia, our leadership had no such leverage, either physically or psychologically.

Then there was the fear of escalating the war and expanding it geographically, thereby involving other countries in the fighting and extending the battle to the seas. It was a fear not shared with our enemies, who from the beginning, as they had made clear, were waging not the "Vietnam War" but the "Second Indochina War."

Our fear of an expanded war was assuaged by faith in Averill Harriman, a former ambassador to Moscow, who presumably had influence with the leadership there. This led to wishful thinking by our policymakers that the western border of South Vietnam adjoining Laos and Cambodia could be protected by the Geneva Accords of 1954 and by the Geneva Agreement on Laos in 1964.

This erroneous assumption resulted in an open hostile flank of more than 700 miles on the Vietnam battlefield, and the enemy's access to resupply routes not only along the Ho Chi Minh trail, that ran through the Laotian panhandle and Cambodia, but also to their use of the port of Sihanoukville in Cambodia. I told President Johnson at a meeting in Guam in March of 1967 that if the flow of supplies to the enemy through the Laotian panhandle was not stopped—a problem growing directly from Ambassador Harriman's "diplomacy"—that the war could go on indefinitely.

Yet another constraint was the desire to reduce the cost of the war, a constraint that proved decisive in the war's final months. Using the budget as the pretext, the Case-Church Amendment to the Fiscal Year 1974 Appropriations Act, named after its anti-Vietnam War sponsors Senators Clifford Case of New Jersey and Frank Church of Idaho (both, incidentally, subsequently turned out of office by the American people), prohibited any funds whatsoever "to finance directly or indirectly combat activities by U.S. military forces in or over or from off the shore of North Vietnam, South Vietnam, Laos or Cambodia."

That was an unambiguous message to Hanoi that it could break the Paris Peace Accords and we would not react, a repudiation of President Richard Nixon's earlier guarantees to South Vietnamese President Nguyen Van Thieu that the United States would ensure the Peace Accords be honored. Then, in the face of the 1975 North Vietnamese massive cross-border invasion of South Vietnam, we were hamstrung by Congressional action. Cut off from its erstwhile ally, South Vietnam collapsed.

Finally, there was a fear of arousing further the well-organized and growing anti-Vietnam War movement at home and abroad. This movement was fueled by several factors. First, Vietnam was an undeclared war, which made it impossible under the law to restrain those like Jane Fonda, Ramsey Clark and others who traveled to Hanoi and, intentionally or not, gave aid and comfort to the enemy and distress to our prisoners of war. Then there was the policy of the political administration to play the war low key, a policy that confused the American people who saw war through the lens of World War II. And, unlike World War II, the lack of an apparent geographical objective led to the perplexing and frustrating fact that the war could not be followed on a map.

Add to this the policy of deferring college students from the draft, which destabilized the campuses and developed a psychological atmosphere that played into the hands of the anti-Vietnam War faction. And—unlike World War II and Korea—there was no media censorship. In the world's first TV war, some journalists reported irresponsibly. Certain TV personalities had more influence on the public than informed and responsible senior public officials. President Johnson stated that when he lost Walter Cronkite he lost Middle America. What a frightening realization!

When it came to public support the final straws that led

to its collapse included the enemy's Tet Offensive of 1968, which was not seen for what it was—like the Battle of the Bulge in World War II, a last gasp by an enemy on the verge of defeat—but instead as evidence that we were losing. Then there was President Johnson's March 31, 1968, announcement that he would not run for re-election followed by the assassination of Dr. Martin Luther King less and a week later on April 4, which threw the nation into turmoil, and the Watergate episode, that destroyed the Nixon presidency. We had succeeded in paralyzing ourselves.

As General Van Tien Dung, who led the final 1975 blitzkrieg that overran South Vietnam, told Mr. Cronkite, a TV personality, some years later: "Our war was an all-out war. Victory was measured politically, diplomatically as well as militarily. Our objective was to defeat the *will* of the United States administration." And, indeed, that is exactly what they did. The United States was defeated psychologically, politically and diplomatically by a clever enemy. It was not defeated on the military battlefield.

Since war is fundamentally a political act, some may say that those facts are immaterial. But they are not immaterial to the warriors of that unpopular war.

The American people should—and, I believe, at long last do—now appreciate the excellent battlefield performance of the Vietnam veterans and understand that it was not they who failed to make good our national commitment to the people of South Vietnam. I was honored to have had such fine young men and women under my command and I believe strongly that the United States can take great pride in those who answered their country's call during the war.

Ninety-seven percent of Vietnam veterans were discharged under honorable conditions. Two-thirds of those who fought in Vietnam were enlisted volunteers (in World War II, two-thirds were draftees). The average age of the World War II soldier was 26 years; the average age of the Vietnam soldier was under 19. The war was a heavy psychological burden for such young people.

In the aftermath of Vietnam, we heard so much about the small percentage affected by PTSD—"post-traumatic-stress disorder"—that the man on the street had been given the impression that most Vietnam veterans are criminals or psychiatric patients. But the fact is that, according to the Veterans Administration and the Federal Bureau of Prisons, fewer Vietnam veterans are in jail than their nonveteran counterparts—only one-half of 1 percent of Vietnam veterans have been jailed for a crime—and there is no difference in drug usage between Vietnam veterans and those of their age group who did not serve. Further, the percentage of psychologically affected veterans does not vary greatly from that experience after other wars.

The overwhelming majority of forces and U.S. government and contract civilians in Vietnam served with bravery, dedication and pride. According to a 1980 Harris survey, 91 percent of Vietnam veterans said they are glad they served. Two-thirds said they would serve again, even knowing the ultimate fate of South Vietnam.

To sum up, there was a pattern of conflicting interests in our society relating to the war in Vietnam. First there was the ideological dimension. America as the champion of freedom and self-determination got us involved but, once committed, ideology recoiled in horror from the cost involved. Second, with politics no longer stopping at the water's edge, the partisan jostling of the political party out of power with the party in power tended to confuse issues in the public mind. The lack of a unifying declaration of war was telling. Third, the decisiveness and the will of the president, and hence the nation, collapsed at precisely the critical time when the enemy was most vulnerable in the aftermath of his failed 1968 Tet Offensive. Finally, our psychological defenses failed. Dissenting elements in our society, aided and abetted by foreign propaganda, were given inordinate visibility.

But now, the global perspective reveals a positive picture as well. John F. Kennedy's caution of 1956 comes to mind: "Southeast Asia is the keystone of the Free World."

Why is it the keystone? Not only because that area possesses many strategic materials—particularly rubber, tin and greater quantities of oil—but it controls the sea and air routes to the Indian Ocean. Without a costly military force on the ground, as we have had for years in Korea, the expansion of Communism has been blocked by circumstances involving little cost to the U.S. and the Free World in recent years, all of which has been in our national interests.

The 10 years that our military efforts blocked the flow of Communism were significant. We gave those countries time to mature, to gain confidence in running their own affairs and to improve their economies. All are thankful to America.

Meanwhile, the reality of life in the "buffer" states of Indochina has been exposed by the boat people, the tragedy of the Cambodian holocaust, and the ineptness of the leadership in Hanoi. Such developments have certainly had significant influence on the apparent disintegration of the Communist world.

As history unfolds it is apparent that America's involvement in Indochina was not in vain.

PART ONE
COMMITTED

Setting the Stage

By Brigadier General David T. Zabecki,
U.S. Army Reserve

In October 1950, it appeared as if the Vietminh had reached a turning point in their war against the French. Operating from bases across the border in Communist-controlled China, the Vietminh forces of General Vo Nguyen Giap swept down upon the string of French border posts that ran along Vietnam's Colonial Route 4. When the smoke cleared away on October 17, the French had lost over 6,000 troops. The defeat stunned the French government, which immediately recalled its High Commissioner for Indochina, Leon Pignon, and the commander-in-chief of the French Expeditionary Corps, General Georges Carpentier. As a replacement for both, Paris sent General Jean de Lattre de Tassigny. Widely considered France's greatest living soldier, de Lattre had commanded the First Free French Army in World War II.

De Lattre arrived in Hanoi on December 17 and assumed both political and military command of Indochina. His 190,000-man Expeditionary Corps consisted of approximately 50,000 French nationals, 75,000 Indochinese, 30,000 African Colonial Troops and 20,000 Foreign Legionnaires. French nationals made up all of his small but effective air force (10,000) and navy (5,000) contingents. The embryonic Vietnamese National Army had a scant

12,000 troops. Most of de Lattre's forces were concentrated around the two major population centers, Hanoi and Saigon. After almost five years of fighting, the Vietminh held a large portion of the countryside, but the French still controlled the majority of the population, as well as almost all the agricultural and industrial potential.

Facing de Lattre, Giap had five main-force 10,000-man divisions. Armed and equipped by the Chinese, four of the divisions (304th, 308th, 312th and 315th) were based about 150 miles north of Hanoi in the mountainous Viet Bac region, close to the Chinese border. The 320th Division was based southwest of Hanoi, just outside the French-controlled Red River delta. Inside the delta, Giap had three independent regiments conducting guerrilla operations and another two independent battalions inside Hanoi for terrorist actions. Over and above this main force, the Vietminh had about 75,000 regional troops and 200,000 village militia. In total, Giap had something like 300,000 under arms at any one time. About the same number of non-combatant porters made up his principal means of supply transport.

As 1951 dawned, the Vietminh held the initiative. Giap's troops were still riding high from their stunning victories along Route 4, and the Vietminh had virtual freedom of movement outside the Red River delta. The French were demoralized and on the run. Giap and other Communist Party strategists felt the time was right to launch the long-heralded general counteroffensive that would finally sweep the French from Indochina. Party propagandists started spreading the slogan, "Ho Chi Minh in Hanoi for the Tet." Giap decided to aim his blow straight for Hanoi by breaching the French Defensive Line at Vinh Yen, near the apex of the triangle, and only 30 miles northwest of the capital.

Two French mobile groups defended Vinh Yen. A mobile group (GM) had 3,000 men organized in three infantry battalions and an artillery battalion. It was roughly the equivalent of an

American regimental combat team of the same period. The town itself was garrisoned by Mobile Group 3, made up of Senegalese units and Moung tribesmen. Mobile Group 1, all North African troops, occupied a series of blocking positions along Route 2, a few miles east of Vinh Yen. Giap planned to drive a wedge between the two forces, pin GM No. 3 against the Dam Vac lake south of the town and then defeat the French in detail. During the last half of December and first part of January, he skillfully moved his 308th and 312th divisions, supported by 180,000 porters, down from the Viet Bac and into position along the Tam Dao ridge. On January 13, 1951, he struck.

The battle kicked off with the 308th Division making a diversionary attack on Bao Chuc, a small outpost about two miles north of Vinh Yen. The French immediately took the bait, and GM No. 3 raced up the road to relieve the 50-man garrison. Halfway there, the 312th Division ambushed GM No. 3 at Dao Tu. Mobile Group 3 only managed to extract itself under the cover of heavy air strikes and artillery fire from Vinh Yen. By the time GM No. 3 staggered back into its original positions, it had lost an entire battalion and the good part of another. The Vietminh attackers quickly occupied the string of hills in front of Vinh Yen and closed the trap on GM No. 3.

The next day, de Lattre flew into Vinh Yen in a light liaison plane and personally took command of the flight. He ordered Mobile Group 2 to move up from Hanoi as a reserve, and he ordered GM No. 1 to drive west along Route 2 and break through to the town. He also called in massive air strikes and ordered an airlift of additional reinforcements from southern Vietnam. By the afternoon of January 15, GM No. 1 had succeeded in clearing Hill 157, which commanded Route 2. On the morning of the 16th, both GM No. 1 and GM No. 3 moved out to clear the remaining hills in front of Vinh Yen. The Vietminh seemed to fall back under the slightest pressure and, by mid-afternoon, the string of hills was in French hands. Two hours later the entire 308th Division came streaming out of the Tam Dao in what became the first human-wave attack of the wars in Indochina.

De Lattre, who had left Vinh Yen, returned immediately and called in the single largest air strike of the French phase of the war. Napalm was used on a large scale for the first time. The French air force used every available aircraft in Indochina, including cargo planes, to dump napalm on the massed Vietminh formations. Giap's troops initially panicked and fled. One shocked platoon leader asked his company commander, "What is this? The atomic bomb?" The air strikes blunted the attack but did not stop it completely. Fighting continued throughout the night. About 0400 on the 17th, the French defenders on Hill 101 ran out of ammunition and had to withdraw. About the same time, the Vietminh took Hill 47. These two hills gave the Communists control of the center of the line, while the French held the two hills (210 and 157) on the flanks.

The 308th Division attacked again at first light. De Lattre committed the fresh GM No. 2, his last reserve, against Hill 47. He sent GM No. 3 to the relief of the isolated French position on Hill 210. He supported both counterattacks with more air strikes and napalm. The French fighter-bombers turned the tide and the 308th Division started to fall back. As the 308th Division was retreating, the 312th Division launched a belated suicide attack that chewed up most of GM No. 3's one good remaining battalion; but the Vietminh counterattack was too little, too late. By noon on January 17 it was all over. The two badly mauled Vietminh divisions faded back into the mountains, having lost 6,000 killed, at least that many wounded, and 500 prisoners.

The attack on Hanoi didn't work, so Giap decided the next best objective would be the port of Haipong, the head of the French logistical lifeline. This time he planned to breach the French defenses at Mao Khe, about 20 miles north of the port.

Another mountain range, the Dong Trieu Massif, provided a good covered approach. Mao Khe was also the center of the coal mine region in northern Vietnam, and its loss would hurt the French. Giap planned to break through the line with his fresh 316th Division and then push on Haiphong with his partially reconstructed 308th and 312th divisions, still weak from the bloodletting at Vinh Yen. At the same time, his 304th and 320th divisions would conduct diversionary attacks over on the west side of the delta.

Mao Khe was weakly defended. Surrounded by a string of outposts, the main position consisted of three strongpoints. The town itself was defended by an armored car platoon of the Moroccan Colonial Infantry. About 1,000 meters north of the town an understrength company of Tho partisans, commanded by a Vietnamese lieutenant and three French NCOs, garrisoned the Mao Khe Coal Mine. On the eastern edge of the town, another understrength company, from the 30th Senegalese Composite Battalion, occupied a fortified Catholic church. The total garrison amounted to only 400 men.

The attack started on March 23 with the diversionary thrusts on the eastern side of the delta. Later that same night, the 316th Division started the process of reducing Mao Khe's outposts. By the 26th all the outposts had been taken. The 316th Division then massed for the main attack, but the French navy spoiled the show. Since Mao Khe was a good distance from the coast, Giap figured he was safe from naval interference. But the Da Bac River, which ran close to Mao Khe, had a channel deep enough for three French destroyers and two large landing craft to move up from the sea. The guns of the French vessels caught the massed Vietminh troops in the open and, combined with additional air strikes, the Communist attack broke up before it even started.

De Lattre, meanwhile, reacted cautiously. He thought Mao Khe was only another diversionary attack because he couldn't pinpoint the locations of the 308th and 312th divisions, which were then hiding in the Mong Trieu Massif. He sent a minimal reinforcement consisting of the 6th Colonial Parachute Battalion (6e BPC) and some artillery batteries. At 0400 on March 27, Vietminh artillery opened up on the coal mine. In the first few minutes of the shelling, the Vietnamese lieutenant was wounded and two of the French NCOs killed. At 0515, the 316th Division launched an all-out attack against the mine. The Tho partisans held out until dawn when French B-26s and Hellcats relieved some of the pressure. At 1400, the 6e BPC tried to move from Mao Khe to relieve the mine, but heavy Communist artillery and mortar fire pinned them down before they got halfway. The paratroopers only managed to crawl back into Mao Khe after dark. Later that night, the Thos, by then almost out of ammunition, conducted a skillful evacuation that took the Vietminh completely by surprise. The defenders slipped away from the mine, taking their wives, children and wounded with them.

The Thos reached Mao Khe unmolested, but they didn't get much of a break. At 0200 on the 28th, the Vietminh opened up against the town and the church with more artillery and mortar fire. The Vietminh followed with human-wave attacks, but the attackers ran into prearranged defensive artillery fire. Some of the attackers got into the town and set it on fire. The fighting continued until morning, house to house, hand to hand; but the attack was spent. By mid-morning the Communist troops withdrew, leaving more than 400 bodies. Total Vietminh casualties probably ran around 3,000. The defenders suffered 40 killed and 150 wounded. Giap had lost again. He never committed his 308th and 312th divisions, perhaps because they were still too weak to commit. More significantly, just as Giap had failed to consider air power at Vinh Yen, he likewise failed to account for naval power at Mao Khe—both arms with which he never had any experience.

The narrow margin of the French victory, caused by de Lattre's caution, only served to convince Giap that the French were still on the verge of collapse. He decided to try once more; only this time he would avoid the errors he made the first two times. In deciding to attack along the Day River, on the southwest side of the delta, Giap was going for a much more limited objective. Rather than the French colonial capital, or the main port, Giap wanted to disrupt the integrity of the French defenses and seize the largely Catholic district of Phat Diem, with its large rice crop. His plan was his most sophisticated, and most complicated, to date. He would use one division for diversionary attacks and hit the Day River side with three divisions on line. The main effort would be made by the 320th Division against the weak line of forts between Ninh Binh and the sea. At the same time, he would use what forces he had inside the delta to cut the French lines of communication (LOCs) and disrupt the forward movement of any reserves.

It took Giap two months to get ready. The 304th and 320th divisions were already on the southwest side. He ordered the 64th Regiment of the 320th Division to infiltrate into the delta and link up with the 42nd Independent Regiment already behind French lines. Meanwhile, he used 40,000 porters to move the 308th Division all the way around the delta, from the northeast side to the southwest.

After some diversionary probes by the 312th Division near Vinh Yen, the main attack kicked off on May 29. The 304th Division, on the left, crossed the river near Phu Ly and drove in the French outposts. The 308th Division in the center hit Ninh Binh and penetrated deeply into the town. The French sent a "Dinassaut" down the river to support Ninh Binh, but the Vietminh ambushed it with recoilless rifles and anti-tank rockets from the west bank. (The Dinassaut were river flotillas of patrol boats and armored landing craft. They were the forerunners of the riverine forces later used by the Americans in the Mekong Delta.) With several of its craft severely disabled, the Dinassaut turned back. A secondary attack south of Ninh Binh put the 308th Division across the river, and the 320th Division on the right flank crossed with little resistance. By the morning of the 30th, Giap had elements of all three divisions across the river. The French defenders managed to maintain a foothold in Ninh Binh, but only at the expense of heavy casualties. Marine Commando No. 3 held the Ninh Binh Catholic Church, but lost 61 of its original 80 men in a single night. A French fort on a high crag above the town had orders to hold at all costs. The Vietminh subjected it to massive mortar shelling. The fort held, but its commander, Lieutenant Bernard de Lattre de Tassigny, died. He had been the only child of the French commander-in-chief. Before they finally withdrew from Indochina, 20 more sons of French marshals and generals would die there.

All went well for Giap the first three days, but then he started to lose control of the situation. On May 31, de Lattre committed three mobile groups, four artillery groups, one armored group and one airborne battalion—a total force equivalent to two divisions. Then the Dinassaut returned, this time with air cover, and started sinking the sampans and small boats that made up the Vietminh's lifeline across the river. The Communist LOCs were being choked off. Ironically, the two Vietminh regiments inside the delta, which were supposed to cut the French LOCs, had no luck at all. Local Catholic militias harassed the two units and even slowed down the 320th Division, buying time for French reinforcements to reach the area.

The climax of the battle came on the night of June 4, when the key position at Yen Cu Ha changed hands several times. By June 6, the French had complete control of the river and had shut down the supply lines for the three Vietminh divisions. Offensive activity ground to a halt. On June 10, Giap ordered his units to withdraw back over to the west bank, and his last troops passed out of the delta on June 18. De Lattre had beaten Giap once again. Total Vietminh casualties probably ran in excess of 10,000. Over 1,000 were captured. Giap failed this time because he underestimated the effectiveness of both the Dinassaut and the Catholic militia.

Giap withdrew into the interior of northern Vietnam, but the French were too weak to follow him and exploit their successes. For the time being, they securely held the delta, but they had only a very limited ability to project power outside of the area. Giap, on the other hand, had five main-force 10,000-man divisions; however, they were all understrength after the bloodletting of the recent offensive. For several months both sides just sat, licking their wounds, waiting for the other to make a move. Giap moved first. On September 22, his 312th Division made a probing grab at Nghia Lo, in the northern highlands, 95 miles west of Hanoi. De Lattre sent in three of the nine airborne battalions that made up his theater reserve force. By October 5 they wrested Nghia Lo from the Communists with relatively little effort. Now it was de Lattre's turn.

De Lattre wanted to lure Giap into another large set-piece battle, and this time, hopefully, crush him. The French National Assembly was debating the Indochina budget about that same time, and de Lattre wanted another impressive victory to bolster his requests for increased support. Rather than wait for Giap to come back to him, de Lattre decided to pick the time and the place. He chose the town of Hoa Binh, on the western bank of the Black River, about 25 miles outside the western leg of the triangular fortification line that ran around the delta.

As de Lattre saw it, Hoa Binh had several advantages. It was within supporting distance of the French defensive lines, and its seizure would be a logical extension of the French zone of control. Hoa Binh also sat between the major Vietminh stronghold in the northeast and Tranh Hoa, the home base of Giap's 320th Division. A thrust in that direction just might isolate and neutralize

20 percent of Giap's combat power. Finally, Hoa Binh was the capital of the Moungs, a tribe fiercely loyal to the French. De Lattre could count on them for local support.

The major disadvantage of Hoa Binh would be supporting it once it had been seized. There were three possible LOCs, but all three had serious weaknesses. Colonial Route 6 ran from Hanoi to Xuan Mai, on the edge of the de Lattre Line, and then out to Hoa Binh. But the stretch outside the delta hadn't been maintained since 1940. The Vietminh sabotaged it in 1946, and the French air force had routinely bombed it ever since. Worse still, high ground overlooked most of the length, and heavy underbrush ran right to the road's edge—perfect for point-blank ambushes. The second major LOC was by water, from Hanoi up the Red River to Trung Ha at the tip of the de Lattre Triangle, and then down the Black River to Hoa Binh. Although it was almost three times as long as Route 6, it was a good way to bring in bulk supplies. But it, too, was lined with dense jungle, right to its banks. The final LOC was by air. Hoa Binh had a small airfield, but direct-fire weapons could easily interdict the field from several hills just southwest of the town.

Despite the potential supply problems, de Lattre went for Hoa Binh. On November 14, three airborne units, the 1st, 2nd and 7th Colonial Parachute Battalions (1er BPC, 2e BPC, 7e BPC), dropped onto the Hoa Binh airstrip. It was the last jump the French made using the old trimotor Junkers-52s. Shortly after that jump, they received a large number of newer C-47s from the United States. At the same time the paratroopers jumped in, a force of 15 infantry battalions, seven artillery battalions, two armored groups and their supporting engineers started pushing down Route 6 from Xuan Mai. On the Black River, two naval assault divisions ("Dinassaut") started to push down from Trung Ha.

By November 16, both forces had linked up at Hoa Binh, and all objectives were in French hands. There had been no resistance from the Vietminh. Although the French had made a mighty lunge, they came up empty handed. They were now faced with the problem of holding on to what they had. Immediately they started fortifying the surface LOCs with a series of strongpoints along both the road and the river. General de Lattre, meanwhile, returned to Paris, dying of cancer. On November 20, he was replaced by General Raoul Salan, who would later head the rebellious Secret Army Organization (OAS) in Algeria.

Giap took his time in responding to the French challenge. He spent almost two months moving his forces into position, carefully avoiding the French strength. This time around, he used all five of his main force divisions. He gave the 316th and 320th divisions diversionary and harassing missions. The 316th Division infiltrated into the French-held delta from the north side of the Red River, while the 320th Division infiltrated from the south, across the Day River. Giap brought his other three divisions down from their strongholds in the mountainous Viet Bac region, near the Chinese border. He deployed the 304th Division along Route 6 and the 312th Division along the Black River. He wrapped the 308th Division around Hoa Binh, with part of it strung out along the river and part along the road. Giap had no intention of attacking Hoa Binh directly; he was going for the French LOCs.

The Communists struck first at Tu Vu, the main French strongpoint near the north end of the Black River line. Two Moroccan rifle companies and a tank platoon defended the west bank (the Vietminh side) position, which was organized into two strongpoints. Tu Vu's main weakness was that the two strongpoints were separated by a small tributary of the Black, and was connected by only a flimsy footbridge. By December 9, two regiments of the 312th Division and one regiment of the 308th Division started moving into attack position. The French detected the movement, and at dawn on the 10th three infantry battalions and the 1er BPC conducted a spoiling attack. They failed to stop the

Communist deployment, however, the five Vietminh battalions launched their attack on Tu Vu at 2100.

The Communist assault started with a heavy mortar barrage. At about 2200, the Vietminh hit the northern strongpoint with a holding attack, while simultaneously launching human waves against the weaker southern strongpoint. Despite French artillery support from the east bank of the Black, the southern strongpoint started to collapse by 0100. The surviving defenders crossed the footbridge to the northern strongpoint, and the Vietminh shifted their attack. The northern strongpoint had the tanks and, for a while, they held the Vietminh at bay by firing directly into the Communist formations and crushing the attackers by rolling over them. Eventually, though, the Vietminh swarmed over the tanks and set them on fire with point-blank blasts from anti-tank rockets. All five tank crews burned to death inside their vehicles. Sometime after 0300, the few Moroccans still alive in Tu Vu abandoned the northern strongpoint and swam out to a little island in the Black River. There they dug in for the final Vietminh assault; but it never came. After dawn, Moroccan patrols slipped back into Tu Vu, but the Communists were gone, leaving over 400 bodies in the position.

The fights along the Black River continued throughout December, but the Vietminh never allowed themselves to become decisively engaged. They would overrun a strongpoint and then fade back into the jungle. The French could easily recapture any lost position, but only at the cost of a brutal and continuous bloodletting. Supply convoys could get down the Black only with heavy escorts from the Dinassaut, fighting every inch of the way. Historian Bernard Fall called the fights along the Black River "the bloodiest river battles since the American Civil War."

While the two forces were slugging it out along the river, part of the 308th Division occupied the high ground commanding Hoa Binh and brought the airstrip under fire. The 304th Division started to put pressure on Route 6. Salan committed his reinforcements, three mobile groups and an airborne group. Five infantry battalions and an airborne battalion held Hoa Binh itself; but the bulk of the French forces were strung out along the river and the road.

In early January, the 88th Regiment of the 308th Division moved against the Route 6 strongpoint at Xom Pheo. The position was held by the 2nd Battalion of the Foreign Legion's crack 13th Half Brigade (13e DBLE). The battalion's 5th and 7th companies occupied well-prepared positions on the high ground overlooking the road. The 6th and 8th companies held positions astride the road itself. The positions were laid out in typical, methodical Legion fashion: four-man bunkers, connected by a network of trenches, surrounded by mines and barbed wire, and screened by aggressive local patrolling. At 0100 on the morning of January 8, a patrol from the 5th Company returned to its position, carefully picking its path through the defenses. A few minutes later a second patrol followed the first back into the position; then, a third patrol came in. The only problem was that the 5th Company sent out only two patrols.

As soon as the Vietminh infiltrators got inside the French lines, heavy mortar fire started falling, and more attacking Communists hit the barbed wire with bangalore torpedoes. Human waves swarmed over the position, heedless of the mines. Within 45 minutes, the attackers overran the 1st and 2nd platoons of the 5th Company, forcing the survivors to fall back on the 3rd Platoon. By 0400 almost all the officers and NCOs were dead, but the survivors of the 5th Company refused to give in. They counterattacked with bayonets and hand grenades. By dawn, most of the defenders were dead, but they had managed to hold the position. The Vietminh withdrew, leaving over 700 bodies. Unfortunately, the Legionnaires' magnificent stand was largely nullified the next day. Another regiment of the 304th Division occupied the high ground overlooking the Kem Pass, between Xom Pheo and the de Lattre Line. They then ambushed and destroyed an entire battalion of the road's screening force, and the Route 6 LOC effectively closed down.

The river line didn't last much longer. By January 10 the Vietminh had forced the French to withdraw from their outposts along the west side of the Black River. On the 12th, they staged a massive ambush against a heavily escorted convoy. Most of the French supply boats were damaged and forced to turn back, and the escorting Dinassaut lost four patrol boats and a heavily armed LSSL. That closed the river LOC, and the jaws around Hoa Binh snapped shut. The day before the river ambush, General de Lattre died in Paris, after receiving a deathbed promotion to Marshal of France. One senior French officer caustically remarked, "I guess Marshal de Lattre died just in time in order not to be saddled with a defeat."

With both the river and the road closed, Hoa Binh started to strangle. Only the airfield remained open, but the Vietminh had positioned artillery and a surprisingly large number of antiaircraft weapons on the commanding high ground. The French started losing aircraft. Salan decided to reopen Route 6, only this time the French would do what they should have done in the first place: clear the underbrush from alongside the road to eliminate the Vietminh's close-in ambush sites. Salan ordered Colonel (later General) Jean Giles to assemble a task force of 12 infantry battalions, three artillery groups, supporting engineers and hundreds of locally "recruited" laborers. On January 18, the Giles Task Force moved out of Xuan Mai and started fighting its way down to Hoa Binh. It took the force 11 days to cover the 25 miles. But even before reaching the objective, Salan finally came to the conclusion he could no longer afford to hold Hoa Binh. He was throwing good troops after dead, troops he desperately needed back in the Red River delta to counter the increased pressures from Giap's infiltrated 316th and 320th divisions.

Salan's problem, then, was to extract himself with minimum damage while under heavy enemy pressure. He devised a plan, called Operation Amaranth, involving a three-phase withdrawal back up Route 6 through a series of reinforced blocking positions as Xom Pheo, the Kem Pass and the approaches to Xuan Mai. One element would move up the road, capture the first blocking position, and hold it open for the remainder of the French troops to withdraw through. The first unit through the first blocking position would continue down the road to seize and secure the second position; and so forth, back to the French defensive line.

The pullout started at 1900 on February 22, with the garrison's support troops, 600 porters and about 1,000 Moung civilians crossing the Black River. The move must have caught Giap by surprise because the Vietminh didn't interfere. At 0600 the next morning the combat forces started to pull out. Two hours later, Giap hit, and hit hard. Under heavy artillery and air cover, the column took two days to reach Xuan Mai. French artillery fired over 30,000 rounds in support of the move. Finally, on the evening of February 24, the last French unit, the 13e DBLE, crossed back over the De Lattre Line and into the relative safety of the Red River delta.

Bernard Fall called Hoa Binh "The Meatgrinder." Both sides claimed victory, but both sides suffered almost 5,000 killed. Giap, however, was the clear victor. By avoiding the French strength and going for the LOCs, he clearly showed he had learned his lessons from his Red River delta defeats. De Lattre, on the other hand, had read too much into his previous victories over Giap. The French still had no ability to project power outside the delta.

In many ways, Hoa Binh was an eerie foreshadowing of Dien

Bien Phu. The situations were similar: a surrounded force, cut land LOCs and a heavily interdicted airhead. Even many of the units were the same. The Legion's 13e DBLE, which fought so well at Hoa Binh, later died at Dien Bien Phu.

Dien Bien Phu Reconsidered

By Douglas Porch

D ien Bien Phu must count as one of history's most studied battles. Indeed, so investigated has been the decision by the French commander in chief in Indochina, General Henri Navarre, in November 1953 to occupy a remote valley in Upper Tonkin—a decision that led inexorably to a battle whose outcome terminated nearly a century of French rule in Indochina—that nothing appears left to be said about it. However, recently revealed documents allow a completely new interpretation of the battle, from both a strategic and an operational perspective. It leaves in tatters the justification Navarre put forward for his occupation of Dien Bien Phu—that his "hedgehog" would force the Viet Minh commander Vo Nguyen Giap to either renounce his invasion of Laos or attack Dien Bien Phu head-on.

The first thing to note is that Dien Bien Phu was not about Laos at all, but about opium. Documents of the *Deuxième Bureau*, French army intelligence, state categorically that Dien Bien Phu was occupied on November 20, 1953, so that the French-sponsored Tai *maquis* could be transferred there from their base at Lai Chau, considered indefensible by the French because it lay at the bottom of a narrow river canyon in Upper Tonkin. This *maquis* was important to the French because it controlled the opium crop whose proceeds financed the French special operations command, the GCMA, under the dynamic Major Roger Trinquier. When French intelligence detected the movement of Viet Minh divisions toward Lai Chau in the autumn of 1953, Navarre felt that he had no choice but to rush to the rescue of his Tai partisans.

Navarre's strategic mistake was to allow the special ops tail to wag the main force dog by placing his forces in a position where they had more to lose from a bad outcome than did the Viet Minh. In other words, while the loss of the opium and the destruction of the maquis in Upper Tonkin, and even the eventual occupation of much of Laos, might have been unfortunate, it would not have proved fatal for Navarre. On the contrary, it could have allowed him to husband his resources in the Tonkin delta and force the Viet Minh eventually to attack his strength there. On the other hand, in trying to protect the two assets of opium and his *maquis*, Navarre not only lost them but also sacrificed much of the cream of the French expeditionary force, a situation that drove the French to the peace table, hat in hand.

A second vital point in understanding this important battle is that if Navarre stuck his head into a noose at Dien Bien Phu, so did the Viet Minh. It is now clear that the strategy that led to Dien Bien Phu was devised not by the Viet Minh but by the Chinese, who had dictated Viet Minh plans since the Communist victory in the Chinese civil war in 1949.

The substantial Chinese military mission to the Viet Minh realized that the French army's dependence on the opium crop opened an opportunity to entice them to a remote battlefield where they could be surrounded and overwhelmed. Consequently, they prevailed upon the Viet Minh leadership to veto Giap's plan for an assault on the Tonkin delta in late 1953 and point his troops toward Lai Chau. But the Chinese were not interested in an operational success for its own sake. Rather, they sought a dramatic French defeat as the *pièce de résistance* of a "peace offensive" that would end the war.

On November 26, 1953, six days after the French occupation of Dien Bien Phu, the Swedish newspaper *Expressen* printed an interview with Ho Chi Minh in which he announced that he was prepared to negotiate an end to the war. But the "victory" envisaged by Beijing, as Viet Minh negotiators discovered to their dismay at Geneva, was one that stopped far short of the unification of Vietnam under Communist rule.

So, if Dien Bien Phu proved a trap carefully laid for Navarre, it proved to be a trap for Giap and Ho Chi Minh as well. In other words, years after the event, it is clear that the real victor of Dien Bien Phu was China, a country that shed no blood there.

Much of the strategic rationale for Dien Bien Phu has been obscured for four decades by postwar polemics over the battle and by the absence of archives. The post-battle autopsy concluded, almost before the garrison had surrendered, that the French high command was divided over the purpose of Dien Bien Phu, and was even, at times, skeptical of the entire operation. This was the line of defense pursued by Navarre's principal subordinate and commander of the Tonkin theater, General René Cogny.

Cogny insisted that he never shared Navarre's concept of Dien Bien Phu as a breakwater against a main force Viet Minh invasion of Laos. Rather, it was meant to be a *point d'ammarage*, or "anchor point," for mobile operations to support French-led Montagnard irregular forces in the Tonkin highlands. Military historians especially have focused on this debate over the strategic purpose of Dien Bien Phu, but the general conclusion has been that the French high command did not speak with a common voice in Indochina. The course of the battle revealed serious professional shortcomings in the army, as well as a serious decline of morale in a heterogeneous expeditionary force.

None of this might have happened, it is alleged, had Navarre been guided toward a more rational strategic choice by better intelligence. Not surprisingly, poor intelligence was an alibi that the French commander in chief proved quick to seize. Navarre complained that while the lack of security consciousness among French forces meant that his moves were an open book for Giap, his knowledge of Viet Minh intentions was limited to radio intercepts of "intermediate echelons" and knowledge of the volume of Chinese supplies once they had crossed the frontier. So, while he knew where Giap's units were, he could not predict what the Viet Minh commander intended to do with them. Nor could he know what support the Chinese were prepared to lend to the insurgents. Both were critical factors, he claimed, in his defeat at Dien Bien Phu.

Contemporary historians have tended to agree that Dien Bien Phu was essentially an intelligence failure. "The one fundamental calculation which underlaid Navarre's decision, the one reason which to Navarre justified the operation," writes American historian Lieutenant Geneneral Philip B. Davidson, who served as Westmoreland's intelligence chief in Vietnam, "was the estimate by his intelligence staff that the operation carried little or no risk."

But how accurate is this view of Dien Bien Phu? And should intelligence share the burden of blame for the disastrous decision? Certainly, in light of the mutual recriminations and the attempts to evade responsibility for the defeat that occurred, the French command appeared to be hopelessly confused and riven over the strategic purpose and operational concepts applied at Dien Bien Phu. But a closer look at the evidence suggests that, on the contrary, there was a remarkable unity of vision over what Dien Bien Phu was meant to do, and that subsequent arguments by the main protagonists of the defeat have obscured that reality.

In fact, the French command had a purpose and believed they possessed the capacity to succeed, and this despite—not in the absence of—accurate assessments of Viet Minh capabilities delivered to the high command by the Deuxième Bureau. Furthermore, Chinese military documents reveal that at Dien Bien Phu the French came within an ace of success. Had it not been for active Chinese intervention in strategic planning, logistical support, tactical direction and, finally, in boosting Giap's faltering resolve, it would have been Navarre, not Giap, who would have emerged as the victor.

Dien Bien Phu was indeed a trap, one set by the Chinese for both Giap and Navarre. But if the Deuxième Bureau failed to pierce the full scope of Chinese-imposed strategy until well into the battle, it did supply more than adequate information for Navarre to have made a more intelligent strategic choice, and for the French command to have turned in a better tactical performance.

The contention that Navarre and Cogny were divided over the purpose of Dien Bien Phu—as a "hedgehog" to stop a major attack, as was done at Na San in November–December 1952, or, as Cogny claimed, an anchor point to support mobile operations—can be dismissed by a study of French army doctrine and the strategic situation of Dien Bien Phu. For instead of the hedgehog/anchor point dichotomy, the French at the time saw Dien Bien Phu as a *base aéroterrestre* that could perform both functions.

Theoretically, a *base aéroterrestre* would have sufficient personnel to permit extensive patrolling, counterattack, and carrying the fight beyond the defensive complex, as the French postwar study of their performance noted: "When the enemy commits major forces, our mobile elements fall back on the entrenched camp. If need be, these are reinforced by land, air, river and maritime routes. . . . The enemy is then forced to under-take veritable siege operations which are long, costly, and diffi-cult, and which require large forces vulnerable to air attack. . . ."

Interestingly enough, even in the aftermath of defeat, the French refused to concede that Dien Bien Phu invalidated the con-cept of the *base aéroterrestre*. The *base aéroterrestre*, the French believed, offered "a solution well suited to the problem of re-establishing our power and our influence in regions which are remote from our bases . . . ," the only way that they could main-tain a semblance of strategic mobility in Indochina.

Clearly, the French saw the *base aéroterrestre* both as an anchoring point and as a hedgehog. The fall of Dien Bien Phu was something beyond the norm, an exceptional case brought on by exceptional circumstances. Navarre insisted that while there were plenty of people around to say "I told you so" after his camp had been overrun, at the time only the head of the air force expressed reservations about supporting a camp at the limit of air range. The main debates appear to have been about *how* the camp was to be defended rather than *if* it could be defended.

And this despite the fact that in late November French intel-ligence began to track the shift of Giap's divisions from the delta northward toward the highlands, a sure indication that the Viet Minh would mount a major effort to seize the region. True, at this stage Navarre did not know that the Chinese were prepared to sustain a major Viet Minh operation at Dien Bien Phu. But as he insisted that Laos was the objective of Giap's thrust, he must have known that the enemy effort might be considerable.

Despite this intelligence, Navarre and Cogny made a series of operational judgments that ultimately proved fatal to the garri-son. These errors were moored in the dual role of the *base aéroterrestre*, which, when combined with the French goal of pro-tecting the *maquis* and the opium crop, contributed to the demise of the camp in at least three important ways.

First, the anchor point portion of the concept implied the appointment of an officer of light armor, Colonel Christian de Castries, as the camp commander, when events proved that an engineering officer expert in siege warfare would have been a happier choice. Second, the use of the garrison in mobile operations in the critical first weeks contributed to the neglect of the defensive positions that so weakened the French. Why should French soldiers already exhausted from patrols and reconnaissance missions worry overmuch about the strength of their bunkers or the depth of their trenches when it was they who held the operational initiative?

The third weakness of the *base aéroterrestre* concept was that it was founded in the belief that the Montagnard resistance, which it was meant to support, was effective militarily. One of the goals of Operation Castor was to evacuate the Tai "capital" from Lai Chau to Dien Bien Phu, which would become a new, more defensible base for partisan activity in the highlands. But when the Tais attempted to depart Lai Chau for Dien Bien Phu in early December 1953, they were ambushed by soldiers of the 316th Viet Minh Division.

The decision in December to persist with Operation Castor, given the state of the Tai *maquis* it was trying to support, was questionable, to say the least. The sad truth for Navarre was that Dien Bien Phu would never serve as an anchor point for anything, much less a friendly *maquis* operating in Giap's rear.

The French postwar study complained that the *maquis* was never able to seriously harass the Viet Minh supply lines to Dien Bien Phu. Despite the monthly investment by 1954 of 1,500 flight hours of C-47s, 300 flight hours of reconnaissance aircraft, numerous B-26 missions and airdrops of close to 300 tons of supplies and ammunition, "at no time did the Viet Minh High Command seem to be disturbed by the operations of our irregular units," the French concluded disconsolately. Roger Trinquier, the

DOUGLAS PORCH

driving force behind the *maquis* experiment, acknowledged the failure of his partisans, but he was not short of excuses—the high command never supported them; and, second, his Meos from Laos got their marching orders to attack the Viet Minh rear only when the battle was virtually lost.

The truth lay elsewhere, however. As has been argued, the problem was that the high command not only supported the *maquis*, it mortgaged its strategy to them at Dien Bien Phu. Trinquier rather undermines his second accusation with the admission that the Meos only agreed to move when they were paid in silver bars, the only currency they recognized. In any case, Trinquier's Meos from Laos had no local knowledge and no local support, which must form an essential element of any successful guerrilla operation. The *maquis* served the French as a political symbol and a source of opium income, not as even a quasi-effective military force.

So if, as the French believed, the fall of Dien Bien Phu was an exceptional case brought on by exceptional circumstances, this leaves intact the "stab-in-the-back" thesis—Navarre's accusations that events in Paris reduced his essentially sound strategy to rubble. Navarre claimed that his decision to parachute drop on Dien Bien Phu was perfectly logical given the situation in November 1953, one that conformed to his plan of drawing Viet Minh troops away from the Tonkin delta and avoiding a major battle.

Cabinet "leaks," which eventually evolved into a full-blown political scandal in the *affaire des fuites*, revealed that the French were overstretched in Upper Tonkin. This was merely an inconvenient indiscretion, however, compared to the blunder that followed Ho Chi Minh's announcement in November that the Viet Minh were willing to negotiate an end to the war. On February 18, 1954, the government foolishly agreed to meet the Viet Minh in Geneva, which, according to Navarre, "overnight upset all my calculations." This gave the insurgents and the Communist Chinese the incentive to commit a disproportionate number of forces to overwhelm the garrison at Dien Bien Phu, and to collect the political payoff.

Chinese sources now show Navarre to have been correct, at least partially. To fully understand the Communist strategy, Dien Bien Phu must be placed in the context of major diplomatic initiatives that followed the end of the Korean War in July 1953. As part of a calculated "peace offensive," in late September Moscow proposed a five-power conference, to include China, whose goal was to reduce international tensions. Beijing supported the Soviet initiative, publicly stating that the Indochina situation should be resolved by a meeting of the big powers.

Chinese pressure was at the origins of Ho Chi Minh's stated willingness in November 1953 to negotiate an end to the war with France. In late January 1954, a four-power conference in Berlin agreed to meet in Geneva to discuss the restoration of peace in Korea and Indochina. The strategy that China forced on Giap sought to put the Communists in the best possible negotiating position—if the French sought to defend their *maquis* in Tonkin and Laos, then they would be overextended and open themselves to defeat. If they hunkered down in the Tonkin delta, then the Communists would carry a very favorable "war map" to Geneva. In short, the Chinese had designed a win-win situation, at least for them. In retrospect, even the French army's official study of the Indochina War blamed the *Deuxième Bureau* for failing to sniff out this carefully crafted ruse, one that conformed to Giap's strategy of enticing the French—and later the Americans—into the outlying regions where they could be isolated and overwhelmed by a superior force.

While it is true that French intelligence did not supply Navarre with a blueprint of the Communist "master plan," to shift the blame for the defeat onto the shoulders of the *Deuxième Bureau*—or French politicians, for that matter—is unfair.

It is true that the French response to the Communist challenge was fragmented and inadequate. However, French intelligence did provide the French commander in chief a picture of the enemy that should have allowed him to make more judicious decisions, had he kept a more open mind. French intelligence documents suggest that Giap was keeping his options open until well into November.

On September 23, French intelligence reported that Viet Minh divisions concentrated around the delta were in a defensive position but had begun to infiltrate some regiments through the so-called de Lattre Line, consisting of blockhouses placed around the delta. "We retain the hypothesis that the campaign can begin by infiltrations in the delta," the report concluded.

On October 22, French intelligence reported that Viet Minh intelligence officers from the 312th and 308th divisions had been reconnoitering attack sites on the northern fringes of the delta, while elements of the 312th were training for urban warfare, which "would seem to indicate that the 312 is preparing to attack urban centers." But French *maquis* attacks against Lao Kay, on the Red River near the Chinese frontier, had caused some Viet Minh troops to be diverted there.

On November 13, it was noted in a report based at least in part on a defector's information that two divisions and part of another were prepared to intervene in the delta, possibly by December 1, while a regiment of the 325th Division stationed near Vinh in Annam had been ordered toward the delta on November 6. But the shift of many of the Viet Minh divisions toward the northwest in late November was immediately detected by the *Deuxième Bureau*, which also drew the proper conclusions from it. "The [Viet Minh] high command has manifestly changed its plan," it declared on December 7. "Rather than aim at the delta, the principal Viet Minh effort seems to be directed toward the Northwest."

At this point, French intelligence attributed the change in plan not to Chinese influence, as we now know was the case, but to the success of Navarre's strategy in the summer and autumn of 1953 of keeping the Viet Minh off balance with a series of spoiling operations and deceptions. The French raid on the Viet Minh supply base at Langson in July (Operation Pelican), a deception run in September 1953 that forced the Viet Minh to shift troops to block a threatened French amphibious operation in northern Annam, followed in October by Operation Mouette, which struck hard at the 320th Division south of the delta, and the attack on Lao Kay near the Chinese frontier, had produced indecisiveness in the Viet Minh high command. Giap renounced his idea of attacking the delta and decided to deal with the softer target of the *maquis* in Upper Tonkin.

Navarre complained that virtually his only intelligence on the enemy came from radio intercepts. But these gave him an enormous amount of information and allowed him to monitor the reactions of his enemy to his every move. On November 28, 1953, barely a week after the surprise French occupation, French intelligence reported that the paratroop drop on Dien Bien Phu initially had puzzled the Viet Minh because its purpose was not readily apparent.

Because they probably expected the French to move directly to Lai Chau, the Viet Minh jumped to the conclusion that Operation Castor was a deep raid like that launched against the Viet Minh supply base at Langson in the summer of 1953. But Giap quickly reached the correct conclusion that the purpose of Castor was to support French-led Montagnard guerrillas in Upper Tonkin. On the day after the landing, according to one report, Giap began to order troops toward Dien Bien Phu in the belief that the French might be forced to withdraw or defend their base. French intelligence believed him especially eager to deal with the guerrillas before they could disrupt his supply lines.

Historians have long echoed Navarre's *cri de coeur* in award-ing low marks to French intelligence for desperately underesti-mating the ability of the Viet Minh to bring such a large amount of troops, artillery and anti-aircraft guns to successfully besiege the French camp. Even a cursory scan of the intelligence papers, however, reveals that these documents provided the French com-mander with enormously useful information, enough to serve as the basis for a sound decision to stand and fight or cut and run.

When the French seized Dien Bien Phu to derail Giap's offen-sive against the *maquis*, Navarre took the risk that his *base aéroterrestre* could take the best that Giap could throw at it. In making that calculation, he held in his hand intercepts that allowed him to trace the movement of Giap's divisions as they disengaged from the delta and threaded their way through the mountains toward Dien Bien Phu in November and December 1953, divisions that included the 351st heavy artillery division and the 367th anti-aircraft regiment.

Navarre's insistence that he was unaware of the potential of Chinese assistance also rings hollow. Six weeks before Castor was launched, the *Deuxième Bureau* had reported an enormous increase in Chinese aid, which "has now lost its character of the improvised supply of heterogenous surplus, and once again underlines the effort of rationalization undertaken by the Viet Minh." And in any case, the possibility of Chinese assistance should always have been in the forefront of Navarre's calcula-tions. As will be seen, Chinese intervention ultimately proved to be the decisive factor in the tactical as well as the strategic phase of the campaign.

Having decided to accept battle, French intelligence gave the high command more than adequate warning of Giap's every move. Radio intercepts of December 22 revealed Viet Minh observers posted on the heights above the valley openly dis-cussing ways of attacking the French position. Even at this early date, they divulged that their priority would be to neutralize Dien Bien Phu's airstrip, the key to the campaign. Navarre was aware that Giap had contemplated a January assault on Dien Bien Phu and that the Viet Minh had been deterred by Chinese advice, by the fact that Giap's artillery was not yet in place, and by an unexpectedly swift French buildup.

Radio intercepts allowed the French to hear about Viet Minh requests for supplies, deliveries of vast quantities of munitions throughout the battle, and the arrival of artillery and reinforcements around Dien Bien Phu in the winter of 1953-1954. Based on these messages, the French constructed an accurate enemy order of battle, including enemy logistical and military capabilities. Even the code names the Viet Minh established for their own units and for the French positions did not baffle French intelligence, including the identity of the man referred to as Mr. Ngoc or Hong Linh, who was none other than Giap himself.

Radio intercepts alerted the French in early January that the Viet Minh had located the bunkering station for the airstrip and the munitions depot, and that enemy unit intelligence officers had been called in to discuss attack plans around a carefully constructed model of the French position. These open discussions revealed to de Castries and Cogny that Giap, at Chinese insistence, would attack the valley, strongpoint by strongpoint, rather than attempt a "human wave" assault designed to swallow the entire position.

The Viet Minh broadcast the results of POW interrogations over the radio and the hours when French guard details changed, so that raids and sabotage missions could be planned for those times. Even when the French systematically ambushed Viet Minh intelligence and raiding parties that crept into their positions at night, it never occurred to the Viet Minh that their radios were being read like a book. "It is possible that spies have denounced Viet Minh activities in the area of Fu Tuu [probably Beatrice]," concluded a radio intercept of March 11. At 7 P.M. on March 13, 1954, the Viet Minh radio broadcast an appeal to their soldiers to "win the battle of Dien Bien Phu." Attack assignments and times were sent out. The Viet Minh artillery barrage that slammed into the French fortified hill called Beatrice, announcing the beginning of the battle, came as no surprise to the French, who knew the precise time and the main axis of the Viet Minh advance.

If the Chinese are to be believed, it is clear that without their substantial assistance, Giap probably could not have won at Dien Bien Phu. And this despite the fact that the French were shoehorned into poorly conceived and constructed defensive positions, lacked air support, were completely dominated by Viet Minh artillery, and only a quarter or so of the French forces, namely legionnaires and paratroopers, put up serious resistance.

Chinese advisers trained Viet Minh troops in tactical methods perfected in Korea, including sniping and engineering techniques. At Chinese insistence, the Viet Minh converted some infantry units to two new artillery divisions. When Viet Minh morale began to falter due to high casualties caused by frontal assault, the Chinese organized a new tactic that spun webs of trenches around French positions so that, isolated, they would fall to attackers who charged from close quarters. These changes were recorded by French radio intercepts and air reconnaissance photographs. It is not clear that the French caught wind of a slackening of Viet Minh resolve as the monsoons approached, a resolve stiffened by Chinese insistence that Dien Bien Phu must be taken before a cease-fire was declared. To make sure that Giap persisted, they trained and equipped two Viet Minh battalions with 75mm recoilless guns and Katyusha multitube rocket launchers for the final assault. On May 7, the garrison surrendered, and de Castries, still wearing his red spahi cap, was taken as he sat in his bunker.

It is obvious that the French had more than adequate intelligence on the Viet Minh, and still it did not save them. Why? Because Navarre failed to make logical decisions on the basis of his intelligence information. He continued to believe, as did the vast majority of French officers, that despite the Viet Minh buildup, Dien Bien Phu would remain inviolate.

The charge that the *Deuxième Bureau* did not warn Navarre that he was headed for disaster is unconvincing. That was simply not the role of military intelligence, whose function was to provide information on which the commander in chief could base his decisions. And if French intelligence did nothing to challenge the firm belief that Dien Bien Phu would shatter Giap's attacks as had Na San in 1952, would it have made a difference? Would such a challenge, assuming that there had been any intelligence officer bold, clear-sighted or foolhardy enough to have made it, have fundamentally altered Navarre's decision? The answer must be no.

In retrospect, it was not Navarre, but Giap and Ho Chi Minh who could more plausibly claim to have been "stabbed in the back." At Geneva the Chinese played their hand at the expense of the Viet Minh. In 1949, China had come to the support of the Viet Minh in part out of solidarity with another Communist insurgency. But Beijing's major motivation was to eliminate Tonkin as a possible base for a Nationalist Chinese resurgence with French connivance.

By 1953, when it was apparent that even the Americans were not prepared to invite the Nationalist Chinese into the Korean War and the French were in no position to do this in Tonkin, Communist China needed time to put its domestic house in order and end its diplomatic isolation with openings to the Western powers. Therefore, Chinese Premier Chou En-lai agreed to the partition of Vietnam, thus undercutting the Viet Minh desire for a united Vietnam under Communist rule. When the Soviets backed the Chinese view, Ho and Giap realized that they had become the final casualties of Dien Bien Phu.

Lost in Laos

As told by Colonel Lawrence R. Bailey,
U.S. Army (ret.) to Ron Martz

I was with the U.S. Army Air Forces during World War II, flying B-29 bombers over Tokyo. I left the service in 1945, only to be recalled as an Army National Guard officer in 1952 for the Korean War. In Korea I flew a Cessna L-19 as an artillery spotter for the 25th U.S. Infantry Division over enemy positions. I remained on active duty after the war—I was a major then—and was assigned to Laos in December 1960 to serve as the assistant Army attaché in the U.S. Embassy in Vientiane, Laos. One of my duties was to fly U.S. Ambassador Winthrop Brown and members of the embassy staff throughout Laos, Thailand and Vietnam.

Laos was then in the midst of a civil war, with rebel Captain Kong Le's "Neutralist" forces, backed by the Soviet Union, in control of the strategically important Plain of Jars. They had allied themselves with the Communist Pathet Lao, nominally under the control of Lao Prince Souphanouvong but influenced greatly by the North Vietnamese Army, which had battled the French for control of Vietnam. The third faction was the Royal Lao under Prince Boun Oum and General Phoumi Nosovan, which was backed by the U.S. Central Intelligence Agency (CIA). Meanwhile, the State Department and the CIA were feuding over which faction to support.

On March 23, 1961, I hitched a ride on *Rose Bowl*, one of several U.S. Air Force Douglas C-47s that were specially equipped for aerial photography and electronic surveillance, operating out of Vientiane. *Rose Bowl* had been searching for an elusive radio beacon on the Plain of Jars that Soviet Ilyushin-14 transports had been using in bad weather to home in on the airport at Xieng Khoung and deliver supplies to the Neutralist forces of Kong Le.

Rose Bowl's crewmen were scheduled to fly to Saigon in Vietnam for some rest and relaxation; I was going along to retrieve a twin-engine Beechcraft L-23D that had been assigned to the embassy in Vientiane but had been undergoing maintenance in Saigon. But *Rose Bowl*'s flight plan called for a circuitous route that took us north and northwest from Vientiane over the Plain of Jars in one last effort to find the beacon.

My fellow passenger on *Rose Bowl* that day was Army Warrant Officer Edgar Weitkamp, 31, of York, Pennsylvania, an administrative assistant in the attaché's office. I didn't know the crew except for the pilot, Air Force 1st Lieutenant Ralph Magee, 29, from Port Sulphur, Louisana, and copilot 1st Lt. Oscar B. Weston, 30, of Norfolk, Virginia. Not until years later did I learn the names of the others: 2nd Lt. Glenn Matteson, 23, of Dallas, the navigator; Staff Sgt. Alfons Bankowski, 31, of Stamford, Connecticut, the engineer; Staff Sgt. Frederick T. Garside, 24, of Plymouth, Massachusetts, the assistant engineer; and Staff Sgt. Leslie V. Sampson, 24, of Richey, Montana, the radio operator.

That morning was bright and clear as we took off from Vientiane's Wattay Airport, unusual for a Laotian spring, when skies usually are clotted with a thick gauze of gray smoke from slashing and burning to prepare the fields for planting. There was no hint of trouble as we turned northeast from Vang Vieng and moved over rebel-held territory at 8,000 feet. Neither I nor any members of the crew were concerned about the flight. Although the United States "unofficially" had some 400 American military advisers assisting the Royal Lao Army, our country was not a combatant in the civil war, and our plane was clearly marked. Although some of our planes had been shot at in previous weeks, the largest weapon used had been a .50-caliber machine gun. There was no indication that either the Pathet Lao or the Neutralists possessed anti-aircraft artillery or knew how to use it.

About 11 A.M., we passed over a small grass airstrip near the village of Phonsavan, northeast of the town of Xieng Khoung. I was sitting just behind the trailing edge of the left wing. Behind me, two crew members had taken off the door and set up a K-17 camera to photograph troop positions. As I reached down to retrieve the sack lunch I had brought along I heard two loud reports on the right side of the plane.

I looked across the aisle at Ed Weitkamp. He had a strange, puzzled look on his face. "They're shooting at us," he said.

"Are we hit?" I shouted.

One of the crew members passed us, heading for the cockpit. "Yeah, right side, pretty bad," he said.

I got out of my seat to inspect the damage. There was a large hole in the outer wing panel, obliterating the U.S. Air Force star. We had been hit by what appeared to be a 37mm anti-aircraft round. There was a second large hole in the fuel cell directly behind the engine. A huge mass of bright orange flames and black smoke was boiling out of it. Someone had suddenly escalated the war, and we were its first victims.

As a pilot, I knew intuitively that the airplane was not going to fly more than a few seconds. *Rose Bowl* was doomed.

"We're on fire! We've got to jump!" I shouted.

The crew members and Weitkamp scrambled for their parachutes. I was already wearing mine. Through some strange quirk of fate, I had chosen a backpack-type parachute when offered one that morning by Magee and wore it throughout the flight. It was the only chute of its type on board. Weitkamp and the crew had chest-pack parachutes and were wearing only the harnesses when the plane was hit. The canopies were stored against the forward bulkhead. There was nothing I could do to help them. One more set of hands clawing at the canopies would only add to the congestion. I went to the open door and threw myself out.

The instant I jumped I felt the plane break into a violent spin to the right. Had I hesitated even a second longer I would have been thrown back inside and trapped by the centrifugal force. Some part of the airplane banged me hard on my left side as I jumped.

As soon as my chute opened I noticed my left arm flopping around uncontrollably. It was broken just below the shoulder. I ignored the useless arm and began searching the sky for the plane and other chutes. The plane was making a terrible howling sound as it fell directly beneath me in a wild corkscrew spin, heading straight into the ground, its engines still at cruise power. There were no other chutes. The plane crashed, carrying six crew members and Weitkamp to their deaths.

I came down hard in a flat, grassy field, surrounded by low, rolling hills studded with clumps of pine trees. I could see smoke from the crashed plane rising from behind a low hill about a mile to the west. I knew no one had survived that crash, but I wanted to get there to see for myself. I was having difficulty moving because of my broken arm and severe bruises and cuts to my lower legs, ankles and feet.

I pulled myself to my feet and took a few steps before collapsing in pain. I couldn't walk, and crawling was just as futile because of my injuries. I lay back in the grass in frustration and tried to organize my thoughts and take a quick inventory of my belongings. My passport had disappeared, but I still had my wallet with my military ID card, a handkerchief and a pocket knife.

With the pocket knife I cut away some of the parachute's shroud lines and immobilized my broken arm by tying it against my body.

When I was finished, I lay back in the grass and waited for help. I waited more than an hour before a search party of about a dozen soldiers came over a ridgeline to the south. I knew I needed medical attention, and these people, whoever they were, were my only chance. I couldn't run with my injured legs and broken arm. I couldn't hide in this open country. I couldn't defend myself with a pocket knife. Escape and resistance were out of the question. When the search party got within about a quarter-mile, I pulled myself up and yelled, "Hey you!" The soldiers froze in place, startled at the sound of my voice. Then they all came rushing at me. My heart sank when I saw them. They wore American-issue olive drab fatigues, and most of them had American-made weapons, but they were Neutralist soldiers.

As they approached, one of the soldiers who appeared to be the leader held up his hands, indicating he wanted me to surrender. I pointed at my left arm and shouted, "It's broke!"

Slowly, the patrol leader raised his rifle and pointed it in my direction. He fired once, the round snapping past my head. In frustration, I said to myself, "The hell with this," and collapsed back onto the ground.

The leader approached and jabbed his rifle toward me, shouting in broken English: "Can kill! Can kill!"

I said nothing, but pointed at my arm again. Finally, he realized I was badly injured and was no threat.

After I was searched, the soldiers motioned with their rifles for me to go with them. I was their prisoner. Unknown to me at the time, I had just become the first American prisoner of war in Southeast Asia. Cases of military and civilian government personnel missing and unaccounted for in Southeast Asia have been assigned case numbers by the Defense Intelligence Agency. I am case No. 0003 in DIA files. The other men on *Rose Bowl* are listed as case No. 0004. Case No. 0001 involves Richard Fecteau and Charles Downey, DIA agents captured in China in 1954. Case No. 0002 is that of Charles Duffy, an American civilian worker at the embassy in Vientiane who went hunting one day in January 1961 and never returned. Fecteau and Downey were actually prisoners of the Cold War, not prisoners of the war in Southeast Asia. And there was never any indication Duffy was a prisoner.

My status was as confusing to my captors as it was to me. Neither they nor I was sure if I was a prisoner of war or a political hostage. Since I was wearing civilian clothes, my captors thought I might be a spy. But as an embassy official I was supposed to be guaranteed diplomatic immunity, but that counted little to rebel Captain Kong Le's followers or to the Pathet Lao.

I was quickly carried to a nearby jeep and driven to a medical clinic at Phonsavan airport, where I was handed over to several North Vietnamese doctors. They cleaned me up and began pumping saline solution into me. Then they gave me a shot, and I passed out.

Later that night, I swam slowly out of the drug-induced fog. My left arm and most of my upper body were locked in a cast, my arm held away from my body at a 45-degree angle. My legs had been washed and cleaned and some type of salve applied to the wounds. The pain had eased to a dull throb.

The next morning I went through the first of what would be six straight days of interrogations. The interrogations were usually conducted by two Pathet Lao officers and one of Kong Le's officers, who did the interpreting. Their initial questions were typical of what I was to hear in all the interrogations I faced over the next month:

How many Americans were in Laos?

Where were the Royal Lao Army forces of General Phoumi Nosovan?

Where was guerrilla leader Vang Pao?

What was the American policy toward Laos?

Some questions I could not answer. Others, I would not answer. As the questioning wore on, my most frequent response was, "I don't know." When I answered "I don't know" too often, the Pathet Lao threatened to kill me. Their threats had little impact, and I continued to feign ignorance, even though I didn't believe giving only name, rank and serial number would work to my advantage in this situation, because I claimed to be a political hostage, not a prisoner of war. I was not a combatant, I repeatedly told my captors. I was an assistant attaché with diplomatic immunity. I adopted the attitude of "How can I be a prisoner of war when my country isn't warring with you?" Neither the Pathet Lao nor the Neutralists bought that argument, but I believed it confused them and had enough impact to ensure I received somewhat better treatment than other Americans captured a few weeks later.

After six days of fruitless questioning, my captors apparently decided they had had enough of me. On the morning of March 30, 1961, I was taken to the Xieng Khoung airport and placed aboard a Soviet-built Antonov-2 Colt. My face was covered with the blue civilian shirt I had been wearing when shot down, and a Lao soldier rode with me to make sure the blindfold remained in place. When we landed after about an hour's flight, I had no idea where I was. I was dumped in the middle of a field of tall grass, and the plane took off, leaving me alone. I couldn't walk because of the injuries to my legs and could barely move because of the cast around my arm and upper body. I was alone and helpless.

It was some time before a jeep carrying several Pathet Lao soldiers came to retrieve me. My new guards were not particularly conscientious about my blindfold, and I was able to lift the shirt to get some sense of my new surroundings. I was in a small village somewhere in the mountains. There were the usual split-bamboo houses with thatched roofs, wandering water buffalo, mongrel dogs, and scrawny chickens scratching in the dirt. But at one point I saw a small Buddhist monument I recognized from photographs I had studied of Laos prior to arriving in Vientiane. That monument, I knew, was in the village of Sam Neua, the provincial capital and Pathet Lao headquarters in northeast Laos, just a few miles from the Vietnam border. There was a moment of elation when I realized where I was. It put me somewhere on the map. At least I knew where I was, even if no one else I cared about did.

I was taken to a two-story stucco house of French design in the center of town and put in a small room on the ground floor. When the guards shut the door, darkness enveloped the room. The only window faced the front of the house and the street, but all the glass had been knocked out and tin nailed over it. A few rays of light filtered in through the left side of the window, where the tin was about 3 inches short of the top of the frame. This was to be my home for most of the next 17 months, a dark, drab isolation chamber in which I was held in solitary confinement.

For the first 30 days of captivity I was flat on my back, lying on the stretcher in the middle of the floor of that room because of the cast and the injuries to my legs. Once a day I was given a ball of rice to eat and boiled water or tea to drink. Occasionally the rice had a piece of water buffalo or sausage in it, but most frequently my only supplement was a turnip-like vegetable or an occasional Russian tin of fish. Dysentery, fevers and colds became constant companions. I weighed 185 pounds when captured, but the weight quickly fell off me.

The only break in those interminable first 30 days came during interrogations. The U.S. Seventh Fleet had moved into the region on President John F. Kennedy's orders, and my captors were particularly interested in it and the number of American troops in Laos. Although I was frequently threatened with death if I did not cooperate, I began to see these interrogations as games to keep me occupied, to help me pass the long, lonely days.

No matter what the question, my favorite answer was, "I don't know." The interrogator's comeback was usually, "What is your guess?" So I'd give him a guess. I told him the Seventh Fleet had 5,000 ships. I told him they were all in the South China Sea. Other days, I told him the fleet had a dozen ships, all of which were in the Mediterranean. It got to be a game to see how many different ways I could describe the Seventh Fleet. If my interrogators caught on, they never told me or punished me.

It was a full 30 days before I was able to stand and shuffle a few steps around the room. Escaping the confines of the stretcher was a major event for me. It made life that much more bearable. I did not want my captors to know I had regained the strength in my legs and could walk again, though. That gave me knowledge they did not have. I was in control of that part of my life, not them. It was some time before they realized I no longer was confined to the stretcher.

Small things began to take on major significance. A nail in the wall and a pinhole in the tin covering the window became two of the most important aspects early in my 17 months of solitary confinement. The nail provided a tool. With it I could make a calendar to keep track of the time that moved ever so slowly. I could also use the nail to enlarge the hole in the tin. I spent days enlarging the hole and fretting over its size. Too large, and the guards would discover it and patch it up; too small, and I would not be able to see through it. When I had enlarged the hole enough, I could stand on my tiptoes and see out into the street. It was like stepping into another life. That peephole became my window to the world. That peephole enabled me through my imagination to leave the cell for hours at a time each day and participate in the lives of those who passed in front of the house.

Instead of lying on my bed, staring at the ceiling and feeling sorry for myself, I was able to escape into the fantasies I constructed about the people of Sam Neua. I gave them families. I gave them jobs. I constructed lives for them and helped them live those lives, even though I was trapped and alone in my room.

When I wasn't peering through the peephole, I was pacing. For hours on end I would pace counterclockwise around the 12-by-15 room, trying to retain some sense of physical well-being while making the time pass. I felt that if I stopped pacing, time would stop. If time stopped, my life stopped. Time became my enemy, not the Pathet Lao, who treated me more with indifference than hostility.

Life in solitary confinement became a progression of events, not days. Events had more meaning than days, and I lived from event to event: the next meal, the next cigarette, the next interrogation, the next morning, the next breath.

Cigarettes became a big part of my life. I was permitted 10 each day, although the guards frequently would not give me that many. Much of each day was consumed by working on my cigarette rations: how much of each to smoke, how deeply to inhale, how much time should elapse between each smoke, how to save the scraps of tobacco from the butts to use to construct an 11th cigarette.

Thanksgiving 1961 proved to be a turning point in my will to survive. I had been held eight months, all of it in that small, dark room. I had not been permitted outside even to use the latrine. I had not been given anything to read or anything to write with. My hair and beard were long and matted. I had not even been given water with which to bathe. My contact with other humans was extremely limited. At least for Thanksgiving, I thought, the guards would give me some extra food, for they knew what day it was.

But as the day wore on, there was nothing—no food, no guards, no cigarettes. I went to the door and pounded on it.

"Food!" I demanded.

There was no reply. I pounded on the door and shouted again. Still no reply and no sound of movement on the other side. I had been abandoned and now was being ignored.

"This is my Thanksgiving, you dirty SOBs!" I shouted, pounding on the door in frustration. "In America, we wouldn't treat a dog like you people are treating me!"

Angry and bitter, I retreated to my cot, vowing to survive so I could tell the world what had happened to me.

After one year in captivity, I was moved out of the small room to a building across the street. The brief exposure to daylight and the momentary freedom gave me hope that something was happening that might lead to my release. Unknown to me, negotiators in Geneva had been trying since the previous May to work out a stable peace for Laos that included a prisoner exchange.

My new home was a cell in what appeared to be a city administrative building. It was smaller than the other room, but just down the hall were two South Vietnamese paratroopers who had been captured several months earlier. One of them spoke some English, and we were able to hold brief conversations. But the best thing about my new surroundings was that I was permitted outside to use the latrine. It was a small thing, but after months of confinement, those walks to the latrine were the high point in my day.

Within weeks of the move, my treatment began improving. I received letters and packages from home. I was encouraged to write letters. I was allowed to bathe and cut my hair and beard.

Finally, on August 12, 1962, I was taken from my cell and driven to the airfield southeast of town where I had arrived 17 months earlier. I was put aboard an Antonov An-2 Colt with several Pathet Lao guards.

I didn't know if we were headed for Peking, Hanoi or "Mossacow," as the guards referred to it, but I was out of that cell. Several bottles of Tuborg beer were rolling around on the floor of the plane. When I looked at them, one of the guards picked up a bottle and handed it to me. I pried open the top and took a swallow. It was warm and flat, but it was the most wonderful thing I had ever tasted. That beer tasted of freedom, of civilization, of life—all the things I had been denied the last 17 months.

The plane landed at the Xieng Khoung airport, and I was transferred to a prison camp known as Latrang. As I was led into the camp, a tall, bearded man who looked to be American came out to meet me.

"Major Bailey, I presume?" he said.

"Yes, Bob [Lawrence Robert] Bailey," I said, smiling.

The man introduced himself as Grant Wolfkill, a cameraman for NBC-TV. He had been captured in May 1961 with Air America helicopter crewmen Edward Shore, Jr., and John McMorrow. They were being held at Latrang with Army Special Forces Sergeant Orville Ballenger, Air America mechanic Lorenzo Frigilano and two Thai soldiers. Ballenger had been captured during the battle for Vang Vieng in April 1961. Frigilano was a Filipino mechanic captured by the Neutralists during the Battle of Vientiane in December 1960.

"You don't know how glad I am to see you guys," I said. It was an incredibly emotional experience to see other Americans and to be able to talk to them after so many months of isolation.

On August 17, 1962, the six of us were loaded on a Russian twin-engine transport, and we took off for Vientiane. When we landed at Wattay Airport, we were met by U.S. Ambassador Leonard Unger, a representative of the new Lao coalition government and other officials. "Some newsmen want to talk to you, but we don't have much time. Your plane to the Philippines is wait-ing," Unger said.

I did not want to go to the Philippines. I wanted to stay in Laos. I wanted to go back to my quarters, pick up my uniforms and carry on with my life where it had been interrupted 17 months earlier. But neither the State Department nor the Army was having any of that. They wanted me out of Laos immediately. My presence would be an embarrassment to the new government. I had not been physically abused while confined, but I had lost 70 pounds and weighed a skeletal 115 pounds at the time of my release. If I remained in Vientiane, I would be a nagging reminder of the civil war and the earliest American prisoners of war.

I was quickly whisked to the waiting aircraft, and within a few minutes Ballenger, the Air America employees and I were on a plane for the Philippines. I was free at last. But Laos was just beginning its descent into hell.

U.S. Complicity

By Colonel William Wilson, U.S. Army (ret.)

Pesident John F. Kennedy confronted a deteriorating situation in South Vietnam from the moment he took office in 1961. In Laos, U.S. friend Phoumi Nosavan was losing ground to a pro-Communist group supported by the Soviet Union. Rioting Buddhists and students were tearing apart South Vietnamese cities while terror squads murdered South Vietnamese officials, and U.S. military advisers died in battles half-heartedly fought by the Army of the Republic of Vietnam (ARVN) against the Viet Cong.

South Vietnamese President Ngo Dinh Diem believed, like the former emperors of China, that he possessed a "mandate from heaven," and he expected the people to follow him as a leader by divine right. Diem's leadership was limited by his use of his family to maintain power. His brother Ngo Dinh Nhu ran the secret police force, and other family members exercised dictatorial control over various provinces. In addition, Diem's practice of forcing military commanders to work in concert with provincial leaders who were primarily politicians was a disaster.

Early in February 1962, the Kennedy administration replaced the Military Assistance Advisory Group in Saigon with a new umbrella agency, the Military Assistance Command Vietnam

(MACV), which coordinated U.S. military policy and assistance in South Vietnam. American advisers had indeed improved the situation of the ARVN, but Diem tended to punish military success rather than reward it—fearing the rise of a general who might take his place.

In May 1963, conditions began to deteriorate rapidly. Early in the month, government officials in Hue allowed Roman Catholics to fly religious flags in celebration of the birthday of the city's archbishop (Diem's brother), but on June 3 the traditional flags to mark the birth of Buddha were banned. Local Buddhists, some 80 percent of Hue's population, complained that the act was discriminatory and, when city officials refused to lose face by admitting their error, took to the streets in protest. The result was nine Buddhists killed by government troops. Rioting soon spread from Hue to Saigon. Although the U.S. government urged Diem to take responsibility, he allowed his Catholic sister-in-law Madam Ngo Dinh Nhu to denounce the protestors as traitors and Communist sympathizers. The rioting spread and became a full political crisis.

In August and October 1963, according to the so-called Pentagon Papers, the United States gave its support to a cabal of army generals bent on removing the controversial Diem, whose rise to power Kennedy had backed and who had been the anchor of American policy in Vietnam for nine years. For weeks, with the president informed every step of the way, the American mission in Saigon maintained secret contacts with the plotting generals through one of the Central Intelligence Agency's most experienced and versatile operatives, Lieutenant Colonel Lucien "Lulu" Conein. An eccentric yet thoroughly professional agent, Conein inspired confidence in his Vietnam contacts, who, in accord with Asian tradition, placed more faith in personal ties than in formal relationships.

Born in Paris, Conein had been raised in Kansas by his aunt but retained his French citizenship. He enlisted in the French army at the outbreak of World War II in 1939, and deserted when France surrendered a year later. The Office of Strategic Services (OSS) recruited him to parachute into France with a French Resistance unit. When the war ended in Europe, Conein joined a company of French and Vietnamese commandos harassing Japanese posts in northern Vietnam. He entered Hanoi in 1945 with the OSS team that worked with Ho Chi Minh, and returned in 1954 on a mission to sabotage the Communist transportation system.

In violation of the Geneva Accords, Conein and his team formed secret "stay-behind" squads of Vietnamese, which were composed of about 200 anti-Communist political activists and code-named the "Hoa" and the "Binh." This mission was his one failure. The team accomplished little. Most team members were eventually compromised and captured. A star performer in the CIA's department of "dirty tricks," Conein also infiltrated covert agents into Eastern Europe and trained paramilitary forces in Iran.

Reassigned to Vietnam in 1962, Conein assumed the cover role of an adviser to the Saigon Ministry of the Interior, a deception that allowed him to gather intelligence on conspiracies against the government. His job was delicate, since he had to be sure that his reports of the coming coup were not leaked to Diem by American sympathizers with the regime.

According to the Pentagon Papers, Washington did not originate the anti-Diem coup; nor did Americans intervene in any way to try to prevent the assassination of Diem and his brother Ngo Dinh Nhu, who, as Diem's chief political adviser, had accumulated immense power. Popular discontent with the Diem regime focused on Nhu and his wife. For weeks the American mission maintained secret contacts with the plotting generals through Conein. Ambassador Henry Cabot Lodge, Jr., had occasion to describe Conein as the "indispensable man." Lodge stressed that Conein had been a friend with General Tan Van Don, figurehead commander of the South Vietnamese army for 18 years, and the general had expressed extreme reluctance to deal with anyone else.

The Pentagon Papers reproduced a sensitive cablegram dated October 5, 1963, from Lodge to the State Department that described a meeting with Conein and General Doung Van Minh. General Minh, who had been held back by Diem because of his popularity with the troops (who nicknamed him "Big Minh"), was chosen to be the leader of the plot against Diem. For some reason, Conein did not respect Minh, who he called a "glorified French army corporal." Oddly enough, Minh had noted that "Lulu Conein is the only American I could really trust." He told Conein that action had to be taken to change the government or the war would be lost to the Viet Cong, because the government no longer had the support of the people. Big Minh did not expect any American support, but he did need assurances that the U.S. government would not attempt to thwart the plan, and that it would continue to provide military and economic aid. Minh also revealed that one reason they had to act quickly was that many regimental, battalion and company commanders were working on coup plans of their own.

The subsequent messages from the White House indicated the National Security Council would support a coup that had "a good chance of succeeding." They also stressed that they would offer no "active promotion of a coup," and the desire for "plausible denial." After one coup attempt failed, the White House told Lodge to discourage the plot if quick success seemed unlikely. Lodge replied that the United States was unable to "delay or discourage a coup."

On August 29, impatient with Washington's disarray, Lodge sent a cable demanding decisive measures. "We are launched on a course from which there is no respectable turning back: the overthrow of the Diem government. There is no turning back because U.S. prestige is already publicly committed to this end in large measure, and will become more so as the facts leak out. In a more fundamental sense, there is no turning back because there is no possibility, in my view, that the war can be won under the Diem administration."

Kennedy approved Lodge's recommendations, giving him complete discretion to suspend U.S. aid to Diem. That gave Lodge a mandate to manage American policy in Vietnam—to topple the Diem regime. In November 1963, the coup proceeded on schedule. On the phone with Lodge, Diem asked about the attitude of the United States. Lodge replied that he was not well enough informed to say, and told him, "If I can do anything for your personal safety, please call me."

Conein, wearing his uniform and an ivory-handled .375 magnum frontier-model revolver strapped to his waist, was summoned to a rendezvous. He carried a satchel containing 3 million piasters, the equivalent of $40,000, in case the insurgents needed funds. He was equipped with two telephones, one linked to the main CIA office and the other to his villa, where a team of American Special Forces personnel was guarding his wife and children. Conein also had a radio in his jeep. As he drove to the headquarters, he transmitted to his superiors a prearranged cipher that signaled the imminent start of the coup.

A short time later, the South Vietnamese generals telephoned Diem and promised to allow him and his brother Nhu to leave the country unharmed if they capitulated. At first, Diem refused to yield. Then, realizing they could not hold out long, he and Nhu slipped into a Land Rover and drove to Cholon, the Chinese suburb of Saigon. After an unsuccessful attempt to negotiate, Diem phoned Minh to say that he would surrender unconditionally and that he and Nhu were in Saint Francis Xavier, a French Catholic church in Cholon. An M-113 armored personnel carrier and four jeeps under Minh's bodyguard commander, Captain Nhung, were sent to the church. As they left, Big Minh signaled Nhung by raising two fingers. By every account, Nhung then sprayed both brothers with bullets.

Ambassador Lodge was quoted in *The New York Times* on June 30, 1964, as stating: "We never participated in the planning. We never gave any advice. We had nothing whatever to do with it." On November 6, 1963, however, Lodge cabled Kennedy, "The ground in which the coup seed grew into a robust plant was prepared by us, and the coup would not have happened as it did without our preparation."

General William C. Westmoreland, who seven months after Diem's assassination replaced General Paul Harkins as commander of MACV, summed up the consequences of President Kennedy's involvement. "In his zeal, the young president made a grievous mistake in assenting to the overthrow of South Vietnamese President Ngo Dinh Diem in 1963," Westmoreland said. "In my view that action morally locked us in Vietnam. If it had not been for our involvement in the overthrow of President Diem, we could perhaps have gracefully withdrawn our support when South Vietnam's lack of unity and leadership became apparent."

Shedding New Light on the Gulf of Tonkin Incident

By Captain Ronnie E. Ford, U.S. Army

The Tonkin Gulf incident of 1964 may rank with the Japanese attack on Pearl Harbor and the assassination of President John F. Kennedy as events that Dr. David Kaiser of the U.S. Naval War College described as "controversies in American political history that dwarf all others."

The claim that the administration of President Lyndon Johnson deliberately triggered the Vietnam War by orchestrating the Tonkin Gulf incident and duping Congress is not a new one. Two recent books—Sedgwick Tourison's *Secret Army, Secret War*, and Dr. Edwin *Moise's Tonkin Gulf and the Escalation of the Vietnam War*—and other new revelations may indicate, however, that the claim is certainly more plausible than could once be proved. Thirty-three years after the fact, modern Tonkin Gulf researchers pointedly ask: Did the United States intentionally instigate the first attack on USS *Maddox* in the Gulf of Tonkin on August 2, 1964? Did Hanoi actually order a second attack on *Maddox* on August 4, 1964? And, if the Communist Vietnamese did not launch this second attack, then did Secretary of Defense Robert S. McNamara knowingly and deliberately mislead the U.S. Congress to obtain support for what would become the Tonkin Gulf Resolution, to ensure President Johnson's re-election and ultimately lead the United States into war?

The story of former South Vietnamese special operation forces, part of an American covert intelligence effort known as Operation Plan 34A (or 34 Alpha), is finally coming to light. Details about the plan are now available, thanks to the release of once-classified documents and disclosures by former Central Intelligence Agency (CIA) and military intelligence officials.

When Hanoi officially switched its reunification strategy to one of armed conflict in 1960, the Communists, through infiltration, began to build an organized regular force that threatened the American-backed Saigon regime in South Vietnam. In 1961, hoping to undermine the Communist Vietnamese government in Hanoi, the CIA initiated a joint sea-land covert special operation with the South Vietnamese government to dissuade Hanoi from its infiltration activities.

The CIA–South Vietnamese covert force conducted airborne, maritime and overland agent-insertion operations. South Vietnamese covert operatives were to gather intelligence, recruit support, establish bases of resistance and carry out psychological operations behind enemy lines. The maritime operation began as an infiltration operation. But beginning in June 1962, with the loss of the vessel *Nautelas II* and four commandos, it evolved into hit-and-run attacks against North Vietnamese shore and island installations by South Vietnamese and foreign mercenary crews on high-speed patrol boats.

While some infiltration operations had some initial successes, such successes were few. The CIA suspected the North Vietnamese were capturing and attempting to turn the agents immediately upon their arrival. By the end of 1963, a National Security Council Special Group, the staff of the special assistant for counterinsurgency and special activities of the Office of the Secretary of Defense, and the CIA were all apparently aware that the covert attacks were unproductive. According to former Secretary of Defense Robert McNamara, "It accomplished virtually nothing." But the operation was not discontinued. According to Tourison, by January 1964 McNamara had taken over the operation from the CIA, and it became known as 34-Alpha. Now in charge, the Pentagon assumed that the overwhelming majority of the airborne commando agents either had been killed or captured or were working for their captors, the Communist North Vietnamese.

Although it appeared that the program had been compromised, new agent teams continued to be recruited, trained and inserted into North Vietnam. By August 1968, approximately 500 of these men were presumed lost. In his book, Tourison poses an interesting question: Were these teams of commandos deliberately used initially to push Hanoi into war and later to test U.S. communications security, or were they simply victims of effective North Vietnamese counterintelligence operations? The answer lies in the story behind what were known as the U.S. Navy's DeSoto patrols.

DeSoto patrols were U.S. naval intelligence collection operations using specially equipped vessels to gather electronic signals intelligence from shore- and island- based noncommunications emitters in North Vietnam. By August 2, 1964, the Communist Vietnamese had determined that the DeSoto vessels were offshore support for a 34-Alpha operation that had struck their installations at Hon Me and Hon Ngu some 48 hours earlier. In retaliation, the North Vietnamese then conducted an "unprovoked attack" on *Maddox*, which was approximately 30 miles off the coast of North Vietnam. During the battle that ensued, one North Vietnamese patrol boat was severely damaged by *Maddox*, and two others were attacked and chased off by U.S. air support from the carrier USS *Ticonderoga*.

On August 4, 1964, *Maddox* and USS *C. Turner Joy* reported a second attack, this one occurring within 17 hours of 34-Alpha raids on North Vietnamese facilities at Cap Vinh Son and Cua Ron. On that day the National Security Agency (NSA) had warned that an attack on *Maddox* appeared imminent. An hour after the NSA's warning, *Maddox* claimed that she had established radar contact with three or four unidentified vessels approaching at high speed. *Ticonderoga* soon launched aircraft to assist *Maddox* and *C. Turner Joy*. Low clouds and thunderstorms reportedly made visibility very poor for the aircraft, and the pilots never confirmed the presence of any North Vietnamese attackers. During the next several hours, the ships reported more than 20 torpedo attacks, the visual sighting of torpedo wakes, searchlight illumination, automatic-weapons fire, and radar and sonar contact.

Despite the recommendation of Captain John J. Herrick, the recently assigned senior officer on board *Maddox*, that the circumstances—including darkness, stormy seas and nervous, inexperienced crewmen—warranted a "thorough investigation," Secretary of Defense McNamara told Congress there was "unequivocal proof" of the second "unprovoked attack" on U.S. ships. Within hours of McNamara's revelations, Congress passed the Tonkin Gulf Resolution, and the United States plunged into the only war it has ever lost.

McNamara's account, backed by the Johnson administration, did not go unchallenged. Before a joint executive session of the Senate Foreign Relations and Armed Services Committee debating full congressional support for the resolution, Senator Wayne Morse (D-Oregon), who had already dubbed the conflict "McNamara's War," declared: "I am unalterably opposed to this course of action which, in my judgment, is an aggressive course of action on the part of the United States. I think you are kidding the world if you try to give the impression that when the South Vietnamese naval boats bombarded two islands a short distance off the coast of North Vietnam we were not implicated." Senator Morse also noted that the American vessels were "conveniently standing by" as support for 34-Alpha operations.

In response, McNamara denied any U.S. naval involvement in the South Vietnamese-run operations, asserting that the DeSoto operations were neither support nor cover for 34-Alpha raids. Tourison sets the record straight on this issue. "The MarOps [maritime operations] were not CIA-supported South Vietnamese operations that the United States had no control over as former Secretary of Defense McNamara claimed," writes Tourison. "These operations were under U.S. control, not South Vietnamese."

McNamara also claimed that the *Maddox* crew had no knowledge of the 34-Alpha raids. McNamara now acknowledges that this claim was untrue, although he maintains that he did not know it at the time. Captain Herrick and his crew did indeed know of the 34-Alpha operations. In fact, retired Lieutenant General Phillip B. Davidson, the former chief of intelligence for the U.S. Army Military Assistance Command, Vietnam (MACV), cites Captain Herrick's observation that Maddox personnel were extremely concerned that the 34-Alpha operations were putting their ship in harm's way. Davidson further endorses Herrick's assessment that this concern may have resulted in an overly nervous crew and unreliable reporting about the second attack in the gulf.

On August 7, 1964, the Senate passed support for Tonkin Gulf Resolution 88-2, with Senators Morse and Ernest Gruening (D-Alaska) voting nay. The House voted 416–0 in support. Prophetically, Senator Morse closed his argument by saying, "I believe that within the next century, future generations will look with dismay and great disappointment upon a Congress which is now about to make such a historic mistake."

The events surrounding the resolution and its passage point to a tragic failure in the U.S. decision-making system of the time.

At a crucial moment in history, U.S. intelligence-collection agencies directly fed raw intelligence data to U.S. policy-makers without submitting that data to thorough and proper analysis. The prevalence of this kind of unpolished intelligence support to government leaders helped open the door to full U.S. involvement in the Vietnam War.

In 1972, Louis Tordella, the deputy director of the NSA, announced that the decoded message on which the NSA's August 4 warning to *Maddox* had been based actually referred to the original attack on August 2. And the "unequivocal proof" of the second attack consisted of decrypted North Vietnamese damage assessments of the first attack (August 2) that were presented to top-level U.S. decision-makers as the alleged second attack was being reported to the Pentagon. According to a *U.S. News and World Report* exposé, former CIA Deputy Director for Intelligence Ray S. Cline verified this series of mistakes in 1984. Given the extreme volatility and pressure of the situation, the fact that some decision-makers were confused by intercepts suggesting two attacks is understandable. That they acted so quickly on rash assumptions—removing the chance for necessary debate and analysis—added insult to injury in an already untenable decision climate.

In his book *Vietnam at War*, General Davidson pointed out that Herrick was a combat veteran who realized that the *Maddox* crew had never before been in combat. He claimed that Captain Herrick's assessment that the "entire action leaves many doubts except for apparent attempt to ambush at the beginning" remains the most valid summation of the second attack.

Understandably, in the United States the Vietnam War as a whole and the Tonkin Gulf incident in particular remain topics of widely ranging interpretation and debate. Former Secretary of Defense McNamara recently visited Hanoi, where he met with Communist Vietnamese Senior General Vo Nguyen Giap. McNamara also invited the Vietnamese to participate in a conference of top Vietnam War decision-makers to, according to press reports of the visit, "correct the historical record." During his visit, Giap told McNamara that "absolutely nothing" happened on August 4, 1964. McNamara later endorsed this statement by his former adversary.

In his recent book, *In Retrospect: The Tragedy and Lessons of Vietnam*, McNamara admitted that the United States "may have provoked a North Vietnamese response in the Tonkin Gulf," albeit innocently. He maintained, however, that "charges of a cloak of deception surrounding the Tonkin Gulf incident are unfounded. The idea that the Johnson administration deliberately deceived Congress is fake." Many disagree. Coincidentally, on the very day McNamara was in Hanoi, American veterans, historians and scholars met in Washington, D.C., for a conference sponsored by the Vietnam Veterans Institute. One of the conference's many prominent guest speakers was Daniel Ellsberg, the former Johnson administration member who leaked the Pentagon Papers to the press. In his presentation, Ellsberg addressed the question of whether the Johnson administration deliberately misled Congress: "Did McNamara lie to Congress in 1964? I can answer that question. Yes, he did lie, and I knew it at the time. I was working for John McNaughton. . . . I was his special assistant. He was Assistant Secretary of Defense for International Security Affairs. He knew McNamara had lied. McNamara knew he had lied. He is still lying. [Former Secretary of State Dean] Rusk and McNamara testified to Congress . . . prior to their vote. . . . Congress was being lied into . . . what was to be used as a formal declaration of war. I knew that. . . . I don't look back on that situation with pride."

Ellsberg was not the only former government official of the era to expose this alleged conspiracy. In 1977, former Under Secretary of State George Ball claimed in an interview televised by the British Broadcasting Corporation: "Many of the people associated with the war . . . were looking for any excuse to initiate bombing. The DeSoto Patrols were primarily for provocation. . . . There was a feeling that if the destroyer got into trouble, that would provide the provocation needed."

Was this provocation needed to initiate bombing, or to assist the Johnson administration during an election year? Either goal certainly seems plausible.

Interestingly, a resolution stating, "Upon request of South Vietnam or the Laotian government to use all measures including the commitment of U.S. Armed Forces in their Defense"—the very resolution that became the Tonkin Gulf Resolution—had been prepared in May 1964, three months before the "unprovoked attacks" ever occurred. At the time, Johnson was running his presidential campaign on a peace ticket. Johnson's main opponent for the presidency, Senator Barry Goldwater, was pushing for an even tougher U.S. stance in Southeast Asia. An "unprovoked attack" by North Vietnam would give Johnson the opportunity to respond with limited force and improve his image with the American people without appearing to agree with his main political opponent, a man the Johnson administration was busy painting as a candidate who would potentially lead the country into a nuclear war.

If this line of thinking was part of Johnson's plan, it was well-calculated. In response to the Tonkin Gulf attacks, the president launched a limited airstrike and warned Hanoi against further aggression. Thus, four months prior to the November election, he appeared firm but not a warmonger. His approval rating with the American people soared from 42 percent to 72 percent, and within three months he overwhelmingly won his campaign for the presidency.

Tourison claimed that the 34-Alpha raids and the DeSoto operations were carefully orchestrated to solicit a North Vietnamese response in the Gulf of Tonkin, a claim that appears at least plausible: "These facts argue that if U.S. communications intelligence resources were able to intercept these messages, Washington also would have known that Hanoi had placed all its forces [on a] total war footing. Intercepted passages would have revealed how closely Hanoi was monitoring the raids undertaken by MACSOG's [MACV's Studies and Observations Group] forces. Further, Washington would have known that Hanoi was closely watching the obvious high correlation between other Seventh Fleet electronic and communications intelligence activities in support of Plan 34A and the full range of covert maritime, airborne, agent, and psychological operations being conducted by MACSOG and the CIA. Information about these actions, in spite of increased questions about the widening war, was closely guarded by a select few in the executive branch who had a need to know."

McNamara explained it differently: "Although some individuals knew of both DeSoto and 34A operations and patrols, the approval process was compartmentalized; few, if any, senior officials either planned or followed in detail the operational schedules of both. We should have."

Tourison's position suggests quite the opposite, and testimony from Daniel Ellsberg seems to back him up: "One of my first jobs in the Defense Department was to carry around . . . the 30 day schedule, regularly, of those operations starting in August [1964]. . . . I carried those plans to Alex Chowpin in the U.S. State Department . . . to McGeorge Bundy . . . and they would initial it. They followed every aspect of it. This is what then both Rusk and McNamara testified to Congress about prior to their vote on a Tonkin Gulf Resolution that was to be used as a declaration of war."

The result of whatever actually did or did not happen in the Tonkin Gulf was that, by overwhelmingly approving the resolution, the U.S. Congress ceded to the president the power that America's Founding Fathers endowed only Congress—the power to declare war. According to McNamara, therein lies the significance of the Tonkin Gulf Resolution: "The fundamental issue of Tonkin Gulf involves not deception, but rather, misuse of power bestowed by the resolution. The language of the resolution plainly granted the powers the President subsequently used and Congress understood the breadth of those powers.... But no doubt exists that Congress did not intend to authorize, without further, full consultation, the expansion of U.S. forces in Vietnam from 16,000 to 550,000 men, initiating large scale combat operations with the risk of an expanded war with China and the Soviet Union, and extending U.S. involvement in Vietnam for many years to come."

Despite passage of the War Powers Act in 1973, the question of presidential versus congressional authority over U.S. military operations remains a topic of serious contention. In 1990, McNamara testified to the Senate Foreign Relations Committee that no president should be able to send American troops to war without congressional approval. He further testified that he believed President George Bush would seek congressional support before sending American troops to conduct combat operations against Iraq. Bush did, and McNamara added, "President Bush was right. President Johnson and those of us who served with him were wrong."

For the Tonkin Gulf incident itself, McNamara endorsed the hypothesis of former Assistant Secretary of State for Far Eastern Affairs William Bundy: "Miscalculation by both the U.S. and North Vietnam is, in the end, at root of the best hindsight hypothesis on Hanoi's behavior. In simple terms, it was a mistake for our administration, resolved to keep the risks low, to have 34 Alpha operations and the destroyer patrol take place even in the same time period. Rational minds could not readily foresee that Hanoi might confuse them ... but rational minds' calculations should have taken into account the irrational. . . . Washington did not want an incident, and it seems that Hanoi hadn't either. Yet, each misread the other, and the incidents happened."

Daniel Ellsberg, at the November 1995 Vietnam Veterans Institute Conference, was far more critical of those who served in the executive branch and notably more apologetic: "What I did not reveal in the Summer of 64 . . . was a conspiracy to manipulate the public into a war and to win an election through fraud . . . which had the exact horrible consequences the founders of this country envisioned when they ruled out, they thought as best they could, that an Executive Branch could secretly decide the decisions of war and peace, without public debate or vote of Congress. . . . Senator Morse, one of the two people who voted against the Tonkin Gulf Resolution told me in 1971, '. . . had you given us all that information . . . seven years earlier, in 1964, the Tonkin Gulf Resolution would never have gotten out of Committee. And, if it had, it would never have passed. . . .' But there was a time in my life later . . . knowing the consequences of all these policies . . . when I did say to myself that I'm never going to lie again with the justification that someone has told me I have to. . . . I've never been sorry I've stopped doing that."

Now that time has passed and some of the individuals involved have re-examined what happened, the shroud of controversy surrounding the events of August 4, 1964, has begun to lift. As mentioned earlier, the former secretary of defense endorsed a joint effort with the Communist Vietnamese to discuss and clear up some of the contentious areas of the Vietnamese conflict. This effort may prove difficult and ultimately fruitless unless the Vietnamese decide to be more candid.

Care must be taken with Communist Vietnamese versions of history. As a typical totalitarian regime, Hanoi is acutely aware of how it is perceived from abroad. The Communists monitor and often censor what is said or written about them by their own citizens. This sort of information-control policy helps to ensure that their "official" accounts of history are accepted by their populace and go unchallenged. They are quick to accept praise, warranted or not. And they are even quicker to deny fault, deserved or not.

In one of their more current official histories, the Communist Vietnamese claimed responsibility for the initial attack in the Gulf of Tonkin, but said that the second was an American fabrication to justify airstrikes on August 5. In an older history, they not only claimed the second attack on August 4-5, 1964, but declared that date as their navy's anniversary or "tradition day," proclaiming it the day "when one of our torpedo squadrons chased the destroyer *Maddox* from our coastal waters, our first victory over the U.S. Navy."

About this assertion, Douglas Pike, the foremost U.S. authority on the People's Army of Vietnam (PAVN), noted, "If the Gulf of Tonkin incident is a myth created by the Pentagon, as some revisionist historians claim, the PAVN navy is now part of the conspiracy." In this same history, the Communist Vietnamese claimed that their navy sank 353 American naval vessels. It is rational to believe that the number of U.S. Navy vessels lost to a fleet of Communist patrol boats, with a total arsenal of 60 torpedoes, was somewhat less.

These and other indicators revealed that, to the Communist Vietnamese, truth is simply a weapon. Given Hanoi's fondness for duplicity, we begin to understand the task faced by intelligence professionals of the Vietnam era—and by modern researchers, historians and former government officials who, with as much as 30 years of hindsight, are trying even today to unravel the events of that conflict.

First to Escape

By Eddie Morin

Isaac "Ike" Camacho was born in the farming community of Fabens, Texas, where crops and cotton-picking are a way of life. Along with his widowed mother and two sisters, he later moved to El Paso, where he attended Thomas Jefferson High School and enjoyed being a part of El Paso's large Mexican-American community.

In 1957, while Camacho was enrolled in the ROTC program, an airborne trooper addressed the group. He made quite an impression on Camacho and three of his buddies, who later joined the Army together and requested airborne training. For Camacho, it was the beginning of a successful military career.

By 1960, Camacho had been promoted to E-5 and was serving as an airborne jump instructor for the old 503rd Airborne (later the 173rd). A friend told him about an elite new unit then being formed that needed personnel. Intrigued, Camacho investigated and shortly became a member of the newly formed 77th Special Forces Group. At the end of the training period, he was ordered to Vietnam.

Initially, Camacho was assigned to the Kontum-Dak To area, in the A Shau Valley. During his second tour in-country in 1963, he was part of the 5th Special Forces Group, serving in the province of Hau Nghia. That unit had established an A-Team camp at Hiep Hoa, in the Plain of Reeds, about 45 miles northeast of Saigon, to train Civilian Irregular Defense Guard (CIDG) personnel to conduct reconnaissance and raids in enemy-controlled areas. Built on the bank of a canal and encircled with barbed wire, the 125-by-100-meter garrison was protected by .30-caliber machine-gun emplacements on all four corners. In addition, two 81mm mortars were located near the gates. There was ample reason for the high level of security, since the camp was located near Cambodia's infamous "Parrot's Beak" region, a major VC staging ground.

In October 1963 a friend of Camacho's who was also serving in the Special Forces, 1st Lt. Nick Rowe, was captured at Tam Phu, on the Ca Mau Peninsula. The following month it was Camacho's turn.

On the night of November 22, moving stealthily under cover of night, several hundred VC infiltrators attacked the Hiep Hoa outpost. Aided by information from their spies, the guerrillas were familiar with the garrison's layout and were also apparently aware that half the camp's troops were out on a reconnaissance mission. Moving in quietly, they quickly killed some of the perimeter guards and then machine-gunned the camp's inhabitants as they emerged from their billets. Several of the Special Forces troops manned a machine-gun position and began trying to stem the tide of invaders.

Camacho, who was the camp's heavy weapons specialist, grabbed a carbine and made his way to the mortar bunker, where he waged a one-man mortar barrage against the enemy. He was still firing approximately 30 minutes later when he was joined by Lieutenant John R. Colby, the detachment's executive officer, who was trying to rally the defending forces. In light of the attack's intensity, and seeing that some of the CIDG troops were fleeing, Colby decided that further efforts to defend the camp would be futile. He handed Camacho a grenade to use for added protection and ordered him to leave while he could.

Camacho left reluctantly. He knew that a couple of Americans were still fighting inside the camp. Once outside the compound, he thought of his friends and could not bring himself to abandon them. He re-entered the enclosure and encountered heavier firepower and exploding mortar rounds. When he suddenly came face to face with some VC, he blasted at them with his carbine. The enemy fire was so overwhelming that he tossed his grenade at the VC and made a dash for cover in a machine-gun bunker. But the VC soon located him, as well as Sergeant George E. Smith, Specialist Claude McClure and Staff Sgt. Kenneth M. Rorback.

"Apparently, I was seen," Camacho later recalled, "because in the next 30 seconds, I was surrounded and flashlights were being shined on me. I was ordered to get up, and as I did a VC grabbed my carbine. He felt the barrel, which was hot, then he said something to the others in Vietnamese. While they were tying me up, one VC gave me a butt stroke with his M-1 and I was out. When I came to, I had blood all over from a gash on the back of my head. Then another order was given, and we were practically dragged across the barbed wire.

"A few minutes later, aircraft came and started dropping napalm and making strafing runs. Our hands were tied at the elbows as tight as could be and they had rope around our necks. We were being pulled like donkeys. Once we got out of bomb range, Smitty and I were told to walk down this little road, and they began to lock and load their weapons. They were going to kill us, but then someone came from the front of the column and gave a different order. We were spared.

"They kept us blindfolded and moved us out—first on foot and then we were placed on an oxcart and covered with a tarp. I was able to move the canvas enough to see even though I was tied. We were going around Nui Ba Den Mountain, and I saw the north star in front of us. We might have been on Highway 22 or just a branch of the Ho Chi Minh Trail. When we entered Cambodia, the VC took off their headgear and began to sling arms. It seemed odd, because in Vietnam they controlled their noise, but over here they were unwinding, even talking. We traveled a long way blindfolded and were told to be quiet. Later that night we moved out on foot again.

"We boarded a sampan to reach this place that looked like an island—it had water all around it. It must have been some kind of haven or R&R center. The VC stacked their weapons and were cooking and relaxing. There were classrooms for training and indoctrination. We were placed in a hooch watched by four guards. They had us locked up with chains. Really, there wasn't much you could do about it with the chains around your ankle and fastened to a huge tree."

Two nights after Camacho's capture, a telegram was dispatched to his mother, Mary Elorreaga, informing her that her son was missing. It revealed only the briefest details of the Special Forces base camp's being overrun and promised that a representative of the U.S. Army would contact her soon.

The four Americans had been taken to Trai Bai, a small camp site near the Cambodian border, no more than 60 miles from Saigon. The Vam Co Dong River lies just east of it. The VC found it ideal as a jungle sanctuary. Everyone in the camp focused their attention on the new arrivals. Camacho's head was still aching, and it seemed to him that their chances of survival were slim.

The four Americans had another reason to be demoralized. The morning after their capture, the VC had received a radio dispatch announcing President John F. Kennedy's assassination. As the Americans were being taken through small hamlets inhabited by people who were sympathetic to the VC, the villagers had turned out to taunt them: "*Kennedy di-et*" ("Kennedy is dead").

Soon after they arrived at Trai Bai, Wilfred Burchett, an Australian writer and Communist sympathizer, and Roger Pic, a French photographer, arrived to document their plight. "I don't remember being photographed," said Camacho, "but the proof is there—all of us Americans in black pajamas. Wilfred Burchett walked up to me and introduced himself. He said that we Americans were in trouble because we were fighting an unpopular war, and that he would try to see what he could do to help us. He asked if I understood. He asked me a few questions, and I answered politely without giving out any real information. He asked me if there was anything he could do for me, and I told him, 'Yes, sir, can you tell me who won the fight between Sonny Liston and Cassius Clay?' He must have been disappointed, because he gave me this look and just walked away."

Shortly after that visit, Kenneth Rorback was summarily taken out and executed in retaliation for Operation Rolling Thunder, the bombing of North Vietnam authorized by President Lyndon B. Johnson. Camacho had to fight depression at that point. "I think what scared me most was when some Cubans came to talk to me," he recalled. "They had on berets like Che Guevara. The incident happened after Burchett left. What they did was sit me down on a stump, and they stood over me and looked down. I guess they were trying to make me feel low while they were on top. This one asked me, '*Eres Latino*?' ('Are you Hispanic?'), and I answered, 'I don't know what you're talking about.' Then he asked me, 'What is your nationality?' and I told him I was Indian.

"He asked me if I knew Fidel Castro, and I said no. He got real mad and said, 'You don't know Fidel Castro?' I told him, 'No, the only Castro I know is the Castro I went to school with in Fabens, Texas.' Next he asked 'Do you like guitar music?' I answered, 'Yes, I like guitar music.' Then he asked, 'Do you like Sabicas?' 'I don't know who Sabicas is,' I told him. 'You like guitar music but you don't know Sabicas?' I said, 'No.' He asked,

'How come you like guitar music?' and I responded, 'Because Elvis Presley played the guitar.'

"They got mad, and I heard them say, '*Este pendejo no sabe nada. Es un baboso bien hecho*' ('This fool knows nothing. He's a natural blithering idiot'). They didn't realize that I could understand what they were saying. One of them said to the other, '*Ya no voy' a hablar con este*' ('I'm not speaking to him anymore'). So he walked around and put his gun next to my temple. '*Hacete para ya!*' ('Move over there!') he said. I told him, 'If you're going to shoot me, just shoot me. I don't know what you're talking about.' I just kept speaking English all the time until they finally said, '*Dejalo, el no sabe nada. El es nada mas que un titere de los Estados Unidos*' ('Leave him alone, he knows nothing. He's nothing more than a puppet for the United States'). My questioner finally spoke in English and said, 'Well, you know you're here as a prisoner of war and these people have been suffering many years. We'll talk to you later.' I think they were trying to break us down mentally.

"The camp was administered by this Vietnamese who called himself 'the commissioner.' He would tell us what a predicament we were in, that they were being bombed all the time and it was hard to provide us with food and medicine. He would say, 'I understand that you've been sick, but you have no business in this country and must pay for your sins. What we expect from you is that you join with your fellow Americans, and now there are many people your age protesting the war, and you should join your comrades in the struggle to let the Vietnamese people live the way they want to.' It cracked me up because they had every bit of information about the anti-war movement.

"The interrogation included efforts to extract a confession, which mainly had to do with burning and looting and killing innocent children, murder and rape and all this other stuff. That's what the context of the confession was. Finally, they wanted us to admit that we had invaded their sovereignty by coming in and doing all these things. I never did sign it. They would pressure me by asking me, 'When are you going to see the light?' I told them the confession did not mean anything to me, and I asked, 'What do you want me to do, lie?' 'No, no,' they said, 'the confession must come from your heart.'

"During the first six months of my captivity, I told them that I was a supply clerk. They asked what kind of work that was, and I told them, 'If someone needed a canteen or a blanket, I would provide it.' They said, 'Oh, you were supplying war materiel?' and I denied it. 'No,' I said, 'It wasn't war materiel, just canteens and stuff like that.' Everything went good for a while until they called me in one day to interrogate me and showed me a copy of *Newsweek* magazine. They said, 'Do you know what this is?' I said, 'Yes, an American magazine.' They said, 'Turn to page 14,' so I did, and there was an article about Hiep Hoa, explaining how we had been captured. It said that Isaac Camacho had been teaching anti-guerrilla warfare. 'We really like this, and your people wrote this!' they said. 'You have been deceiving us!' They almost starved us to death after that article appeared.

"Then the *Chicago Tribune* and *The New York Times* had articles about Mike Mansfield and Ernest Gruening, two anti-war politicians. Every time they would get something like that, when we went into interrogations they would show it to us. They would boast, 'Even these people's hearts are for the VC—these are the true patriots.' It was very demoralizing.

"The camp was located under triple-canopied forest. You couldn't see the sky unless you were out on a work detail. It was always dark. I was kept in a cage just big enough to sleep and get some exercise. The first six months were probably the hardest, because they kept us in isolation. The only time I would see somebody is when they were going down to the well to wash up or clean the little cup they gave us. Then they decided to put us to work with a guard watching us so we couldn't talk.

"The first chance we had, we would talk to each other—'Hey, how are you doing? You all right?'—things like that. At first the guards would whack us across the back for talking, but they soon decided we weren't going to escape, and then we could talk a bit. Eventually we were able to carry on a conversation.

"We were fed just enough so we would be strong enough to work. One detail involved building a bomb shelter, and we had to go out half a mile in the woods to cut logs. It was on work details like this when we would get to see the sky. You don't know how nice it is to see a piece of blue out there in that type of situation. We'd look out and say, 'God, the sky looks beautiful.' The logs we cut had been knocked down by bombing or lightning, so we wouldn't bother the natural foliage.

"I was held in a cage approximately 8 feet by 6 feet in area. Originally, I had been placed in a one-man cell, but they put us in two-man cells to relieve the guard force. The cage was constructed of wood. They very seldom used bamboo except for maybe the rafters. The logs were hammered together with wooden pegs, not nails, and held really tight. The thatched roofs kept us dry during the monsoons. It would really pour, but by the time the water filtered through the branches and reached the cage, the roof would protect us.

"There was a hole dug at one end of the cage that we used as an air raid shelter. A couple of times we had to use it. They always had a small lamp on in our cage so they could observe us, and they would yell '*Pica*' when a plane approached. That meant we should turn off the lamp and take cover. During one Skyraider attack, we jumped into the hole, but the chains on our legs weren't long enough—our feet were sticking out. We knew that snakes and scorpions might be in the hole, but we still had to take cover. One bomb landed so close that the nose cone reached our cage. The foliage was scattered and you could smell smoke the next day because of the powder residue.

"We did more wood cutting and dug some wells. Another detail involved working on their rice mill. I couldn't believe how much rice they had. It was a mountain. It made me angry to see these guys pass my cage carrying sacks of flour or rice, condensed milk, vegetable oil for cooking, and all with lettering, saying: 'Donated by the people of the United States.' As a matter of fact, they made a rucksack out of this material so I could carry my personal items on work detail.

"My physical condition deteriorated horribly. I was underweight and had gone through malaria, hepatitis and beriberi. I was really afraid of beriberi because my skinny legs would inflate and I could take my finger and poke it down almost all the way and it would leave a deep dimple there. Later, it would slowly come back out. It was caused by vitamin deficiency.

"They served us *nuoc mam* sauce and plenty of rice. Sometimes it would be a mixture of half-rice and half-salt. They used to give us these old dried fish with worms crawling out of the mouth and eyes. When I relieved myself I could see the worms in my excrement.

"When I saw the VC eating some peppers, I knew what to do. I asked them what it was they were eating and they told me that they were called '*ot*' and did I want some. After I ate them, I put on a good show and acted like it was real hot. I threw myself on the floor and started asking for some water. My cage was now surrounded by VC, and they were all laughing. They gave me more, so I ate it. Besides being a vegetable, I knew it was the hottest remedy available, and it would clean out my system and kill all the worms.

"Once I went on a hunger strike because of the food they regularly fed us. I told them, 'I know you can give us better food than this.' The commissioner came over and wanted to know what I was doing. He pointed to the rice and said, 'What's that?' I answered him sarcastically, saying, 'You mean you've lived in Vietnam all your life and don't know what it is? It's rice!' He said, 'We've worked so hard to bring the rice to you, and you're throwing it away.' I told him, 'I can't eat rice anymore. That's why I'm throwing it away. I'm going to die.' That evening we got a decent meal with meat in the rice. It could have been one of those giant rats that they killed or maybe a wild hog, we didn't know. We knew that they ate a lot of different meat. They had elephant meat, snake, wild deer, chicken and a lot of vegetables besides. An army just can't fight on a diet of only rice, they'd never make it. Sometimes when the breeze was blowing in from the mess hall toward the cage, you could smell something good cooking. When you're hungry, that's when your sense of smell gets real sensitive.

"I learned some useful words in Vietnamese when I was a POW. I'm hurt, I'm sick, I want water, I need medical help. The guards didn't lend themselves that much to helping us learn, and the interpreter was more interested in learning English. On work details I would see the VC picking up things from the ground, and I knew that they were getting edible things. Soon I was attempting the same thing. I would motion to them and ask, '*To?*' and they would say, '*No can to, dao.*' That meant I would get sick if I ate whatever it was. I learned what was good and what was harmful. Later on, that knowledge would be helpful.

"I had a hunch that someday they would take the chains off of us while we were in the cage, and so I had been looking for a weak spot in the cage. One day I found it. Newer cages had been built, and I knew that more prisoners would be coming into camp. They drew our cages closer together and took off our chains to use on two new arrivals, a Marine captain named Cook and an Army private first class named Crafts.

"I pried this one bar in the cage until I could loosen it and pull it upward and tie it with a little cord that I had. It gave me a little space that I could crawl over, and when I got out of the cage, I could push the crossbar down with my feet and just go around it.

"We had only a rough concept of what the date was. The new prisoners helped us figure it out, and we fashioned a calendar. I had wanted to escape on July the Fourth, but it was actually on the July 8 that I left.

"Smitty, my cellmate, knew that he would be seriously handicapped if he tried to escape, since he had no boots. He knew he wouldn't get far with the plastic slippers that he wore. We both knew that the guards were going to be checking. He stayed awake all night to make sure the lamp would stay lit and the guards wouldn't have to come in.

"We had our mosquito nets pulled down, and I left an extra pair of black pajamas bundled up on my cot to give the illusion that I was still there. It was monsoon season and raining hard. The guard's post was nearby, and it was hard to see if he was inside because of the way the building was shaped. I was so glad that I kept my old boots. I had rice, a piece of mirror and some tobacco paper to spell out 'POW' on a black plastic sheet. I asked Smitty again to stay awake and keep the lamp lit, and then I left.

"Thunder and lightning lit the trail where we used to go on work details—that's where I headed. After going out around 300 meters, I slipped into the jungle. There was a wall there where we used to take our breaks and look for patches of the sky. I knew my boots were leaving tracks, but they couldn't be traced with all the water coming down.

"I must have walked about 45 minutes through the downpour when I realized that I had made a 360-degree turn and was now back in the camp area. That really broke my heart. I was thinking, maybe I should get back in the cage and try some other time. I knew it would go real hard on me if I was detected. I decided to try again. I knelt to pray and think before going on. It went through my mind, 'Think of escape and evasion tactics,' and it seemed like the Lord was listening. I saw the little leaves as they were falling down from the storm, floating away. Then it hit me. That's it—follow the water! I followed one little stream as it led into a bigger one, and then finally I came into a running brook that poured into a big fork of the Saigon River. I jumped in and swam with the current. I knew there would be nobody there to stop me in that kind of weather, and I tried to get as much distance as possible.

"When I got out of the water I was loaded with leeches. I thought I had millions. I ran into the woods and began to pluck out the bloodsuckers. They were everywhere! I decided to stay in the woods and walk along the river. What I wanted to do was get my bearings when I came to a spot where I could see the sun. I had to go south or southeast—that's the only way the river flowed. I knew I couldn't stay too near the river because that's where they would be looking for me.

"I saw this little trap for small animals like muskrats and knew that people were nearby. By the second day I could hear search parties looking for me. I would hide whenever I heard them. I climbed trees at night to get away from tigers and other animals. I walked through this arroyo and I thought, 'Nice sand, good ground like the arroyos in the U.S. southland. This is good—now I can make some time.' But I had gone only a few yards when I saw some tiger tracks. I decided to change course.

"During the first couple of days, fruit was abundant. I would fill my pockets. There was one that looked like a small orange or nectarine, also some like kiwi fruit and some mangos. I knew what mangos were, since I had eaten them all my life.

"I had only a stick to defend myself with. On the third day out I was feeling dehydrated. I was lost and wanted to do some navigating. That evening, I heard a round go off in the distance and decided to travel in that direction. It had been cloudy when I started off that morning. By afternoon, when the sun came out, I realized that I had been traveling in the wrong direction.

"On the fourth day, I just packed up what I had been carrying with me in a tree and began walking. I came across a puddle of water and was glad, since I had run out. I noticed that the water was loaded with mosquito larvae, but I drank it anyway.

"I kept on going, and around 10:30 or 11 A.M. I saw an American plane—it may have been a Cessna L-19—flying real low at treetop level. I could read the U.S. Army markings on it. I began walking in that direction it was headed.

"I came to a hardtop clay road, and I thought how it might be the same one that I had taken north toward Song Mau. I could see an abutment on the road, and when I got closer I saw some markings, something about a corps of engineers. That was the first sign of civilization I had seen since my capture. I sat back down in the jungle and I thought, 'I can't blow it now.'

"First I saw a dump truck coming down the road. There were no soldiers riding on it, so I thought it must be a civilian truck. I stayed in the jungle to study things and kept going until I neared a rubber tree plantation. Keeping near the road, I moved ahead, hiding behind trees, until I saw a little Vietnamese flag and a gate with some gun emplacements and bunkers.

"I figured that I had made it to safety, but I wanted to be careful. Then I saw a little moped coming. I was getting ready to knock this guy off his moped just in case he wasn't friendly when I noticed a small car following it with a Red Cross symbol on its bumper. I jumped into the road and started waving a branch to signal him. He spoke to me in French, asking if he could help me. I knew a little French, and I told him I was an American and I needed help. I was real nervous that he would turn in the opposite direction, but he reassured me. He asked again, '*Vous être un Americain?*' and I answered, '*Oui, je suis un Americain.*'" He gave me a ride to the Vietnamese compound and hollered at the guard to let them know who I was. He took me right to the village chief's house. The village chief spoke good English. I told him I had been captured at Hiep Hoa.

"He told me that there was no American compound at Hiep Hoa, and I answered, 'maybe not, but there was one when I got captured.' He said that I didn't look American, so I showed him my tattoos. I looked out the window and saw some berets. I told him, 'If you don't believe me, ask the Green Beret over there.' He asked the Green Beret to come in. When he saw me, he cried, 'Ike, is that you?' I answered, 'Yeah, it's me.'

"They took me to the Special Forces camp at Minh Tranh. Sergeant First Class Rocky Laine and some of the other fellows I knew were there. They were all happy to see me and got me a hot shower and a new uniform. They served me a big breakfast plate of eggs and ham. I couldn't eat it. My brain was saying I want it, but my stomach was rejecting it. I got real sick, and they took me to the Third Field Hospital in Tan Son Nhut for a checkup.

"The helicopter that took me to the hospital was actually on a mail run to Da Nang when the guys diverted it. The pilot took me to Da Nang, and I saw Sergeant Thompson, an old friend of mine. He hugged me before I was rushed out. Once I arrived at the hospital, Colonel Mike De La Peña came to see me within half an hour.

"I can only describe the whole episode as something that occurred in a dream. That's the only way I know how to put it. In my hospital room, Colonel De La Peña was standing over me like a father figure and there were tears in his eyes. I guess that's when everything finally caught up to me, because I broke down, too."

After being debriefed, Isaac Camacho was promoted to master sergeant, and he later received a field promotion to captain. Authorities told him not to speak about his encounter with the

Cubans. He was shipped to Okinawa, where it was determined that his stomach had shrunk to the size of a 6-year-old's during his 20 months of captivity. One doctor warned him that he would probably have stomach problems for the rest of his life.

As the first GI to escape from a VC POW camp, Camacho returned home to a hero's welcome. He was congratulated by El Paso Mayor Judson Williams, Congressman Richard White and President Johnson. The El Paso *Times* reported that his mother said, "Thank my good God! My prayers have been answered! He is my only boy, my only son, I have always been proud of him. I am the happiest mother in the world. I prayed day and night for 20 long months."

Camacho's former commanding officer wrote a letter urging that he be awarded the Medal of Honor. But that never happened, perhaps because of a lack of witnesses. For his gallant defense at Hiep Hoa, however, Camacho did receive the Silver Star. In 1999 he was also awarded the Distinguished Service Cross. Many people still feel that he should have received the Medal of Honor for the bravery he displayed in support of his comrades.

After all he has been through, Isaac Camacho is remarkably upbeat when he looked back on his experience. Speaking of a visit he had from George Smith, his friend who was in captivity with him, Camacho said: "I always say that I'm in debt for the way he sacrificed for me. That gave me all night to get away. We had a blast talking in El Paso. He told me about the reaction of the guards the morning after I escaped."

"That was the funniest thing I ever saw in my life," Smith said. "They checked out the cage inside and out. They just couldn't see how the hell you got out! They had about five or six guys down in the hole to see. Even the commissioner went down in the hole to see if you were there. They didn't even know which guard to blame because they had all been on duty and changed posts. They got the smallest guy in the camp and tried to force him through the bars to see if his head could squeeze through, and of course it couldn't. They never once knew where the exit was. I wanted to laugh, but I couldn't."

PART TWO
ESCALATION

The War's "Constructive Component"

By Peter Brush

Accoring to the 1939 U.S. Army field manual on military operations, the ultimate objective is the destruction of the enemy's armed forces in battle. Decisive defeat—according to the manual—breaks the enemy's will to continue fighting and forces him to sue for peace. Tactics based on that doctrine served the United States well in World War II, but by the 1960s, with the advent of Communist "people's wars" and "wars of national liberation," some of the Army's underlying beliefs needed to be re-examined. In regional conflicts such as those, the objectives were sometimes quite different. Mao Tse-tung wrote in *On Protracted War*: "Weapons are an important factor in war, but not the decisive factor; it is people, not things that are decisive. The contest of strength is not only a contest of military and economic power, but also a contest of human power and morale."

The most effective strategy for opposing Communism in these regional wars had two components. The destructive component would address the conventional military threat, while the constructive component was concerned with the political, economic, social and ideological aspects of the struggle. The Marines understood this duality. According to British counterinsurgency expert Sir Robert Thompson, "Of all the United States forces [in

Vietnam] the Marine Corps alone made a serious attempt to achieve permanent and lasting results in their tactical area of responsibility by seeking to protect the rural population."

The Americans and South Vietnamese seemed to understand the importance of the relationship between the government and the civilian population, but were unsuccessful in translating this understanding into practice. With the Communists, self-interest demanded that they impose severe controls on the use of violence toward the population. "Normally Communist behavior toward the mass of the population is irreproachable and the use of terror is highly selective," Thompson maintained. The Communists depended on the goodwill of the Vietnamese rural population far more than did the American and Government of (South) Vietnam (GVN) troops.

In February 1965, the United States began Operation Rolling Thunder—the sustained bombing of North Vietnam. Many of the U.S. Air Force and GVN aircraft making those attacks were based at Da Nang, which was considered vulnerable to retaliatory attacks by the Communists. Since there was an insufficient logistical base to support the arrival of heavily armed U.S. Army units, Marine Corps forces were dispatched to support the Air Force.

By mid-1965 there were 51,000 U.S. servicemen in Vietnam; 16,500 Marines and 3,500 Army troopers were on defensive missions, while the rest functioned in an advisory capacity to the GVN and as airmen flying and supporting combat missions. The Marines were assigned responsibility for I Corps, the military region of South Vietnam comprising the five northernmost provinces. The remaining three military regions were the responsibility of the U.S. Army.

By 1966, General William C. Westmoreland's Military Assistance Command, Vietnam (MACV) had completed the construction of the logistical infrastructure necessary to support Army troops. The Army, denied the opportunity to invade North Vietnam, applied the doctrine of conventional operations that had worked against the Japanese and Germans in World War II and against the Chinese in Korea: the efficient application of massive firepower. The goal of this search-and-destroy strategy was the attrition of insurgent forces and their support systems at a rate faster than the enemy could replace them, either by infiltration of North Vietnamese forces or by recruiting local replacements. The strategy of attrition offered the prospect of winning the war more quickly than with traditional counterinsurgency operations.

The Communists, nevertheless, were largely successful in controlling the fighting during the war. General Lewis Walt, commander of the U.S. Marine Corps in Vietnam, noted, "The fact is that every enlargement of U.S. military action has been a specific and measured response to escalation by the enemy." Whether the United States was leading this escalation or merely responding to it, more than 80 percent of the firefights were initiated by the Communists.

The U.S. government seemed aware of the value of pacification efforts—programs that were designed to bring security and government control and services to the Vietnamese countryside. In 1966, Secretary of Defense Robert McNamara offered the following evaluation of the situation in Vietnam: "The large-unit operations war, which we know best how to fight and where we have had our successes, is largely irrelevant to pacification as long as we do not have it. Success in pacification depends on the interrelated functions of providing physical security, destroying the VC apparatus, motivating the people to cooperate and establishing responsive local government."

Both the U.S. Army and the Marine Corps understood that the war in Vietnam could not be won solely by defeating large units of the enemy. Attention to counterinsurgency operations would be necessary to remove the political influence of the National Liberation Front (NLF), particularly in the rural areas of South

Vietnam. The Army remained convinced throughout the war that the emphasis should remain focused on conventional warfare and the interdiction of the enemy's external supply mechanisms. The Army felt large-unit operations were the key to victory and thus paid little attention to small-unit operations.

The U.S. Marine Corps, on the other hand, had adopted a strategic approach that emphasized pacification over large-unit battles almost from the outset of its arrival in Vietnam. Previous Marine deployments in Haiti, the Dominican Republic and especially Nicaragua had involved elements of civil development and an emphasis on the training of local militia. General Walt held that many of the lessons learned in the "banana wars" were applicable to the fighting in Vietnam. These lessons were spelled out in the U.S. Marine Corps Small Wars Manual (1940): "In regular warfare, the responsible officers simply strive to attain a method of producing the maximum physical effect with the force at their disposal. In small wars, the goal is to gain decisive results with the least application of force and the consequent minimum loss of life. The end aim is the social, economic, and political development of the people subsequent to the military defeat of the enemy insurgent forces. In small wars, tolerance, sympathy, and kindness should be the keynote of our relationship with the mass of the population."

This was not merely a humanitarian policy. One Marine general noted that there were 100,000 Vietnamese within mortar range of the Da Nang airfield. Anything that would encourage a friendly civilian attitude toward the Marines would clearly assist the more conventional mission of the Marines.

Shortly after the Marines' arrival in 1965, Combined Action Platoons (CAPs) were created to help gradually enlarge the Marines' coastal enclaves through "clear and hold" operations. Each CAP unit consisted of a 15-man rifle squad assigned to a particular hamlet in the I Corps. CAP units worked with platoons of local Vietnamese militia (Popular Forces, or PFs). CAP Marines were volunteers with combat experience who were given basic instruction on Vietnamese culture and customs. These combined units conducted night patrols and ambushes, gradually making the local Vietnamese forces assume a greater share of responsibility for village security. Their mission was to destroy the NLF infrastructure, organize local intelligence networks, and train the PFs.

CAPs were immediately successful. General Walt described the results as "far beyond our most optimistic hopes." Two years after the initiation of the CAP program, a Department of Defense report noted that the Hamlet Evaluation System security score gave CAP-protected villages a rating of 2.95 out of a possible 5.0, compared with an average of 1.6 for all I Corps villages. There was a direct correlation between the time a CAP stayed in a village and the degree of security achieved, with CAP-protected villages progressing twice as fast as those occupied by the PFs alone.

The casualty rate for CAP units was lower than that of units conducting search-and-destroy missions. British General Richard Clutterbuck noted that although Marine casualties were high, they were only 50 percent of the casualties of normal infantry battalions on large-scale operations. The proportion of Marine participants who extended their tours in the CAP program exceeded 60 percent, and there were no recorded desertions of PF soldiers from CAP units. The NLF never regained control of a hamlet that was protected by a CAP unit. By the end of 1968 there were 114 CAP units in I Corps, providing security for 400,000 Vietnamese—15 percent of the population of I Corps.

One of the best combat narratives of the Vietnam War, *The Village*, by F.J. West, Jr., describes the history of one CAP unit in a typical Vietnamese village: "General Lewis Walt, commander of the III Marine Amphibious Force, was in the habit of asking his district advisors to comment on the effectiveness of Marine battalions in I Corps. In June, 1966, Walt visited Major Richard Braun, advisor to the Binh Son district chief in Quang Ngai Province. Braun told Walt that the Marines would be more effective if they worked with the Vietnamese rather than searching for Viet Cong on their own. When Walt asked for specific recommendations, Braun suggested sending a platoon of Marines to the village of Binh Nghia.

"The ARVN [Army of the Republic of Vietnam] had been chased out of Binh Nghia two years previously. A platoon of the Viet Cong lived there regularly, and often a company or more would come in to resupply or rest. Binh Nghia belonged to the NLF, and was the full-time government of five of the seven hamlets in the region and controlled the boat traffic moving on the Tra Bong River."

On June 10, 1966, Corporal William Beebe led a group of Marine volunteers from their base camp to the Vietnamese village of Binh Nghia. All the Marines were seasoned combat veterans who had been chosen for their ability to get along with the villagers. With the arrival of the Marines, the village police chief felt strong enough to move his security forces from a nearby outpost into the village proper. Chief Ap Thanh Lam called a meeting of the villagers, explained that his men and the Americans had to come to stay, and asked for volunteers to construct a new fortified headquarters. Forty civilians joined the Marines, policemen and Popular Forces in constructing a fort. Work progressed on the fort by day, and by night combined Marine-PF patrols went hunting for the enemy. Initially, the Marines and PFs were distrustful of each other, but over time they came to respect each other's particular strengths. The Marines used the PFs as "eyes and ears" because they could not always depend on them to advance with the Marines. But the PFs were valuable at point, according to West's narrative, "due to the belief that a Vietnamese soldier could spot a Viet Cong at night before an American could." From the beginning, the Marines' training ensured that they could shoot better than the Viet Cong, and after hundreds of village patrols, the Marines were learning to move as well as the Viet Cong.

The Marines liked duty in the village. They enjoyed the admiration of the PFs, who were unwilling to challenge the Viet Cong alone. The Marines hunted the VC as the VC for years had hunted the PFs and village officials. The village children did not avoid the Marines, and the children's parents were more than polite. The Marines had accepted too many invitations to too many meals in too many homes to believe they were not liked by many and tolerated by most. Their conduct had won them admiration and status in the Vietnamese villages.

In September 1966, the NLF attempted to force the Marines out of the village. Eighty local VC joined with 60 North Vietnamese Army troops in an attack on the fort, which was defended by six Marines (the others were away from the fort on patrol) and 12 PFs. Five Americans and six PFs were killed, but the position held. The day after the fight, the commander of the 1st Marine Division, Maj. Gen. Lowell English, entered the smoldering fort to speak to the Marines. General English remarked that perhaps the combined platoon was too light for the job, too exposed, and overmatched from the start. He was considering pulling them out, he said; they could stay at the fort, or go. One Marine stated the position of the group: "The general was a nice guy. He was trying to give us an out. But we couldn't leave. What would we have said to the PFs after the way we pushed them to fight the Cong? We had to stay. There wasn't one of us who wanted to leave."

Rifles and grenades were to be the weapons of the Americans at Binh Nghia. The village stayed intact throughout some of the heaviest fighting in Vietnam—there was never an airstrike called for Binh Nghia during the war. Although the region was marked "VC" on military operational maps, it was also marked in red as out of bounds for harassment and interdiction artillery fire because American ground forces patrolled the area.

By March 1967, it appeared that the enemy had modified their strategy toward the Binh Son district in general and toward Binh Nghia in particular. The VC had previously sought out contact with the CAP unit, but now avoided the patrols. Vietnamese military intelligence reported that the NLF political cadres had attended a conference in January where it had been decided to discontinue the spreading pacification efforts with local troops. Rather, the guerrillas were to gather intelligence and act as guides and reinforcements for the main forces. At the January conference, the Binh Nghia CAP unit had been denounced more bitterly than any other U.S. or GVN program. The unit was hurting the NLF militarily—its patrols and ambushes prevented NLF use of the Tra Bong River and blocked one route to the air base at Chu Lai. The Marine presence impeded food collection, taxation and recruitment. NLF attempts to re-establish control over the area after the attack on the fort in September were a failure.

By October 1967, district and Marine headquarters felt that the job of the CAP unit at Binh Nghia was finished. The village was pacified and the Marines were needed elsewhere. In December 1967, U.S. Army troops and Korean Marines moved into the area, while the U.S. Marines moved farther north, toward the Demilitarized Zone (DMZ). A captain from district headquarters felt that security in the DMZ had not improved, since the Army troops were too far in the hills and the Koreans were behind a massive defensive barrier.

By 1971 the war had passed by Binh Nghia. The Americans were gone. The VC guerrillas and PF soldiers were gone. The fort constructed by the CAP unit and the Vietnamese was gone. But the village was intact and had survived the fighting.

For the Army, pacification remained an added duty, not a primary task. Resources committed to civic action, it was felt, were resources not available to accomplish the military's major mission. The Army's aggressive approach to pacification is reflected in the Strategic Hamlet Program, which involved the forcible relocation of Vietnamese peasants into armed refugee camps around the district towns. The Army believed that draining Mao Tse-tung's "sea" in which the guerrilla "fish" swam would allow massive firepower to destroy the remaining enemy inhabitants in these free-fire zones. Since the Strategic Hamlet Program was a failure even before U.S. Army ground units arrived in Vietnam, it is not surprising that the Army put minimal faith in the efficacy of civic action.

Army leadership was united in its disapproval of the Marine CAP program. General Westmoreland believed that pacification should be primarily a South Vietnamese task, saying, "I simply did not have enough numbers to put a squad of Americans in every village and hamlet; that would have been fragmenting resources and exposing them to defeat in detail." Westmoreland felt Marine tactics were insufficiently aggressive, that their practices "left the enemy free to come and go as he pleased throughout the bulk of the region and when and where he chose, to attack the periphery of the [Marine] beachheads." Major General Harry Kinnard, commander of the Army's 1st Cavalry Division (Airmobile), was "absolutely disgusted" with the Marines. "I did everything I could to drag them out and get them to fight. . . . They just wouldn't play. They just would not play. They don't know how to fight on land, particularly against guerrillas." Westmoreland's operations officer, Maj. Gen. William Depuy, observed that "the Marines came in and just sat down and didn't do anything. They were involved in counterinsurgency of the deliberate, mild sort."

Marine General Victor Krulak was the most articulate spokesman for pacification. Krulak was a former special assistant for counterinsurgency to the U.S. Joint Chiefs of Staff and, by

1965, the commanding general of the Fleet Marine Force, Pacific. He felt that Westmoreland's strategy of attrition would fail because it was Hanoi's game. The Communists' strategy in Krulak's view was to seek "to attrit U.S. forces through the process of violent, close-quarters combat which tends to diminish the effectiveness of our supporting arms." By killing and wounding enough American soldiers over time, they would "erode our national will and cause us to cease our support of the GVN." For Krulak, a strategy of pacification was the only way to succeed, and in 1966 he presented his views to Secretary of Defense McNamara in an attempt to force Westmoreland to adopt a pacification strategy for the whole of South Vietnam. In the summer of 1966, a meeting was arranged between Krulak and President Lyndon B. Johnson. After hearing Krulak describe his plan for winning the war in Vietnam, Johnson "got to his feet, put his arm around my shoulder, and propelled me firmly toward the door," Krulak later recalled.

In the test of wills between Westmoreland and Krulak, the Army general possessed a formidable weapon—a general's fourth star. Westmoreland was popular with the press, the public, and especially with President Johnson. Eventually the Marines gave up their attempts to more widely implement their pacification strategy and fell in line with the Army.

It is ironic that the Marines, who favored a long-term, small-unit approach to combat in Vietnam, were ordered by the Army to implement Operation Dye Marker, better known as McNamara's Line. This plan called for the construction of a barrier along the DMZ employing minefields, sensors and barbed wire to reduce NVA infiltration from North Vietnam into the South. Marines and Navy Seabees (U.S. Naval Mobile Construction Battalion personnel) provided the manpower to strip a 600-meter belt, or "trace," of its vegetation, taking large numbers of casualties in the process. Eventually—after the investment of 757,520 man-days and 114,519 equipment-hours—the project would be abandoned.

In many ways, Marine Corps strategy and tactics were more appropriate to the reality of the Vietnam battlefield than those of the U.S. Army. The CAPs, though, were not uniformly successful and were too scattered to have a maximum impact. Several months after the CAP program was instituted, the United States noted a large enemy buildup in the DMZ. Westmoreland decided this area should receive the focus of the U.S. effort in I Corps, which obligated the Marines to move northward.

Civic action remained a sideshow to U.S. efforts to wage conventional war. To acknowledge the effectiveness of pacification would deny the appropriateness of U.S. military doctrine and ignore the historical successes of the U.S. Army. Civic action was a time-consuming process, and time is a precious commodity in an industrial society. Civic action had promise, however. Had it been adopted on a wide scale, the war would have been different, but it is a matter of speculation as to whether civic action would have ultimately affected the outcome. Less speculative is the applicability of the strategy and tactics that prevailed.

Sir Robert Thompson remarked: "It was never clearly understood by the American administration, and certainly not by the Army, that the whole American effort, civilian and military, had to be directed towards the establishment of a viable and stable South Vietnamese government and state, i.e., the creation of an acceptable alternative political solution to the reunification with North Vietnam under a Communist government. Instead, through the bombing of the North and a war of attrition within the South, the whole effort was directed to the military defeat of the Viet Cong and North Vietnamese divisions infiltrated into South Viet Nam. Even if such a military defeat had been possible, it would not have achieved victory without a political solution."

The U.S. Army in Vietnam was configured as it had been to wage warfare in Europe. Its insistence on waging large-unit battles ensured that the enemy would avoid the deployment of its forces in large units when it was to its advantage to do so. Using massive firepower to inflict large numbers of casualties on the enemy resulted in civilian casualties and social disruption. The United States was seen as an ally of the GVN; but neither government was seen as an ally by the civilian population. The more the United States took control of the war to avoid the defeat of the GVN by the Communists, the easier it was for Hanoi to portray the United States as a neocolonialist power and the GVN as merely a puppet regime.

With the end of the Cold War, the humanitarian functions of the U.S. military have assumed increased importance in low-intensity conflicts. Recent troop deployments to Iraqi Kurdistan, Bangladesh and Somalia are testimony to the utility of civic action. The nontraditional use of military force represents a fusion of political and military assets that can further the foreign policy goals of the United States.

It Became Sinful: A Reporter's Story

As told by George McArthur

A veteran war correspondent, George McArthur covered the Korean War for three years as a reporter for The Associated Press. In 1963 he was the AP bureau chief in Manila, and as the war in Vietnam began to heat up he found himself more and more on temporary duty in Saigon. In March 1965, he was transferred permanently to Vietnam as chief of the AP's Saigon bureau. He was there when the Marines landed at Da Nang that month and reported from Vietnam for the next 10 years. In 1969 McArthur became the war correspondent for the Los Angeles Times *and covered the fall of Saigon in April 1975. Now retired, McArthur talked with San Jose State University Professor Larry Engelmann about those final days.*

—Editor

The January 1973 agreement known as the Paris Peace Accords cemented the feeling in my mind that the Vietnam War was down the tube. I think that I made up my mind—it was about that time. I say I made up my mind, but I never made up my mind completely. I was up and down depending on the evidence of the day at any given moment as to whether it could or could not be done. I always felt that it would be nice if we could pull it off because there were about 25 million people there that didn't want the bad folks to come trooping down and impose upon them a government they didn't want. I just decided we didn't have the will, and a lot of this came from Major General John Murray, the U.S. military attaché in Saigon. Gen. Murray had a lot to do with my own thinking because I was on very good terms with Murray and he was telling me about the ammunition and how things were going, and it was going very badly. I then came to the conclusion, which I sort of held until the end, that, all right, if we're not going to pull it off, then let's get the hell out of here totally, and in toto. Because at that point it became sinful. You're simply killing more people and you're not accomplishing anything.

I felt up until about 1972—I can't pin it down exactly—that something might be accomplished, that a Southern entity outside of the Hanoi orbit might be maintained. And you didn't find anybody in a position of responsibility in Saigon outside of ideologues like the U.S. ambassador to South Vietnam, Graham Martin—he might give you his grand scheme for the war. Ordinary people thought of it in terms like I've just enunciated, that we were trying to salvage something out of this horrendous wreck, and the only thing that was salvageable would be some kind of entity that would allow these people to flourish, and some kind of a free-enterprise society, because they are a tremendously industrious people. They don't fit into anybody's mold. The Southerners are totally unlike the Northerners.

And you couldn't write that during the war either. If you wrote that there was an ethnic difference in Vietnam itself, you were laughed out of town in Washington. The French were much more sophisticated about this. They knew it. They knew that the Northerners had certain characteristics and the Southerners had certain characteristics—part of my current belief, and my belief then—and I came to the same conclusion as Ambassador Jean-Marie Merillon, the French ambassador at that time, who was one of the more perspicacious men, that the Northerners are going to find the South indigestible. And that is precisely what has happened. No matter, they still cannot refrain from supping the forbidden fruit. But the North is not going to digest the South. It's just not going to happen.

One thing I did believe—I think everybody did at the time—that, having given up hope—and a lot of the Vietnamese gave up hope, too—I felt the North would be a little bit more understanding when it came down because there was a feeling in Saigon at the time among those who stayed, "All right, we gave it our best shot, and we lost. Now let's see what we can do to build the country and to get over this. And if we're going to have to put up with these ... Communists, we'll do it. We'll take orders, we'll do whatever they please, if they're just reasonable men in any shape, form or degree." The South was ready, almost to a man, to cooperate with any kind of reasonable occupation. And the North squandered that opportunity for stupid ideological reasons. They felt they had to engage in a certain amount of education, this that and the other. They took off more of their friends than their enemies.

I stayed in-country until '75. The final night, I continued to do my reporting. I wouldn't have lived there for 10 years if I had felt my life was in imminent danger. You accept a certain amount of hazard, but I was a fairly cagey old goat by then; I knew how to take care of myself, and I avoided getting into a pitched battle with the North Vietnamese. I never saw much point in that. I flew up to Da Nang in the spring of 1975. I also flew up to Hue in that period. But when the final collapse started up, I was back and forth and all over the country. In that situation, your timing had to be good . . . you had to be sort of a baseball player. You get in and get out. If you get out 24 hours before the place collapses, your timing is good. My timing was always superb.

I covered the congressional delegation that came through—Millicent Fenwick and Bella Abzug and others. I was over in Phnom Penh, and they were there the day the last civilian aircraft left Phnom Penh. They had a military aircraft down at one end of the field with Bella and Phil Habib, Paul McCloskey, Millicent with her pipe, that whole bunch. They were over there. That place was well down the tubes.

But I went out to the airport to catch my plane, and the damn thing had been canceled. In addition to the canceled flight, my driver and I got rocketed on the way out there, so I wasn't in any good mood. But I went back into that back corner of the field where I knew the C-47s were. Phil Habib is an old friend of mine, so I said, "Phil, I've got to have a ride on that plane to get back to Saigon." So he says, "Okay, we've got plenty of room." So I clambered aboard the plane, and I was sitting right behind Bella Abzug and two or three guys. It's only a 50-minute flight back to Saigon, and they were saying things up there; I didn't join in the conversation at all. But they were so shallow and vapid and had nothing to do with what was going on over in Phnom Penh. There was no doubt that they were right that the place was going down the tubes, but it made me so mad when I came back and filed my story. That night I had a ruptured ulcer. I went around to a friend's house with my wife, Eva Kim—we were married after the war—and had a drink and keeled over. And I'd lived with that ulcer for 20 years. So that night it got me. And I always blame it on Bella Abzug. Perhaps I'm being uncharitable.

Remember also, at the time the final offensive began, Graham Martin was back in the United States, and my wife was his secretary. Martin and I got to be friendly enemies, and we were still friendly enemies until his death in March 1990. The night before he left for the States, he said there was no way that South Vietnam could be defeated militarily. And, although I phrased it more politely, I told him he was full of crap.

Having left me with that pearl of wisdom, he then departed for the United States. He was gone for about four weeks, is my recollection. Didn't even leave word where he was. Washington was trying to find him. Eva was calling all over Carolina from Saigon trying to locate him. So he came back, and Da Nang was in the process of collapse at that time. Martin's first reaction to anything was, "I'll go there and I'll personally lead the troops." He would be the worst troop leader the world has ever known. But his first reaction was to get up to Da Nang: "I want to go up to Da Nang, I'll bring order." And he was argued out of that by the calmer heads in the embassy.

A half-dozen other times he wanted to do that. The final day when the whole world knew that Tan Son Nhut had been blown to smithereens, he had to get in his limousine and go ride the runway out there, serving no purpose whatsoever, but he had to report to the president, "I've seen the runway and it's unusable." I could have told him that from five miles away. The damn rocketing jolted me out of bed that night. You couldn't listen to that without knowing precisely what was going on, if you've been around it. And Martin knew, but he had to grandstand. So he came back right in the middle of all that crap.

In retrospect, I'm inclined to agree with part of what he said. He said the Americans couldn't give the impression that they were bugging out. So he gave everybody orders, disregarded politely in many instances, that they were not to ship their goods out. They were not to do a damn thing. So life at the embassy maintained its regular pace. And I'll say one thing for Martin. He lost every damn thing that he owned. His wedding pictures, things like that, silver frames—you know the stuff, you go into an ambassador's house and all those pictures of him and Harry J. Whoever, signed "to my dear friend Graham." All of that was gone. Everything that Martin had in terms of mementos. I'm positive.

I don't make any claims to prescience as to the exact date that Saigon would fall, but let's say I knew within two weeks that it was going to happen. I didn't know how it was going to happen. At that time I still felt that I'd fly out on a C-130 from Tan Son Nhut. But I didn't know. I knew also that all the guys in the press corps were making up their own minds. And those guys that made up their minds to stay, bless their hearts, I was all for them. They were very brave guys. At that time, remember, I had just come out of the hospital where I had that ruptured ulcer, and I could barely hobble around the last month I was there. So I delude myself that perhaps I would have stayed if I had been in reasonable shape. I made up my mind two weeks before the end that when the time came I was getting out. And Eva, of course, helped me in that decision. Despite the fact that I did not feel there would be a blood bath in Saigon, I didn't think it was going to be too gentle, either. I was rather surprised at how gentle it was toward the newspaper types.

Eva and I were living together. It was no great secret. And I knew I was going to wait until she got out. As I say, it just never entered my mind. I never attended a briefing or that kind of thing. I knew that Brian Ellis, the CBS guy, was doing Trojan work in getting out Vietnamese employees. I was aware that these things were going on. But in terms of my own personal departure, I simply wasn't concerned.

We spent the night of April 28 at Eva's house and got up that morning—we got up at 3 o'clock in the morning when they shelled Tan Son Nhut. And we both had had shoulder bags ready for a week, and we knew that was it. So Eva, being Eva, went in and got an extra pair of shoes and took her shoulder bag, and she drove off to the embassy about 5:30 in the morning because she knew it was going to get started early. Then I followed her about half an hour later, went by my house, had a little breakfast, and gave my cook all the money I had, and then I drove to the embassy in my little Volkswagen. This was about 6:30, and it was still wide open there. So I parked the Volkswagen and went out in the city with an embassy type. He and I patrolled the city until about noon. And when we came back we had trouble getting in the embassy. He had the big official car and pass, so the Marines cooperated to get us in. They were keeping everybody else out.

Then about noon I got in there. I didn't go out again. By that time it was a sea of humanity. Eva was up on the seventh floor. I stayed downstairs. I didn't want to bother her, and I didn't want to bother Martin, although I could have gone up there any time I wanted. So I stayed down there taking notes and watching all manner of funny things. The Filipinos whom we were evacuating showed up in two big vans and had all their stereo equipment. They had a bass fiddle and all that stuff. Well, the security guy, Marvin Garrett, said, "Junk that crap." And the Filipinos were practically in tears.

The Japanese ambassador drove up to pay a courtesy call, and when he came up he was wearing a bulletproof vest and a white helmet. It was a hilarious day. It was a farcical day. It was just like the beginning. They wouldn't cut down the big tamarind tree in the embassy yard. Can we cut down the tree? No, you can't cut down the tree. Well, finally they said, we're going to cut down that damn tree; I don't care what Graham Martin says. I avoided Martin's office. Finally, about 9:30 in the evening—it was dark and obviously the circle was getting tighter and tighter all the time—there was nobody coming and going and I couldn't do anything. So I said, well, I'll go up to Eva's office and spend the rest of the time with her and see what's going on. So I went up to her office—I'd say it was about 9:30—and there were half a dozen guys in there. The consul, who had an old guardsman's mustache, I've forgotten his name, he went over and got half a bottle of gin, and some guy brought about that much in a bottle of Scotch. They raided the embassy liquor supply. This was no cocktail party. This was a wake. We were sitting there with paper cups having a drink, and we all needed it bad. I don't think anybody had more than two.

By the end, Thomas Polgar (the CIA station chief) and Graham Martin hated one another. Polgar had been the faithful servant for a long time, and in the end he said, "I better put some distance between myself and that man because that man is trouble." So Polgar began to go his own way. Martin, on the other hand, was trying to blame everything on Polgar. And he called me into his office and he started to talk about Polgar, and he says, "If it hadn't been for that SOB Polgar. . . ." Polgar down at the end of the hall saw me go into Martin's office, and he came running down there, and at that point Graham cut off the conversation.

When we got out on the troop ship, it was the same thing. Polgar spent half his time on the troop ship where we were when we were evacuated, watching Martin. Martin didn't get to poison the press with stories about Polgar, and vice versa. Martin left with all the embassy documents. Well, he got those because he was afraid he was going to get into it with Henry Kissinger or with the CIA, and those documents had the ammunition that he felt he would need. That's why he stole those documents.

I wrote several stories at that time saying that was what was going on. You got the Kissinger camp. You got the CIA camp. The Martin camp. And they're all dumping on one another. And everybody is trying to blame everybody else. When we got back to the States, of course, you quickly discovered back here that nobody wanted an investigation of anything. The idea of a major defeat—in Britain we'd have had an Imperial Commission—in the

United States, and you didn't even have a congressional hearing. Not one. Nothing.

I mean, you've got malefactors, people who screwed up, no question about it, and that included Polgar and Martin and the whole bunch. It would have made Watergate look pale. They all had dirty linen that they wanted to hang out. Everybody was ready to blame everybody else. As it turned out, they didn't have to blame anybody because neither the Congress, nor the presidency, nor the press, nor anybody else wanted to investigate. And they never have.

After that experience with Polgar in the embassy, Martin and I came out of Martin's office and once again I went over and stood by Eva's desk. Polgar disappeared, Martin went back into his office, he came back out and it was about 10 in the evening. And he turned to Eva and he said, "Miss Kim, I don't think I'll have any more dictation today. Why don't you go?" Those were his parting words to her that night.

Well, after that she got her bag. The evacuation "chute" was a stairwell right by the office, so we just went over and got in that stairwell and went up. I was going to get out with her. Martin's poodle was tied up in there, and I'd learned to like that poodle a little bit, named Nit Noy—Thai for "little bit."

Nit Noy was a great favorite of Janet's, Martin's daughter, who was a good friend of mine, and of Dorothy's, Martin's wife, and that SOB Martin was going to leave Nit Noy there. He denied it, but I knew he was going to leave Nit Noy there. I said, "Do you want me to take the dog out?" He said, "I'd sure appreciate it." So I got Nit Noy on the leash—and I didn't feel bad about displacing somebody else. I knew that the doctor downstairs had a miniature dachshund he had put in his bag. He kept the little miniature dachsie doped up all day long because he didn't know when he was going to have to leave, and they didn't want the dog barking. So the little dachsie was sleeping in the bag, and I knew the doc-

GEORGE MCARTHUR

tor. Well, he showed me the dachsie because he knew I had dachshunds too. Slept right through the evacuation.

When we finally got up on the roof and aboard our helicopter, Eva was sitting on my right and I was holding Nit Noy in my lap. Incidentally, Nit Noy is black. They didn't even see him. I mean, I could have carried a 105 howitzer on there. People did not "see" details at that moment. I could have carried your mother-in-law; I could have carried an elephant on there. It wouldn't have made any difference. It was just, get aboard the chopper and get out. So I took out the ambassador's dog, which caused me grief on the carrier, but that's something else again. The chopper took off, and of course I'm a newspaper type so I was looking down at the streets, and there was literally a ring of fire around Saigon. The dumps out at Bien Hoa were going up in flames. It was a fireworks display surpassing anything you're ever going to see. And I was checking out spots on the ground, this that and the other, thinking what I'd do if we went down. We circled for about five minutes because they sent us out in pairs and we were waiting for the second chopper to get off the roof, say five minutes—probably was 60 seconds but it seemed like a longer period.

But as we were circling the city, I was drinking in that spectacle that was the end of 10 years of my human experience, and, let me tell you, the adrenaline was flowing through me; I couldn't have gone to sleep, and I didn't sleep at all that night, as a matter of fact.

They took us to *Blue Ridge*, the command ship for the evacuation; then they took us back to the carrier *Midway* because *Midway* was going to be one of the first ships into Subic Bay, in the Philippines, and obviously all the correspondents wanted to be on the first ship to Subic. Naval communications was losing our copy like mad. When I got to Subic, they hadn't received one damn word that I'd filed. The Navy said they were going to provide communications—and never believe that. Don't file your book by naval communications. I was lucky I had saved my back-up copies, so as soon as we got to Manila, I just started refiling all that stuff. I stayed busy for two days refiling stuff that I had filed from the ship.

Of course, then there was a big emotional letdown. It lasted for a year or longer. And almost everybody who had been there in that period experienced it—remember I'd been there for 10 years. Eva had been there for 12. Our good friends were people who were not the fly-by-nights but people that we had known, dedicated people most of them, who had been there a long time. So among that group of people are those who are still wrapped up in the Vietnam thing. It wasn't what the GIs call post-stress what-not, but when you have devoted 10 years of your life to a story and the story ain't no story anymore, you're going to have a tremendous letdown. That's one of the reasons I retired. I can't write about Vietnam to this day. I've tried and can't do it.

I don't think any of those people will ever recover. Let me define the word "recover" a little bit better. They'll certainly not get over it. They'll carry it to their graves, and it will affect them. It affects me and the way I treat people—my tolerance for certain things, intolerance for others. It changed my character, not 180 degrees, but I took a sharp turn. I don't think it was toward or away from any specific things. I suffer fools less well now than I did before. On the other side of the coin, I don't get angry anymore. I haven't gotten angry since 1975. You couldn't make me angry. You could hit me on the head with a baseball bat and I'd call you names, but you wouldn't make me angry. I just don't get angry. I don't think I have the capacity for that kind of emotion.

I've always been a fatalist, but I'm sure it deepened that tendency in my psyche. And I'm more patriotic than anything. Patriotic in the sense I never want to see that happen again. I know we betrayed them. I know the promises we made to the Vietnamese and the promises we were unable to keep. The betrayal may not have been intended, but it still was there.

Personally, I did not have a sense of betrayal so much as the deepest kind of disappointment, like when you've committed something when you're a kid that's just so bad that you're ashamed to face your mom and pop; you want to go out and hide, you want to run away. I didn't want to face myself. I didn't want to face a lot of people. I felt an awful lot like the CIA man I talked to out there who left fairly early in the game, and he said he left because he'd reached the point that he didn't like to talk to anybody about anything, that he knew what they were going to say already anyhow—about Vietnam. Because he was a really knowledgeable man. He knew where the bodies were buried. I belonged to that group of people. We talked to one another in a form of code. You didn't have to go through great convolutions to explain that the NVA (North Vietnamese Army) and the VC (Viet Cong) were bad people. You didn't have to go into great philosophical convolutions that communism is not necessarily a beautiful system of government. This code that a lot of these people had was simplified and also helped you get by with people like Graham Martin. I could talk to Martin when other people couldn't because I accepted about 50 percent of his givens. I wasn't going to argue with Martin about whether communism is good or bad. I know that Martin was no archreactionary. He stood about 100 degrees to the right of me, but no matter. We didn't have to argue about it.

As for my fellow journalists, I was disappointed. I had lived with this condition for five years at the time. Remember, I had been bureau chief of the AP, and restraining some of my younger colleagues had just been a pain in the ass. I remember one young kid came out there and he turned in a lead one night that just said, "Surrounded Saigon . . . so and so." And then he got into a long argument with me about whether Saigon was surrounded or not. I said, "Look, I'll get in the car and drive you down to My Tho, that's 40 miles south, right now. If they're surrounded, it's a pretty big ring." But he insisted that, since the Viet Cong controlled the countryside by night and they were then lobbing shells into Saigon, the city was surrounded. I said, "Well you're not going to say it." So he had to soften it.

I had fights like that all the time with people who were not trying to write things that were wrong but who were just convinced in their own minds that certain simplifications were acceptable. And I wouldn't accept them as the bureau chief of AP. Then when I went to work for the *Los Angeles Times*, and I won't go into names in this particular instance, I had an experience with a member of our staff who wanted to do certain things and I was not going to permit that, so I didn't.

This had been a running battle with me for five or six years. I've never been one to accept the conventional wisdom, but there was a journalistic wisdom that permitted certain people to say anything they wanted about Vietnam. And it persists to this day. Errors in fact were accepted. You can refer to the embassy compound out there as "gold-plated"—use the phraseology they used to describe—well, I considered that slipshod and slapdash reporting. The press was generally guilty of a vast amount of that.

But the other part of the trail of disgust—I'm not particularly proud, as I said earlier, of people like Gloria Emerson, and there were a lot of them out there. Morley Safer is not one of my heroes. Walter Cronkite is not one of my heroes. When Cronkite broadcast in Hue during the Tet Offensive, he arranged to have a shelling of the ridgeline behind him. This was his famous trip when he supposedly changed his mind. Baloney. He'd made up his mind before he ever came out there. But the Marines staged a shelling at 4 in the afternoon, and he was up on top of our mission building in Hue doing his stand-upper, wearing a bulletproof vest and a tin pot. And I was up there doing my laundry. Crap! It was a four-story building and you had to hang it out to dry and nobody else was going to do it for you.

Why did they do it? That's one of the questions I ask myself repeatedly and continually. Why I see things from a certain perspective, and Harry Horse Hockey over there sees them from a totally different perspective, I don't know. But I know that a lot of those guys went out there and covered a far different war than I covered.

I continued to write. I went back out to Southeast Asia and I covered Bangkok, and I did the refugees out of Phnom Penh, which people wouldn't believe either. I went to Thailand because that was the center, and I wanted to tidy up the story, so to speak. I stayed in Thailand for three years and then I retired. But I didn't do a good job in Thailand. I just didn't have much zip. People weren't believing the stories I was writing. They wouldn't believe Pol Pot's tendencies in Cambodia.

This was public knowledge a year before; somehow or other America exploded with it. All you had to do was read AP and UPI (United Press International). They were filing virtually two or three paragraphs a day. I was filing it. A lot of other people were filing it. It didn't mean anything because the mind-set in America at the time was, well, we lost the war: first, we don't want to pay any attention; and second, other Communists are not that bad. Pol Pot has to be a nice little fellow, crackpot maybe, but can't be all bad. I'd written stories about the ruthlessness of the Khmer Rouge—and this too is a part of the public record—way back, I guess about '66, '67, '68.

I'd been reporting that stuff all along. I had not been reporting it, I think, with the vigor I should have. When I went to Thailand, one reason I retired is that I didn't feel I was doing a good job anymore. I wanted to go somewhere else. I've gone down to the Vietnam Veterans Memorial. I take people down there regularly. It's just on my tour. If you live in Washington, people come to see you. I take them down there on a regular basis. I don't have any feelings about avoiding it. And when I go down there I cry.

Ambush at Albany

As told by S. Lawrence Gwin, Jr.

The first division-sized U.S. Army unit to see combat in Vietnam was the legendary 1st Cavalry Division (Airmobile), often called the 1st Air Cav or 1st Cav. Ordered to Vietnam in June 1965, the division was formed from the elite 11th Air Assault Division, which had been conducting airmobile training at Fort Benning, Georgia. The unit arrived in August and September and immediately set up base camp in the An Khe area. Not all of the units of the 1st Cav were formed from the 11th Air Assault. Some battalions came from other Fort Benning units that had received no special training. After several weeks of shakedown training around the "Golf Course" at An Khe, General William Westmoreland ordered the 1st Cav into battle—Operation Shiny Bayonet—in what has become known as the Pleiku Campaign. Essentially, the overall intent of the campaign was to find and test the PAVN (Peoples Army of Vietnam—the North Vietnamese Army) units recently infiltrated into Vietnam, a series of brigade recon-in-force operations. In reality, it served as the first test of the 1st Cav as several units encountered the North Vietnamese units. The best known of these encounters occurred at the base of the Chu Pong mountain. There, the so-called Battle of the Ia Drang, the 1st Battalion, 7th

Cavalry, stood and fought PAVN. According to official accounts, the 1st Battalion, 7th Cavalry, fought off numerous assaults by PAVN regimental units, killing more than 1,000 PAVN, while suffering 79 killed and 125 wounded. The more severe encounter came several days later when Kinnard ordered the sister battalion, the 2nd Battalion, 7th Cavalry (2/7), which had also been at X-ray, to move from there to LZ Albany. Upon arrival, it ran head on into a reinforced PAVN battalion. Within 20 minutes, 151 troopers lay dead and 121 were wounded. The two lead companies, A and C, had been, for all intents and purposes, wiped out during the surprise North Vietnamese attack. Few American units during the Vietnam conflict would experience so many casualties in one day as occurred at LZ Albany. Curiously, it remains one of the least-known battles of the war. One of the survivors of the battle was Larry Gwin, the executive officer of the lead company that triggered the PAVN attack. He was also one of the few in that unit who came out of the ordeal without being wounded. In a recent talk with Vietnam *Senior Editor Alexander Cochran, he recalled that terrible afternoon.*

Vietnam: When did you join the Cav?
Gwin: I was already in Nam when they arrived. I had been a battalion adviser with MACV (Military Assistance Command, Vietnam) in the Delta for 10 weeks. In mid-September, out of the blue, I got orders to join the 1st Cav in An Khe. I was part of an attempt by MACV to infuse the Cav with combat-experienced officers.
Vietnam: That would have meant that you joined the Cav just as they were arriving in-country.
Gwin: Actually, I was in An Khe before the division arrived in full. On about the 14th or 15th , masses of helicopters and trucks arrived. I was assigned to the 2nd Battalion, 7th Cav, immediately

upon arrival. I remember that I had fresh jungle fatigues while those poor bastards were still wearing the old field uniform!

Vietnam: What was your impression about the Cav at this time?

Gwin: You have to remember that these poor guys had been on a ship for months coming across the Pacific. They were sure that there was a VC behind every bush. During the first week, everyone was shooting at each other. Actually the Cav's transition was very good. My impression was that the Cav had been reorganized from the 11th Air Assault. This was a hard-core U.S. unit. These guys were pros, like the 82nd Airborne. I was assigned as the XO in A Company, 2nd Battalion, 7th Cavalry. My company commander was Captain Joel Sigdinis.

Vietnam: Well, what about your outfit, the 2nd Battalion, 7th Cavalry? People talk about it being an "unlucky battalion" formed from a mechanized battalion.

Gwin: I remembered noting that there were a lot of fat NCOs! Then I found out that the 2/7th had been organized from the 2nd Infantry Division, then also at Fort Benning, not the 11th Air Assault. And the morale was terrible. The troops were okay. But the senior leadership was lacking. The battalion commander was an autocrat whom everyone detested.

Vietnam: What about the first month in-country?

Gwin: We cleared brush around the "Golf Course." We went on a few operations so that everyone got a chance to get on and off a helicopter. We did a lot of flying out from base camp to patrol bases. We conducted several combat assaults in "Happy Valley." This was a good idea. You have to remember that 2/7th had not had any airmobile training! These were not experienced troops. We suffered our first casualties. And our NCOs slimmed down very fast.

Vietnam: In early November, the 1st Cav launched the Pleiku Campaign—Operation Shiny Bayonet. Weren't there several major contacts with the NVA, at Plei Me Special Forces Camp, and then in front of the Chu Pong Mass going on?

Gwin: Not really. Then General Kinnard, the division commander, came down and briefed the battalion officers one day. He told us that the 1st Brigade had run into hard-core PAVN units, there had been heavy contact, and you guys were going in soon. We were then moved forward overland by truck from An Khe through the Minh Yang Pass to Pleiku. Then we moved by chopper to somewhere in the bush only five klicks from the Chu Pong and LZ X-ray.

Vietnam: This was to be the 2/7th's first combat operations?

Gwin: Yeah, and we were apprehensive. I then learned that the 1/7th had been in heavy contact, that they were suffering casualties, and that we were going in at dawn to help them out. We could hear sporadic reports on the radio about what was happening. My company commander was from the 1/7th, knew the troops and was concerned. The next morning we were lifted into X-ray. As soon as we landed, I heard rounds popping over my head, and the guy next to me got hit!

Vietnam: The 1/7th had landed the day before and then had withstood a series of determined NVA ground attacks that afternoon and evening. Did you have any sense of this when you stepped off the chopper at X-ray?

Gwin: I remember the carnage of combat, a line of 15 dead Americans with ponchos over them. The Chu Pong was being pounded with air and artillery. There was occasional incoming fire. We knew that we were into something, though most of it was over by then. Soon we were joined by more fresh Cav troops from the 2/5th . That evening, a platoon from the 1/7th that had been cut off for 24 hours came in, and I saw the "1000 yard stare" for the first time. They were staggering from exhaustion, dragging their dead with them. That evening—the night of the 15th—we dug in on the perimeter and waited. The night was very still. We thought that we were going to be hit that night, and we stayed up, 100 percent alert. At 4:30 in the morning, the PAVN hit the other side of the perimeter and, for the next two hours, there was just a sheet of iron overhead. Then at dawn, we had a "mad minute."

Vietnam: That has got to be some sobering moments for all. The point should be made that you all have been up for more than 36 hours at this point.

Gwin: Right. And the next night, the 16th, we stayed 100 percent alert but nothing happened. That evening, the remainder of the 1/7th had been flown out. The morning of the 17th, Joel Sigdinis learned then that B-52 bombers were coming in to wipe X-ray out and we were going to move overland to a place called LZ Albany.

Vietnam: How many men were there in your company and battalion?

Gwin: I guess that there were about 400 in the battalion and Alpha had 120 men. We were to be the lead company, spearheading the march.

Vietnam: What did you think your mission was? This seems to be one of the unknowns as that would at least influence the method of movement, tactical or otherwise. Was this just a "walk in the sun?"

Gwin: We were going to walk to Albany to be picked up and flown back to Pleiku for a rest. But we moved tactically. Our company led the battalion out in a wedge. We expected to run into the PAVN, and we moved in tactical formation. The terrain was mainly forest, clear visibility up to 100 yards, with waist-high grass. After about two or three klicks, it got hotter and the terrain changed remarkably as the forest got much thicker. The canopy got triple, the undergrowth got very thick—festooned with hanging vines and Spanish moss. The undergrowth enshrouded us, and all was obscured in a dim, eerie light. Visual contact became very important. We were very tired.

Vietnam: Your troops had to be exhausted at this point.

Gwin: As exhausted as we were, the prospect of Pleiku kept us going. Then I heard that our recon platoon had captured two PAVN soldiers, and I went forward to see them. They were two skinny little men. They didn't seem dangerous but were well equipped, with khaki uniforms, canvas harnesses, potato masher grenades, ammo pouches, sneakers—the full load. I remember being nervous. These buggers were PAVN, hard-core all the way. Joel thought that they were deserters.

Vietnam: I believe that they later turned out to be scouts, one of which had escaped and warned the remainder of the battalion about your presence?

Gwin: I remember that Lt. Col. Robert McDade, the battalion commander, along with his interpreter and the battalion intelligence officer, came forward to question them. I moved away from them, so I don't know what they said. The battalion commander interrogated them for 20 to 30 minutes. What we didn't know then was there were more than two and that interrogation time gave them time to go back and warn the PAVN battalion commander that we were coming.

Vietnam: Then these prisoners did not warn you about what was about to happen?

Gwin: We were deadly serious. We had seen PAVN at X-ray, both dead and alive. There was a distance period some 20 to 30 minutes during the walk from X-ray to Albany where everything went quiet. I remember asking, "Where are the helicopters?" In a few minutes, we resumed our trek forward. Within another 500 yards, and less than 30 minutes later, we reached Albany. Just as we got there, we could see the clearing. We sent two platoons around to secure the LZ, and Colonel McDade moved forward into the open area that had a clump of trees in the middle. I followed them into the clearing.

Vietnam: What did the LZ look like?

Gwin: A large grassy field that sloped gently downward to the left. A large clump of trees arose from the middle of the field about 100 yards away. I saw the battalion commander and his team move toward the trees. Our mission was to go to Albany and secure it. So I moved out into the open. The field was fine for an LZ. I estimated that it could take up to eight ships at a clip. We'd be out of there in no time. We'd been in the center clump less than two minutes when a few rounds erupted from the jungle that I'd just left. I figured it was PAVN stragglers. Then the jungle seemed to explode in a crescendo of small-arms fire, as if everyone in the woods had opened up with every weapon they had. Mortar rounds started landing in the LZ. The jungle literally opened up with 500 people shooting at each other. We now knew that this was the signal for the PAVN to charge.

Vietnam: We now also know that the soldier who had escaped your capture had returned to his battalion and that you walked into an ambush that the PAVN probably had 30 minutes to set up.

Gwin: It was very clear that we had run into something big, but it was very confusing because the rounds were in back of us.

Vietnam: In other words, your lead company plus the battalion command group had been cut off from the rest of the battalion?

Gwin: The fire fight was raging around us. And as the noise grew, so did the confusion. Incoming rounds were exploding overhead, but we couldn't tell where they were coming from. It was clear from our communication with our platoons that they were in real trouble, talking about lots of enemy, taking casualties, all in the matter of 10 or 15 minutes. One platoon thought that our battalion was shooting at them! I could see the battalion commander 20 yards to my rear. He was putting out the word to cease-fire because he thought that our companies were shooting at each other! I could see 30 or 40 PAVN troops right where we had just been! I jumped up and yelled at Colonel McDade that there were PAVN troops over there. Confusion continued along with screams of "Cease-fire!" The shooting continued all around us, unabated, rolling back and forth around the perimeter.

Vietnam: What about the 1st Platoon, which had moved to the other side of the LZ?

Gwin: At first, Joel told me helplessly, "1st Platoon's surrounded." Then the mortars started and the firing picked up furiously to our front where the 2nd Platoon was. Grenades were exploding. Wounded men were screaming in pain. Others were calling out or shouting hysterically. Suddenly, the "whump" of incoming mortar rounds stopped, but the fire fight continued. After about 10 minutes, Joel looked at me and said, "I've lost the 1st Platoon." Two NCOs came back several hours later and reported that they were the only ones left. One NCO was left behind wounded. Those were the three survivors from the platoon.

Vietnam: The 1st Platoon was where the PAVN main ground attack came?

Gwin: Right. But there was also movement where we had just left, in the tree line. I remember seeing men in uniforms, mustard-colored uniforms with floppy hats, in the tree lines, 10, maybe 20 men moving upright on the far side of the landing zone, the very spot we'd just left. And they continued in the open where we had come from, into the company that was behind us.

Vietnam: That would have been against C Company, which was training your company into Albany?

Gwin: I now saw three guys running across the field. One was the forward air controller. I pointed him toward the battalion commander. I knew that we needed air support. I remember seeing the battalion executive officer lying on his back. I thought that he was dead. I thought that we were next. We had lost radio contact with our 2nd Platoon. I could see PAVN coming across the LZ to our front also. I realized that they were all around us. Several long bursts of M-60 machine-gun fire erupted from our left as our recon platoon somehow managed to move back from its position in the forest. The platoon sprinted back, dragging dead and wounded. We consolidated around an anthill about 80 yards in diameter.

Vietnam: What did you have in mind at that point?

Gwin: Joel and I decided to make a last ditch perimeter, to consolidate our defenses so that we might have a chance. We'd been thinking about that last resort, a bug-out escape route. Then I looked across the field and saw, emerging from the tree line a hundred yards away, the 2nd Platoon leader. He began to jog across the field, though he seemed to be floating in the high grass. Behind him, I could see enemy soldiers. Why they didn't see him, I'll never know. Behind him were two men, one crawling on his hands and knees, the other with his arm dangling useless at his side. The leader had lost most of his men. He only had those two men with him. It turned out that they left one badly wounded man whom the PAVN tried to execute, shooting him through the eye. We found him the next morning, still alive.

Vietnam: What did you plan to do?

Gwin: I thought this was worse than any nightmare I could have dreamed. In 20 minutes, we'd been cut off and surrounded, lost two of our four platoons, half of our people. God only knew what was happening to the rest of the battalion. They were strung out behind us when PAVN hit. They had to be pinned down and totally confused.

Vietnam: In fact, C Company behind you was almost completely wiped out that afternoon. They started off with 110 guys and lost 100, 50 killed and 50 wounded. They clearly were in the killing zone.

Gwin: They had nine guys left, as I recollect. I began to worry about ammunition. Spent cartridge casings lay all over the place, and we were firing up a storm. We'd have to conserve ammo if we were going to get out of this mess alive. I could see North Vietnamese soldiers wandering around outside our perimeter, and I began to shoot at them. It was now clear that we had lost our two platoons, and Joel now explained this to the battalion operations officer. The radio crackled for everyone to throw smoke, any color. Smoke grenades popped all around us as our perimeter was completely marked by a ragged circle of red, green, yellow, white smoke billowing from canisters, its acrid smell sharp against the stench of cordite. Tac Air was on the way. Salvation was at hand. There it was, an A1-E Skyraider, diving toward the tree line. All the firing was drowned out by its roar. At about 100 feet, it let go of the silver napalm canister and climbed sharply back into the sky. Blazing napalm rolled into the trees and began to seep downward, slowly, like stalactites of flame. A second Skyraider followed closely behind, dropping its two canisters slightly to the left of the first deadly strike. They were tight on target, hitting the spot where we'd exited the forest. Within five minutes, napalm had ringed our position.

Vietnam: What effect did this have upon the PAVN attack?

Gwin: In numb fascination and horror, I watched. Canister after canister crashed into the treetops, and the jungle floor seemed to writhe. The napalm was devastating, terrifying. Each aircraft seemed to come a little closer, fly a little lower, drop a little more accurately. Each pass burned another swath of safety. It was beautiful. A heavy PAVN machine gun opened up and fired every time a Skyraider made a pass. On the last pass, a napalm canister landed dead center on the gun. With that bull's eye, the air strikes suddenly stopped.

Vietnam: Did this end the action?

Gwin: I don't know how long we listened, watched, waited. A hush seemed to settle over the field. PAVN had gone. A few small fires still burned as the dim haze of cordite and dust settled over the battlefield. The strikes clearly broke the back of the North Vietnamese attack. I can never express all the confusion and chaos that went on in that first 10- or 20-minute period. The few times that I saw the battalion commander, he appeared to be functioning, probably talking to the brigade. I've read the report that he had lost it. But it was so confusing that I can't blame him for that. You have to understand that the North Vietnamese were fresh troops and we were not. I don't care who was in command of that battalion—the same thing would have happened. The North Vietnamese hit us so hard and so fast, and we incurred so much damage so fast. However, the battalion executive officer and the FAC got us the A1-Es that made the difference with the napalm.

Vietnam: What happened then?

Gwin: It was quite eerie. It was like we were waiting for the next shoe to drop. Finally another company from our battalion came in by choppers. I remember them flying around several times before landing. The fact they had been able to land without taking any hits told me that the North Vietnamese had pulled back. The new company commander took charge of the perimeter. We had lost almost all our troops. Then we dug in for the night. Actually, I fell asleep for the entire night.

Vietnam: You'd been up for 48 hours at that point?

Gwin: That's right. The next morning, we went out and searched outside the perimeter. It was then that we really sensed what had happened. We saw all those dead Americans and very few North Vietnamese. It has been clear from the fire fight that we had suffered horrible casualties. As we started bringing in the dead, it became every bit clearer.

Vietnam: What became clearer? You faced a determined foe that day at Albany?

Gwin: I recently learned that the North Vietnamese unit we ran into had been ambushed themselves by the 1st Brigade several weeks earlier and were spoiling for a fight. And they were good, damn it they were good, brave and disciplined. They stood up to the air strikes. Their execution of the ambush maneuver was excellent. If we had not been in the open, we would have been wiped out period. They shot at every A1-E. They weren't running. They were trying to shoot down the airplanes.

Vietnam: How did Albany end for you?

Gwin: There were about 30 of us left in the company. We were pulled out into another LZ, Crook, for another night. I was wondering when this was all going to end. The next day we flew back to Pleiku. Then we trucked back to An Khe. Everyone was shocked. We had one line company of 120, and nine guys survived; another of 100 plus and 20 guys survived, all in one battalion. We were met by the division band, only 150 guys left of the battalion. General Westmoreland came several days later—it was Thanksgiving—and told us what a wonderful job we had done. Of course, he meant the 1st Battalion at X-ray, who had won on the ground. As bad a bloodying as we took, however, the morale was incredible. When I got back to An Khe on the first night, everyone got drunk and was so pleased to be alive. The morale was sky high. We'd come through combat and we'd survived. We had kicked ass. We'd busted PAVN's best.

Vietnam: How do you compare X-ray to Albany?

Gwin: I was at both X-ray and Albany. X-ray was a well-run operation. Albany was a debacle, but only because of the exigencies. I saw no cowardliness at Albany. In retrospect, I wish that we had artillery and more immediate air cover. If we had used artillery, that might have made a difference. After Albany, we were much more professional! Those NCOs that survived Albany became stalwarts, the backbone of the battalion. From the hardened crucible came the leadership for subsequent operations.

Rolling Thunder

By Colonel William Wilson, U.S. Army (ret.)

O n February 7, 1965, McGeorge Bundy, the U.S. national security advisor, dispatched a memorandum to President Lyndon B. Johnson recommending a policy of sustained reprisal against North Vietnam. As Bundy said: "We cannot assert that a policy of sustained reprisal will succeed in changing the course of the contest in Vietnam. It may fail, and we cannot estimate the odds of success with any accuracy—it may be somewhere between 25 percent and 75 percent. What we can say is even if it fails, the policy will be worth it. At a minimum it will damp down the charge that we did not do all that we could have done, and this charge will be important in many countries, including our own. Beyond that, a reprisal policy to the extent that it demonstrates U.S. willingness to employ this new norm in counterinsurgency—will set a higher price for the future upon all adventures of guerrilla warfare, and it would therefore somewhat increase our ability to deter such adventures. We must realize, however, that ability will be gravely weakened if there is failure for any reason in Vietnam."

A month later, Bundy's recommendation became a reality. Operation Rolling Thunder was the code name for U.S. air operations over North Vietnam, which began in March 1965 and involved Air Force and Marine aircraft flying from bases in South Vietnam and Thailand, and Navy aircraft flying from carriers in the South China Sea. The operation was designed to interdict North Vietnamese transportation routes in the southern part of North Vietnam and thereby slow infiltration of personnel and supplies into South Vietnam. In July 1966, Rolling Thunder was expanded to include North Vietnamese munitions dumps and oil storage facilities. In the spring of 1967, it was further expanded to include power plants, factories and airfields in the Hanoi-Haiphong area. Earlier expectations were that the bombing would constitute the primary means for the United States to turn the tide of the war. This was overtaken by the president's decision to send in substantial U.S. ground forces. Rolling Thunder was counted as useful and necessary, but the consensus was that it was a supplement, not a substitute for efforts in South Vietnam.

Rolling Thunder was hobbled from the start by its target selection system. Indeed, with the maze of procedures for coordination and approval, it is difficult to understand how permission was ever granted for a target strike. As Assistant Secretary of Defense Paul Warnke explained to Secretary of Defense Clark Clifford in March 1968, "Every Tuesday and Friday the Joint Staff has been sending me (Warnke) a current list of the authorized targets on the target list which have not been struck or restruck since returning to a recommended status. After our review this list is also sent to your office. . . . In the normal course of events, new recommendations by the Chairman of the Joint Chiefs of Staff (CJCS) for targets lying within the 10- to 4-mile prohibited circles around Hanoi and Haiphong respectively, or in the Chinese buffer zone, have been submitted to [your office] and to my office in ISA [International Security Agency]. ISA would then ensure that the State Department had sufficient information to make its recommendation on the new proposal. . . . State Department and White House approval also were required before the Chairman's office could authorize the new strikes."

Such bureaucratic log rolling had rendered the bombing campaign ineffective from the start. A secret Defense Department seminar assembling the cream of the technical scientific community concluded in the summer of 1966 that the bombing of North Vietnam had had no measurable effect on Hanoi. The study said the Johnson administration's continual expansion of the air war during 1965 and 1966 was based on a "colossal misjudgment" about the bombing's effect on Hanoi's will and capabilities. Although his suggestion was not acted on until March 31, 1968, Secretary of Defense Robert McNamara sought in October 1966, to persuade President Johnson to "stabilize" the bombing of North Vietnam and seek a political settlement.

The North Vietnamese were paying a price. They had been forced to assign some 300,000 personnel to the lines of communication in order to maintain the critical flow of personnel and material to the South. "Now that the lines of communication have been manned, however, it is doubtful that a large increase or large decrease in our interdiction sorties would substantially change the cost to the enemy of maintaining the roads, railroads and waterways or affect whether they are operational," the Pentagon Papers said. "It follows that the marginal sorties—1,000 or even 5,000—per month against the lines of communication no longer have a significant impact on the war."

When this marginal utility of added sorties against North Vietnam and Laos was compared with the crew and aircraft losses implicit in the activity (four men and aircraft per 1,000 sorties), McNamara recommended that the level of bombing of North Vietnam not be increased. "At the proper time," he said, "I believe we should consider terminating bombing in all of North Vietnam . . . or at least in the Northeast zones for an indefinite period in connection with the covert moves toward peace."

The Pentagon Papers include extracts from a CIA report titled, "An Analysis of the Rolling Thunder Air Offensive against North Vietnam," dated March 16, 1966. The report declared that "although the movement of men and supplies has been hampered and made somewhat more difficult (by our bombing), the Communists have been able to increase the flow of supplies and manpower to South Vietnam. Air attacks almost certainly cannot bring about a meaningful reduction in the current level at which essential supplies and men flow into South Vietnam."

A "Bomb Damage Assessment in the North" by the Institute of Defense Analysis summarized, as of July 1966, that the U.S. bombing of North Vietnam had had no measurable direct effect on Hanoi's ability to mount and support military operations in the South at the then current level: "Since the initiation of the Rolling Thunder Program, the damage to facilities and equipment in North Vietnam has been more than offset by the increased flow of military and economic aid, largely from the USSR and Communist China.

"While conceptually it is reasonable to assume that some limit may be imposed on the scale of military activity that Hanoi can maintain in the South by continuing the Rolling Thunder Program at the present, or some higher level of effort, there appears to be no basis for defining that limit in concrete terms, or for concluding that present scale of VC/NVN activities in the field have approached that limit.

"The available evidence clearly indicates that Hanoi has been infiltrating military forces and supplies into South Vietnam at an accelerated rate during the current year. Intelligence estimates indicate that North Vietnam is capable of substantially increasing its support." The secret papers went on to say that the economic and military damage sustained by Hanoi in the first year of the bombing was moderate and the cost could be (and was) passed along to Moscow and Peiping (Beijing). The major effect on North Vietnam was to force Hanoi to cope with disruption to normal activity, particularly in transportation and distribution. The bombing hurt most in its disruption of the roads and rail nets and in the very considerable repair effort which it required. The regime, however, was singularly successful in overcoming the effects of the U.S. interdiction.

Much of the damage was to installations that the North Vietnamese did not need to sustain their military effort. The regime made no attempt to restore storage facilities and little to repair damage to power stations, evidently because of the existence of adequate excess capacity and because the facilities were not of vital importance. For similar reasons, it made no effort to restore military facilities, but merely abandoned barracks and dispersed military material usually stored in depots.

The effects of the bombing, through 1965, on the morale of the North Vietnamese people appear to have been mixed. The bombing clearly strengthened popular support of the Communist regime by rousing nationalist and patriotic enthusiasm to resist the attacks. Because air strikes were directed away from urban areas, morale was probably damaged less by the direct bombing than by its indirect effects, such as the evacuation of the urban population and the splitting of families.

A secret CIA/DIA [Defense Intelligence Agency] report, titled, "An Appraisal of the Bombing of North Vietnam through 12 September 1966," stated that "there is no evidence yet of any shortage of POL [Petroleum, Oil, Lubricants] in North Vietnam and stocks on hand with recent imports have been adequate to sustain necessary operations. There is no evidence during the past month of serious transport problems of the movement of supplies to or within North Vietnam. There is no evidence yet that the air strikes have significantly weakened popular morale."

In January 1967, the Pentagon account discloses, the CIA produced a study estimating the military and civilian casualties of the air war in North Vietnam had risen from 13,000 in 1965 to 23,000 or 24,000 in 1966, including "about 80 percent civilians." In all, that meant that the air war expanding in the next 15 months would result in nearly 29,000 civilian casualties.

The study reports that the total number of individual flights against North Vietnam in Operation Rolling Thunder rose from 55,000 in 1965 to 148,000 in 1968, total tonnage dropped rose from 33,000 to 128,000, the number of aircraft lost rose from 171 to 318, and direct operational costs rose from $460 million to $1.2 billion. Succinctly summarizing the CIA study, it said the bombing in 1966 "accomplished little more than in 1965."

Operation Rolling Thunder was cut back in April 1968 by a partial bombing halt and ended in November 1, 1968. From 1965 to 1968 some 643,000 tons of bombs were dropped on North Vietnamese targets at a cost of 922 aircraft lost to North Vietnamese action. Like the war itself, Rolling Thunder lacked focus, and therefore never achieved its intended objective.

Operation Bright Light

By Steve Edwards

Today the exploits of the U.S. Navy SEALs (sea, air, land) on operations in Southeast Asia are legion. People who have heard some of the stories and heard General William Westmoreland's comments about SEALs being the "most effective fighting force in my command" might be surprised to learn that SEALs practically had to fight their way into the fighting.

U.S. Navy SEAL teams were commissioned on January 1 and January 3, 1962, with Team One assigned to the West Coast and Team Two to the East Coast. Within days, Team One had dispatched a platoon for training South Vietnamese SEALs—called Lien Doi Naguoi Nhai (LDNN)—for clandestine raids into North Vietnam, but for four years that was the total of SEAL commitment to Vietnam. By early 1966, both teams had new commanders and both were chomping at the bit to get into the conflict.

There were several problems. The SEALs had been commissioned to conduct small-unit unconventional warfare in a maritime environment. Nobody in the Navy, outside of the SEALs, knew what that meant; and if they did, they did not know how to apply it to Vietnam. The other problem is one that has always plagued elite unconventional units—prejudice. When officers of the regular Navy thought of the SEALs, they thought of prima donnas. Much of the criticism along these lines was not unde-served.

The SEALs descended from the Underwater Demolition Teams (UDTs) of World War II. The teams had been conceived with very specific tasks in mind, such as clearing the Normandy beaches prior to the invasion. This was not conceived to be a continuing commitment and capability after the war. In fact, it was not until the early 1970s that a career path was designed within naval special warfare.

By early 1966, Lieutenant Jim Barnes, who was the second commanding officer (CO) of SEAL Team One, had made a proposal to COMUSMACV (the Commander, U.S. Military Assistance Command Vietnam) to use SEALs in the Rung Sat Special Zone (RSSZ). The RSSZ, also known as the "Forest of Assassins," was critical to the continuing war effort from South Vietnam—the RSSZ could control the approaches to Saigon through the Long Tao River since Saigon is approximately 50 miles inland. The problem was that the RSSZ was a difficult operating environment, with deep mangrove swamps, and was an area conceded to the Viet Cong (VC).

On February 19, 1966, Lt. Barnes and his team of three officers and 12 enlisted men, deployed to South Vietnam and initially set their operation up at Vung Tau, at the mouth of the Long Tao River. This would be the one and only time that the commander of one of the SEAL teams would deploy to South Vietnam with one of his platoons while leaving his executive officer (XO) in charge of daily operations at the SEALs' home base at Coronado, California. From this deployment, the "Lessons Learned" file written by Lt. Barnes would form the basis for standard operating procedures for the platoons that followed.

It was learned that the standard SEAL deployment period of six months was the perfect time span because of the intensity of operations. Each platoon should attempt to do 60 operations during a six-month deployment, although this was considered really humping it. The SOP (standard operating procedure) for a SEAL platoon operational evolution was for half the platoon (one squad) to go out for night ambush, prisoner snatches, etc., while the other squad stayed back and rested but was ready to act as reserves if needed. Many secret methods were learned on how to do battle with a wily foe like the VC in his home environment—the swamp at night. But some of the most important lessons learned by Barnes and his men were methods for development of intelligence. In fact, it was from this first deployment that Barnes expounded the dictum that the single factor which could most affect the success of a SEAL platoon deployment was the development of intelligence.

Ironically, Barnes had specifically precluded the use of intelligence developed from South Vietnamese or indigenous people because of his fear of mission compromise. This was a very understandable fear but one that he would specifically recant in his "Lessons Learned" report. He said, "It is essential that Vietnamese Intelligence sources be used whenever possible. Every effort should be made to develop rapport with counterparts in this field and win mutual confidence."

Barnes would eventually see his original one platoon detachment—Det Delta—grow to nine platoons covering the entire Mekong Delta, including the RSSZ.

Fortunately for the SEALs, others had seen Barnes' vision of the importance of native intelligence. On May 23, 1967, MACV installed the CIA-inspired Civil Operations and Revolutionary Development Support (CORDS) organization with responsibility for pacification efforts in Vietnam. One program installed by Robert Komer, CORDS' director, was the Chieu Hoi, or "open arms," program. The Chieu Hoi program encouraged the Viet Cong Infrastructure (VCI) to rally or defect to the allied side. Many did, and became invaluable sources of intelligence.

SEALS would visit provincial Chieu Hoi rallying centers to interview the ralliers (Hoi Chan) as potential scouts for SEAL missions in the delta. A Hoi Chan was free to do what he wanted, but life as a SEAL Kit Carson scout was not bad. Kit Carson scouts, former VC who volunteered to work as scouts for the United States, got free room and board and were well-paid by the platoon leader. SEAL platoon leaders learned early on that the Vietnamese piasters, drawn from the Naval Operations Support Group at Binh Thuy and signed for by the Kit Carson scout (KCS or Kit), could produce real results if used effectively. By the late 1960s and early 1970s, most Kits working with SEALs were accepted by the SEAL platoon as regular SEALs. Kits ate, drank, slept and fought next to their SEAL platoon. This relationship became even more important as SEALs were increasingly asked to perform "Bright Light" missions.

"Bright Light" was the code name for operations mounted to rescue American prisoners of war. In the late 1960s, American leaders expressed their concern for American POWs by ordering that intelligence relating to the POWs be exploited fully. This meant that an operational unit like a SEAL platoon had only to label a mission Bright Light to secure any assets (helicopters, boats, etc.) it needed. In practice, this could often result in a circuslike atmosphere, since everyone wanted to be part of a successful Bright Light op. Majors would be flying helicopters normally flown by enlisted men, and lieutenant commanders with no prior experience would be commanding PBRs (river patrol boats).

It was into this atmosphere that the "Whiskey Platoon" of SEAL Team One deployed to the Republic of Vietnam in November of 1970. Whiskey's officer in charge (OIC) was Lieutenant Richard Couch. An Annapolis graduate, rare for those times, Couch had volunteered for SEAL teams after serving as first lieutenant and ASW (anti-submarine warfare) officer aboard the destroyer *Mansfield* (DD-728). All SEAL platoons when transferring back to CONUS (continental United States) would have the final task of training their SEAL replacements. It would be up to the OIC of the departing platoon as to how he wanted to do it, but it usually came down to two methods. Either the platoon would fly home while leaving its OIC and a senior enlisted man behind to do a week or so of training, or the whole platoon would stay and integrate a few members each night in a series of operations. (Incidentally, when SEAL platoons went home, they all flew back to Coronado together in their own airplane along with their weapons.) The OIC of the departing platoon, Lieutenant Tom Richards, who would eventually be commander of SEAL Team One, chose the latter method.

The area of operation (AO) was the Ca Mau Peninsula on the southern tip of Vietnam. The base of operations was "Solid Anchor," which at one time was based on barges in the same spot on the Cua Lon River and was called "Sea Float." The AO was dominated by mangrove swamps, voracious bugs, 12-foot tides and VC. At this point in the war, the Ca Mau Peninsula was strictly "Victor Charlie" turf except for a few villages. Most of the base assets had been turned over to the Vietnamese navy with American advisers.

The remaining U.S. direct-action forces on Solid Anchor were two SEAL platoons and a HAL-3 (helicopter attack, light) detachment, known as Seawolves, that flew helicopter gunships. The "Wolves" were fearless, and many SEALS owe their lives to them. Needless to say, the relationship worked both ways. If word came in that a Seawolf had gone down, some comfort had to be derived from the certain knowledge that every available SEAL was doing his best to get to the stricken man. Rounding out the list of assets was a Boat Support Unit commanded by Lieutenant Bob Natter, a close friend and Annapolis classmate of Couch's, and six Kit Carson scouts.

It was one of the Kits along with SEAL Walt Gustaval who

had wandered into a village and developed information from a fisherman about a POW camp he had seen up a certain canal. The fisherman was from a village on the north shore of Square Bay, and he claimed the camp was on the south shore of Square Bay. (Square Bay is the notch in the map on the western side of the southernmost tip of Vietnam.) The fisherman said he would lead the SEALs to the camp. This was the kind of information that was music to SEAL ears. When the intelligence source was willing to lead the SEALs in, they knew that there was reason for a high level of confidence in the information—confidence that the camp was there, that there were prisoners, and that it wasn't an ambush.

On November 21, 1970, the members of Whiskey Platoon began to map their strategy. The plan was that they would cross Square Bay after dark in the medium SEAL support craft (MSSC) while towing sampans that were to be used for silently paddling up the canal for a dawn strike. Natter used secure communications with the base to clear the team into the area and to secure Seawolf and chopper assistance. The boat crew prepared the MSSC, checking everything from the engines to the ammo bins. The medium SEAL support craft was designed specifically for SEAL operations. It was a steel hull of catamaran configuration powered by twin-muffled 427-Cobra gasoline engines. The typical MSSC would carry two .50-caliber machine guns, two M-60 machine guns, and often a General Electric minigun. The MSSC could really make "the rubble rumble."

The rescue attempt would be made by six SEALs, three Kits, the fisherman guide, and Couch's Vietnamese interpreter. A second SEAL squad would stand by at Solid Anchor to rappel in by helicopter if help was needed.

At 2200 hours, the team loaded the boat, dressed in typical SEAL fashion: small canteen with drinking tube clipped to shirt lapel, grenades of all sorts (SEALs love grenades), pop flares, ammunition and blue jeans. Blue jeans made a lot less noise than "cammies," especially when wet. A number of different weapons were carried, including Chicom AK-47s and M-16s; the heavy-weapons man carried the M-60 machine gun that had been modified and shortened and fitted with a flex tray for those loud-talking, fire-suppressing 7.62 long rounds. Couch carried that favorite of all SEALs, the Stoner assault rifle, which fired 5.56mm rounds at the cyclic rate of 1,100 per minute. The raiding party rounded out their fashion ensemble with camouflage face paint.

Some 30 yards from the south side of the bay, the team switched to the sampans, with the lead sampan holding the fisherman guide, Couch's best Kit, and the platoon's point man. The second sampan held Couch and his interpreter along with the SEAL radioman and another Kit. The third sampan held three SEALs and the other Kit.

An incoming tide helped the sampans to slip silently into the 15-foot canal, and they were making such good time that Couch was getting ready to order that they hold up to await dawn. Suddenly, there was subdued commotion in the lead sampan. After much heated whispering, Couch determined that they had gone up the wrong canal. To make matters worse, the team had lost radio contact with the MSSC. With dawn now approaching, the pressure was building on Couch to abort. This mission was dangerous enough if all went well.

Watt Gustaval, who was now on his third Vietnam deployment, was of the opinion that they were very close and that this one "felt like a good one." The decision was made to go through with the mission. The team now had to work hard against the current but finally found the mouth of the right canal 100 meters from the first. Still no radio contact had been made with the medium support craft, however.

The canal twisted and turned with some 90-degree bends. With first light 30 minutes away, the team was approaching the objective when the silence was broken by a cough out in the dark. It was the cough of someone asleep—probably a sentry. Couch signaled the lead sampan to move in and they slid ahead into the night. Within five minutes, a small red dot of light signaled that the sentry was secured.

Couch's sampan joined the lead sampan and he climbed into the rickety structure that was the guard post. His penlight revealed a scared and confused VC sentry, handcuffed and gagged and surrounded by the lead sampan crewmen, who were interrogating him. This was a defiant VC—he wasn't giving any information.

Couch tried everything from increasing threats of violence to offers of money—no dice. Finally, in frustration, Couch took his K-bar knife and placed it at his throat. No dice. Just then one of the Kits asked if he could try. Relieved, Couch stepped aside. The Kit leaned down and spoke to the VC in Vietnamese, "You know who I am and what I will do if you don't talk." Suddenly the VC couldn't tell the SEALs enough about the camp.

The camp was 100 meters farther up the canal and did have POWs, all ARVN (Army of the Republic of Vietnam) in cages separated from the rest of the camp. There was a small security force with only a few light automatic weapons.

The SEALs regagged the VC, tossed him in the third sampan and headed up the canal. Couch was still worried about having no radio. No radio meant no boat support and no Seawolves, so he decided to ready a pop flare. The boat could find them from the flare. The plan called for the flare to go up after first contact, with the team advancing in a skirmish line.

In the false dawn's light, the camp appeared ahead. The sampans were grounded silently, and the team prepared to advance.

Couch stood cautiously to survey the situation and accidentally dropped the pop flare. It made the sound of an empty beer can dropped on a patio deck on a quiet night. He picked it up quickly and fired it into the air.

Tracers started flying everywhere, with the VC's tracers colored green and the SEALs' tracers red. The Kits charged into the camp firing, while the SEALs madly looked for the prisoner cages. The camp was quickly overrun, and the team set up perimeter security. Natter had spotted the flare and placed the Seawolves over Couch's position while Natter made his way up the canal in the medium support craft. The radio had now come up and a "slick" (an unarmed UH-1 helicopter) was called in with the other SEAL squad to help out if the VC rallied and returned.

Couch had one of the SEAL's fire up that indispensable SEAL Mekong Delta weapon, the chain saw, and had him start cutting trees for a helicopter landing pad to extract the two VC prisoners, 19 ex-ARVN POWs and an old woman and her daughter who had been pressed into cooking duty by the VC.

It took an hour and a half for the helos to pull everyone but the SEALs and Kits out of there. The helos couldn't completely land but would hover about 5-6 feet off the ground as the crews helped people in. The SEALs would leave by the medium support craft—the plan was to back down the 2,000 meters of the canal to Square Bay. However, both Couch and Natter were worried about the possibility of a VC ambush set up along the canal, so they had the Seawolves blast both banks with their .50-caliber machine guns.

In the din of the Seawolf fire, Couch and Natter saw what appeared to be muzzle flashes from both banks. They both jumped to the medium support craft's forward machine guns and started blasting away. So intent were they that they failed to notice the rest of the SEALs laughing in the back of the boat. The

Seawolves were firing APIT (armor-piercing incendiary tracers) that exploded on impact—thus the muzzle flashes.

The SEALs made it back to Solid Anchor. The Whiskey Platoon members would find it difficult to match the success and excitement of their first combat operation.

Re-examining the Effects of Agent Orange

By Colonel Richard D. Duckworth, U.S. Air Force (ret.)

Operation Ranch Hand, the name given to the U.S. Air Force herbicide distribution in Vietnam, began initial evaluations of herbicides in combat with missions in early 1962, becoming fully operational in 1965. The first Air Force aircraft lost in the war was a Ranch Hand C-123, which went down on February 2, 1962, killing its three crewmen. Nine more Fairchild UC-123s and 23 more airmen were lost before Ranch Hand was finally canceled in January 1971. The Ranch Hand unit—the 12th Special Operations Squadron—became one of the most highly decorated Air Force squadrons of the war, receiving four Presidential Unit Citations, three Air Force Outstanding Unit Awards with Combat Vs for valor, and three Vietnam Gallantry Crosses with palms.

The primary use of herbicides in Southeast Asia was to destroy vegetation and deny cover to the enemy. An additional aim was crop destruction, to deny the enemy food. Herbicides were recognized as important new weapons in the war.

The final authority for herbicide operations in Southeast Asia was MACV, through its U.S. Army Chemical Corps office. Once requests for herbicide spraying were approved by the commander of MACV, the Chemical Corps office sent coordination instructions, including a priority target list, to Seventh Air Force head-quarters. The Seventh, through its Tactical Air Control Center (TACC), directed the Ranch Hand squadron in planning and executing spray operations.

Ranch Hand missions were usually flown in formations of two to six UC-123s (the replacements for C-123s) flying side by side about 80 yards apart, and they were normally accompanied by a forward air controller and fighter cover. During the delivery portion of the mission, the UC-123s flew at about 125–130 knots and at the lowest altitude possible (usually 100–150 feet above the foliage) in order to disperse the herbicide efficiently. Because of their slow speed and low altitudes, the aircraft were fired upon during virtually every mission. One of the squadron's aircraft, *Patches*, suffered more than 600 hits in nearly 10 years of spraying operations. *Patches* survived the war and is now in the Air Force Museum at Wright-Patterson Air Force Base in Dayton, Ohio.

A 1,000-gallon pressure pumping tank in the cargo bay directed the herbicide to the wings and a tail spray bar for distribution. Ground crews who loaded the chemical into the pumping tank often got some of it on their skin and clothing. ARVN troops, who were normally assigned to load the aircraft, worked with the herbicides for years without complaining of any problems. Many times U.S. Air Force crews were also exposed to the fumes of the herbicide while it was being loaded or sprayed. No measures such as protective clothing were instituted to protect those who were exposed to it—after all, the Seventh Air Force Tactical Air Operations handbook stated that the defoliant was "completely harmless to humans and animals."

The process of aerial spraying and defoliation was certainly not new. Defoliants had been used in American agriculture for years, yet no one had attributed any health problems to their use. Throughout the war in Vietnam, in addition to questions Americans raised concerning the effectiveness of the spray operations, there was also a constant flow of enemy propaganda against the herbicide project. The Communists denounced the defoliation missions as chemical-biological warfare.

The main herbicide defoliants, named Orange and White for the colored stripes painted on their shipping drums, were sprayed on jungle vegetation. Agent Blue was a desiccant (drying chemical) used on crops such as rice and narrow-leaf plants. Approximately 20 million gallons of herbicides were sprayed in Southeast Asia, 92 percent by the Air Force and 8 percent by the Army. About 60 percent of the herbicides used was Orange, nearly 30 percent was White (sometimes used as a substitute for Orange, but made up of different chemicals) and about 10 percent was Blue.

By late 1969, scientists who visited South Vietnam and Cambodia were using the word "agent" in articles describing the defoliation missions. "Agent" simply means a biologically active principle, but both popular and scientific publications began referring to the various types of defoliants as agents. Agent Orange became the most widely known of the chemicals when it was labeled by one publication as "an imminent hazard to human health, mainly due to the trace contaminant dioxin (TCDD)." Under heavy scrutiny from the scientific community—as well as by some others who perhaps had other agendas—the use of Orange was discontinued in Southeast Asia by orders from the U.S. Department of Defense on April 15, 1970.

Agent Orange and its military significance should have become just a footnote in the history of the Vietnam War. On May 9, 1970, the Ranch Hand defoliation operations were terminated, just weeks after the Department of Defense's suspension of the use of Orange. The MACV commander permanently canceled Air Force fixed-wing defoliation missions on July 17, 1970. The inactivated Ranch Hand squadron (now a flight) was still responsible for crop-destruction missions, but only 70 sorties were flown over the next six months. The last mission was flown on January 7, 1971. Because several Army units, including the Americal Division, were exposed to Agent Orange during unauthorized use in mid- to late 1970, the MACV commander ordered all remaining stocks of Agent Orange in South Vietnam—some 25,000 drums—consolidated and placed in centralized locations where access to them could be closely controlled.

Supplies of the Orange herbicide remained in South Vietnam until April 1972, when the last of the 25,000 drums (approximately 1.4 million gallons) were shipped to Johnston Island in the Pacific. In addition, 15,500 drums of herbicide that had been stored at a naval facility in Gulfport, Mississippi, were shipped to Johnston Island and then burned at sea in July 1977. On September 3, 1977, the herbicides shipped from Vietnam were also incinerated at sea. The Air Force estimated the total cost of storage and destruction of the herbicides at more than $8 million. But the destruction of the herbicides did not end the controversy surrounding Agent Orange. Although the Vietnam War was over by then, the use of Orange remained a thorny topic, particularly in the media. And new victims of herbicide use now began emerging—Vietnam veterans.

Most of the accounts appearing in the media about Ranch Hand, Agent Orange and its effects have been one-sided and often misleading. For example, an article published in the October 1996 issue of *Vietnam* described Ranch Hand crewmen engaged in very questionable activities. According to the author, Tony Spletstoser, crews of UC-123s that were not rigged for spraying would simply dump herbicides from drums over the rear loading ramp, allowing the vortexes surrounding the aircraft to suck the chemicals out of the drums, creating their own spray. I have been unable to locate anyone in the Ranch Hand Association who has ever heard of a crew member in either a C-123 or UC-123 using this procedure. According to association members, the Air Force C-123s and UC-123s carried herbicides only in 1,000-gallon MC-1 Hourglass spray system tanks, never in barrels. But I can imagine—although I have no knowledge of this ever having actually been done—how an Army helicopter crew might try such a method if the chopper was not rigged for spraying.

That article also stated that even when the Ranch Hand crews used spray equipment, it was impossible for the crew members not to be covered with herbicides in the course of the missions. This is not true. While the crewmen were certainly exposed to fumes and spilled herbicides when filling the spray tanks, it is doubtful that Ranch Hand aircrews were ever drenched or covered with the chemicals unless a tank was ruptured by enemy groundfire and the herbicide leaked into the cargo compartment. It was possible for crewmen to be drenched with hydraulic fluid if small-arms fire hit the reservoir or lines in the cargo compartment. Ranch Hand aircraft were hit more than 7,000 times during their operations.

Yet another incorrect statement in that article was that UC-123s flew their missions at slightly more than 85 knots. The normal spraying speed was 130 knots. A speed of 85 knots would be more consistent with helicopter spraying.

Finally, if anyone in the U.S. Army sprayed any Agent Orange in the Mekong Delta in December 1970, it was in violation of the MACV commander's orders. The commander of MACV authorized the Army to spray only White and Blue herbicides after April 1970 and until U.S. troops departed Vietnam in 1973. The Seventh Air Force and the Ranch Hand squadron were not responsible for or even informed about the Army missions.

Whether they are veterans of Vietnam or the Gulf War—who have their own health problems to deal with—or simply interested citizens, readers should decide for themselves the truth about the effects of Agent Orange and other herbicides on humans who have been exposed to it.

I feel qualified to respond to the misinformation circulating about Ranch Hand and Orange because I was directly involved in the herbicide missions. I was a Ranch Hand aircraft commander with the 12th Special Operations Squadron at Da Nang, and I was later assigned to Seventh Air Force headquarters as the last Ranch Hand herbicide project officer. Following the deactivation of the squadron on July 31, 1970, I was transferred to the Seventh Air Force's Directorate of Tactical Analysis.

After reading a number of articles on the controversy, including some containing grossly inaccurate information on Agent Orange and the Ranch Hand operation, I decided to get the latest available mortality information on the subject. I eventually obtained the Air Force Health Study publication titled *Mortality Update*, 1996. This report covers four medical exams of Air Force personnel following exposure to the herbicide in Vietnam. Physicals were done in 1982, 1985, 1987 and 1992, with a 15th-year exam held in 1997-98 and a final physical scheduled for 2002. The overall purpose of the ongoing study is to determine whether individuals serving in Ranch Hand experienced adverse health effects as a result of their participation in that project.

Ranch Hand crew members constitute the only group whose herbicidal exposure could be accurately determined by type, time and frequency. As Paul Cecil has written in his book *Herbicidal Warfare*, simulated spray mission experiments indicated that exposure levels for the Ranch Hand airmen were as much as 1,000 times greater than the maximum levels experienced by ground personnel in the target areas, whether friendly or enemy. It should be remembered that the Ranch Hand missions could not be flown over allied troops or areas populated by South Vietnamese.

I have been a participant, as have more than 90 percent of Ranch Hand veterans, in the Air Force health study since it began in 1982. The medical examinations, conducted at the prestigious Scripps Research Clinic in La Jolla, California, take nearly three days to complete. The implications inherent in the medical data gathered during these tests is becoming clearer all the time. The July 1996 edition of the Air Force *Mortality Update* stated: "This study has not demonstrated health effects which can be conclusively attributed to herbicide or dioxin (a contaminant in Agent Orange) exposure. The over-all mortality experience of Ranch Hands is not significantly different from that expected. As of December 31, 1995, 118 (9.4 percent) of the 1,261 Ranch Hands have died; the expected number of deaths is 119.95. The observed expected number of deaths among all Ranch Hands were not significantly different from accidental deaths, suicides, and deaths caused by malignant neoplasm and circulatory system disease. However, there were borderline significant increased deaths due to circulatory system diseases in non-flying enlisted Ranch Hands. In contrast to previous reports, deaths caused by digestive disease and deaths due to ill-defined and unknown causes in pilots are no longer significantly increased."

The report did note a possible association between dioxin exposure and diabetes, as well as a relationship between dioxin exposure and heart disease. In reviewing the death rate of former Ranch Hand crew members, the report compared the 989 members involved in the study to a group of 1,276 airmen who flew C-130s but were not involved in defoliation missions. The association with diabetes appears to suffer from some statistical variances and needs some explanation.

Armstrong Laboratory, located at Brooks Air Force Base at San Antonio, Texas, is responsible for the 20-year Air Force health study. Although the investigators were looking primarily for cancer and birth defects, over time they discovered an increased rate of diabetes in the Ranch Hand subjects. When the scientists reported their findings in the media in May 1997, they said that the Ranch Hand members had a 50 percent higher chance of developing diabetes than did airmen not exposed to the herbicide.

The 1,276 men in the control group had a median result of 4 parts per trillion (or ppt) dioxin body burden in their blood, the same level for the average American citizen. Of these 1,276 men, 169 (or 13.2 percent) had contracted diabetes. In comparison, the Ranch Hand group had a median result of nearly 13 ppt, and 146 former Ranch Hand crew members (14.7 percent) had diabetes. However, nearly half the men (442) in the Ranch Hand group had less than 10 ppt of current body burden, and this group also included only 40 airmen with diabetes (a 9.5 percent rate). This was nearly 30 percent lower than the C-130 group with approximately the same dioxin level. Because they were unable to correlate any disease with a dioxin level lower than 10 ppt, the scientists decided to remove this low-dioxin-level Ranch Hand group from the final comparison.

Forty-nine former Ranch Hand crewmen from another group of 284 airmen (29 percent of the total Ranch Hand group) developed diabetes. Their blood dioxin burden levels were greater than 10 but less than 94 ppt. This group had a 17.2 percent diabetes rate, roughly 30 percent higher than the control group. However, the scientists decided to eliminate this group from a final comparison so as to concentrate on the last group of 283 Ranch Hand airmen. This remaining group, which constituted 28 percent of the total Ranch Hand group, had blood dioxin levels greater than 94 ppt. Fifty-seven men in this last group developed diabetes, for a 20.1 percent rate.

It was this group alone that accounted for the startling "50 percent higher rate" that was announced to the media. I do not know why the scientists chose to use the last group of men as the basis for this claim, but I do know that it was not totally correct to say, as the *Air Force Times* reported, "Airmen involved in the spraying of Agent Orange in Vietnam have a 50 percent higher chance of contracting diabetes than people not exposed to the herbicide."

It is more accurate to say that, of the 989 Ranch Hand airmen studied, the 283 with a blood dioxin burden level of nearly 100 ppt or greater are the only ones who have a 50 percent higher chance of contracting diabetes. This is a very important distinction to make when looking at the entire group of Ranch Hand crewmen. Only 146 of those individuals contracted diabetes. This number represents only a 14.7 percent rate, slightly more than one percent higher than the rate of the C-130 control group.

A considerable amount of research on Agent Orange and the other herbicides used in Vietnam has been undertaken by both governmental and nongovernmental organizations. According to the final report, issued in 1994, of the Domestic Policy Council's Agent Orange Working Group, at that time there were 38 ongoing projects and 189 completed projects. More than $127 million had been spent on the completed projects, $86 million on the continuing projects, and an estimated additional $70 million would be required to complete ongoing projects. Recent Department of Veterans Affairs information also indicates that at least 200 more research studies have scrutinized every conceivable aspect of Agent Orange's presumed effect on veterans. So while the Air Force's health study may be considered the best of these studies because of its in-depth epidemiological investigation, its 20-year length and the definite exposure of the participants to defoliants, the Ranch Hand investigation is by no means the only research effort I have studied.

From my review of the literature from each of these projects, it appears that no medical conditions or areas are left to be researched. The National Academy of Science's (NAS's) Institute of Medicine, in its 1994 report Veterans and Agent Orange— Health Effects of Herbicides Used in Vietnam, reviewed all relevant scientific research: national, international, public and private. In its first recommendation to then Secretary of Veterans Affairs Jesse Brown, the academy fully endorsed the continuation of only one study by name—the Air Force Ranch Hand study. It also recommended that a similar study be done on members of the Army Chemical Corps.

In its 1996 Update Report, as in its earlier report, the NAS assigned each health outcome considered in the report to one of four categories based on the scientific evidence of an association with Orange or the other herbicides that were used in Southeast Asia. In making these assignments, the NAS considered a large range of public and private occupational, environmental and veterans' studies.

The categories are:

- Sufficient evidence of an association
- Limited or suggestive evidence of an association
- Inadequate or insufficient evidence to determine whether an association exists
- Limited or suggestive evidence of no association

On the basis of the NAS's 1996 report, the secretary of Veterans Affairs authorized an expansion of a list of conditions presumed to be the result of exposure to herbicides during military service. With the addition of prostate cancer and acute and subacute peripheral neuropathy, along with spina bifida in the children of Vietnam veterans, the list of conditions presumed to be related to exposure increased from seven to ten.

These ten conditions: chloracne, Non-Hodgkin's lymphoma, soft tissue sarcoma, Hodgkin's disease, porphyria cutanea tarda, multiple myeloma, respiratory cancers (including cancers of the lung, larynx, trachea, and bronchus), prostate cancer, peripheral neuropathy (acute or subacute), and spina bifida, are now recognized, presumptively, as being service-connected for Vietnam veterans based on exposure to Agent Orange or other herbicides that contain dioxin. But there is still no direct evidence of cause for any of the ten conditions, only what the NAS terms "sufficient or limited/suggestive evidence of an association."

According to an article in the January 1991 issue of *Disabled American Veterans* magazine, of these ten conditions, there appears to be a 50 percent higher chance of some Vietnam veterans' developing non-Hodgkin's lymphoma. However, the highest incidence of this has been among Navy personnel who served offshore and thus were least likely to have been exposed to Agent Orange.

Today, Vietnam veterans are not required to prove exposure to Agent Orange, since it is assumed that all military personnel who served within the borders of Vietnam or in adjacent waters from 1962 to 1975 were exposed to some extent. Of the 8.74 million Americans on active duty during the war, only 3,403,100 actually served in the Southeast Asian theater and only 2,594,000 were physically in South Vietnam and adjacent waters.

After reviewing all the studies cited in the January 1997 Veterans Affairs *Agent Orange Briefs* (a total of 20 covering the 10 conditions) and the *Agent Orange Reviews* from 1982 to 1997, it seems to me that these publications still do not show evidence that the NAS categories do, in fact, represent an indisputable scientific way to classify these medical conditions. It appears that the publications require little evidence to scientifically classify these diseases as associated with Agent Orange. Less than 5 percent of the studies examined provide any evidence of even a remote connection between the disability or disease studied and Agent Orange and other herbicides.

One would think that by now something more than a "presumptive finding or relationship" would have been discovered if, in fact, Orange and other herbicides were the culprits. Isn't some conclusive evidence normally required to pronounce something or someone guilty?

The lack of hard evidence has not stopped the media from issuing ill-informed stories about Agent Orange. In the February 12, 1997, issue of the *Wall Street Journal*, an article appeared titled "Body Count: In Vietnam, the Agony of Birth Defects Calls an Old War to Mind." The reporter wrote, "Vietnamese scientists believe that as many as 500,000 children may have been born with dioxin-related deformities since the mid-1960s." He also described the countryside as a "sea of toxic defoliants." Without any mention of direct scientific proof, the presumption was, once again, that Agent Orange was the culprit.

A Vietnam veteran who had served as an intelligence officer with the 25th Division in an area of concentrated Ranch Hand activity took exception to the article in the *Wall Street Journal* and wrote to the paper. In a letter to the editor published in the March 5, 1997, edition, he stated how sad it was to read such a sensationalized story on the *Journal*'s front page, an article that seemed to implicate U.S. armed forces as "baby killers." He wrote that, although he could not help but feel sorry for the children suffering from birth defects, it was outrageous to mix their tragedy with rank speculation, propaganda and junk science.

The former intelligence officer said he had traveled extensively in the areas that were heavily sprayed and never smelled or tasted Agent Orange at any time, let alone "for weeks," as suggested in the article. Furthermore, he saw none of the disreputable activities described, and he concluded that it was more likely to have been Communist economics, rather than Agent Orange, that ruined rice production in South Vietnam until recently.

No matter what might be your view concerning Orange, it is worth considering the following passages from Paul Cecil's *Herbicidal Warfare*. Cecil, who flew more than 1,000 combat sorties in airlift operations and Ranch Hand and is the Ranch Hand Association historian, stated: "Operation Ranch Hand proved successful in its primary purpose of reducing the concealing vegetation used by the enemy to mask his facilities, lines of communications, and avenues of attack. Most field commanders were enthusiastic about the results . . . and requests for additional [defoliation] sorties continued to arrive from the field until the program was canceled. The reduction in enemy activity in defoliated areas was repeatedly documented. While it is impossible to determine to what extent it saved lives, there can be no doubt that it did. However, the benefits of reduction in injury and death among American ground forces were overwhelmed by the controversies over environmental damage and possible indirect, long-term harm to human health."

Cecil continued: "The special irony of the Ranch Hand herbicide program is that it was a technique that offered a way to blunt the guerrilla and terrorist effectiveness without direct injury to enemy, ally, or innocent. It is not wholly absurd to suggest that if it had not been used, many would have criticized the Kennedy-Johnson-Nixon administrations, the Air Force, and MACV for failing to utilize such a cheap and economical weapon."

The adverse publicity surrounding Agent Orange and herbicidal warfare in general should not detract from honors due to the dedicated men of Ranch Hand who wrote a unique chapter in the history of air warfare. As *Vietnam* editor Colonel Harry G. Summers, Jr., wrote in his editorial in the October 1996 issue, "the line between truth and fiction often becomes blurred." He quoted former Secretary of Defense James Schlesinger as saying, "Everyone is entitled to his own view, but everyone is not entitled to his own facts." Colonel Summers continued, "while the U.S. government has *failed to find a link* [emphasis added] between Agent Orange and the various disabilities suffered by the veterans of the war," there were others "who think, regardless of the government's account, that such a link does indeed exist."

COLONEL RICHARD D. DUCKWORTH

The most recent statement from the Ranch Hand study, released in December 1997, indicated that some former crew members with high dioxin levels—those experiencing an increased risk of diabetes—would have fat samples removed during the fifth round of physicals, which were scheduled to take place between May 1997 and April 1998. The specimens are to be analyzed to help understand whether dioxin actually causes diabetes.

It was also disclosed that a new study of the relationship between paternal exposure to dioxin and low birth weight and infant death found no relation between dioxin exposure and those adverse outcomes. Another study found no relation between dioxin exposure and chloracne in Ranch Hand veterans. A cancer study found no relationship between malignancies and dioxin exposure, while another paper awaiting publication shows no relation between dioxin exposure and immune suppression. Another paper found no relation between a study group (Ranch Hand, Comparison) and mortality. Further studies of cardiovascular disease, psychological or gastrointestinal abnormalities, fertility and peripheral neuropathy are in progress.

My primary interest is in clarifying the facts about the Ranch Hand missions and revealing the most recent sources and factual data concerning Agent Orange. Clearly, much misinformation is still being circulated about the use of herbicides in Vietnam and their effects on humans.

Perhaps careful consideration of the information presented here will provide readers with a better understanding of Vietnam veterans' health problems as they are related to Agent Orange, by helping sort out the fact from the fiction.

On Patrol with the Kiwi Infantry

By Jon Latimer

When the first U.S. Marine combat units landed at Da Nang on March 8, 1965, America's allies in the Pacific pledged to contribute a further 7,250 troops, including an Australian battalion. The initial contingent consisted of the 1st Battalion, Royal Australian Regiment (1st RAR), with the 105th Battery, Royal Australian Artillery, as well as logistics and medical personnel, engineers and a small armored contingent. The following month the 161st Battery, Royal New Zealand Artillery, arrived. Despite the Australians' and New Zealanders' wide experience in counterrevolutionary warfare, the number of soldiers from the Australia–New Zealand Army Corps, or ANZAC–named after the organization originally formed for the Gallipoli operation of World War I–was not considered sufficient for the unit to operate on its own in Vietnam.

By that time, both the NVA and the VC had demonstrated an ability and willingness to engage in battalion- and even regiment-sized actions. During its first year in-country, the fledgling ANZAC force operated closely with the 173rd Airborne Brigade, based at Bien Hoa, proving extremely effective in search-and-destroy operations around Saigon. The ANZAC troops impressed the Americans with their superb field craft and the efficiency of their artillery's close support, while they in turn benefited from the seemingly unlimited air transport and the professionalism of the U.S. Army's air arm.

Meanwhile, Australia's participation in the Vietnam War had become very unpopular back home. Additional troop deployments were restricted until after the Australian federal elections of March 1966, in which Vietnam was a crucial political issue. Resistance to participation in the war was principally from the political left and proved very vocal, particularly from organizations with strong links to the Communists. After a right wing Liberal-Country Party coalition formed a strong government, Australia underlined its commitment to its U.S. ally by creating the 1st Australian Task Force, which authorized adding the 5th and 6th Battalions to the 1st RAR, later supplemented by a company group from the 1st Battalion, Royal New Zealand Infantry Regiment. The 1st RAR was then replaced by the 7th Battalion. The Australian units included a high proportion of national service conscripts who had volunteered for service overseas.

The New Zealand units, on the other hand, were comprised exclusively of professional soldiers normally stationed in Singapore or Malaysia. The initial deployment on May 8, 1967, consisted of Victor 1 Company, which formed part of the 2nd RAR/NZ (ANZAC) Battalion, followed six months later by Whiskey Company. These units were then attached to the 4th RAR/NZ (ANZAC) Battalion when it took over from the 2nd RAR in May 1968, and the 6th RAR from May 1969 to 1970. The 2nd RAR then returned for a further tour before its final withdrawal in 1971.

The creation of a brigade-sized grouping meant that the ANZAC troops—sometimes called the Kiwi infantry—could now take responsibility for their own area of operations. They were assigned to Phuoc Tuy province, a coastal region southeast of Saigon. Rear echelon operations were established at Vung Tau, on the coast itself, but the Task Force headquarters and base of operations was at Nui Dat, where it was more centrally located and better able to swiftly move support to the provincial capital at Ba Ria.

When the ANZAC troops arrived, they found themselves in a hot spot of VC activity, an area that had long proved troublesome to the allies. The VC appeared to have already won the war in Phuoc Tuy. Unperturbed, the ANZAC troops immediately began taking aggressive action in the area, launching patrols and ambushes—employing techniques learned in Malaya. They effectively denied the VC not only the freedom to operate but also the ability to supply their forces in the area. Although the region around the base at Nui Dat was frequently patrolled, most Kiwi infantrymen spent the majority of their one-year tour in Vietnam in the field.

A typical offensive operation in which the Kiwis participated was Operation Marsden, which took place between December 1 and 27, 1969. The operational area selected by the Australian Task Force command was a complex VC system defending a base near Nui May Tao Mountain that was supplying VC forces in Long Khanh, Bien Hoa and western Binh Tuy, as well as Phuoc Tuy. There were also believed to be two VC hospitals in the area. It was somewhat remote but still close to Highway 1 and the beaches of the South China Sea, enabling the VC to supply their forces with large quantities of stores by sampan and vehicle. Authorities believed that support troops defending the base area might be backed up by regulars from the 274th NVA Regiment who periodically came in to resupply.

The 6th RAR/NZ (ANZAC) Battalion was designated the principal ground search unit for Operation Marsden, supported by M-113 armored personnel carriers from B Squadron, 3rd Cavalry Regiment; Centurion tanks from A Squadron, 1st Armoured Regiment; the 101st Battery, Royal Australian Artillery, with 105mm howitzers; an American 155mm artillery platoon; the 1st Field Squadron, Royal Australian Engineers; and Australian and American helicopters.

Beginning on November 30, the Kiwis established Fire Support Base Picton in what was designated area of operations (AO) Gulliver to support the arrival of an armored vehicle convoy on December 1. New Zealand's Whiskey Company was inserted into FSB Picton that day by Bell Iroquois helicopters of No. 9 Squadron, RAAF, and landed without incident. Kiwis began patrolling southwest, to the edge of AO Gulliver, before moving northwest.

The night after they arrived, each platoon set up independent patrol bases to resume sweeping the Song Rai and Suoi Luc rivers the following morning. They discovered a large munitions cache, including grenades, mines, rockets and explosives. As the Kiwis continued patrolling, they found additional caches located along the edge of the Song Rai.

Victor Company was airlifted into FSB Picton on December 3, together with an ARVN Battalion that it had been responsible for training. Victor Company troops led the ARVN troops in a sweep operation southwest of Nui May Tao and located an unoccupied enemy bunker system.

By December 8, ANZAC forces had killed 13 enemy troops in fleeting contacts with the D440 VC Battalion. The Australian companies located the main VC munitions dumps and part of a hospital. Meanwhile, Whiskey Company had completed its search of the northwest and was airlifted out. Whiskey's role was now changed to following up an Australian company and establishing blocking ambushes on suspected VC trails, in an effort to trap enemy troops trying to avoid the Australian company's sweep. Those operations continued without success until the Kiwis were withdrawn on December 27. As usual, the ANZAC troops celebrated the end of the mission with a barbecue.

Victor Company had made contact with the enemy on December 18, when Kiwis cornered the VC hospital's commanding officer and his adjutant and killed them in a brisk firefight. When they continued their patrol the following day, Victor Company's troops located a complex of 30 huts, the main part of the hospital, as well as a substantial drug cache, which had been concealed in some nearby caves. The patients, who had been abandoned by the VC, were evacuated. On December 21, a prisoner led scouts to an arms cache, where they captured another VC soldier.

Patrols continued until Christmas Day, when operations were suspended to observe a truce imposed throughout Vietnam. The troops of Victor Company celebrated with a church service and Christmas dinner. Hostilities resumed the following morning, with patrols sweeping the rugged terrain around Nui May Tao once more. The Kiwis captured five more VC from a logistics unit that had been responsible for the enemy base camp on December 27. Victor Company was airlifted back to its own base camp the next morning.

The operation was regarded as a success in that it disrupted the VC supply line and hospital facilities in Phuoc Tuy province, although as always, the area was then left for the VC to reoccupy and resume their activities. In fact, the medical supplies seized represented the largest such haul of the war and included items from France, China and the United States, including goods donated by American anti-war groups. Altogether, the 6th RAR/NZ suffered four men killed and nine wounded, mostly by mines. Eventually a total of 35 New Zealand infantry soldiers were killed in the conflict and 187 wounded, many seriously. Kiwi veteran George Babbington later said: "The greatest personal loss to me was when my section commander, George Hoerara, was killed after only two weeks in Vietnam. At the time I was only a short distance behind him when he stepped on a mine. It was a shock to us all. One minute he was there, the next minute he was gone. At the time I thought, 'What am I doing here?' afterward thinking, 'Is it worth it, will I stay for the whole game?' I was hurt by the loss."

As can be seen from the description of Operation Marsden, most of the Kiwi soldiers' time in the field consisted of patrolling and setting up ambushes. Both require high levels of training and competence in navigation, marksmanship and field craft. Kiwi troops seldom used mines except in ambush positions, when they used Claymores. Former Kiwi infantryman John McGuide recalled, "We were terrified when we deployed in an American area of operations because they were slack in recording where they had laid minefields."

It takes great care and skill to set up an ambush properly. The ambush position must be occupied quietly and troops need steady nerves to maintain vigilance and allow the enemy to enter the killing ground before opening fire. Kiwi troops often set up night ambushes, which are particularly nerve-wracking for the attackers, to cover VC supply routes.

Kiwis tried to cover all possible approach routes with cutoff parties and to prevent any indiscriminate fire from a unit's automatic weapons by marking their arcs of fire with wooden aiming stakes. Both Aussies and Kiwis were principally armed with the semiautomatic British variant of the FN rifle and M-60 machine guns. If one of their ambushes was successfully sprung, the Kiwis generally either carried their assault through the enemy position or withdrew to a prearranged rendezvous point.

A Kiwi infantry platoon commanded by Lieutenant B.E. Hall was involved in an ambush against a VC platoon on the night of June 1, 1969. Unfortunately for the Kiwis, the ambush was sprung by one of the cutoff groups rather than the main platoon position, and the VC—after losing two dead—immediately counterattacked with automatic fire and rocket-propelled grenades (RPGs). Hall quickly brought his M-60s to bear on the enemy soldiers and was able to withdraw his cutoff group before leading an assault with another section through the initial ambush site to drive off the enemy. The VC lost several more confirmed dead, and blood trails discovered by the Kiwis after the battle suggested there were probably additional casualties. Hall's platoon suffered no losses.

While the Kiwis were very skilled in this form of warfare, so were the VC. They had a formidable reputation for using such tactics to wipe out entire road convoys. If a Kiwi patrol was caught in an ambush, survival depended on quick thinking as well as effective training. Kiwi troops were conditioned to aggressively respond by reflex—getting out of the killing zone and immediately engaging the enemy. An outflanking maneuver they rehearsed proved effective against small-scale ambushes but not against concealed bunkers. Kiwis were caught under fire from such fortified positions on a number of occasions, and in those cases artillery support or airstrikes were generally necessary if the enemy decided to make a fight of it.

When Sergeant T.H. Tuhiwai's platoon was ambushed while crossing a deep ravine on March 19, 1969, Tuhiwai himself was among the first five casualties, hit by shrapnel from an RPG round. Fortunately for his platoon, he was an exceptional leader, and despite his injuries he quickly organized his men into a defensive perimeter to prevent them being overrun. A second platoon nearby was pinned down by heavy mortar fire and unable to assist, so Tuhiwai's men had to face a fierce assault by about 100 VC by themselves. Several more Kiwis were wounded in the hail of fire as Tuhiwai moved among his men, encouraging and directing their fire. Unable to follow up on their initial success, the VC were reluctant to take on the smaller New Zealand force and retreated after about an hour. In that instance, the Kiwis inflicted a tactical defeat on ground of the enemy's choosing and without the benefit of fire support. The Kiwis recovered all their wounded, and Tuhiwai subsequently received a Distinguished Conduct Medal for his leadership and courage during the firefight.

Operation Duntroon was another large-scale, multi-unit operation that Kiwi troops participated in. Victor Company, 2nd RAR/NZ, commanded by Major R. Worsnop, was inserted by helicopter into Xa Bang on the afternoon of January 10, 1968, initially assigned to defend the western perimeter of the battalion base area. The following day the unit was airlifted into LZ Cook, where the Kiwis were to serve as the lead company of a battalion air assault. On landing, they were to head out to the southwest to set up ambush blocking positions. Difficult ground and thick vegetation slowed them down, but they were secure in ambush positions by nightfall of the 12th. The next evening saw the first contacts. Reacting to the sweep underway in the area, a VC platoon was moving along a track, trying to avoid the cordon to the west. Foolishly using torches, the guerrillas walked straight into a section-strength ambush set by the 4th Platoon, which opened fire at a range of 10 meters. Seven VC were cut down immediately and the remainder scattered into the bush, covered by a single brave individual who crawled into a ditch and returned fire. He was killed by a deluge of grenades. The Kiwis then conducted a thorough search of the area and recovered a dozen weapons.

That ambush had been successful largely because the number of troops was kept to a minimum at the ambush site itself, with the remainder of the platoon positioned to provide close support if needed. When the VC platoon subsequently split up into smaller groups and tried to break out again, those squads were caught by a second ambush set by members of the 5th Platoon. One VC was killed and three more wounded, while the other four fled. The platoon commander's sweep yielded two AK-47s, two RPD light machine guns and a wheel-mounted machine gun, plus various grenade launchers and rounds. As he was conducting this sweep, two more VC returned to the site to try to recover their lost equipment. They wounded three of the Kiwis before being driven off early on the morning of the 14th.

Victor Company's 6th Platoon began a sweep at 0700 hours, moving through thick jungle. After 20 minutes the lead scout spotted a VC soldier treating a wounded comrade barely 10 meters to his front. The remainder of the section deployed while the scout fired two rounds from his M-16 (the weapon usually carried by scouts) and another soldier fired a single 7.62mm SLR (Self-Loading Rifle) round through the thick vegetation. The wounded VC was killed and the second man fled through the bush, under fire by the section M-60. Later that same morning, the 5th Platoon engaged a single enemy soldier while conducting their own sweep, but he too escaped. Ten minutes later the 4th Platoon had one final contact with a single enemy soldier who escaped.

On January 15 the 4th Platoon searched a nearby area and discovered 20 unoccupied fighting bunkers, complete with overhead cover, which they destroyed. The next day Kiwi troops maintained blocking positions in the same areas. At 0930, when two VC were spotted moving toward one position, the Kiwis opened fire. They later recovered medical supplies and documents from what appeared to be a medic team that had recovered casualties and equipment in an area previously swept by the Kiwis. Again the Kiwis maintained the ambush positions the following day, also sending out patrols. At midmorning the 4th Platoon's patrol base spotted three VC moving cautiously about 50 meters away and directed artillery fire on them.

Finally, the Kiwi company headquarters received orders to commence a two-day search-and-destroy operation in a designated area and then concentrate on LZ Cook late on the afternoon of the 19th. The company rendezvoused at 0800 on the 18th and moved toward its new area. Kiwi troops found some indications that small groups of VC were moving through the area from the west, but as the company continued to sweep its area, it got held up by the thick vegetation. The unit did not arrive at LZ Cook until the afternoon of the 21st, when it was airlifted out to Luscombe Field.

Operation Coburg commenced only three days later. Flying out at 0900, the Kiwis headed northwest to a landing zone at FSB Andersen, from which it patrolled east, pausing to allow C Company, 2nd RAR, to move out of its proposed route. By 1700 Kiwi troops had established an ambush blocking position, which they were supposed to hold until Major Worsnop received radio orders to commence the search-and-destroy phase of the operation.

The next afternoon, the 5th and 6th platoons moved out to lay ambushes on nearby trails. On the morning of January 26, 1968, the 6th Platoon stopped two oxcarts driven by Vietnamese woodcutters. After verifying that the woodcutters were genuine, the Kiwis allowed them to proceed. Moving through thick secondary jungle in patrol formation an hour later, the lead scout spotted two VC dressed in black and armed with M-1 carbines just 10 meters away. He opened fire with his M-16 as the other members of the section put their M-60 into action, spraying the area where the two VC had gone to ground. The section commander informed the platoon commander of the situation. Subsequently, Kiwis recovered two M-1s and some enemy documents. Meanwhile, the remaining section of the 6th Platoon, deploying to follow up the contact, observed enemy movement to their rear. Quickly redeploying, they engaged the enemy with small-arms fire and called for artillery support, which arrived promptly. After that, the VC disappeared into the jungle.

The 5th Platoon now began its move to the northeast, soon followed by company headquarters and the 4th Platoon. Once again, the troops were traveling through difficult terrain where they could move only about 400 meters per hour. The Kiwis took up three ambush positions late in the afternoon, then received orders to join C Company, 2nd RAR, which had located an enemy encampment.

Following breakfast on the 27th, the 5th Platoon struggled through to that location at midday, only to find that C Company had successfully withdrawn from the enemy camp. After that, they proceeded with the search-and-destroy operation, which resulted in an additional move east the next morning. At around midday, the 4th Platoon contacted the enemy. The rear section had begun to move across the area when one of its members was surprised to see two VC approaching along the track, completely oblivious to the presence of the Kiwi company. The Kiwis quickly opened fire, killing both enemy soldiers. They recovered another M-1, more documents and a satchel containing a large quantity of detonators.

During the afternoon the company continued patrolling. Members of the unit were crossing a T junction when five VC soldiers dressed in green approached from the north. The Kiwi company second-in-command and his group fired on them, killing two men, but two Kiwis were wounded by an RPG round. Armed only with M-16s, a single SLR and no machine gun, the Kiwis lacked the firepower to dominate the fight, and the remaining VC were able to withdraw, with one of them providing covering fire with an AK-47. However, they abandoned a quantity of Claymores, detonators and plastic explosives.

Victor company patrolled the area for four more days without incident, until it was ordered to support B Company, 2nd RAR, during an attack on an enemy camp. Following a short barrage, the 6th Platoon was supposed to attack the south side, and after it secured its objective, the 4th and 5th Platoons were to assault the north side. Moving methodically, the 6th platoon cleared its objective, capturing a large quantity of medical supplies, and the 4th and 5th Platoons began their sweep. They encountered six enemy troops and killed one before the remainder fled. After the complex was secured, a lone VC soldier wandered into the camp, possibly meaning to surrender. However, when he was barely 10 meters from an M-60 group, he turned and ran, and the M-60 cut him down.

The company moved once more into an ambush site to the east and barely had time to get settled when 5th Platoon sentries spotted five VC approaching. They opened fire and withdrew, killing one and wounding a second enemy soldier. But covering fire from the nearby M-60 stopped when the gun jammed, and one of the Kiwi sentries, Private H.D. Hirini, was killed by the wounded VC before he was subdued. The remainder of the VC made good their escape. On February 4, another VC was killed in a brief encounter, and the next day, when the company was due to join the 2nd RAR/NZ headquarters, two more VC were killed by mines. On the 6th the Kiwis encountered and killed two more VC, but Gunner E. Ellwood from the 161st Battery was also slain in the brisk exchange of fire.

The climax of the operation was the long anticipated clash with VC troops in strength on the morning of February 7. At dawn the Kiwis were subjected to a ferocious barrage from dug-in VC that wounded six of the ANZAC troops. They returned fire at the VC through dense vegetation to their front, calling down artillery support from the attached ATF battery. B Company of the Australians came to their assistance, and helicopter gunship support also arrived to drive off the already retreating VC. The casualties were medevaced and ammunition resupplied. Finally, in the afternoon of February 9, Victor Company was flown out to FSB Andersen, where they remained for another six days in a base defense role until a road move to Nui Dat finally ended their involvement in ANZAC operations in-country.

After being cut back to a single company in-country in

November 1970, New Zealand's presence in Vietnam came to an end in December 1971. On May 5, 1992, the Battle Honor "South Vietnam 1967-70" was bestowed upon troops of the 1st Battalion, Royal New Zealand Infantry Regiment. Although recognition of the Kiwis' achievements may have been somewhat overdue— thanks mainly to the public antipathy for the Vietnam War— surely no one could deny that these consummately professional soldiers had earned that honor.

Airlifters to the Rescue

By Sam McGowan

F or all practical purposes, Khe Sanh was totally dependent upon air support for its existence," noted General William W. Momyer, deputy commander of MACV (U.S. Military Assistance Command Vietnam) and Seventh Air Force commander. "By the fall of 1967, enemy activity around Khe Sanh forced us to decide whether the base should be evacuated or defended. We thought of Dien Bien Phu and its isolation, but decided we could do the job with intensive air support."

Operation Niagara, as the air effort in support of the Marine base at Khe Sanh was dubbed, is usually thought of in terms of the enormous bomb loads dropped on the surrounding enemy positions, but equally critical was the aerial resupply of its defenders by Air Force and Marine airlifters.

If there was anything that kept the morale of the Marines at Khe Sanh alive during the darkest hours of the siege, it was the sight of a load of parachute-borne cargo containers drifting to earth from a low, overcast sky. Even when bad weather and enemy fire prevented Air Force and Marine airlifters from landing, the beans and bullets that were necessary for the survival of the combat base continued to come in. No doubt the outcome of the Siege of Khe Sanh would have been quite different without the airlift operation.

Before making his decision to hold Khe Sanh in the face of an obvious enemy buildup, the MACV commander, General William C. Westmoreland, was briefed by a historian about the Battle of Dien Bien Phu. Study groups within his own command, as well as the chiefs of staff, believed that General Giap would attempt to re-enact the full Dien Bien Phu scenario around the Marine combat base.

There were many similarities between the two: Like Dien Bien Phu, Khe Sanh was isolated; both were located in valleys surrounded by high, mountainous terrain. Because the enemy controlled the countryside, Khe Sanh was cut off from all resupply except by air, as had been Dien Bien Phu. But though there were similarities, the American situation was much better than that of the French 14 years before. Though Khe Sanh was isolated, the distance to the nearest allied bases could be measured in tens of miles instead of hundreds, and flying time between the combat base and the nearest supply base involved minutes, not hours.

And General Westmoreland had an asset in abundance that the French had lacked—adequate airlift resources to keep the Marine base supplied during an extended siege.

In 1954, French air transport squadrons were equipped with twin-engine C-47 transports: rugged and reliable airplanes to be sure, but also very slow and limited in payload for the 400-mile round trip required to supply the isolated base at Dien Bien Phu. In 1968, General Westmoreland had at his disposal a massive airlift apparatus, including three full wings equipped with fast, modern four-engine C-130 Hercules turboprop transports capable of carrying 35,000-pound payloads over fairly long distances—yet they would have to fly only a little more than 100 miles to get to Khe Sanh from Da Nang.

Weather conditions at Khe Sanh were expected to be bad during the late winter months, and MACV assumed the enemy would take advantage of them. Evidence of increasing enemy anti-aircraft resources around the combat base would present a formidable obstacle—the historian pointed out that a major problem for the French at Dien Bien Phu had been their failure to suppress enemy groundfire. And so far this was also true at Khe Sanh in early 1968. But Westmoreland had confidence in the ability of the airlifters of the Air Force's 834th Air Division (AD), as well as in the Marines' own C-130, CH-53 and CH-46 crews, to get through.

The airlift apparatus upon which General Westmoreland was depending to keep Khe Sanh supplied had been in place in South Vietnam since 1966, when the 834th Air Division was activated to control all airlift within South Vietnam. Commanded in 1968 by Brigadier General Burl McLaughlin, the 834th consisted of two airlift wings—the 325th Air Commando Wing and the 483rd Tactical Airlift Wing—along with the 2nd Aerial Port Group. In addition to the two airlift wings, equipped respectively with C-123 Providers and C-7 Caribous, the division also had operational control of four-engine C-130 Hercules transports that were based out of country with the 315th Air Division, but whose main duties were to provide aircraft and crews for in-country airlift operations.

In addition to the Air Force airlift units, the Marines maintained a detachment of their own KC-130 tanker/transports at Da Nang. Like their Air Force counterparts, the Marine airlifters were based out of country, on Okinawa at Futema Marine Corps Air Field—just a few miles up-island from Naha Air Base, where the Air Force's C-130-equipped 374th Tactical Airlift Wing was based. (The other two Air Force wings were the 314th, based on Taiwan, and the 463rd, based in the Philippines at Clark and Mactan.) Marine airlift also included squadrons equipped with CH-53 and CH-46 heavy-lift helicopters. Marine helicopter crews would do yeoman's service keeping outposts around the combat base supplied, while CH-53s would lift cargo into the base from nearby Dong Ha throughout the siege.

Although the world was not to hear of Khe Sanh until late 1967 and early 1968, the airfield had been a frequent stop for air-lifters from the commencement of U.S. activities in early 1962. A U.S. Army Special Forces and CIDG (Civilian Irregular Defense Group) camp there was serviced by C-123s of the 311th Air Commando Squadron at Da Nang. In mid-1967 the Marines began building up the base they had established at Khe Sanh a few months earlier. The buildup was entirely dependent on Air Force and Marine airlift to move troops in and out and to bring in construction materials and other supplies. Air Force and Marine C-130s and Air Force C-123s airdropped supplies to the construction crews in late 1967, gaining experience that would be invaluable less than six months later.

By January 1968, Khe Sanh was a regular stop for Air Force C-130 crews, with an average of 15 missions per day being scheduled into the base, as well as for the C-123 crews who had been operating there for years. Khe Sanh already had a reputation among the airlift crews, partly because of the known presence of the enemy and partly because of the airstrip itself. Located on top of an 800-foot rise, the runway was difficult to approach because it lacked ground references, while the steep drop-off at the end of the runway often caused downdrafts in wickedly shifting winds. In addition, the runway was only 3,000 feet long—barely long enough for safe C-130 operations, but with little margin for error.

In mid-January, MACV began building up the defenses at Khe Sanh. On the 16th, C-130s lifted in a third Marine infantry battalion to reinforce the two already there (along with an artillery battalion). A fourth battalion was proposed, which raised the question of the feasibility of adequate airlift resupply. MACV advised General Westmoreland that the 15 C-130 missions per day would be adequate, although 75 extra missions would be required to build up the 30-day stock to accommodate the additional troops. But on the 20th the North Vietnamese Army (NVA) blew up the main ammunition dump. Suddenly the airlift effort became critical.

When the dump detonated, debris was scattered all over the base, including the runway. Only two-thirds of it was usable, and that portion was littered with debris. A six-plane C-123 emergency resupply mission managed to land at nightfall by flare light, in spite of bad weather and incoming enemy fire complemented by constant explosions in the still-burning ammunition dump. Other supplies were brought in by Marine helicopters, but no C-130s landed at Khe Sanh that day.

For three days, only C-123s and helicopters could operate into Khe Sanh. Yet the smaller transports managed to bring in 88 tons of critically needed supplies, while Marine helicopters brought in more than 500 members of the fourth Marine infantry battalion. On the 23rd, C-130 operations resumed. Over the next eight days, Air Force deliveries to Khe Sanh averaged 50 tons, with 18 C-130 landings per day during that same period.

Khe Sanh was blessed with unusually good weather during those first few days of February. Early morning ground fog was the only obstacle, but the presence of a Marine GCA (ground-controlled approach) radar unit made landings possible with ceilings as low as 500 feet. A pair of Air Force officers with the 834th AD, Majors Myles Rohrlick and Henry Van Gieson III, thought of a new possibility for the Marine GSA in the event that landings at Khe Sanh should become out of the question. In late January and early February the two airlifters conducted a series of test airdrops at Khe Sanh, using the GCA to position the C-130 drop planes over a known point from which the aircrew navigators could compute a heading and the amount of time to a drop zone. Experience gained from the tests would be a major factor in the later successful supply effort. After the initial tests were conducted with C-130s, the 834th developed similar procedures for the C-123s.

By early February, Khe Sanh had the attention of the world, including the White House. On February 4, the 834th was advised that the airlift effort in I Corps, particularly in the Khe Sanh area, was "vital to the U.S. national interest." In response to this White House order, the 834th began120 percent overscheduling in I Corps and issued a directive that missions were not to be diverted out of that area without special authority. All C-130 missions scheduled into Da Nang were forbidden to be used for stops at intermediate points on the way. All Khe Sanh missions were designated as "Emergency Resupply," the highest priority in the airlift designation.

The Tet attacks had little effect on the Khe Sanh resupply effort, though airlifters countrywide were affected as much as anyone else, and perhaps more so. At Tan Son Nhut, a 29th TAS C-130B had just lifted off when the base was attacked. The crew remained over the base and acted as a combination control tower/forward air controller until an AC-47 gunship came on the scene. For the remainder of the morning and into the next day, the crew, under the command of Major Frank Blodgett, shuttled Vietnamese marines from Vung Tau to reinforce the base defenses at Tan Son Nhut.

For six airlift officers on temporary duty in-country as airlift liaison officers, the Tet attacks in the Cholon district were nearly disastrous. Although the 463rd Tactical Airlift Wing aircrews quartered in the Merlin hotel were told to move onto the base in anticipation of the attacks, the six pilots and navigators failed to get the word. Consequently, they were in their rooms on an upper floor of the hotel when the attacks came. Fortunately, VC forces who occupied the lobby and first floor of the hotel for several hours failed to look upstairs!

Throughout the Tet Offensive, C-130s were used to move troops and supplies to meet attacks throughout the country. A C-130 lift moved elements of the 101st Airborne north from Song Be to

Quang Tri, while dozens of C-130 and C-123 missions brought reinforcements and supplies into Phu Bai airfield in support of the battle to retake Hue.

There was a benefit from the Tet attacks. In response to the sudden increase in tempo of the war, the Pentagon rushed additional forces to the Pacific, including several squadrons of Tactical Air Command (TAC) C-130s from bases in the U.S. to augment the Pacific Air Force C-130 squadrons of 315th Air Division. The newly arrived TAC C-130s were immediately put to work in South Vietnam, where two new C-130 operating locations were opened at Tuy Hoa and Nha Trang in addition to the bases at Cam Ranh and Tan Son Nhut, bringing the total of C-130s in-country at one time to 96. That many of the TAC C-130 crewmen were recently returned from duties in Southeast Asia made their presence even more important.

During the first 12 days of February, all deliveries to Khe Sanh involved landings on the short runway after an approach through heavy groundfire. Once on the ground, the airplanes became targets for enemy artillerymen doing their level best to destroy the transports the NVA knew were vital to the outcome of the battle. It was during that period that the Marines at Khe Sanh began referring to the camouflaged Air Force C-130s as "mortar magnets."

On February 5, Lieutenant Colonel Howard M. Dallman's C-130 crew distinguished themselves at Khe Sanh. As the airplane landed, machine-gun fire from nearby positions struck the fuselage, setting fire to wooden ammunition boxes that made up the load. Flames spread quickly through the inside of the airplane. While the flight mechanic, Staff Sgt. Charles Brault, and the loadmaster, Staff Sgt. Wade Green, went back to fight the fire, Lt. Col. Dallman taxied the airplane to the very end of the runway, as far as possible from the combat base. Once the fire was out, the crew dropped the cargo ramp and rolled off the pallets of still-smoldering cargo, then taxied to the cargo area. Enemy fire continued to strike the C-130 throughout their ordeal, which was still far from over.

Enemy fire had flattened a tire; the crew changed it—using an extemporized jacking rig. The entire time the plane was on the ground, enemy incoming continued to fall all around. Then, as they were taxiing for takeoff, a round hit in front of the nose of the airplane, sending a spray of shrapnel over the C-130 and knocking out one engine. Dallman was making preparations for a three-engine takeoff when the copilot, Captain Roland Behenke, managed to restart the damaged engine. Still receiving hits and low on fuel, the airplane struggled into the air and to safety. For their efforts, Dallman received the Air Force Cross and his crewmen were awarded Silver Stars and Distinguished Flying Crosses.

Five days after the experience of Dallman and his crew, a U.S. Marine Corps KC-130F was hit by groundfire while landing at Khe Sanh with a load of "elephant turds," (i.e., 500-gallon rubber bladders filled with fuel). Several rounds hit the cockpit and cargo compartment, starting a fire and rupturing one of the fuel bladders, which spilled its contents and fueled the fire. Onlookers saw several explosions as the stricken Hercules rolled down the runway after landing. The pilot, Chief Warrant Officer Henry Wildfang, managed to escape through the side windows of the cockpit, as did the copilot, while the navigator and flight mechanic escaped through the crew door after the pilots opened it from outside. The flight mechanic died later, as did one of the passengers who escaped the crash. In all, seven men died in the disaster.

The day after the loss of the Marine KC-130, another Air Force C-130 was seriously damaged by groundfire that killed two passengers and injured the loadmaster. Crew members managed to put out the resulting fire with assistance from two members of the Air Force detachment. Yet, when the fire was out, the airplane was incapable of flight—tires had blown, the engines had received shrapnel damage and the hydraulics had been shot out. Over the next two days the crew worked on their airplane, assisting ground personnel who had been flown in from Da Nang to make the repairs. One mechanic worked on the tail of the airplane at night—easily visible to snipers—using a flashlight. On the second day, a new fire erupted when the airplane was hit by mortar fire. Yet, after two days on the ground at Khe Sanh, Captain Edwin Jenks and his crew managed to get the badly damaged airplane off the ground and safely to Da Nang. There, mechanics counted 242 bullet and shrapnel holes—then stopped counting! Jenks and his crew were nominated for the Silver Star.

After being advised of the near-loss of Jenks' C-130, General Momyer ordered that all Air Force C-130 landings at Khe Sanh cease. General Momyer reasoned that the C-130 was "a national resource" and would be needed for future wars. Besides, the four-engine transports could supply the combat base by airdrop. On the other hand, the smaller C-123s had been declared obsolescent even before the U.S. effort in Southeast Asia began, and they needed less runway than the C-130s and could spend less time on the ground. Consequently, C-123 landings were still allowed when shelling and weather conditions allowed. And for a time the Marines continued landing their own C-130s.

Throughout the siege, the C-123 crews would land at Khe Sanh when possible, along with an occasional Caribou. Yet the C-123s were incapable of carrying the kind of tonnage necessary to keep the base supplied; the bulk of the supplies would have to be airdropped.

By 1968 the prevailing method of aerial delivery in the Air Force was the container delivery system, or CDS. A single C-130 could drop as many as 14 A-22 containers, each filled with up to 2,200 pounds of rations, ammunition, fuel or other cargo, on a single pass. CDS was the primary method of delivery at Khe Sanh. Earlier experiments using GCA to position the airplane for a drop allowed CDS deliveries even when weather conditions were very poor.

Another airdrop method was LAPES, a low-altitude parachute extraction system in which the C-130 would approach the drop zone as if to land, but level off just above the ground long enough for an extraction parachute to pull a single platform out of the airplane. LAPES afforded delivery of large items with pinpoint accuracy. There was one problem with LAPES—the platforms would slide for some distance over the ground until the extraction parachute brought them to a halt. On February 21, a C-130 inbound for a LAPES mission inadvertently struck the ground, tearing off the airplane's rear ramp and causing the load to extract early and break apart. The careening cargo killed one Marine and injured another. In mid-March, an extraction parachute separated from the load during the extraction, allowing the platform to go wild, smashing into a bunker and killing a man inside.

Another problem with LAPES was that the system required a special electrical harness, and with the increased demand, these harnesses soon were in short supply. In early March, 10 sets of LAPES harnesses were destroyed by incoming fire as they set in the cargo area awaiting transportation to the rear for reuse. LAPES was itself a derivative of an earlier system TAC had developed in the early '60s that used a hook to snare an arresting cable and extract the load. Though the system, known as GPES for ground proximity extraction system, had been discontinued, the equipment was stored in warehouses at TAC bases in the States. The equipment was airlifted to Southeast Asia. In mid-March, an Air Force combat-control team, assisted by Marines and Seabees, installed the arresting cable across the runway at Khe Sanh while the 274th TAW at Naha trained crews for the missions.

On March 30, the first GPES mission was flown to Khe Sanh.

It was so successful that the Marines reported that only two eggs from a crate placed on the pallet arrived with broken shells! Over the next several days, more drops were flown, some of which met with problems as the crews adjusted to the new system. On the second drop, the moorings for the arresting cable were pulled from the ground and had to be reburied. After the first few days of use, the Marines and Air Force concluded that GPES was superior to LAPES for the conditions at Khe Sanh.

Because of their low altitude deliveries, the LAPES and GPES missions and C-123 landings were more spectacular, but it was the CDS method that delivered most of the cargo that arrived at Khe Sanh during the siege. Even though CDS crews were not required to land and risk exposure to shelling and fire while on the ground, the drop missions nevertheless involved great danger for the crews. Groundfire was a constant threat throughout the run-in and during the drop itself, while low clouds and low visibilities in an area of high terrain made the drop missions even more hazardous. At least bad weather provided a cloak that made the low-flying C-130s and C-123s invisible to enemy forces on the ground. (Fortunately, the enemy had few radar-aimed guns around Khe Sanh.)

While most CDS missions were successful, on occasion a load would be dropped too early or too late, resulting in an even more hazardous recovery operation by the ground personnel who were already exposed on the drop zone. Some loads had to be abandoned, no doubt to be recovered by enemy forces. One CDS load fell within the combat base; five men were killed by the heavily laden pallets.

In spite of the weather and threat from groundfire, no Air Force C-130s were lost at Khe Sanh during the siege (though a C-130B from the 463rd TAW crashed during landing shortly after the base was relieved). Air Force aircraft losses were confined to C-123s. Three were lost in less than a week. On March 1, mortar fire knocked out an engine of a C-123 as it lifted off the runway; the pilot forced the airplane back onto the ground, where it was eventually destroyed by shelling. Fortunately, the crew survived, as did all the passengers. On the 6th, a C-123 was hit by ground-fire several miles east of the base. The airplane spiraled to the ground and exploded, killing all 49 people aboard. The loss occurred when the pilot had to break off his first landing attempt when an unannounced Vietnamese light aircraft suddenly appeared. Later that same day, shelling damaged a C-123; further shelling destroyed the airplane before it could be repaired and flown out of harm's way. Those three were among four fixed-wing transports lost at Khe Sanh during the siege.

While the fixed-wing airlift for Khe Sanh resupply was essentially an Air Force show, Marine KC-130 crews did their share. Fuel was the primary cargo for the Marine Herks, largely because they were not equipped with the 463L cargo handling system that allowed the Air Force C-130s to "speed offload" palletized cargo by simply lowering the aft ramp and taxiing out from under the pallets as they rolled out onto the ground. For a time the Marine transports were actually under the control of the Air Force tactical airlift officer at Da Nang, even to the point that he wrote evaluations of the Marine pilots! Interservice rivalry was not a factor in the Khe Sanh airlift. Since Marine C-130 crews were initially trained by the Air Force, the capabilities of both services were identical—except that Marine pilots were less experienced in assault landings than their Air Force counterparts.

Khe Sanh was completely cut off from all resupply except by air for 77 days. For much of this time, no C-130s landed at the combat base, and there were many days when the smaller C-123s were also unable to land. In late February, Air Force C-130 landings resumed for four days, but they were again suspended when the Air Force mission commander at Khe Sanh predicted that continued landings would soon result in the loss of one of the huge airlifters. With enemy troops as close as 35 yards to the perimeter, the transports were subject to small-arms and artillery fire while on the ground.

Khe Sanh was relieved in early April by 1st Cavalry Division troopers of Operation Pegasus. Such a massive effort had not been seen before in Vietnam and would not be seen again until the Eastertide Offensive of 1972, when Air Force C-130 drops would supply Vietnamese forces at An Loc in the face of anti-aircraft weapons that were more sophisticated than any others used during the American phase of the war.

Desperate Hours During Tet
Inside MACV Headquarters

As told by General Walter T. Kerwin, U.S. Army (ret.)

A general's chief of staff requires a diverse set of skills—tactical, supervisory, coordinating, leading and negotiating. He must fulfill many roles, on occasion acting as the commander's most ardent advocate, harshest critic, closest adviser and alter ego. Major General Walter T. "Dutch" Kerwin, who served as General William C. Westmoreland's chief of staff during the 1968 Tet Offensive, understood those challenges very well.

Kerwin's assignment as MACV chief of staff topped an action-filled career. He graduated from West Point in 1939 and received a commission in the field artillery. When World War II broke out, Kerwin rose quickly to become the 3rd Infantry Division's artillery operations officer, participating in campaigns in North Africa, Sicily, Italy and southern France.

No operation was more trying than the landings at Anzio, Italy, in 1944. After an almost effortless landing, the Allies found that well-dug-in Germans were holding the Alban Hills, blocking the route to Rome and claiming an unrestricted view of the beachhead. The German advantage in observation made artillery fire a significant threat to Allied troops. The challenge of organizing effective counterbattery fire against the enemy guns thoroughly tested Kerwin, bringing out the best of his organizational and tactical skills.

Wounded in southern France, Kerwin returned to the United States. After World War II he rose through the ranks of America's postwar Army to command the 3rd Armored Division and serve as assistant deputy chief of staff for operations on the Army Staff before deploying to Vietnam.

In an interview conducted by Lieutenant Colonel James Jay Carafano, General Kerwin recalled the difficult and complicated world of the MACV chief of staff. Kerwin's May 1967 assignment was no matter of chance. He previously had served under MACV's deputy commanding general, Creighton Abrams, who had a reputation as a difficult and demanding boss. Kerwin, however, thrived on pressure and challenges. The two officers had long ago earned each other's respect and confidence, and Abrams had become a friend and mentor. When Abrams was posted to South Vietnam, Kerwin received three days' notice to follow him.

Dutch Kerwin arrived in Vietnam as the level of the U.S. Army's involvement in the war was nearing its peak. While military operations were expanding throughout South Vietnam, the theater's complicated organizational arrangements strained to keep up. Although General Westmoreland, or "Westy," was the military leader most visibly connected with the war, his command, MACV, did not directly control all the forces involved. The air and naval units, for example, answered in part to the theater commander in chief in Hawaii.

Kerwin was appalled by the inefficiency of the organization when he arrived in-country. "The Marines were sitting up there in I Corps almost entirely by themselves," Kerwin recalled. "The bombing and other fire support was being run out of many other organizations. It was split . . . initially MACV was in a small headquarters downtown [in Saigon], and, in my opinion, not organized to get the best out of everything." According to him, the staff was simply not taking full advantage of the preponderance of power available from the various forces crammed into the theater. Theater rotation policies that moved officers through the MACV staff in less than a year did not help. "In retrospect," Kerwin said, "the one-year tours were a mistake." The staffs were never as cohesive and competent as the ones he had seen in his service with the 3rd Infantry Division during World War II.

Nor did Kerwin find the command relationships at MACV as strong as they should have been. Abrams had left for Vietnam believing that he would shortly relieve Westmoreland as MACV commander, with Kerwin as his own hand-picked chief of staff at his side. The change in command, however, was delayed for more than a year. "Although General Abrams was completely loyal to Westmoreland," Kerwin recalled, "there was not the closeness that there probably should have been between the two of them. There were many times—which I knew of, being the chief of staff—that General Westmoreland did not take General Abrams into his confidence. General Abrams knew that he wasn't being utilized in the true sense of being a deputy commander."

In addition to supporting both generals, Kerwin was called on to perform chief-of-staff duties for the ambassador to South Vietnam, Ellsworth Bunker, and Ambassador Robert William Komer, MACV's civilian deputy commander in charge of Civil Operations and Revolutionary Development Support programs. Although Kerwin remained fiercely loyal to all four of his bosses, his duties were complex and difficult, considering that these men seemed to have different agendas, personalities, philosophies and priorities.

Moreover, as Kerwin lamented, his bosses "didn't necessarily speak the same language." From the quiet and introspective Westmoreland, to the blunt and down-to-earth Abrams, to the abrasive and volatile Komer, it was usually Kerwin who was caught in the cross-fire. "It took an inordinate amount of time," the MACV chief of staff recalled, "before I, as the chief of the whole headquarters, was able to exercise some sort of coordination and staff functioning, and all those things that should be done in that headquarters got done." Moving MACV from its cramped facilities in Saigon to larger and better organized quarters near Tan Son Nhut helped, but staff coordination remained a chronic challenge in his new position.

TET BEGINS

MACV's problems seemingly culminated on January 31, 1968, during the Tet cease-fire that marked the traditional Vietnamese celebration of the Lunar New Year. The day before, MACV had received reports of sporadic attacks, including some near Da Nang. Before dawn on January 31, VC insurgent forces and NVA Regulars launched a series of coordinated surprise attacks across South Vietnam. They hit more than 100 cities, towns and hamlets, as well as military bases and the U.S. Embassy in Saigon.

"Well, we knew something was coming," recalled Kerwin. "They [the NVA forces] were moving out all over the place. [On the night of January 30, 1968] I went down to my house, down almost in the center of Saigon. Of course, it was Tet night and they'd blow firecrackers all over the place as they do in Hawaii. I woke up about 2 in the morning, wondering what all of this bang, bang, bang was, and I just ordinarily thought it was the firecrackers, because I had heard them before. Then the phone rang, and they said that we were under attack and I'd better get down here right away.

"My Vietnamese driver slept in the other part of the building, and I got dressed in a hurry and out the door we went—got the jeep and started down the long drive. I quickly saw that was not the thing to do, particularly since up ahead of us on the right-hand side of the main drag there was a military police outfit. They were under attack. So I tried to figure out what the hell to do. I thought, If I get off on the side streets, I'm liable to get killed myself. And I'm not sure in the middle of the night (it was a dark night in January) whether I can even get back to headquarters or not.

"So we quickly turned around and went back close to the house and waited for a while. Things didn't improve. It must have been 45 minutes or something like that. They were firing all over the damn place. We finally got out of there, and of course I went right down to the TOC to find out what the hell was going on. It was very difficult to do that, because everybody was being attacked everywhere."

At about 3 A.M., General Kerwin got a call from the JCS, who asked what was going on. "I said: 'To be frank with you, I'm not sure what the hell's going on. Everybody seems to be unaware. We're doing the best we can to get you the information. I'll have to call you back.'" Soon after that, he learned that the U.S. Embassy was under attack.

"Westy went down there because he thought if we lost that, it would appear that we'd lost the whole damn battle," Kerwin recalled. "He called me and said to get hold of General Fred Weyand, who had II Field Forces. He said to get the troops down here at this embassy.

"So I got hold of Fred on the radio, and by that time Fred had gotten the word. He sent down some troops. From there on out, my main job was to get a tactical picture. So, that was what I did—get the staff really ginned up and get hold of various commanders. I got the picture for Westy because he was down there at the embassy. From then on out, the rest of that day, I slept in the headquarters and never got home."

Getting the staff organized was a considerable challenge, since many of the officers had a difficult time making their way to MACV headquarters on the 31st. "After the battle," Kerwin recalled, "that led to the establishment of a trailer park at the new headquarters [at Tan Son Nhut Air Base, a few miles to the north]. I said: 'We can't have this. Next time we may get a hell of a lot of people killed.' Of course, that's a part of combat, but the question was how to get people in hand so we could do something. So I said, 'Let's establish a trailer park up there for everybody.' But of course, that didn't help us at the time. . . . You just shift as best you can. You tap everybody on the shoulder down in the operations center and say, 'Get a hold of those guys—tell Khe Sanh I want this and I want that, and so forth.'"

As the situation developed that day, General Kerwin recalled, "In some places we weren't quite sure what was going on. It didn't look too bad—we hadn't lost anything, I mean anything major. Of course, the battle for Hue developed more and more as time went on, and that turned out to be one hell of a fight. [As for] the embassy, of course, it was just psychological. . . . If we lost that place, if the people inside got killed in our own embassy, that would be one hell of a blow psychologically. But that was not our problem [at MACV headquarters]. It was our job—the whole damn staff—to get information."

TURNING TO THE OFFENSIVE

As Kerwin pieced together the scope of the enemy operation, he updated the MACV commander and the JCS in Washington. In the days that followed, American troops, South Vietnamese forces and a small contingent of other allied units gradually regained the initiative across the entire country. While there were some serious battles in the south, they were not of primary concern. The greatest challenge was keeping the north-south main supply routes open. As long as the allies could keep control of the highway and continue to move troops and supplies, Kerwin believed the situation in the south could be stabilized. Operationally, Westmoreland was most concerned about the attack on the city of Hue and the siege of the U.S. base at Khe Sanh (which Kerwin called Westmoreland's "pet project"). Both were in the northern part of the country.

In addition to the Marines already fighting in the north, MACV redeployed the Army's 1st Cavalry Division from South Vietnam's central coast. Kerwin recalled that it was a difficult situation, mixing Army and Marines, as well as South Vietnamese forces, on the fly. "It could have gone down the tube up there," Kerwin said.

The Marines, the Vietnamese forces and the more than 45,000 Army troops that MACV funneled into the area strained both the theater's tactical control and its logistical support structure in the following weeks. MACV also found itself battling incessantly to ensure that commanders gave the South Vietnamese forces enough air and artillery support so that they could make real contributions to the operation.

Worried that the northern provinces might fall to a North Vietnamese invasion, Westmoreland extended his operational control over the region by establishing a MACV forward headquarters at Phu Bai, just south of Hue. Troops in the area were under the command of Marine Lieutenant General Robert E. Cushman of III Marine Amphibious Force (MAF). Westmoreland, however, ordered Deputy MACV Commander General Abrams to assume control over all forces in the area and conduct the fight for the northern provinces.

It was General Kerwin who suggested establishing the MACV forward headquarters. "It was always a question of accountability," he said, recalling discussions of that move. "This was a big step. If we were going to coordinate all of these people up there, somebody had to do it, and Abe had the stature to do it. We had Army, Navy, Air Force, Marines and everybody up there, [but] we didn't seem to be making much headway, if any. The question was, who's coordinating all of it, who's running that thing up there? It's an eyesore, it's left over, the rest of the place is pretty quiet. We've won that battle. So we talked about it and I said, 'Well, we've got to establish a headquarters up there and make sure things get under control.' Westy said, 'Abe, how about you?' Abe said, 'Sure.'

"Abe was a real team player. He established a headquarters up there. Meanwhile, it was my job to make him a staff. So I gave him my J3 [joint operations officer] and some staff. Some of them he personally asked for."

On occasion, General Kerwin became personally involved in the joint operations. "One day," he recalled, "there was a squabble going on up in the north about controlling the TACAIR [tactical air support]. You had the Army with their helicopters. You had the Navy and Marines. It was a hell of a problem with the coordination of the air campaign up there. So we had a meeting. Westy was there, Abe was there, and a couple of people from the embassy, as usual. Abe said, 'Let's send Dutch Kerwin up there.' Abe had read this book [General Lucian Truscott's *Command Missions*] and saw my name in there and what I had done in the middle of the night [at the Battle of Anzio during World War II], changing artillery plans for the division commanders."

Abrams apparently had assumed that if Kerwin could straighten out the artillery firing at the Anzio beachhead as a lieutenant colonel, he could make sense out of the air coordination in Vietnam as a two-star general. "I called up the Marines and the Army and everybody else and I said I wanted a meeting," recalled Kerwin. "They assembled this huge crowd in a great big general purpose tent. They must have had 150 or 200 people there. I started out by saying, 'You can't meet with this many people.' At the end of that meeting—which lasted all day and part of the night—we hadn't gotten anywhere.

"I came back to the headquarters and told Abe that it would

require people who would settle down and stop fighting over pre-rogatives and things of that type. So I asked him to send three people down—Army, Air Force and Marines—one each, three people. They came down to the headquarters.

"Finally, after much debate, we came up with a set of rules about who was going to do what. It turned out pretty well, but I must admit that it could have been much better if we'd stopped working on everybody's prerogatives."

As U.S. and South Vietnamese troops pushed back the enemy in the north, the MACV staff turned their thinking to future operations, including thinking about the unthinkable—the use of nuclear weapons. Kerwin, who had considerable experience in working with nuclear weapons, assembled a small planning team to consider the potential for employing tactical nuclear weapons against North Vietnam in the event the enemy attempted to repeat the Tet maneuver.

"The idea was," Kerwin recalled, "that, suppose we did get authority. What would we do? It was shortly after Tet. We thought this was a good time to see what we could plan at a place called Vinh, on the coast. I got about four guys out of the staff, two of them Air Force—nuclear business was big in the Air Force—one Army, and one Marine."

This team's purpose, said Kerwin, was contingency planning "in case we had a catastrophe. It wasn't a full-time job. We met two or three times a week just to discuss things and see what the planners had come up with. Basically the plan looked at using a few tactical Air Force weapons, bombs that we could drop on one focused, constricted area."

The choice of targets for such an operation, according to Kerwin, "depended on whether we had sufficient troops or not. One place we looked at was near Vinh, because that was the only main avenue of approach on the DMZ. Also, that would be a place where you could use a nuclear weapon, because you would have a target that was of sufficient size. You bottle up the enemy and then block the approach."

Eventually, the plan to use nuclear weapons was dropped when "somebody, somewhere heard about it." Looking back, Kerwin said: "I guess we should have expected that. We were told pretty firmly to knock it off."

THE AFTERMATH

Tet offered a variety of lessons for Kerwin and the MACV staff. Despite all its shortcomings and obstacles, MACV had launched an effective counteroffensive under difficult conditions, demonstrating great operational agility and flexibility. On the other hand, though the invasion had been successfully repulsed, the campaign again highlighted the flaws Kerwin saw in MACV's operational design. These included the challenges of getting the South Vietnamese army into the fight, the cost of not thoroughly coordinating all fighting, Vietnamization and pacification efforts, and the difficulty of holding the initiative when the enemy had the freedom to withdraw to safety beyond the borders of North Vietnam, Laos, Thailand and Cambodia.

Kerwin also witnessed MACV's rapidly deteriorating relations with the press. The American media generally portrayed Tet as a horrendous military setback. As a result, Americans back home were becoming increasingly disillusioned with the war effort.

After Tet, Kerwin remained as chief of staff during the transition between Westmoreland and Abrams, helping the new commander begin to address the flaws they both saw in MACV's operational approach to the war. Later on Kerwin served in combat as the commanding general of II Field Forces, a corps-level command. After returning to the United States, he held a succession of high-level posts, retiring as the vice chief of staff of the U.S. Army in 1978.

In retirement Kerwin has remained an influential figure, supporting the post–Vietnam War revitalization of the Army, encouraging the renaissance in thinking on operations, and—perhaps most important—supporting a return to an emphasis on the basics of soldiering, professionalism, integrity and character.

Viet Cong Assault on the U.S. Embassy

By Don North

On January 31, 1968, the Army of North Vietnam (NVA) and Viet Cong (VC) attacked the U.S. Embassy in Saigon and more than 100 other targets throughout South Vietnam. The assault became known as the Tet Offensive, named after the Vietnamese celebration of the lunar New Year.

When the bloody fighting finally ended 24 days later, the Communist troops had been driven from all major South Vietnamese cities, and U.S. military analysts declared victory. But there was little doubt that the NVA and VC had scored a stunning psychological success.

Because U.S. politicians and commanders had oversold progress in the war as a way to quiet domestic dissent, the savage Tet fighting shocked millions of Americans and widened Washington's credibility gap on Vietnam. Within weeks, President Lyndon B. Johnson would bow out of his race for re-election. Tet was the beginning of the end of the Vietnam War.

But Tet had another long-term consequence. In the years that followed, U.S. military officers would insist bitterly that critical reporting about Tet and the war in general caused the American defeat, that the U.S. news media had betrayed the nation, that reporters had gone from being the Fourth Estate to acting like an enemy fifth column. In turn, the correspondents who covered Vietnam, many of whom now assume highly influential roles in their news agencies, are more distrustful of U.S. military officials than their older or younger counterparts.

Army historians would eventually conclude that the war was lost by poor strategy and excessive casualties, not by disloyal journalists. "It is undeniable," wrote Army historian William Hammond in 1988, "that press reports were ... more accurate than the public statements of the administration in portraying the situation in Vietnam." But by 1968, the charge that the press lost Vietnam had become an article of faith to many Vietnam veterans.

As a reporter in Vietnam for ABC and NBC News, I was there to experience Tet at most of the major battlefields, from Khe Sanh on January 30 to Hue on February 25, as U.S. Marines secured the southeast gate of the Citadel to end the siege of Hue. But it was at the U.S. Embassy at dawn on January 31 that one of the most important engagements of the war took place.

At a greasy car repair shop at 59 Phan Thanh Gian Street just before the VC attacks on Saigon, 19 VC sappers climbed into a small Peugeot truck and a taxicab to begin the short drive to their objective, the U.S. Embassy. Wearing black pajamas and red armbands, they were part of the elite 250-strong C-10 Sapper Battalion. Most of them had been born in Saigon and were familiar with the streets of the crowded city.

Two days earlier, heavy baskets, supposedly containing tomatoes, as well as bamboo containers of rice, had arrived at the home next door to the repair shop. They also contained all the AK-47s, B-40 rocket-propelled grenades and satchel charges the 19 sappers would need for their mission that evening. Shortly after midnight the soldiers were briefed for the first time on their combat mission against the American Embassy. There were no mock-ups of the location, no instructions on what to do after gaining entrance to the compound, no word of reinforcements or an escape route and no confirmation that this would be a suicide mission.

The embassy assault would be only a part of the sapper battalion's assignment to spearhead the attack on Saigon, backed up by another 11 battalions, totaling about 4,000 troops. There had been little time for rehearsal. What they lacked in planning would be made up for in the intensity, scope and audacity of the attacks.

The battalion's mission that morning was to gain control of six objectives: the U.S. Embassy, the Presidential Palace, the national broadcasting studios, South Vietnamese Naval Headquarters, Vietnamese Joint General Staff Headquarters at Tan Son Nhut air base and the Philippine Embassy. The attackers were to hold these objectives for 48 hours until other VC battalions could enter the city and relieve them. The survivors of the attack were to be instantly promoted.

Of all the targets, the overriding importance of the U.S. Embassy could not be overstated. The $2.6 million compound had been completed just three months earlier, and its six-story chancery building loomed over Saigon like an impregnable fortress. It was a constant reminder of the American presence, prestige and power. Never mind that Nha Trang or Ban Me Thout or Bien Hoa would also be attacked that morning. Most Americans couldn't pronounce their names, let alone comprehend their importance. But the U.S. Embassy in Saigon? For many Americans, this would be the first battle of the Vietnam War they understood.

En route to the American Embassy, the sappers were spotted driving without lights by a South Vietnamese civilian policeman. This member of the South Vietnamese National Police force, referred to as "the white mice," chose to avoid problems and stepped back into the shadows as the truck and taxi passed by. The sappers had similar good fortune confronting the embassy's first line of defense. After turning onto Thong Nhut Boulevard, they encountered four police officers, but the policemen fled without firing a shot.

At 2:45 A.M., the sappers wheeled up to the front gate of the U.S. Embassy and opened fire with AK-47 machine guns and a B-40 rocket-propelled grenade launcher. Outside the embassy entrance, two American military police of the 716th Battalion— Spc. 4 Charles Daniel, 23, of Durham, North Carolina, and Pfc. Bill Sebast, 20, of Albany, New York—returned fire while backing through the heavy steel gate and locking it behind them. At 2:47 they radioed "Signal 300"—the MP code for enemy attack. A tremendous explosion shook the compound as the sappers blew a 3-foot hole in the wall with a satchel charge. Daniel shouted into the MP radio, "They're coming in—help me!" and the radio went dead.

The first two soldiers of the C-10 Battalion who went through the hole were believed to have been the two senior members, Bay Tuyen and Ut Nho. They and the two American MPs were killed in a close and deadly exchange of gunfire. The remaining sappers had more than 40 pounds of C-4 plastic explosive, more than enough to blast their way into the chancery building. Without any clear orders since their leaders had been killed, they took positions behind big circular flower tubs on the embassy lawn and fired back at the growing force shooting at them from rooftops outside the embassy.

Just minutes later, at about 3 A.M., chief U.S. Embassy spokesman Barry Zorthian phoned news bureaus from his home a few blocks away to alert them. Zorthian had few details, but he told us what he knew: The embassy was being attacked and was under heavy fire.

ABC News Bureau chief Dick Rosenbaum called me after Zorthian had phoned him. The ABC bureau, located at the Caravelle Hotel, was only four blocks from the embassy. And as it turned out, cameraman Peter Leydon and I were in Saigon because of what we thought had been a stroke of bad luck at Khe Sanh the day before.

For months any journalist with decent sources was expecting something big at Tet. The ABC bureau and most other news agencies were on full alert, R&Rs were canceled and I had celebrated Christmas with my family in nearby Kuala Lumpur, Malaysia, on December 1, so I could be in Vietnam, ready for the big enemy push when it came sometime before, during or after Tet. Plenty of captured enemy documents circulating in the months before Tet indicated something big was afoot. One of the most respected and credible military sources at the time was Lieutenant General Fred C. Weyand, commander of American forces in III Corps, the area around Saigon. In the weeks prior to Tet, General Weyand told many journalists what he was telling General William C. Westmoreland: "The VC are maneuvering in large units with reinforcements of North Vietnamese and new weapons. Enemy documents and prisoners indicate that a major Communist offensive is coming soon, probably against Saigon." There were strict rules against reporting U.S. troop movements, but Weyand told us, off the record, that he was shifting 30 American battalions into better defensive positions around Saigon.

In the weeks before Tet, the various civilian and military intelligence agencies, both American and South Vietnamese, knew most of the facts about the enemy but didn't understand their significance. Because of hostility and rivalry between the agencies, they rarely shared or compared intelligence and were never able to assemble it into a cohesive mosaic. They knew through an avalanche of captured documents the enemy's intentions for 1968, but they did not know that their capabilities were anywhere close to matching these intentions.

In the New Year's Eve roundup of ABC News TV correspondents around the world, I predicted heavy fighting in Vietnam in the new year. "Documents captured at Dak To recently indicate the North Vietnamese and Viet Cong are now entering what they call the 'sprint phase of the revolution,'" I said. "Intensification of the fighting seems the intent here of both sides as 1968 begins. Don North, ABC News, Vietnam." It was to be the Year of the Monkey—a year in which we all experienced more history than we could digest.

The week before Tet had been strangely quiet. With nothing else to do, I took a camera crew over to the Phu Tho racetrack in Cholon to produce a little news feature on the "crookedest horse race in the world." Widespread drugging of the horses produced some weird results, and often a lame horse could enter the winner's circle if it could still stand up by the end of the race. A week later, the Phu Tho racetrack was used as a staging center and resupply base for the VC during the Tet Offensive. Even on that quiet Sunday afternoon it was likely the VC had been infiltrating Saigon and the racetrack—chances are that the heavy better in line with me at the parimutuel window that afternoon was an NVA colonel. Arriving back at the ABC bureau I was dispatched immediately to the airport for a flight to Khe Sanh, which was where General Westmoreland was expecting the main thrust of an enemy strike during Tet.

In Khe Sanh on January 30, ABC News cameraman Peter Leydon and I came under a heavy barrage of NVA artillery fire. When we dived into a trench, the lens of our 16mm film camera broke off, forcing us to cut short our stay in Khe Sanh. We returned to Saigon on the Lockheed C-130 "milk run" that evening.

Because of the broken camera, we thought we would be missing the NVA's push against Khe Sanh. But flying the length of Vietnam that night, it seemed like the whole country was under attack. As we took off from the Da Nang air base, we saw incoming rockets. Flying over Nha Trang shortly after midnight, we could see fires blazing. We heard about the attacks through radio contact with ground control.

But at 3:30 A.M. on January 31, we were back in Saigon, wheeling out of the Caravelle Hotel in the ABC News jeep with a new camera. Just off Tu Do Street, three blocks from the embassy, somebody—VC, ARVN, police or U.S. MPs, we weren't sure who— opened up on us with an automatic weapon. A couple of rounds pinged off the hood of the jeep. I killed the lights and reversed out of range. We returned to the ABC bureau to wait for first light.

As dawn was breaking around 6 A.M., we walked the three blocks to the embassy. As we approached the compound, we could hear heavy firing, and green and red tracers cut into the pink sky.

Near the embassy, I joined a group of U.S. MPs moving toward the embassy's front gate. I started my tape recorder for ABC radio as the MPs loudly cursed the ARVN troops who were supposed to provide embassy security. The MPs claimed the ARVN had "D-Dee'd" (slang for running away under fire) after the first shots.

Green-colored VC tracer bullets were coming from the embassy compound and the upper floor of buildings across the street. Red tracers stitched back across the street. We were in the cross-fire.

Crawling up to the gate with me was Peter Arnett of the Associated Press (AP), who was glad to have the company of another journalist who wasn't competing with the AP. Peter had been covering the war for more than five years and had picked up a Pulitzer Prize for his reporting. Arnett was a prolific, competitive and fair journalist, often filing more than a dozen stories for the AP every week. In spite of his later problems at CNN that would bring into question his credibility as a reporter of Vietnam-related stories, I believe his eight years of daily reporting from Vietnam are without par in the annals of war correspondence.

Lying flat in the gutter that morning with the MPs, Arnett and I didn't know where the VC attackers were holed up or where the fire was coming from. But we knew it was the big story.

Arnett and other AP staffers had been the first to alert the world of the attack on the U.S. Embassy. At 3:15 the first bulletin had gone out a full 40 minutes ahead of competitor United Press International (UPI). "First Lead Attack: Saigon (AP) The Viet Cong shelled Saigon Wednesday in a bold followup of their attacks on eight major cities around the country. Simultaneously, a suicide squad of guerrilla commandos infiltrated the capital and at least three are reported to have entered the grounds of the new U.S. Embassy near the heart of the city. U.S. Marine guards at the Embassy, opened only late last year, engaged the infiltrators in an exchange of fire."

Several MPs rushed by, one of them carrying a VC sapper piggyback style. The VC was wounded and bleeding. He wore black pajamas and, strangely, an enormous red ruby ring. I interviewed the MPs and recorded their radio conversation with colleagues inside the embassy gates. The MPs believed the VC were in the chancery building itself, an impression that later proved false. Peter Arnett crawled off to find a phone and report the MPs' conversation to his office. At 7:25, based on Arnett's calls from the scene, the AP transmitted the first report that the VC were inside the embassy. "Bulletin: Vietnam (Tops 161) Saigon (AP) The Vietcong attacked Saigon Wednesday and seized part of the U.S. Embassy. U.S. Military Police on the scene said it was believed about 20 Vietcong suicide commandos were in the Embassy and held part of the first floor of the Embassy building."

The question of whether the VC were in the chancery building or only in the compound took on symbolic importance. I have replayed the tape of that day in 1968, and there is no doubt the MPs believed the VC were in the chancery.

A helicopter landed on the embassy roof, and troops started working down the floors. MP Dave Lamborn got orders on the field radio from an officer inside the compound: "This is Waco, roger. Can you get in the gate now? Take a force in there and clean out the embassy, like now. There will be choppers on the roof and troops working down. Be careful we don't hit our own people. Over."

As we prepared to join the MPs rushing the gate, I had other concerns. "OK, how much film have we got left?" I shouted to cameraman Peter Leydon.

"I've got one mag [400 feet]," he replied. "How many do you have?"

"We're on the biggest story of the war with one can of film," I groaned. "So it's one take of everything, including my stand-upper." There was no time to argue about whose responsibility it was to have brought more film.

I stepped over the United States seal, which had been blasted off the embassy wall near a side entrance. We rushed through the main gate into the garden, where a bloody battle had been raging. It was, as UPI's Kate Webb later described, "like a butcher shop in Eden."

As helicopters continued to land troops on the roof, we hunkered down on the grass with a group of MPs. They were firing into a small villa on the embassy grounds where they said the VC were making a last stand. Tear gas canisters were blasted through the windows, but the gas drifted back through the garden. Colonel George Jacobson, the U.S. mission coordinator, lived in the villa, and he suddenly appeared at a window on the second floor. An MP threw him a gas mask and a .45 pistol. Three VC were believed to be on the first floor and would likely be driven upstairs by the tear gas. It was high drama, but our ABC News camera rolled film on it sparingly.

I continued to describe everything I saw into a tape recorder, often choking on the tear gas. I could read the embassy ID card in the wallet of Nguyen Van De, whose bloody body was sprawled beside me on the lawn. Nguyen was later identified as an embassy driver who often chauffeured the American ambassador and who had been a driver for 16 years. The MPs told me Nguyen Van De had shot at them during the early fighting and was probably the inside man for the attackers.

Amid the tension, I was distracted by a big frog hopping and splashing through pools of thick blood on the lawn. It was one of those images that never gets properly filed away and keeps coming back at odd times.

A long burst of automatic-weapons fire snapped me back to reality. The last VC still in action rushed up the stairs firing blindly at Colonel Jacobson, but he missed.

The colonel later told me: "We both saw each other at the same time. He missed me, and I fired one shot at him point-blank with the .45." Jacobson later admitted that his Saigon girlfriend had been with him at the time and witnessed the entire drama from beneath the sheets of their bed.

The death toll from the embassy battle stood at five American soldiers killed along with 17 of the 19 sappers. The two surviving but wounded sappers were later questioned and turned over to the ARVN.

On the last 30 feet of film, I recorded my closing remarks in the embassy garden: "Since the lunar New Year, the Viet Cong and North Vietnamese have proved they are capable of bold and impressive military moves that Americans here never dreamed could be achieved. Whether they can sustain this onslaught for long remains to be seen. But whatever turn the war now takes, the capture of the U.S. Embassy here for almost seven hours is a psychological victory that will rally and inspire the Viet Cong. Don North, ABC News, Saigon."

A rush to judgment before all pieces of the puzzle were in place? Perhaps. But there was no time to appoint a committee to study the story. I was on an hourly deadline, and ABC expected the story as well as some perspective even in those early hours of the offensive—a first rough draft of history.

My on-the-scene analysis never made it on ABC News. Worried about editorializing by a correspondent on a sensitive story, someone at ABC headquarters in New York killed the on-camera closer. (Ironically, the closer and other outtakes ended up in the Simon Grinberg film library, where they were later found and used by film director Peter Davis in his Academy Award–winning movie *Hearts and Minds*.)

The film from all three networks took off from Saigon on a special military flight about noon. When it arrived in Tokyo for processing, it caused a mad, competitive scramble to get a cut film story on satellite for the 7 P.M. (EST) news programs in the States. Because we had only 400 feet to process and cut, ABC News made the satellite in time, and the story led the ABC-TV evening news. NBC and CBS missed the deadline and had to run catch-up specials on the embassy attack later in the evening.

Meanwhile, at 9:15 A.M. in Saigon, the embassy was officially declared secure. At 9:20, General Westmoreland strode through the gate in his clean and carefully starched fatigues, flanked by grimy and bloody MPs and Marines who had been fighting since 3 A.M. Standing in the rubble, Westmoreland declared: "No enemy got in the embassy building. It's a relatively small incident. A group of sappers blew a hole in the wall and crawled in, and they were all killed. Nineteen bodies have been found on the premises— enemy bodies. Don't be deceived by this incident."

I couldn't believe it. "Westy" was still saying everything was just fine. He said the Tet attacks throughout the country were "very deceitfully" calculated to create maximum consternation in

Vietnam and that they were "diversionary" to the main enemy effort still to come at Khe Sanh.

Most journalists in Vietnam at that time respected Westmoreland—he often generously gave long interviews, which would invariably explain the success of his command. But an incident about six months prior to Tet left questions in my mind concerning the commanding general's understanding of the role of the media in wartime.

The military and the media have since the beginning of recorded history had a difficult and conflicting relationship. The reporter's job is to gather information, while the soldier's concern is to hold back information that could possibly help the enemy or demoralize the home front and—sometimes—to hide his own mistakes or incompetence. A U.S. military censor in Washington, D.C., in 1938 expressed the ultimate military disdain for the American public's right to know: "I wouldn't tell the people anything until the war is over and then I'd tell them who won." In 1914, Richard Harding Davis of the New York *Herald* wrote, "In war the world has a right to know, not what is going to happen next, but at least what has happened."

A memo signed by Westmoreland was delivered to the ABC News Bureau and to most other agencies in mid-1967 suggesting that news reports of inefficient Vietnamese ground troops were not helping the war effort. "If you give a dog a bad name, he will live up to it," Westmoreland suggested, recommending that more positive reporting be done on our Vietnamese allies.

Most of us had been with crack South Vietnamese airborne or marine units and had described them accordingly. We thought the ARVN 1st and 21st divisions were effective, but we considered the 2nd, 5th and 18th divisions slacker units, plagued with high desertion rates and questionable commanders who rarely moved aggressively out of their base camps.

Westmoreland's ill-advised memo was largely ignored by Saigon journalists. In fact, the MACV chief of information, Major General Winant Sidle, had strongly urged Westmoreland not to issue the memo. A television report on an ARVN unit doing nothing doesn't make great news, however, so it was more likely that the better units got more coverage anyway.

Even after Westmoreland's pronouncement that the chancery had not been breached, Peter Arnett and the AP seemed heavily committed to their earlier lead and continued to quote the MPs and others at the embassy who believed the sappers had penetrated the first floor. As Arnett would explain later, "We had little faith in what General Westmoreland stated, and often in the field we had reason to be extremely careful in accepting the general's assessments of the course of a particular battle." Much of the later criticism of the press for its handling of the embassy story fell on Arnett for supposedly exaggerating the VC action with his report from the MPs. But a report is only as good as its sources, and the MPs' fears and warnings were trusted.

Later, at the MACV press briefing, the so-called "Five O'clock Follies," Westmoreland appeared in person to emphasize the huge enemy body counts as U.S. and ARVN forces repelled the Tet Offensive. But MACV had been caught manipulating enemy casualty figures before, and many reporters were skeptical.

To add to Westy's growing credibility gap, it was also reported at his press briefing that the city of Hue, in the northern part of South Vietnam, had been cleared of enemy troops. That false report had to be retracted, as the enemy held parts of Hue for the next 24 days.

Not to be outdone by Westy's vigorous control of the Tet story, Ambassador Ellsworth Bunker called a "background" briefing for select reporters at the embassy three days after the attack. "Our reports from around the country indicate the South Vietnamese people are outraged by the deceitful Viet Cong violation of the sacred Tet Holiday," Bunker said, identified only as a "senior American diplomat." He added, "No important objectives have been held by the enemy and there was no significant popular support."

The ambassador ignored the fact that Hue was still under enemy control and, in Saigon, residents had not sounded the alarm while 4,000 VC and NVA troops infiltrated the city. In later interviews with Saigon residents, I found none who thought the VC had been particularly deceitful in breaking the Tet truce to gain the element of surprise.

Many were, however, alarmed at how vigorously U.S. and ARVN firepower had been directed against VC targets in heavily populated urban centers of Saigon, Can Tho and Ben Tre—attacks that killed and wounded thousands of Vietnamese civilians and created a half-million refugees.

My TV and radio report on those interviews was titled "U.S. mission, more out of touch with Vietnamese than ever." But it also never made it on the ABC-TV evening news. It arrived in New York but was never scheduled for broadcast and was later reported lost. It was, however, broadcast as an "Information Report" on the ABC Radio News Network, which tended to be more open to critical stories from the staff in Vietnam.

After the last enemy troops were rooted out of Hue, the U.S. government could finally declare that the Tet Offensive was indeed a clear-cut American military victory. Westmoreland would claim that 37,000 of the enemy had died, with U.S. dead at 2,500.

It was obvious that the enemy operations had dealt Washington a decisive psychological blow. Somehow, more than 70,000 VC, backed by regular units of the NVA, had been able to coordinate a nationwide offensive with attacks on 36 provincial capitals and 64 district towns.

The political consequences of Tet were made worse by the cheery public-relations campaigns that had preceded the offensive. Although some senior U.S. commanders, like General Weyand, warned of a coming offensive against Saigon and had repositioned some U.S. forces, Westmoreland and Johnson had been determined to keep up a happy face.

At times, it seemed as if Westmoreland and Johnson were the only ones oblivious to the intelligence reports pouring into the MACV headquarters about an upcoming VC offensive. In late November 1967, Westy had been enlisted by Johnson in a spin campaign to put the war in the most favorable light possible. The general spoke to Congress and to the National Press Club—and dutifully painted a rosy picture of the war's progress. *Time* magazine honored Westmoreland as its man of the year.

Just days before Tet, Johnson gave a State of the Union address in which he avoided telling the American people what his military advisers were telling him—that there would be a large enemy offensive. The official optimism would double the shock felt by American citizens about Tet. In the offensive's wake, U.S. strategy was subjected to a new and critical re-examination.

There were stunning political consequences, too. On March 31, President Johnson announced that he would not run again. In the following week, polls showed a drop-off in public support for the war. Soon, policy-makers in Washington were hedging their bets and voicing more discontent about the war. Following that official shift, TV news correspondents were given more time for war criticism.

Contrary to what some critics of the media believed, it was not that TV editors had suddenly become opponents of the war. Rather, their Washington sources had decided to shift toward opposition and that change was simply reflected in the reporting. TV news followed the change—it did not lead it.

Ten years later, when I produced a TV documentary on the Tet Offensive, one of 26 programs in the series *The Ten Thousand Day War*, General Westmoreland was still bad-mouthing the media for the events of that morning. "This was the turning point of the war," he told me. "It could have been the turning point for success, but it was the turning point for failure. By virtue of the early reporting . . . which was gloom and doom and which gave the impression that Americans were being defeated on the battle-field. It swayed public opinion to the point political authority made the decision to withdraw." In a lengthy critique of the press, Westmoreland made it clear we were his worst enemy. "At one time we had 700 accredited reporters, all practicing, seeking and reporting news as they were accustomed to in the United States, all looking for sensational stories. If we continue the practice of reporting only the off-beat, the unusual or the bizarre in any future war, well, then the American public are going to be influ-enced as they were during Vietnam. I think the bottom line on this subject is how an open society, and how our political democ-racy are vulnerable to manipulation by an autocratic flow of society."

Westmoreland not only failed to understand journalism in our society, but he also failed the lessons of history. Even grave defeats have been perceived as victories of the spirit when clear-cut goals—and shortcomings—are shared with the public. But there was little to inspire confidence in the nation about the mil-itary's claims of victory at Tet.

On March 25, 1968, just two months after Tet, a Harris poll showed that the majority of Americans, 60 percent, regarded the Tet Offensive as a defeat for U.S. objectives in Vietnam.

Westy's insistence that the media somehow betrayed the troops in the field still rings true with many senior U.S. mili-tary officers. In the book *The War Managers*, retired General Douglas Kinnard polled the 173 Army generals who commanded in Vietnam. Eighty-nine percent of them expressed negative feelings toward the printed press and even more—91 percent—were negative about TV news coverage. Despite those findings, Kinnard concluded that the importance of the press in swaying public opinion was largely a myth. That myth was important for the government to perpetuate, so officials could insist that it was not the real situation in Vietnam against which the American people reacted, but rather the press' portrayal of that situation.

In a research paper for the Joan Shorenstein Center at Harvard, William Hammond of the U.S. Army Center of Military History described "a breakdown in the basic spirit of cooperation and communication that had made MACV's Guidelines for the Press so successful in Vietnam."

In a paper titled "Who were the Saigon correspondents, and does it matter?" Hammond observed, "Flailed both by the Nixon White House and increasingly by officers in the field for their supposed disloyalty, reporters had encountered generals who would no longer give interviews, staff officers who declined to respond to the most innocuous questions in a timely manner, and official dissembling on a range of topics that stretched from the so-called 'light at the end of the tunnel' to the supposedly secret wars in Laos and Cambodia . . . as a result many reporters lost faith in their government's word."

The psychological impact of the 1968 Tet Offensive was considered a contributing factor in South Vietnam's collapse seven years later. In 1975, a minor setback in a battle near Ban Me Thout escalated into the ARVN's panicked retreat and the fall of Saigon a few weeks later.

Tet should have taught a hard lesson to American leaders: Responsible leadership in wartime will recognize problems clearly and publicize events that are likely to have a serious impact on the nation. Public relations spinning only makes matters worse.

But American leaders extracted a different lesson: the need to control images coming from the battlefield. The bad rap the press got in the wake of Tet stuck and became the rationale for the military's hostility toward the press. The fallout is still with us, in tighter battlefield censorship of war dispatches and a denial of access to soldiers in the field—changes that have reduced public information about more recent conflicts, including the invasions of Grenada and Panama, the Persian Gulf War and NATO's Serbia bombing campaign.

In 1968, a few months after the Tet Offensive, although the hole in the wall had been repaired, bullet holes still pockmarked the facade of the U.S. Embassy. In the lobby a plaque commemorating the U.S. soldiers who died defending the embassy that morning had been erected. It read: "In memory of the brave men who died January 31, 1968, defending this embassy against the Viet Cong: Sp4 Charles L. Daniel MPS, Cpl James C. Marshall USMC, Sp4 Owen E. Mebust MPC, Pfc William E. Sebast MPC, Sgt Jonnie B. Thomas."

On the same wall nearby someone had framed a quotation from "Seven Pillars of Wisdom," by Lawrence of Arabia: "It is better that they do it imperfectly than that you do it perfectly. For it is their war and their country and your time here is limited."

Storming the Citadel

By Michael D. Harkins

It was a chilly morning and the skies were a lead gray as the convoy slowly snaked its way along Highway 1. Captain Gordon D. Batcheller, Commanding Officer of Company A, 1st Battalion, 1st Marine Regiment (1/1), was worried. His orders were to relieve the MACV (Military Assistance Command Vietnam) compound at Hue and link up with ARVN (Army of the Republic of Vietnam) units north of the city. But he had little information to go on. Moving up the main coastal highway that ran from Da Nang all the way through Dong Ha in the north, where the 3rd Marine Division Headquarters was located, things were unusually quiet. Batcheller knew "something was up." The previous day, January 30, 1968, North Vietnamese and Viet Cong units had taken advantage of the Tet (Vietnamese New Year) cease-fire to attack cities and towns throughout Vietnam. Fighting raged everywhere.

As Batcheller's understrength company advanced, they fortuitously met four M-48 tanks of the 3rd Tank Battalion, 3rd Marine Division, also heading north. As they approached Hue, the polyglot force experienced harassing sniper fire that wounded several Marines, but the convoy hurriedly pushed on and crossed the An Cuu Bridge spanning the Phu Cam Canal on the outskirts of Hue. It was evident from large holes in the cement that the enemy had tried to destroy the bridge but, luckily for Alpha Company, they had failed. A downed bridge would have delayed them for hours, even days. Ahead of them was majestic Hue City, the old Imperial capital of Vietnam.

The column halted as Batcheller assessed the situation. There was no one visible in the streets. Odd, he thought, since Hue was the third-most populated city in the country. An eerie silence prevailed. As Batcheller gave the order to move out, the Marines climbed aboard the tanks and, as the clanking machines roared forward, the leathernecks raked the surrounding structures with automatic-weapons fire as they rode through the narrow streets.

Suddenly, a B-40 rocket ripped into the lead tank, shattering Batcheller's eardrum and fatally wounding his radio operator. His legs were severed at the knees. Both sides exchanged a tremendous fusillade of small-arms fire. The NVA began dropping mortar rounds among the Marines, as the tanks' 90mm cannons and .50-caliber machine guns opened up to support Alpha Company. All radio sets were jammed with Vietnamese voices. Pinned down, the infantrymen dragged their wounded to safety behind the tanks, in ditches, anywhere to escape the deadly barrage. As the morning sun burned away the overcast, giving way to a pale blue sky, the first day in the struggle to retake Hue City had begun.

Not realizing it, the leathernecks of 1/1 had walked right into a deathtrap. The 800th and 802nd battalions of the North Vietnamese Army (NVA), 6th Regiment, had launched a two-pronged assault from the west in the early morning hours of January 30. Storming through the lightly defended gates, their plan was to destroy the ARVN's 1st Division near the Citadel. However, both NVA units were repulsed by the ARVN's elite Black Panther Battalion and their drive was abruptly halted. Brigadier General Ngo Quang Truong, 1st ARVN Division Commander, a short, wiry individual, had heeded the reports of mass NVA/VC troop movements and consolidated his forces in the HQ compound. Although half his men were on leave because of the Tet holiday, he managed to deploy his units and keep the enemy at bay.

While this fight was raging on, two additional units, the 804th and K4B battalions of the NVA 4th Regiment, swept in from the south and east, attacking the MACV compound where 200 Americans held off the enemy throughout the night. Meanwhile, another NVA unit, the 806th Battalion, set up blocking positions on roads leading out of the city to the north and yet another enemy unit, the KC4 Battalion, did the same in the south, along Highway 1. In all, nine enemy battalions were firmly entrenched in the town.

About noon, news of Alpha Company's dilemma had reached Task Force X-Ray (1st Marine Division Forward HQ) at Phu Bai. Lieutenant Colonel Marcus J. Gravel, Commanding Officer of 1/1, quickly set out with his Operations Officer Major Walter J. Murphy and Company G, 2nd Battalion, 5th Marines (2/5), attached to Gravel's command.

Racing up Highway 1, 2/5 reached the beleaguered Marines and, providing cover fire, were able to drive the NVA back. The wounded were evacuated, and Batcheller, peppered by shrapnel, was medevaced to the 1st Marine Medical Battalion at Phu Bai. Pushing forward, the infantrymen reached the MACV enclave and hastily established a perimeter. They also secured the Navy boat ramp and the base of the Nguyen Hoang Bridge, an important move, since directly across from it was the Citadel. A small park near the boat ramp was utilized as an LZ (Landing Zone). A few Marine and ARVN tanks formed a semicircle around the LZ to protect it from enemy fire across the Perfume River. The Marines had gained a small foothold.

On the second day of the battle, February 1, 1968, the Marine headquarters at Phu Bai was in a quandary. They had little information as to what was happening at Hue. Brigadier General Foster C. LaHue, Assistant Commander of the 1st Marine Division, thought his Marines were in control of the south side and the enemy would soon be finished because of "no resupply capabilities." Also, Saigon issued a press release saying the "enemy was being mopped up." Marine Amphibious Force (III MAF) HQ at Da Nang concurred, stating: "[Marines] were pushing VC out of Hue this morning." Even Lieutenant General Hoang Xuan Lam, overall head of I Corps, thought the enemy had been routed with the exception of a "platoon" holding out in the Citadel. They were all woefully incorrect.

Despite this optimism, two additional companies, Fox and Hotel of the 2nd Battalion, 5th Marines, were alerted for immediate duty in Hue. As the C-46 Sea Knight helicopters approached the embattled city, several Marines were wounded in their seats as bullets tore through the thin-skinned "birds." Landing on the university soccer field, the heavily laden infantrymen scrambled from the rear door and bolted for cover near the MACV HQ. That night was spent organizing for the following day's attack.

Lieutenant Colonel Ernest C. "Big Ernie" Cheatham, Jr., 2/5 Commander, and Colonel Stanley Smith Hughes, 1st Marine Regimental Commander, arrived on the scene. Smith's orders were simple and straightforward—clear Hue's south side. To Cheatham's 5th Marines went the bulk of the task: push west from the MACV compound, following the Perfume River all the way to the Phu Cam Cathedral. Their main route would be along Le Loi Street paralleling the river. Unknown to the Marines, this was the site of the NVA HQ and the location of the majority of their troops. Gravel was given the assignment of keeping Highway 1 open for traffic, since Alpha 1/1 had suffered the most casualties and was undermanned.

The attack commenced on February 4, but this was not the type of combat 2/5 had been accustomed to. Since arriving in

Vietnam, it had been a frustrating game of cat and mouse for the leathernecks. Booby traps, hit-and-run tactics, and nightly ambushes were the mainstay. Some Marines would go months without ever seeing an enemy soldier. This time it would be different—the fighting would be house-to-house and the NVA and VC had no intention of retreating.

Hunched over maps scrounged from a nearby Shell gas station, Cheatham was dismayed. Confronting his Marines were 11 blocks of enemy-held territory and they had excellent fields of fire for their mortars, recoilless rifles and automatic weapons. It had to be secured house by house, street by street and block by block. Captain Michael Downs, Fox Company, was slated to assault the Treasury complex, and Captain Ron Christmas' Hotel Company would move on the public health building. Golf Company would be in reserve. The use of supporting arms was restricted—no bombing or strafing runs by jets, no naval bombardments and no heavy artillery. Saigon wanted to save the city from complete ruin.

"You must dig the rats from their holes," Cheatham informed his company commanders.

Advancing up Le Loi Street, the Marines of F 2/5 used smoke grenades to shield their movements, as platoons scrambled to gain access to buildings. A mechanical "mule," a small flatbed vehicle, brought up a 106 recoilless rifle and it silenced several NVA machine-gun nests. Bazooka men, armed with a 3.5 rocket launcher, provided additional support fire. However, it was the aggressiveness of the "grunts" that ousted the enemy from their lairs.

"The NVA in Hue were mean, motivated bastards," said one combat correspondent, continuing "but, the plain fact is, we were better."

The streets sprang to life with the unremitting noises of combat. The fighting grew in intensity as squads of Marines converged on the buildings. It was precision, as four men covered the exits, two rushed in hurling hand grenades and several others followed with their M-16 rifles on full automatic. "Timing," said Cheatham, "has to be as good as a football play."

While 2/5 was moving westward along Le Loi Street, Gravel's 1/1 command, two and a half platoons of Alpha Company, was ordered to take the Joan of Arc School, just 100 yards from the MACV compound. Approximately 100 NVA soldiers were quartered there, pouring fire onto Smith's HQ. Tanks and recoilless rifles pounded the structure. The roof was completely blown off as glass and cement flew everywhere. Rushing in, fire teams blazed away, and the fighting was at close quarters. Screams of the wounded, the incessant "pop-pop" of the M-16s mixed with AK-47s, exploding grenades, LAWs (Light Assault Weapons) and B-40 rockets filled the air. One by one the enemy was flushed out of the rafters, classrooms and school grounds. Bodies were everywhere. The leathernecks suffered 22 casualties. Huge, gaping holes covered the wall where the crucifix was hanging. It was still intact.

That afternoon, the remaining platoon of Alpha Company, along with Bravo Company, arrived at Hue. That evening, as red and green tracers filled the night, the 12th VC Sapper Battalion blew the An Cuu Bridge. The land route from Hue to Phu Bai had been cut; but not before five reinforced Marine companies had crossed it. If the NVA had destroyed the bridge several days earlier, the results might have proved disastrous.

By February 6, 2/5 had in its possession the Treasury complex, the university library and the hospital. Hotel Company was given the assignment of assaulting the Thua Thien Province capital, a two-story building with enemy troops on the top floor. Beside its tactical importance (this was the NVA Command Post), it was a major irritant to the Marines. The red and gold-starred flag of North Vietnam was fluttering from the flagpole. And the Marines wanted it.

Tear gas was fired at the structure as the attack commenced; however, the weather was not cooperating, and a cold wind blew the gas away from its objective. Donning gas masks, Lieutenant Leo Myers' First Platoon sprinted through an iron gate, across the street, to an open courtyard facing the capitol. Captain Christmas, using the radio in the rear of the vehicle, directed a tank forward. Several 90mm rounds exploded against the masonry walls as the leathernecks rushed through the front door. The first two were cut down by small-arms fire. A flurry of fragmentation grenades was hurled, M-60 machine guns spewed empty brass shell casings in every direction and the NVA fell back. As fire teams hunted down the stragglers, Gunnery Sergeant Frank Thomas pulled down the NVA flag and replaced it with the Stars and Stripes.

On February 7, VC sappers detonated another bridge that spanned the Perfume River. Luckily, the Navy boat ramp was in full operation. As replacements and supplies motored in and out of Hue, sporadic enemy fire from the opposite shore was directed at the vessels, but it had little effect. Also, choppers from the Marine helicopter squadrons ferried in reinforcements and took out wounded.

As the infantrymen progressed in both directions along the south bank the fighting began to slacken off. But a considerable "mop up" would have to be implemented before the area could be considered safe.

In the wake of the battle, there were other major problems that arose. Thousands of homeless refugees who had fled the fighting had to be cared for. At one Catholic church alone 5,000 were housed and another 17,000 camped around the university. Food and medicine were in short supply and had to be brought in. Navy doctors and corpsmen, U.S. civilians from the Public Health Office, an Australian doctor and Vietnamese medical personnel worked wonders.

By the second week, the once beautiful "lotus flower" was in a shambles. Shell-pocked buildings, remnants of houses, debris scattered all along the tree-lined avenues that once teemed with shoppers, and bullet-riddled walls were evident throughout the city. Then there were the dead and wounded. Navy doctors and corpsmen went without rest to patch up Marines. Some begged to return to the outfits and be with their friends. Others with minor injuries never even bothered to report them. They stayed in the battle.

Although the south side of Hue was declared officially secured on February 10, pockets of snipers continued to plague Marine patrols trying to root them out. To add to the confusion, enemy troops mingled with the population and, as a result, innocent people were killed or wounded. On one street, a father held his blood-splattered child as he stared vacantly at the ground after getting caught in a crossfire.

"A woman knelt in death," wrote one reporter. "A child lay ... crushed by a fallen roof. Many of the bodies had turned black ... rats gnawed at the exposed flesh." The people of Hue were suffering.

With the An Cuu Bridge damaged, only one overpass remained over the Phu Cam Canal that permitted entry into Hue City's south side. Called the Ga-Hue, it was located on the extreme northwest bank, where the waterway emptied into the Perfume River. It was imperative it be kept safe. One platoon from Hotel 2/5 cleared a one-block area around the important causeway. Establishing a perimeter, the Marines repulsed numerous counterattacks through the night, aimed at dislodging them from their position. With the arrival of dawn, they had held, and were relieved by 1/1. With this bridge, the land route between Hue and Phu Bai could remain open, although it was out of the way, while combat engineers repaired the An Cuu roadway.

Brigadier General Truong and his 1st ARVN Division, cut off and surrounded on the north side of the city, were making a defiant stand of their own. One Black Panther Company, led by Captain Tran Ngoc Hue, repelled Communist units at the Citadel airfield. A wounded ARVN officer, Lieutenant Nguyen Hi, with a collection of office clerks, drove the enemy back when they gained entry to the medical area. Truong maintained radio contact with his people and each unit fought its way back into the compound. From here, Vietnamese paratroopers, marines and rangers clashed with a tenacious enemy to gain control of the Citadel. Whole companies became stranded and had to claw their way back using grappling hooks to scale walls within the maze of parapets. Finally, on February 9, his army weakened to the point of exhaustion, Truong grudgingly requested U.S. assistance. The 1st Battalion, 5th Marines (1/5), were ordered up to Hue.

From Phu Loc Combat Base, two platoons from Company B, under Captain Fern Jennings, were helicoptered into the ARVN HQ stronghold. The 3rd Platoon, coming under intense fire, was forced to pull out after the pilot was wounded, and limped back to base camp. On the south side, Major Robert H. Thompson, Commanding Officer of 1/5, conferred with Colonel Hughes. It was decided that Thompson would take Companies A and C, via Navy LCUs (Landing Craft, Utility), join up with Company B and attack southward, pushing the NVA toward the Perfume River. Here, the enemy would be caught between 1/1 and 2/5 on the opposite side.

The morning of February 12 was similar to most mornings in Hue during the battle—cold, windy, with a misty rain. The Marines boarded the LCUs for the short trip to the northern tip of the Citadel, where they quickly disembarked at a ferry landing. Thompson and his men made their way to the ARVN CP where Thompson met with Truong. The feisty Vietnamese general informed him that the Communists had two battalions in the Citadel and another to the west, resupplying them. The enemy held the northeast and southeast walls near the Imperial Palace. Thompson was responsible for securing the northeast wall—2,500 yards long, 20 feet high with widths from 50 to 200 feet. With the 1st ARVN Airborne Battalion attached, the three Marine companies (Company B's 3rd Platoon arrived with Thompson) would make a frontal assault down the wall. Meanwhile, the 3rd ARVN Regiment would continue attacking to the southeast, moving in their direction, on their right flank. Once the Imperial Palace was taken, they could begin their southward sweep.

That evening, the Marines received some good news. Lieutenant General Lam, after meeting with South Vietnamese President Nguyen Van Thieu, authorized allied forces to use whatever weapons were available to them in the Citadel. The only exception was the Imperial Palace. It was still off-limits.

Tuesday, February 13, Captain J. J. Bowe and Alpha 1/5 proceeded down the northeast wall. Upon advancing only a few yards, the entire area erupted in an ear-shattering barrage of AK-47 automatic rifles, B-40 rockets and mortars that cascaded from a large tower onto the Marines below. The ARVN unit that was supposed to have taken the southeast cordon was pulled back. No one told Thompson. In only 10 minutes, Alpha Company was cut to pieces with 30 casualties. Preparatory fire from 155 howitzers and 5-inch shells from Navy destroyers offshore were placed directly in front of Marine lines. By day's end, the "grunts" of 1/5 held the wall 75 yards from where the ARVN unit had retreated. Thompson summoned Company D, still on the south side, to join him.

Captain Myron C. Harrington, Delta Company's leader, reached Bao Vinh Quay where Thompson had landed the previous day, near dusk on the thirteenth. Throughout the fourteenth, his men rested and reorganized in the ARVN sanctuary while

Bravo and Charlie 1/5 once again hurled themselves at the NVA bastion. Six-inch projectiles from a cruiser slammed into the ominous-looking tower that was hampering the leathernecks' progress. Fighters from the 1st Marine Air Wing dropped rockets, napalm and CS (nonlethal tear gas) inside the wall. Still no headway could be made.

The following day, Harrington's Marines crept cautiously down the northeast barricade after ships in the South China Sea and artillery from the 11th Marines sent rounds crashing into the tower. Chunks of brick and cement crumbled to the ground and houses nearby were razed. Two F-4 Phantoms roared overhead and released canisters of napalm and 500-pound bombs on the seemingly invincible spire.

As if untouched by the pounding they had just received, within a few minutes the NVA let fly a broadside upon the Marines. A driving, miserable rain made the going treacherous, as the screams of the wounded and the cries of "Corpsman!" permeated the air. Tanks lurched forward to lend support, sending 90mm rounds screeching at the fortified Communist bulwarks. Men with 3.5 rocket launchers and disposable LAWs moved back and forth to help trapped infantrymen. Second Lieutenant Jack S. Imlah's 1st Platoon slugged their way through the rubble and placed themselves at the rear of the tower. From here, the Marines lobbed grenades into spider holes where individual NVA soldiers would emerge like a jack-in-the-box, let loose a few bursts, and rapidly disappear. After nearly three hours of continuous combat, the tower was in Marine hands. From its summit, which made an excellent observation point, the Imperial Palace could be seen through the fog.

An enemy message was intercepted on the sixteenth and relayed to Major Thompson: ". . . original commander of the force inside Hue . . . killed . . . many officers killed or wounded . . . [new commander] recommended [his units] to withdraw. Senior officer ordered new commander . . . in Hue . . . to remain in position and fight." The outcome was inevitable. The NVA and VC, who had lost 219 confirmed dead as well as an undetermined number of wounded, knew they were going to die.

For the next four days, the leathernecks of 1/5 hammered away at the northeast wall. Each day was an exact duplicate of the day before: artillery and naval gunfire, followed by infantry assaults with tanks, bazookas and mortars. Many of the men, numbed with fatigue, could barely walk. The constant flow of wounded kept the medical teams busy. To expedite things, the more serious cases were set aside and those who had any hope of surviving at all were attended to immediately.

After one week's fighting, the Marines had suffered more than 300 casualties. Companies were now at half-strength. Morale was low. "We've got to get some help," said one anguished Marine. "They're going to annihilate 1/5." But there were no available additional troops that could be committed to help.

In spite of all this, when ordered to attack, the Marines attacked. Finally, on February 21, Thompson's grizzled grunts had in their possession the northeast wall. However, the ARVN units had literally stopped and waited and, to their horror, the Marines of 1/5 were told to turn right and take the southeast wall as well. Reinforced by Company L, 3rd Battalion, 5th Marines, the infantrymen set out for the Imperial Palace. As they pressed forward, 106 recoilless rifles and tanks fired round after round at the temple. As the sun appeared in the sky and the weather cleared, Captain John Niotis, Lima Company commander, called in air strikes. Coming as close as possible without damaging the cherished building, fixed-wing aircraft discharged napalm against the palace wall. The jellied gasoline mixture created fireballs that leaped high in the air very near to Marine lines. As the Marines pressed warily onward, each building had to be cleared. Again, it was house-to-house. Grenades were tossed through broken windows while fire teams kicked down doors and rushed in, shooting anything that moved.

As they slowly inched forward, the riflemen noticed a huge structure with a tile roof and decorative carvings. The Marines ventured in, discovering the walls completely covered in gold leaf, and two thrones perched atop a raised dais. The room was also garnished with caricatures of lions and dragons richly adorned in red and gold lacquer. In one of the corners were the crumpled bodies of two dead NVA soldiers. One sergeant sauntered over and nudged the motionless corpses with the barrel of his rifle. The leathernecks had reached the venerated throne room of the Vietnamese Emperors.

Led by Captains James Coolican, a Marine advisor, and Tran Ngoc Hue, a Hoc Bao Company (Black Panther) stormed over 200 yards of open terrain to conduct the final assault on the Imperial Palace. Many present knew this was "strictly public relations." To the South Vietnamese government, it was a matter of pride to have an ARVN unit seize this historic place. But every Marine there knew 1/5 had taken the Citadel. The grunts watched as the NVA flag was torn down and replaced with the yellow and red banner of South Vietnam. It was fastened and hoisted—ironically—over the Palace of Perfect Peace. Everyone cheered. The city of Hue had been recaptured. It had lasted 26 days.

But the true agony of Hue was not to be fully realized until the Communists had fled. During the occupation by NVA/VC troops, thousands of civilians were massacred by death squads. The district worst hit was Gai Hoi, a large triangular residential zone northeast of the Citadel. Because it had little military importance, it was left untouched and not liberated until the end of the battle. Government officials, teachers, priests, nuns, doctors, foreigners and anyone aiding the Americans were singled out for execution. Coaxed from their homes by loudspeakers and radio broadcasts and, in some cases, forcibly abducted, they were led away never to be seen again. With hands tied behind their backs, they were removed to a remote area and shot, bludgeoned or buried alive. As late as September of 1969, mass graves were being discovered. In one, the skulls and bones of 428 people of Phu Cam stretched as far as a football field, scrubbed clean by a running stream. In all, 2,800 citizens of the city were systemically and methodically murdered. It was genocide in its most barbaric form.

Upon being relieved, the Marines returned to the rice paddy war they were all too familiar with. During Operation Hue City, the Marines lost 147 killed and 857 wounded (these figures don't take into account those serving with support units or who died of wounds later in hospitals). The South Vietnamese units suffered 384 killed and 1,800 wounded. The exact count of enemy dead may never be known, but records show the NVA/VC dead to be 5,113, an unknown number of wounded and 89 captured.

In 1969, the Hut battle streamer was affixed to the Marine Corps flag and every outfit that participated in that fight was awarded the Presidential Unit Citation, which read in part: "The men of the 1st Marines and 5th Marines [Reinforced] soundly defeated a numerically superior force ... by their effective teamwork, aggressive fighting spirit and individual acts of heroism ... achieved an illustrious record of courage and skill which was in keeping with the highest tradition of the Marine Corps and the United States Naval Service."

But it was the dirty, bearded and exhausted Marine grunt who deserves the accolades. With rifle in hand and a "tight knot" in his stomach, he overcame his fear and drove the invaders from Hue.

Turning Point of the War

By Colonel Harry G. Summers, Jr., U.S. Army

O ne of the great mysteries of the Vietnam War is how the allied military victory during the Tet 1968 Offensive, a victory so complete that for the rest of the war the Viet Cong guerrillas never again played a significant military role, ultimately was turned into an American political defeat. The stock answer is that it was all the fault of the media. But there's more to it than that.

While the media unquestionably played a role, the real answer has to do with the collapse of the nation's "national command authority," the top level chain of command, including the president, the secretary of defense and the Joint Chiefs of Staff (JCS).

"What was striking—and important—about the public White House posture in February and March 1968 was how defensive it was," noted Peter Braestrup in *Big Story* (Yale University Press, 1983), his landmark work on Tet. "In retrospect, it seemed that President Johnson was to some degree 'psychologically defeated' by . . . the onslaught on the cities of Vietnam."

That in itself was strange. Compared to previous American battlefield setbacks, the Viet Cong (VC) and North Vietnamese Army (NVA) 1968 Tet Offensive was rather tame. In this century alone there was the disastrous Japanese sneak attack on Pearl Harbor in 1941, where the United States lost most of the Pacific Fleet; the surprise German counterattack at the Battle of the Bulge in 1944, where the Allied advance was halted and two whole regiments of the U.S. 106th Infantry Division surrendered to the enemy; the initial defeats in Korea in July 1950, where the commanding general of the 24th Infantry Division was captured and the entire Eighth U.S. Army decimated and pushed back into the Pusan Perimeter; and the cataclysmic shock of the Chinese Communist Forces intervention in November 1950, which inflicted terrible casualties and drove Eighth Army and X Corps out of North Korea.

In each case the initial news media accounts were filled with hysterical prophesies of doom and defeat. And Tet 1968 was no exception. But previously these initial reports had been countered by government statements that the situation was under control and that things were not as bad as they seemed and that we'd soon be back on the road to victory.

But there was no such political counterattack after Tet 1968. Instead of rallying the nation, as Franklin Delano Roosevelt had done after Pearl Harbor and the Battle of the Bulge, and as Harry S. Truman did after Taejon, Kuni-ri and the Chosin Reservoir, Lyndon Baines Johnson remained reclusive in the White House.

"If he did not appear in public to be as depressed as those subordinates whom he later chided for their gloom, he did not strike a decisive public stance," noted Braestrup. "He emphasized the need to stand firm, but he did not spell out what this meant, or how the battlefield situation was changing, as he saw it, in Vietnam. He left a big void, which others hastened to fill."

Why did the Tet Offensive have such a profound effect? For one thing, LBJ's heart was not really in the war in the first place. Believing it was jeopardizing his "Great Society" social programs, all he really wanted was for the war to go away. But war is not for the faint of heart. As the great military theorist Karl von Clausewitz noted more than 150 years ago in *On War* (Princeton University Press), "The more modest your own political aim, the less reluctantly you will abandon it if you must."

But the fault was not Lyndon Johnson's alone. Contributing to and compounding his "psychological defeat" was the perfidy—by definition the "deception through faith"—of his principal national security advisers, Secretaries of Defense Robert S. McNamara and Clark Clifford, and General Earle G. Wheeler, the chairman of the Joint Chiefs of Staff (JCS).

To understand why these political happenings in Washington were to have such a profound effect, one must have a basic appreciation of the fundamentals of war. Traditionally Americans have seen war and politics as things apart, but in reality they are inexorably linked, for war in its essence is what Clausewitz called "a true political instrument, a continuation of political activity by other means."

Further clouding our understanding is the fact that the Vietnam War is usually explained in terms of the revolutionary guerrilla war theories of Ho Chi Minh and Mao Tse-tung (Zedong). But as has been argued elsewhere in more detail in my *On Strategy: A Critical Analysis of the Vietnam War* (Presidio/Dell), the key to understanding the Vietnam War in general, and the 1968 Tet Offensive in particular, lies not in the then new and trendy counterinsurgency theories propagated by civilian academic experts and their soulmates within the military, who arrogantly believed that with the tools of social science they could change the world. The answer instead lies in the age-old fundamentals of military science.

Paradoxical as it may seem, the explanation for the Tet debacle was formulated more than 150 years earlier. Writing in 1838 about what he called *centers of gravity*, "the hub of all power ... on which everything depends," Clausewitz described

COLONEL HARRY G. SUMMERS

several such centers. "In small countries that rely on large ones, it is usually the army of their protector. Among alliances, it lies in the community of interest, and . . . the personalities of the leaders and public opinion.

"It is against these that our energies should be directed," he went on to say. "I would . . . state it as a principle that if you can vanquish all your enemies by defeating one of them, that defeat must be the main objective in the war. In this one enemy we strike at the center of gravity of the entire conflict."

Albeit by accident, that is exactly what the NVA and VC did with their 1968 Tet Offensive. While they could not and did not defeat the army of South Vietnam's protector (the U.S. military) on the battlefield, they did strike fatal blows at the *community of interest* between the U.S. and South Vietnam, at the personality of the U.S. commander in chief, Lyndon B. Johnson, and at American public opinion. As Clausewitz predicted, these centers of gravity proved decisive.

"War is nothing but a duel on a larger scale," said Clausewitz, "but a picture of it as a whole can be formed by imagining a pair of wrestlers. Each tries through physical force to compel the other to do his will; his immediate aim is to throw his opponent in order to make him incapable of further resistance." President Johnson had not only been thrown by the enemy's 1968 Tet Offensive, but pinned as well. And his handlers were no help at all.

The comparison with earlier wars is telling. After the disasters in World War II, President Roosevelt could count on the support and advice of his longtime friend Admiral William D. Leahy, his personal chief of staff and ad hoc chairman of the Joint Chiefs of Staff, as well as the backing of the chiefs themselves, General George C. Marshall and Admiral Ernest J. King.

And during the Korean War President Truman could count on Secretary of Defense George C. Marshall, who had been the Army chief of staff during World War II, and on General of the Army

Omar N. Bradley, the chairman of the Joint Chiefs. But President Johnson lacked such a solid base of support to fall back on.

Most Americans do not realize that unlike President Franklin D. Roosevelt in World War II and, to a lesser extent, President Truman in the Korean War, President Johnson did not directly command the armed forces through the JCS—originally including the chairman, the Army Chief of Staff and the Chief of Naval Operations, but after 1947 also including the Air Force Chief of Staff, and after 1952, the Commandant of the Marine Corps.

With the National Security Act of 1947, as amended, the Congress created the Department of Defense, and the president delegated his command authority over the armed forces to the newly created Secretary of Defense. The Secretary of Defense became in fact, if not in name, the nation's military commander in chief. President Harry S. Truman quickly realized that fact after the initial disasters of the Korean War in 1950. He fired Louis Johnson, a political patronage appointee, and appointed General of the Army George Marshall to head that critical wartime post.

During the Korean War the chain of command extended from the President as commander in chief to the Secretary of Defense and then to the unified geographic commands—i.e., the European Command, the Far East Command, etc.—through the Joint Chiefs of Staff. At that time an "executive agent" system prevailed in which the JCS designated a service chief—the Army Chief of Staff in the case of the Korean War—to provide the link between the unified commander and the JCS.

But the Defense Reorganization Act of 1958 abolished the executive agent system that had worked so well during the Korean War and in effect took the JCS out of the chain of command. The Vietnam War was the first (and only) war conducted under this new system.

Unfortunately, the Defense Reorganization Act coincided with a shift in focus of the responsibilities of the Secretary of Defense. In the late 1950s and early 1960s the concern was not with fighting a war but with managing the defense budget. Accordingly, a succession of businessmen—General Motor's Charles "Engine Charlie" Wilson in the Eisenhower administration and Ford's Robert S. McNamara in the Kennedy administration—were appointed to that post. Known for his "whiz kid" team of accountants, bookkeepers and systems analysts, McNamara was a ruthless and efficient administrator.

But that was only part of his job. McNamara was retained in office after Kennedy's assassination, and when the United States opted for direct military involvement in Vietnam, McNamara's primary focus as Secretary of Defense should have shifted from management to his leadership responsibilities as the military commander in chief.

As defense secretary he was the U.S. counterpart of North Vietnam's defense minister, General Vo Nguyen Giap. The absurdity of the situation is apparent. Giap, the hero of Dien Bien Phu, was a military genius whose will to win never waivered. "During the war against the Americans," noted Stanley Karnow in Vietnam: A History (Viking), "[Giap] spoke of fighting ten, fifteen, twenty, fifty years, regardless of the cost, until 'final victory.' "

But by McNamara's own later admission, Giap had him whipped from the start. McNamara confessed during the 1984 CBS-Westmoreland libel trial that he became convinced as early as 1965 or 1966 that the war "could not be won militarily." In other words, three years before Tet, the will to win of the U.S. military commander in chief had already been broken.

That was fatal, for war at its essence is a contest of wills. And the will of the commander is crucial, especially when things go wrong. "It is the ebbing of moral and physical strength . . . that the commander has to withstand—first in himself, and then in all those who directly, or indirectly, have entrusted him with their thoughts and feelings, hopes and fears," said Clausewitz. "The inertia of the whole gradually comes to rest on the commander's will alone. The ardor of his spirit must rekindle the flame of purpose in all others. . . . Only to the extent that he can do that will he retain his hold on his men. . . . Once that hold is lost, once his own courage can no longer revive the courage of his men, the mass will drag him down to the brutish world where danger is shirked and shame is unknown."

McNamara reached those depths early on. Instead of telling Johnson of his long-held reservations about the war, he kept silent while at the same time sending the troops under his command into a war he himself believed unwinnable.

The inescapable conclusion is that he kept silent in order not to jeopardize his subsequent appointment by Johnson as chairman of the World Bank.

"Since leaving the defense department in 1968," he said in the August 3, 1992, edition of *Newsweek*, "with the exception of my testimony during [the Westmoreland] libel trial against CBS, I have not spoken of these matters." But instead of apologizing for past actions, he bragged about what a sensitive and politically correct guy he had been.

At the same time he was ordering America's sons and daughters into battle he was consorting with leaders of the anti-war movement, including, in his own words, "Senator J. William Fulbright, chairman of the Foreign Relations Committee; the Reverend William Sloane Coffin, chaplain at Yale; the young Quaker who subsequently burned himself to death below my window at the Pentagon; Sam Brown, a friend of my children, who after leading marches of protest against the president and me, would dine at my home."

A month after the Tet Offensive began, McNamara resigned as Secretary of Defense and was replaced by Clark Clifford. But that was no improvement. A longtime Washington wheeler-dealer and Johnson crony, Clifford admitted in his 1991 memoir, *Counsel to the President* (Random House), that he was brought in because Johnson wanted "a Secretary of Defense who supported his policy." But instead, as Clifford himself makes clear, President Johnson was betrayed again.

"At a time when what was needed was new leadership and a new strategy in Vietnam," notes Lewis Sorley in a review of Clifford's book in the September 1991 *Army*, "Clifford set about ensuring that . . . American involvement in the war and American support for the South Vietnamese would be progressively and inexorably eroded. What is more significant he did this not in furtherance of his president's policy and direction but in defiance of it, forcing the president into one untenable position after another and ultimately usurping the role of commander in chief. This may be deduced from Clifford's own testimony, given proudly and without apology."

"I want to impress upon the president that our posture is basically so impossible that we have got to find some way out," Clifford told his staffers. But, "far from convincing Johnson," Sorley notes, "Clifford simply hamstrung him." As Sorley concludes: "It is one thing to seek to influence the formulation of policy, quite another to faithlessly undermine that policy once formulated. Clifford represents himself as being very proud in doing the latter."

Sad to say, the support President Johnson received from the JCS was no better. While the chiefs of staff did not consciously betray their commander in chief, neither did they provide him with the kind of straightforward military advice to which he was rightfully entitled.

The most damning critique of the role of the JCS during the

Vietnam War was made by one of its own members, Army General Bruce Palmer, Jr. "The JCS seemed to be unable to articulate an effective military strategy that they could persuade the commander in chief and secretary of defense to adopt," he said in his 1984 work, *The 25-Year War: America's Military Role in Vietnam* (University of Kentucky Press).

"There was one glaring omission in the advice the JCS provided the president and the secretary of defense. . . . Not once during the war did the JCS advise the commander in chief or the secretary of defense that the strategy being pursued most probably would fail and the United States would be unable to achieve its objectives."

"The only explanation of this failure," Palmer concluded, "is that the chiefs were imbued with the 'can do' spirit and could not bring themselves to make such a negative statement or to appear to be disloyal." But by withholding their negative views from President Johnson, they were the very embodiment of disloyalty, guilty of what the U.S. Military Academy's honor code calls "quibbling," a form of lying by evasion where the entire truth is deliberately left unstated.

Far from rallying to the president's support at Tet, the JCS further undermined his will and resolve and, in so doing, unwittingly gave what would prove to be the *coup de grace* to further American involvement in Vietnam. Instead of convincing Johnson that things were not as bad as they seemed, they used the enemy attack as a pretext for pushing for mobilization of the reserves to shore up America's depleted strategic reserves.

From their standpoint, that deception was justified. As Palmer points out, the JCS had earlier "lost control of the overall strategic direction of American armed forces as the burgeoning force demands of Southeast Asia quickly consumed the strategic reserve of forces in the United States previously earmarked for the reinforcement of Europe or Korea, or for an unforeseen contingency elsewhere."

With the Tet crisis coinciding with the North Korean seizure of the USS *Pueblo* and with intelligence reports indicating a developing crisis in Berlin, "the administration could not be certain," noted Herbert Y. Schandler in *The Unmaking of the President: Lyndon Johnson and Vietnam* (Princeton University Press), "that these events did not represent a concerted Communist offensive designed to embarrass and defeat the United States not only in Vietnam but elsewhere in the world."

With that threat in mind, said Schandler, the chairman of the JCS, General Earle G. Wheeler, and the chiefs of staff "saw Tet as an opportunity to force the president's hand and achieve their long-sought goal of a mobilization of the reserves." To that end they "laboriously solicited an 'emergency' request for reinforcements from a supposedly beleaguered field commander."

The U.S. commander in Vietnam, General William C. Westmoreland, was led to believe that "the administration was ready to abandon the strategy of gradualism it had been pursuing and perhaps allow him the troops and authority he had long wanted in order to end the war in a reasonable timeframe."

"I envisaged a new approach to the war that would take timely advantage of the enemy's apparent weakness," said Westmoreland, "for whereas our setback on the battlefield was temporary, the situation for him as it developed . . . indicated that the enemy's setbacks were traumatic."

But General Wheeler had his own agenda. "In his report to Washington," said Schandler, "General Wheeler emphasized the gravity of the situation in South Vietnam and said nothing about a new strategy, about contingencies that would determine the level of forces required there, or about reconstituting the strategic reserve for possible use independent of Vietnam. Indeed his report contained a very somber and pessimistic picture of the South Vietnamese government and army."

"Wheeler's report had really ominous overtones to it," Clark Clifford told Schandler. "It seemed to me he was saying that the whole situation was a precarious one, and we had to have additional troops. I thought (and everyone did) that he was saying he needed 206,000 additional troops in Vietnam. Whatever the reasons, he made a case for 206,000 more men. He came back [from a February 1968 visit to Saigon] with a story that was frightening. We didn't know if we would get hit again, many South Vietnamese units had disappeared, [and] the place might fall apart politically."

Westmoreland had been set up. In stressing the negative aspects of the situation in Vietnam, Schandler concluded, Wheeler "saw Tet and the reaction to it as an opportunity, perhaps the last opportunity, to convince the administration to call up the reserve forces and . . . allow some military flexibility to meet other contingencies. Vietnam was the excuse, but was not necessarily to be the major beneficiary of a [reserve] call-up."

But he was too clever by half. General Wheeler's ploy backfired badly. Instead of precipitating a reserve call-up as he had intended, his report triggered a major re-evaluation of the war. "Give me the lesser of evils," President Johnson told Clifford, his incoming Secretary of Defense. "Give me your recommendations." As Schandler pointed out, "It would become one of the most controversial episodes in recent American history."

What made it especially controversial, noted Dave Richard Palmer in his landmark 1978 work, *Summons of the Trumpet: US-Vietnam in Perspective* (Presidio), was not so much the hot debate within the administration, but the fact that "it was almost as quickly pre-empted by a press leak. A disgruntled official told

The New York Times of the military's request for 206,000 rein-forcements, although failing to mention that it was supposed to support a proposed change in operations.

"The news broke in headlines spread across three columns of the Sunday edition of 10 March 1968. For all intents and pur-poses, that story ended the debate—and killed Westmoreland's plans for a dynamic new strategy.

"Looked upon erroneously but naturally by readers as a des-perate move to avert defeat," said Dave Palmer, "news of the request for 206,000 men confirmed the suspicions of many that the result of the Tet offensive had not been depicted accurately by the president or his spokesmen. If the Communists had suffered such a grievous setback, why would we need to increase our forces by 40 percent?

"For years officials had been uttering rosy public statements; for years the war had dragged on. Just three months before, in fact, [General Westmoreland] himself had returned to America to assure the public that all was well, that the end was in sight. Now the war had exploded, and that same general was asking for still more men to wage a still wider war.

"It was too much. The public rebelled. From that moment on the majority of Americans no longer supported the president in his conduct of the fighting. In the election year of 1968 there could be no further escalation of the conflict, not if the Democ-rats hoped to retain the White House."

"We had won a major victory," says Clark Clifford in his autobiography, over his successful fight for control of the text of the presidential speech that marked the beginning of American disengagement from Vietnam. But that "victory" soon turned to ashes.

In a television address on March 31, 1968, President Johnson announced, as a bid for peace, a partial cessation of the bombing of North Vietnam. He also took himself out of the race for a second term. As Dave Palmer concludes, "the nation and its president had received a wrenching psychological defeat, had suffered a galling defeat of the very soul. That the defeat was largely self-inflicted made it no less real or crippling."

Missile Ambushes: Soviet Air Defense Aid

By Sergei Blagov

Although it is widely recognized that North Vietnam received sizable aid during the war from the former Soviet Union (USSR), the actual role of Soviet combatants and weaponry experts in building up Hanoi's air defense still remains underreported. During the Soviet era, the history of USSR military involvement in Vietnam—notably in air defense—was considered sensitive and kept secret. In the wake of the Soviet collapse, when Communist Party archives were partly opened to scholars, few researchers or journalists bothered to investigate Soviet involvement in the Vietnam War.

Historians agree that the USSR contributed weapons essential to North Vietnamese defense against air attack, including radar systems, AAA, SAMs, and MiG fighter aircraft. Without this materiel, the North Vietnamese air defense would hardly have been feasible.

Between 1965 and 1973 a total of some 22,000 Soviet military experts went to Vietnam, most of them as air defense personnel, according to the Russian Union of Vietnam War Veterans. Some Soviets were in combat, and 18 were killed in action. Soviet military personnel in North Vietnam, whose numbers averaged somewhere between 2,000 and 3,000 throughout the war, faced the tricky job of protecting the skies over North Vietnam. In Southeast Asia the United States waged the greatest air war in history. It lasted from 1961 until 1972, longer than any other air campaign. Estimates of ordnance dropped on all of Southeast Asia vary from 8 to 15 million tons. In contrast, during World War II the United States and its allies dropped less than 3 million tons of bombs on the much larger combined land masses of the European, North African and Asian theaters.

The arrival of Soviet air defense experts in 1965 marked a turning point in relations between Moscow and Hanoi. When President Lyndon Johnson ordered retaliatory airstrikes on August 5, 1964, in the wake of the Tonkin Gulf incident, it produced a somewhat muted response from the Kremlin. Even the statement of Tass, the Soviet news agency, on the Tonkin Gulf incident was delayed.

Until he was ousted in October 1964, Soviet leader Nikita Khrushchev was reluctant to get involved in Indochina, lest doing so might jeopardize the improvement in Soviet-American relations in the wake of the 1962 Cuban Missile Crisis. The Kremlin, for example, in July 1964 rejected the North Vietnamese request to open a representative office of the National Liberation Front of South Vietnam in Moscow. (It was opened in December of that year.)

With Leonid Brezhnev's emergence as the new Kremlin boss, signifying a change of Soviet policy in Indochina, Moscow became more willing to get involved. The Kremlin probably was eager to prevent Beijing from becoming North Vietnam's main partner in the Communist camp, and Hanoi cunningly capitalized on the deepening Sino-Soviet schism.

When Soviet Premier Aleksei Kosygin visited Hanoi in early 1965, the challenge of American airstrikes was discussed. The visit coincided with the Flaming Dart operations of February 1965, mounted in response to VC attacks against Pleiku and Qui

Nhon. A 19-day pause in the bombing followed to see what response the North Vietnamese would make. Not surprisingly, Hanoi made no response, as North Vietnamese leaders were looking forward to getting new anti-aircraft weapons from the USSR.

Following Kosygin's return to Moscow, the Politburo and the Central Committee of the Communist Party, the main Soviet decision-making bodies, issued directives to send military advisers and to supply SAMs to Vietnam. Paradoxically, just a few months before, in late 1964, the North Vietnamese general staff had informed the Soviet military attaché in Hanoi that there was no longer any need for Soviet military experts to stay in the country, and that they should leave without replacement by other Soviet advisers as soon as they completed their current business. It probably was a well-calculated form of blackmail—and it worked.

In April 1965 the first group of advisers, some 70 officers and the equipment of an air defense regiment, arrived from the Baku air defense region. They were selected because of the relative similarity between subtropical climates of Azerbaijan and Vietnam. The unit was supposed to establish a training center—but soon it, as well as another regiment, became involved in combat.

The Americans first detected the SAMs in April 1965. On July 24, SAMs were fired at four U.S. McDonnell F-4 Phantoms over Vietnam, shooting down three. This marked the first time American planes were attacked by SAMs.

"We were defending the skies over Hoa Binh and Son La northwestern provinces," said Alexander Krylov, who served as a radar engineer in Vietnam from September 1966 to September 1967. "Our batteries were supposed to down electronic countermeasures [ECM] planes so the missile sites around Hanoi could do their job," he said.

The Soviet experts described the tactics of the first engagement as "missile ambushes." The U.S. pilots did not expect any danger and carelessly flew at medium (9,000 to 12,000 feet) altitudes, making ideal targets for the missiles. The missile crew under Colonel Fyodor Ilinykh downed 24 aircraft in the first months of the SAM deployment. In one engagement in Ninh Binh, the Thanh Hoa area Soviet crew under Colonel Ivan Proskurin downed four warplanes with three missiles.

The missile ambushes proved to be a good tactic, Krylov said. "We were moving in the nighttime only, 20 to 30 kilometers a night, led by Vietnamese sentries with white flags."

"Living conditions were appalling," Krylov noted. "Once we stayed at a buffalo barn, and then a village school seemed an excellent facility for us." The Soviets were paid a slim 800 dong a month. To make matters worse, Krylov recalled, Russian military paymasters sometimes were refused the money from the Vietnamese bank, as the tellers claimed that the transfer from Moscow had failed to come through. "Buffalo meat was a highlight of local cuisine, although we could purchase beer and cigarettes at local food stalls," he said.

The technical and tactical characteristics of the SA-2M (whose Soviet designation was SA-75M) were not advanced as compared with U.S. planes, according to retired General Mark Vorobyov, the senior Soviet military expert in charge of missile modernization from 1967 to 1969. But in 1965, the SA-2M initially proved very effective, downing a plane with only one to two missiles fired on average. The factor of surprise seemed decisive, according to Vorobyov.

In all initial engagements, the missile launchers were manned exclusively by Soviet crews. Later, step by step, the North Vietnamese started taking over the job, according to Nikolai Kolesnik, chairman of the Russian Union of Vietnam War Veterans. It was a process laden with controversy.

On August 31, 1965, the Soviet ambassador to Hanoi, Ilya

Shcherbakov, reported that on the eve of the first combat engagement some people, presumably Chinese military experts, secretly checked the Soviet missile complexes and told the North Vietnamese that the weapons were obsolete and unreliable. On July 24, a North Vietnamese commander had bluntly asked Shcherbakov if the missiles were reliable enough for combat. Furthermore, North Vietnamese personnel refrained from taking part in the initial engagements, thus sabotaging a plan they had agreed to earlier to set up joint missile crews.

Between 1965 and 1972 the Soviets supplied North Vietnam with a total of 95 missile complexes and 7,658 SAMs. Initially they were the SA-2M Dvina and later SA-2 Desna, designed by Pyotr Grushin's Fakel Design Bureau. The complexes included sophisticated radar that detected the range, altitude, speed and azimuth of American planes. But neither the Dvina nor the Desna was the most advanced Soviet design. Hanoi never got the more up-to-date Volkhov.

It is widely believed that the Soviet Union flooded North Vietnam with the latest designs of surface-to-air missiles, rockets and artillery, as well as a large array of especially sophisticated arms and combat hardware for its air defense system. Oral history and other sources suggest otherwise. The Vietnamese military reportedly complained that they were getting missiles of obsolete design. In some cases, General Vorobyov recalled that the Vietnamese even removed fresh paint from missile components and discovered old marks, suggesting that the equipment may have come from East Germany or Poland. According to Shcherbakov, the missile systems supplied by the Soviet Union were actually secondhand, produced between 1956 and 1958.

On the other hand, maintained Nikolai Kryukov, an air defense officer who was in Vietnam from 1968 to 1969, "There were no secondhand missiles in Vietnam. The claims of unreliability were groundless. The Vietnamese themselves were handling the missiles without proper care, letting them fall from the track, for instance."

North Vietnamese AAA, though growing in numbers, included many obsolete guns. During 1965 the number of anti-aircraft guns north of the DMZ rose from 1,000 to well over 2,000. However, Soviet military experts recall that the 45mm AAA gun supplied to Vietnam was a World War II–era design.

The main reason for Moscow's failure to supply North Vietnam with the newest armaments was the Kremlin's fear that the Vietnamese might leak Soviet military secrets to the Chinese. Furthermore, the missiles initially were shipped to Vietnam by rail through China, and the Soviets were reluctant to have their newest weapons vulnerable to possible inspection by the Chinese.

"We had an unconfirmed report that the Vietnamese permitted Chinese crews to handle Dvina complexes in the Haiphong area sometime in 1967," Vorobyov recalled. "The Chinese fired a number of rockets but failed to hit any U.S. aircraft, as these missiles from earlier shipments were not modernized to cope with ECM," he said. Obviously, incidents like that did nothing to improve mutual trust between the Communist allies.

Nonetheless, the North Vietnamese, with Soviet assistance, mounted what American scholar Douglas Pike called one of the most sophisticated and effective anti-aircraft defenses in the history of warfare. It was a multilevel, dynamically integrated defense that included radar warning systems, MiG fighters, SAMs, AAA of various calibers and small-arms fire. The system created a complex environment in which any aircraft tactics designed to escape one type of threat would bring a plane under threat from another layer of the system.

In order to evade radar detection and resulting AAA fire, SAMs and MiG attacks, U.S. pilots flew at low, terrain-hugging altitudes when first entering North Vietnamese airspace. Shortly before reaching the target, they would pop up to identify it visually and then dive on it in their bombing runs. AAA guns were most effective weapons in bringing down American aircraft. Their presence forced U.S. aircraft to fly above AAA range, but that brought the planes within the range of the SAMs.

The Soviets were not exclusively responsible for building up the North Vietnamese air defense. Other combatants from the Communist bloc were in North Vietnam, including Chinese and North Korean AAA personnel. "On one occasion our missile site was protected by North Korean AAA gunners, but I never heard about North Korean pilots," Kolesnik recalled.

From the mid-1960s, the North Vietnamese air force—which received Soviet advisers and Soviet-supplied MiG-15s, MiG-17s, and after December 1965, the more modern MiG-21s—posed a constant threat. The Soviet air force presence in Indochina commenced in 1961, when roughly 100 pilots started to fly personnel and supplies from North Vietnam into northeastern Laos in an ironic replication of Air America's covert operations.

According to the estimates of the Soviet Embassy in Hanoi, as of January 1, 1968, the total value of Soviet assistance since 1963 was in excess of 1.8 billion rubles, with military supplies accounting for 60 percent of the total. Between 1953 and 1991, the USSR supplied North Vietnam, and later the unified Vietnam, with 2,000 tanks, 1,700 armored vehicles, 7,000 artillery pieces and mortars, 5,000 anti-aircraft guns, 158 SAM complexes, 700 warplanes, 120 helicopters and more than 100 naval vessels.

Despite the importance of Soviet arms shipments to Hanoi, bilateral military ties were not going very well at that point. The USSR Defense Ministry and the embassy in Hanoi repeatedly informed Moscow about "the Vietnamese friends' insincere attitude" toward the Soviet Union, the Soviet people and the Defense Ministry. They documented North Vietnamese reports belittling the role and importance of Soviet military assistance and discrediting the performance of Soviet arms and military hardware. They also reported that the North Vietnamese had prevented Soviet military experts from inspecting captured U.S. military hardware and showed suspicion toward Soviet military representatives. But later, when the Vietnamese realized the need to modernize their missile systems to counter the improving ECM and anti-missile capabilities of American warplanes, the Soviets got limited access to the U.S. equipment.

The Soviet experts also complained to Moscow about violations of storage rules for Soviet military hardware, the wasteful use of missiles and ammunition, and the failure to heed the experts' advice on the use of military hardware. Vorobyov recalled that a Vietnamese regimental commander in the Haiphong area once complained to him that Soviet missiles malfunctioned. "Hey, wait a minute. When did you perform the last routine technical checkup?" Vorobyov asked. It turned out that the regimental commander, a former political commissar, had simply ignored the maintenance rules. Water was found in the missile fuel tanks.

Furthermore, the Vietnamese stubbornly tried to employ missiles against targets such as the Lockheed SR-71 reconnaissance aircraft, which simply could not be hit by that type of missile. "We told them that they could not hit an SR-71, but they continued to fire at these aircraft, just wasting missiles," Vorobyov recalled. The last Vietnamese attempt to down an SR-71 took place on January 27, 1969.

All these frictions were well-kept secrets, however, and did not prevent Hanoi from making incessant requests for more arms supplies. The initial deadly effectiveness of the missile ambushes was augmented by the fact that political constraints effectively prevented a concentrated use of U.S. air power over the North. Certain areas, chiefly around the populous centers of Hanoi and Haiphong, as well as a buffer zone near the Chinese border, were officially termed "sanctuaries" into which no raids could be mounted. Targets were carefully controlled, often by the White House itself, and selected elements of the North Vietnamese war effort, including port facilities and initially even air defense systems, were off-limits.

The Vietnamese also raised camouflage and concealment to an art. SAMs were moved around, and some sites were equipped with dummy missiles. "It was our idea to set up dummy sites and they were quite good," said Alexander Krylov. "There were even kegs full of sand, and small bombs were detonated there to imitate launches, precisely at the same time as actual launch," he said. "Even some 300 to 400 meters off the site we wore steel helmets, as metal fragments were pouring like rain."

"We were moved . . . during the night, and we rarely knew where we were in northern Vietnam," Kolesnik recalled. "We never faced the task of preparing positions. The Vietnamese were doing the job, camouflaging the sites with banana leaves."

The Vietnamese, however, did come up with some unorthodox air defense tactics. The port authorities in Haiphong reportedly delayed the unloading of Soviet vessels, evidently believing that the longer they held the large-tonnage ships flying the Soviet flag in the port and its vicinity, the less risk of damage Haiphong would run from U.S. bombing raids. Moreover, they usually placed those Soviet vessels in close proximity to the most dangerous areas (e.g., near anti-aircraft guns), in hopes of ensuring their own safety in case of air raid. During air raids, Vietnamese military boats fired at the Americans from behind Soviet vessels, using them as shields.

By the end of 1965, a total of 56 SAM sites had been reported by American pilots. "There were only 16 combat missile positions then, and the rest were dummy sites," Kolesnik recalled. A policy of rapid site displacement and dummy construction by the North Vietnamese posed problems to American pilots, who never knew exactly when to expect a SAM attack. The employment of missile ambush tactics against the Americans proved effective in the first stages of their air war against the North. By the end of 1966 the Americans had lost 455 aircraft to the various defense systems north of the DMZ.

Attack or threatened attack by MiGs and SAMs often forced U.S. pilots to abort their missions. Often U.S. pilots responded to the presence of SAMs by simply not attacking certain areas. "Of course, American pilots were afraid of our missiles, and they often jettisoned their ordnance up to 30 kilometers away from the designated target," Kolesnik said.

"The locals were furious with the U.S. pilots. But they also believed the pilots carried cash and gold. Thus the locals were keen to kill U.S. pilots to loot their belongings, while the authorities were eager to capture them alive," Krylov said.

The Americans responded with tactical and then technical countermeasures. In order to counter the SAMs, U.S. aircraft equipped with ECM devices flew in formation with other planes. This provided a measure of security against the SAMs but reduced the planes' maneuverability and made them more vulnerable to attacks by MiGs. When a SAM was actually coming at them, American pilots performed a tight turning dive to outmaneuver the missile. But this tactic had the undesirable effect of bringing them down again into the range of AAA. Nevertheless, the results were clear: By mid-1966 the ratio of downed planes to missiles fired dropped to 4-to-6.

Missile effectiveness dropped further because of U.S. attacks with anti-radiation missiles that homed in on the radar signals. "Noticing the launch of anti-radiation missiles, we just turned our radars off, which impaired the accuracy of U.S. missiles and protected our crews against attack," Kolesnik recalled.

Still, with the aggressive use of ECM, SAM effectiveness plummeted further to a 1-to-10 ratio by the end of 1967. The North Vietnamese complained to the Soviets that efficiency was dropping because the missiles were old and unreliable. "I was constantly telling them that it was caused by ECM," Vorobyov recalled.

The Soviet and Vietnamese response was twofold: changed SAM tactics and modernized missile complexes. The tactical response, developed by the Soviet experts and Vietnamese officers, included using a false radio launch signal. This deceived U.S. pilots into performing the tight turning dive to outmaneuver the nonexistent missile, which again brought them down into AAA range.

To counter the anti-radiation missiles, the missile crews turned their radars on and off or did not activate the SAM terminal guidance radar until some 10 seconds before launch. That impaired accuracy, but it protected the missile crews against anti-radiation missile attack and denied warning to the U.S. pilots. To counter American ECM, the crews fired SAMs in barrages when aircraft were close to the target area. In 1967 the NVA added optical tracking devices that did not depend on electronics.

Soviet military leadership saw the Vietnam War as an opportunity for combat-testing Soviet military hardware. Those systems were being improved constantly, taking into account the capabilities of the American warplanes. The Soviets also had a chance to obtain data on up-to-date U.S. weaponry by inspecting the captured equipment.

"As an expert, I was not interested in aircraft hardware, only in ECM devices," Vorobyov recalled. "These devices never survived crashes, and the Vietnamese gave us a limited access to data obtained from POWs, though we never met U.S. pilots," he said. According to Vorobyov, on December 22, 1967, the NVA deputy chief of staff in charge of air defense, Phung The Tai, told them about the interrogation of POWs. Captured pilots were "asked hard questions" about ECM devices, notably their frequencies. The "simple pilots" turned out not to be well versed in ECM specifications.

In 1967 the Soviets sent a permanent mission of researchers and designers to analyze SAM employment and suggest design changes. That December, an experiment was carried out under combat conditions as Soviet experts sat in an SA-2M command post. They were not firing missiles, but just analyzing frequencies of the ECM. As a result, they designed a new device that enabled a missile to home in on electronic countermeasures signals. The Soviets made six significant changes in the SAM system, later used in the next generations of the complex SA-2 Desna and SA-2M Volkhov.

Following the 1968 Tet Offensive, President Johnson on November 1 ordered a halt to all air, naval and artillery bombardment of North Vietnam. When President Nixon suspended the Paris peace talks on May 8, 1972, and authorized a renewed air offensive known as Operation Linebacker, the U.S. Air Force and Navy were permitted for the first time to mine Haiphong and other North Vietnamese ports. The North Vietnamese walked out of the Paris talks on December 13, and Nixon, in an effort to force them back to the conference table, initiated a further series of concentrated air attacks. The Linebacker II operation spanned an 11-day period, from December 18 to 29, 1972. For the first time Boeing B-52s were permitted to strike the Hanoi-Haiphong area. The process was costly, however. On January 15, 1973, the bombing of North Vietnam was stopped, and eight days later a cease-fire agreement was signed in Paris.

"Soviet missile crews contributed greatly to successful defense against the Christmas bombings in December 1972," said retired General Anatoly Khyupenen, former chief Soviet military adviser in Vietnam. During this battle, known in Vietnam as an "aerial Dien Bien Phu," the Vietnamese claim to have downed 81 aircraft, including 34 B-52s. Most of the B-52s were shot down by missiles.

According to Colonel Le Van Tri, commander of the North

Vietnamese air defense forces, the modernization of the SAM complexes proved timely. In 1972 the success ratio rose to 1-to-4.9. The Vietnamese fired 2,059 missiles to hit 421 targets. The statements of Le Van Tri and his deputy, Colonel Nguyen Van Hien, were recorded by Vorobyov on February 7, 1973, during a bilateral conference on missile employment in North Vietnamese air defenses.

Between July 1965 and January 1973, a total of 6,806 missiles were fired, were destroyed by U.S. pilots, or simply broke down according to Vorobyov's records. By January 1973, North Vietnam still had 39 operational SA-2M sites. The rest had been destroyed in combat or had become nonoperational through poor maintenance. General Vo Nguyen Giap, when meeting with Soviet experts at the February 7 conferece, told them that the Paris agreement could not have been signed without "Hanoi's victory of anti-aircraft missile batteries. It was a political victory."

The actual role of Soviet military anti-aircraft personnel has been virtually ignored by historians. Evidence suggests, however, that the Soviet military involvement in Vietnam was often a story of rather thorny relations with the "Vietnamese friends," despite mutual pronouncements of combat fraternity. Those uneasy relations, with the background of growing Sino-Soviet rivalry, were complicated further by the constant need to improve the efficiency of Soviet-made missile complexes to face American anti-missile measures. Even in their reliance on Soviet experts in building up their air defense—an issue of vital importance for North Vietnam during the war—the Vietnamese seemed to insist upon being, as Edward Lansdale once noted, different and unpredictable.

PART THREE
THE ROAD TO DISENGAGEMENT

Massacre at My Lai

A first-person account of the investigation by
Colonel William Wilson, U.S. Army (ret.)

I was to hear stories from such a wide variety of people that it became impossible for me to disbelieve that something rather dark and bloody did indeed occur sometime in March 1968 in a village called 'Pinkville' in the Republic of Vietnam."

These words were from the letter that former combat infantryman Ron Ridenhour sent to the president, 23 members of Congress, the secretaries of state, defense and Army, and the chairman of the Joint Chiefs in March 1969. "One morning in the latter part of March," Ridenhour continued, "Task Force Barker moved out from its firebase headed for 'Pinkville.' Its mission: to destroy the trouble spot and all of its inhabitants . . . the other two companies that made up the task force cordoned off the village so that 'Charlie Company' could move through to destroy the structures and kill the inhabitants . . . one of the companies [sic] officers, 2nd Lieutenant Kally [Calley], rounded up several groups of villagers (each group consisting of a minimum of twenty persons of both sexes and all ages) . . . Calley then machine-gunned each group. It was so bad that one of the men in the squad shot himself in the foot in order to be medivaced out of the area so he would not have to participate in the slaughter . . ."

Ridenhour's letter was forwarded by then Army Chief of Staff General William C. Westmoreland to the Army inspector general's (IG) office with orders to investigate. I saw it in the "Read File" the morning it arrived, and read it in shocked disbelief, disgust and anger. One description was particularly sickening as Ridenhour described the death of a 3- or 4-year-old child: "clutching his wounded arm while blood trickled between his fingers. . . . He just stood there with big eyes, staring around like he didn't understand. . . . Then the captain's RTO [radio-telephone operator] put a burst of 16 [M-16] fire into him."

I read the letter four times and picked up the phone for an appointment with Major General William Enemark, the inspector general.

At 10 A.M., I entered General Enemark's office, saluted and explained that I had asked to see him regarding the letter from Ridenhour. The general observed that it painted a sordid picture of our forces and added that General Westmoreland and several congressmen were very upset. I requested assignment to the case, pointing out that I was the only investigator he had with infantry combat experience. In my time I'd seen civilians killed, but those deaths had been accidental, and I thought it was important to have someone who was confident that he could separate atrocities from wartime incidents requiring lethal force. If the Pinkville incident were true, it was coldblooded murder.

General Enemark cautioned me that if he gave me the job, I must keep an open mind, and to remember that everything in that letter was hearsay. He wanted me to move fast; if the information leaked before we got the facts, "it will do a lot of damage to any subsequent disciplinary actions."

The general approved my request in writing with a letter of instructions that included a requirement to keep the investigation and the disclosures confidential until I completed the case and apprised him of my conclusions. I conferred with my division

MASSACRE AT MY LAI

chief and he assigned a court reporter named Smitty for the case. Smitty was near retirement, a cheerful Washington, D.C. local, and pretty good company—which was very good luck because it turned out that we would spend the next three months living in motels, listening to degrading, inhuman and obscene testimony.

I gave the IG administrator a requirement to get me a roster of C Company, 1st Battalion, 20th Infantry Regiment (1/20), the company Ridenhour described, as it existed on March 16, 1968, and to request Army locator files that would provide the present addresses of the men on the roster. I called Army Map Service and arranged for topographic maps of the Quang Ngai area, and then went to my desk to think.

Ridenhour's letter had mentioned seven names. The information in the letter had originated with four of these men. The first step was to interrogate Ridenhour; then find the four men who had provided the information. The letter indicated Ridenhour was in Phoenix, Arizona. I needed details and addresses; perhaps he would know the location of his four buddies. I kept repeating to myself: this is not a criminal investigation, there is no cross-examination, you are not trying to convict anyone, only determine the facts.

A study of available maps of the provincial divisions of Vietnam was hastily completed. Quang Ngai province was located in the northern part of the II Corps Tactical Zone. My Lai was a hamlet of Son My village, approximately nine kilometers northeast of Quang Ngai, a city on the South China Sea. At that time, Son My village was composed of four hamlets. My Lai 4, the objective area for my investigation, was, in fact, a subhamlet in the Tu Cung hamlet. The name "Pinkville," used by the troops, pertained to subhamlet My Lai 1 in My Lai hamlet. It was called "Pinkville" because of the reddish-pink color by which it was shown on the topographic map, indicating its population density. The troops erroneously used the term for most of the subhamlets in the area. Enemy strength in Quang Ngai province during this period was estimated between 10,000 and 20,000, of which 2,000 to 4,000 were regular forces, 3,000 to 5,000 were guerrillas and 5,000 were assigned to administrative units.

There was no problem locating Ridenhour through directory assistance in Phoenix. I spoke to him and he knew the location of the men who had described this atrocity: Charles Gruver was in Oklahoma City; Michael Terry was in Orem, Utah; William Doherty was at Fort Hood, Texas, and Michael Bernhardt was at Fort Dix, New Jersey. Army records indicated that Sergeant Larry La Croix was at Fort Carson, Colorado. I called for appointments; all were available to provide testimony. The witnesses were told they would be contacted on my arrival. Military witnesses can be ordered to appear before an IG investigator, but civilians may or may not cooperate. I was pleased that these men were eager to assist.

Ridenhour's letter was dissected to extract the specific allegations and establish the routine questions with which to begin the interrogations. I decided to truthfully state that the investigation was ordered by General Westmoreland because these men knew, served under, and had confidence in this officer. I also decided to wear full uniform and decorations to let them know immediately that they were talking to a combat soldier. Several of the men said that if I were not wearing the Purple Heart and Combat Infantry Badge, the information they gave me might be different because they would feel as if I wouldn't understand. Each witness was told not to disclose or discuss his interrogation because of the damage it would do to any subsequent legal actions.

Ridenhour's letter was dated March 29, 1969 (one year and 13 days after the My Lai assault). General Westmoreland's office acknowledged receipt to Ridenhour on April 12, stating an investigation was underway. General Westmoreland officially turned the case over to the inspector general on April 23. I interviewed

Ridenhour in Phoenix on the 29th of April, exactly one month after the date of his letter. Considering mail time, distance, scheduling and interoffice routing, the matter was being handled with dispatch, even if, unfortunately, I was starting 13 months after the event.

My interrogation of Ridenhour was conducted in the evening in a downtown-Phoenix hotel. The interview lasted nearly two hours and was a careful review of his letter to assure that I had covered all the allegations. He was most convincing but, at this point and time, all allegations were hearsay.

Michael Terry was questioned on May 1 in Orem, Utah. I quoted his statement in Ridenhour's letter: "Most of the people they came to were already dead.... The platoon left nothing alive, neither livestock or people ... close to us was a group of Vietnamese in a heap and some of them were moaning. Calley [2nd Lt. William L. Calley, Jr.] had been through before us and all of them had been shot but many weren't dead ... it was obvious they weren't going to get any medical attention ... I guess we sort of finished them off." Terry acknowledged that this was the information he gave to Ridenhour. I had no doubt Terry had tried to put the dying Vietnamese out of their misery.

We left Orem for Fort Carson, Colorado, where Sergeant Lawrence La Croix was interviewed on May 2. Ridenhour had talked to him in June 1968 at the USO in Chu Lai. I referenced Ridenhour's letter relating Sergeant La Croix's description of the killings. He had been a witness to Calley's gunning down at least three separate groups of villagers: "The people in the groups were men, women and children of all ages. As soon as he felt the group was big enough Calley ordered an M-60 (machine-gun) set up and the people killed.... When the first group was put together, Calley ordered Pfc Torrez ... to open fire on the villagers.... This Torrez did but before everyone in the group was down he ceased fire and refused to fire again ... Lieutenant Calley took over the

M-60 and finished shooting the remaining villagers ... Calley didn't bother to order anyone to take the machine-gun when the other two groups of villagers were formed. He simply manned it himself and shot down all villagers in both groups."

Sergeant La Croix acknowledged this statement was correct and also testified that at some point during that morning someone in a helicopter had complained over the radio: "From up here it looks like a blood bath. What the hell are you doing down there?" I had to find this man—he would be a key witness.

Smitty and I caught an early flight for Oklahoma City and interrogated Charles Gruver on May 3. Obviously, the contacts were moving as planned. I called the Washington office and told them to order Captain Thomas Willingham, stationed at Fort Meade, and Sergeant Michael Bernhardt, stationed at Fort Dix, to report to me on May 8 at the IG's office in Washington.

Gruver acknowledged seeing the 3-year-old wounded boy machine-gunned by the RTO. He stated that the information he gave Ridenhour concerning Calley was hearsay but that he trusted the people who told him.

Our flight from Oklahoma City was late, so I did not question Spc. 4 William Doherty at Fort Hood until May 5. Doherty had been with Michael Terry when they entered My Lai 4, after the initial assault. He confirmed that nearly every living thing in the village had been shot—cows, chickens, dogs, babies, and unarmed women.

Sergeant Bernhardt was interrogated on the 8th. By that time I had the names of 60 to 70 percent of the men from C Company. Again, I quoted Ridenhour's letter: "Bernie had absolutely refused to take part in the massacre ... he thought it was rather strange that the officers of the company had not made an issue of it."

Bernhardt acknowledged this as being true. He had entered the village after the action had started because Captain Medina had sent him to the landing zone to check a booby trap. He summarized the day: "We met no resistance and I only saw three captured weapons. We had no casualties. It was just like any other Vietnamese village—old papasans, women and kids. As a matter of fact, I don't remember seeing one military-age male in the entire place, dead or alive."

He testified that he saw Charlie Company doing strange things. They were going into hooches and shooting them up. They were gathering people in groups and shooting them. "It was point-blank murder and I was standing there watching it."

There was a key witness in Georgia—Captain Ernest Medina, the C Company commander. These interrogations took place on May 12 and 13 at Fort Benning. Medina was attending the Infantry Advanced Officers School, a nine-month course. I asked him about the allegation that he had shot a woman lying on the ground. He admitted that he had shot a body that he assumed was dead but when he turned to walk away he thought he observed, from the corner of his eye, the woman's hand moving under her body. He fired because he thought she may have been preparing to throw a grenade.

Colonel Oran K. Henderson was ordered to report to the IG's office on May 26 from U.S. Army Headquarters in Hawaii. I asked him to portray on my map the Son My operation as he remembered it. He denied being told anything about his troops wantonly killing large groups of civilians. He denied a machine-gun confrontation between chief Warrant Officer 2nd Class Hugh C. Thompson, Jr., and Calley. He did remember Thompson telling him that his soldiers in the operation on the 16th were "like a bunch of wild men and were wildly shooting throughout the area." Henderson said, "I recall, I asked Thompson if he knew the results of the units he supported." Henderson informed Thompson that 20 civilians had been killed and 120 Viet Cong (VC). Thompson replied that the bodies he saw on the ground were not VC but old men, old women and children. Henderson said, "When he was talking to me he was in tears."

Arrangements were made for Lieutenant Calley to be returned to the United States from Vietnam and report to the IG's office on June 9.

Thompson was given special orders to report to me June 11 from Fort Rucker, Alabama. I kept him in Washington three days while he related how he'd tried to accomplish on the spot what Ridenhour did a year later. He was not successful—I do not think any honest eyewitness could have been—but he made extraordinary efforts. He said that as he flew over the hamlet in his helicopter, he began seeing wounded and dead Vietnamese civilians everywhere, with no sign of an enemy force. He decided to mark the locations of wounded civilians with smoke so the GIs could start treating them. "The first one I marked was a girl that was wounded," Thompson testified, "and they came over to her, put their weapon on automatic and let her have it."

Thompson landed his helicopter near a drainage ditch filled with corpses. Nearby he saw several terrified women and children cowering in a bunker. An American lieutenant and some troops were approaching. Thompson asked the officer to help get the women and children out. "The only way you'll get them out," said the lieutenant, "is with a hand grenade." Thompson returned to the helicopter and told his gunners to fire on the Americans if they got any closer. Then he evacuated the Vietnamese.

This pilot was not assigned to C Company; he was an outsider. I needed him to identify Calley—if Calley was the man who was seen performing these acts. I arranged for a lineup.

On June 13, Thompson picked out Calley from a lineup as the officer at the drainage ditch in May Lai 4. Thompson also reported seeing a captain shoot a woman at close range while she lay on the ground. Without identifying Medina, I repeated his testimony regarding the movement of the woman's hand. Thompson responded, "Nothing is impossible." Thompson testified that he spent 20 to 30 minutes the following day telling Colonel Henderson his account of the massacre at My Lai 4.

Thompson estimated the number of bodies in the ditch to be between 75 and 100. I found Thompson immensely impressive; he was the only hero of that awful day, and his testimony was damning. The trick would be to corroborate it.

Roy L.A. Wood was interrogated in Richmond, Virginia., on June 11. He was a rifleman in Calley's platoon. He stated: "Medina didn't like Calley who was always doing things wrong. I wonder how he got through Officer Candidate School. He couldn't read no darn map and a compass would confuse his ass."

I found Chief Warrant Officer 2nd Class Dan R. Mullians at Fort Walters, Texas, and cut special orders for him to report to me in Washington on June 18. He was flying a helicopter in support of C Company that morning. He heard no shooting and didn't receive any fire. He noticed the numerous bodies scattered in and around the village, in particular the ditch with bodies piled 5-to-6-feet deep. He stated that Thompson was enraged and said over the radio that if he saw the ground troops kill one more woman or child he would start shooting (the ground troops) himself.

Private First Class Lawrence M. Colburn, Thompson's door gunner, was brought to Washington from Fort Hood on June 19. He also corroborated Thompson's testimony. I showed him a number of photographs and he picked out Medina and Calley as the officers involved in the shootings. He had gotten out of the aircraft and walked toward the ditch with the crew chief.

The crew chief had crawled into the ditch. He was knee deep in people and blood. They had found a young child alive, buried under the bodies. "He was still holding onto his mother. But she was dead."

The boy, clinging desperately, had been pried loose. Thompson later testified, "I don't think he was even wounded at all, just down there among all the other bodies, and he was terrified." Thompson and his men flew the baby to safety.

Major Glen D. Gibson, Thompson's company commander, was located at Sixth U.S. Army Headquarters and was ordered to report to Washington on June 25. There was a conflict between his and Colonel Henderson's testimony. Henderson testified that sometime that evening he had asked Major Gibson, commander of Thompson's aviation company, to look into this matter of his gunships firing and also whether they had observed "any of my soldiers shooting at civilians." Henderson stated he told Gibson of the charges made by Thompson and had asked for a report from "each of the pilots, within 24 hours." Henderson further stated that Gibson had reported "none of them had heard or seen any indiscriminate shooting, nor had they participated in any. He got a complete negative response from his people." On this matter Gibson persistently denied having any conversations with Henderson about My Lai 4.

Ronald D. Grzesik was a fire-team leader in Calley's platoon. He was interrogated June 26 in Springfield, Massachusetts. Prior to the attack on My Lai 4, he heard Medina tell the men "to go in and destroy the village; to make it uninhabitable," but did not recall an order to destroy the inhabitants. For Grzesik, My Lai 4 was the end of a vicious circle that had begun months earlier. "It was like going from one step to another worse one," he said. "First you'd stop the people, question them and let them go. Second, you'd stop the people, beat up an old man, and let them go. Third, you'd stop the people, beat up an old man and then shoot him. Fourth, you'd go in and wipe out a village."

While Grzesik was closing into the village with his team, he was told to go to Calley. He did so, but when Calley ordered him to go to the ditch and "finish off the people," Grzesik refused. "I really believe he expected me to do it," Grzesik said with amazement. Calley asked him again and Grzesik again refused. Calley then angrily ordered him to take his men and burn the village.

About three quarters of the way through My Lai 4, he suddenly saw a soldier named Paul E. Meadlo. Meadlo was crouched, head in his hands, sobbing like a bewildered child. "I sat down and asked him what had happened," recalled Grzesik, who had felt responsible because he was the team leader. Meadlo told him that Calley had made him shoot people.

I was struck by the image of this man Meadlo, crying by the bodies of the dead; he was possibly the crucial witness I needed to present the truth of My Lai. Further interrogation disclosed that Meadlo had lost his foot by a land mine the following day. While being loaded on the evacuation helicopter he allegedly shook his fist at Calley and screamed, "God will punish you for what you made me do!" He was evacuated and discharged from the service. He would remember the day as none of the others would because he would not be influenced by the "barrack room" discussions that followed the operation.

I interviewed Denis R. Vasquez (formally captain) on July 1 in Williamsburg, Virginia. He was the task force's artillery liaison officer and testified that his forward observer reported 69 Viet Cong killed by artillery. To the experienced soldier, this was a high body count for a short three-to-five-minute artillery barrage—I couldn't accept it.

The evening of July 16 in a motel in Terre Haute, Indiana, is a time I would like to block forever from my memory. Meadlo, his right foot and self-respect gone, came to the motel determined to relieve his conscience and describe the horrors of My Lai. He stated that Calley left him and a few others with the responsibility of guarding a group of about 80 people who had been taken from their homes and herded together. He repeated Calley's instructions. "You know what I want to do with them," Calley said and walked off. Ten minutes later he returned and asked,

"Haven't you got rid of them yet? I want them dead. Waste them!" After this statement, Meadlo raised his eyes to the ceiling of the room and began to cry. His body literally shook with sobs as he continued. "We stood about 10 to 15 feet away from them and then he started shooting. Then he told me to start shooting them. I used more than a whole clip—used four or five clips."

I was shocked. I stopped him and told him to wait outside the room with Smitty. I called Washington and contacted Colonel Carney (the IG military attorney) at home. I told him a witness had confessed to murder and I had not warned him of his rights. My instructions were to give him his warnings and see if he would repeat the confession. After he was warned that anything he said could be held against him in a court of law, he said, "I don't care." He repeated his confession.

There was no doubt in my mind that a massacre had been committed at My Lai 4. I dejectedly returned to Washington on July 17, two and a half months after I interviewed Ridenhour. Something in me died when I watched Meadlo regress to the revulsion of the massacre at My Lai on March 16, 1968. I had prayed to God that this thing was fiction. It was fact.

I returned to Washington to report my findings. The report was to go to the chief of staff, the president and Lieutenant General William R. Peers. On August 19, I flew to Fort Benning to brief the legal officers there about the case. Under army regulations, the commanding officer of Fort Benning and his legal staff were the ultimate authority for reviewing the evidence and filing charges against Calley.

On November 26, 1969, the Secretary of the Army and the chief of staff issued a joint memorandum directing General Peers to explore the nature and scope of the original Army investigations of what occurred on March 16, 1968, in Son My village. I was ordered to participate in this inquiry; I stated, to no avail, that four months of this nightmare was enough. It was decided early that in order to determine the extent of the coverup, the investigation must determine what had occurred in the entire Son My area on March 16 and 17, 1968. The Peers' inquiry discovered that an equally vicious massacre was conducted by a second company (B Company) or Task Force Barker on the same day. Peers reported that a part of the crimes visited on the inhabitants of Son My village included individual and group acts of murder, rape, sodomy, maiming, assault on non-combatants and the mistreatment and killing of detainees. Eventually, some two-dozen officers and men were charged with murder or assault with intent to commit murder at My Lai 4. Only one was convicted: Calley.

In the words of General Peers, "The failure to bring justice to those who inflicted the atrocity casts grave doubts upon the efficacy of our justice system."

A Newsman Goes to War

As told by Jim Bennett to Larry Engelmann

I love der Boom Boom." That was Pulitzer Prize–winning Associated Press photographer Horst Fass' reason why he had spent so many years covering the war in Vietnam. "And that's what the newsmen did want, the blood and the guts," said Jim Bennett, who covered the war in Indochina longer than any other television news correspondent.

No stranger to "blood and guts," Bennett joined the Navy in 1943 and was assigned to USS *Renshaw* before that destroyer was torpedoed by a Japanese submarine in the South China Sea in 1945. Eighteen of his shipmates were killed in the attack, but the captain and the surviving crew members managed to keep afloat and make it back to port.

After the war and a short stint at the University of Rochester on the GI Bill, Bennett began his career as a newsman. For the next 16 years he moved from paper to paper, ending his career as a print journalist with the Los Angeles *Herald Examiner.* In 1965 the chance came to work in television news, and he joined the news staff at KNBC in Los Angeles. Two years later, he was posted to NBC's Saigon bureau for a six-month tour. His Indochina odyssey had begun, first with NBC News in Vietnam and then with ABC News in Vietnam and Cambodia.

"There were some crazy things that were happening," said Bennett, now retired, of that initial six-month tour. "I guess Vietnam had a tendency to make boys out of men and men out of boys in a lot of ways. A lot of correspondents, young reporters who went, couldn't hack it and terminated their tours very early." Bennett believed that many correspondents went for the wrong reasons. "I don't think they necessarily went because the story attracted them as much as they saw an easy way to gain fame and fortune," he said. "And when it turned out you had to do something to gain the fame and fortune, to actually cover the damned war, that's when a lot of them became discouraged and bailed out."

After completing his initial tour, Bennett was still hungry for more. Having seen the country and the war, he wanted to follow through, to follow up and report the progress of the American effort in Vietnam. Within a few weeks of returning to the States, he was agitating for another assignment in Vietnam.

"There probably was a lot more innocence at the time among most of us who were there," he remembered. "It hadn't yet dawned on us that this might be a losing proposition. More and more there was the escalation and we were still buying into 'the light at the end of the tunnel.' There was still a real air of optimism, I think, on just about everybody's part."

Bennett talked to some of the print journalists who were openly skeptical about the war. The pencil press was beginning to question the explanations for the war's escalation. But Bennett didn't necessarily see things that way during his own first tour: "I came away with a feeling of dissatisfaction that it was a job undone. I hadn't had enough. I hadn't seen enough to come to any other definitive conclusion."

He had been back in California only six months in 1968 when Bob Mulholland, West Coast director of news for NBC, came to Bennett and asked if he would like to go back to Vietnam. He arrived in the spring of 1968, shortly after the Tet Offensive launched by the North Vietnamese Army and Viet Cong. Bennett discovered that in the short time he had been back in the United States the situation in Vietnam had changed in subtle ways. The behavior of the newsmen was different.

"There was a hurry to get someplace—everybody was rushing around frantically trying to make a name for himself because they didn't think it was going to last much longer," he said. "Then they began to see that the tunnel was a hell of a lot longer, and you couldn't see any light at the end of it anyway." He found more cynicism among the newsmen than he had noticed earlier.

Bennett didn't share that cynicism at first. "I couldn't yet come to grips with the fact that this tremendously powerful military machine could not take the measure of this country, this little country," he recalled. "Never mind the dedication on the part of the North Vietnamese and Viet Cong. I didn't quite understand it at that point. It took me a little bit of time to come to grips with that. Maybe that does hark back to my own time in World War II and my belief that military machines are designed to win wars—not lose them. I didn't understand the extent of the politicizing of the war back here in the States. I didn't understand how far that had gone either.

"We had everything in place. There wasn't any reason why the military establishment—built up to almost 500,000 men with all of the sophisticated weaponry we had and all of this great technology—didn't literally wipe out the enemy. But the military was being contained; it couldn't fight beyond a certain limit; it couldn't use all its great technical ability. A couple of bombs in the Red River delta in North Vietnam would have settled the whole thing in a great hurry. But I didn't understand what the constraints were, why we couldn't drop our smart bombs or go beyond the 17th parallel."

Bennett went up to I Corps, near the Demilitarized Zone (DMZ), several times. He saw firsthand that American forces were honoring the DMZ. "We were not infiltrating north—maybe some of the long-range patrols and things like that; the Green Berets may have been carrying out some clandestine affair behind the lines, but those were Special Forces events," he said. "But there was no mass movement of our troops going on. That was the DMZ, and we were honoring it. However, I remember standing just yards away, looking through the night scopes and seeing plenty of movement going on at that time by the North Vietnamese. They used the DMZ as an infiltration route. I thought at the time: 'Why should we honor this if they're not honoring it?' When you're in a pissing contest with a skunk, don't bring Chanel No. 5 to the fight. When you've got the best tools available, it's foolish to try to limit the war. You can't have a limited war. You give me a limited bullet, and I'll give you a limited war."

Bennett said that in I Corps he found "these great young men who were still willing to give their best and to lay it on the line, but they had nothing to back it up. Their country wasn't morally reinforcing them. They were fighting a war without being given any reasons for it. It was a war fought in name only. They understood, probably a lot earlier than some of the people in the news business, that they were being shackled. I looked at them and understood that here they are in Vietnam and willing to put their lives on the line, and not quite understanding why. What does this mean in the overall context of things, what does it mean to us? They didn't understand things like 'domino theory.' They were just told they were fighting communism. That's not enough reason. Some of them were over there thinking, 'What the hell am I doing here? I'm not mad at these people, it's not my country.' And I think that's when things began to come apart. That's when the disillusionment really began to set in.

"Wars are fought to be won, not lost. So when the politicians began to shackle and hinder this machine that we had put together to win the war, put restrictions on it so that it couldn't be won, then I began to have a very different view of things—maybe my anti-war feelings began to come out at that point. I remember thinking, 'I'm going to burn my son's draft card before I'll let him get involved in this kind of stupidity. I'm not going to let him be ground up in this kind of machine.'"

Along with his own growing cynicism, Bennett found that corruption was rampant within the Vietnamese government. He didn't believe this was entirely the fault of the Americans. "Vietnam was corrupt before we got there," he said. "There was a black market with the French. Things were just as corrupt under the French as under the Americans." On the other hand, he found that Americans participated almost enthusiastically in the black market. Even the newsmen, who often were self-righteous about the corruption in their reports. "Reality dictated that we would be participants in it—particularly when our own news organization was encouraging us to use the black market when they were orienting us to go over," Bennett said. "They told us, 'You will be living off the economy, and there is a black market.' They didn't go much beyond that, but they made you aware of the fact that there was a black market and you probably could save money by participating in it. There was only one person I know who publicly pulled the plug, and that's because he got in a bind. He was an AP [The Associated Press] photographer who finally testified at some congressional committee about the media's involvement in the black market's exchange. I knew people who made a bundle, and some made a living out of it."

Bennett reported on the Laos invasion of 1971—Lam Son 719. "For the press corps, that was the worst one of all," he remembered. "It was a bad one. It was then obvious that we were spitting into the wind on Vietnamization. It was a joke. They tried to ban us from going into Laos with the Army of the Republic of Vietnam (ARVN), so it was very, very difficult to get in. You could find the odd chopper pilot who would take you in, but it was very dicey. That's where the three newsmen were lost at one time—Larry Burrows, a Time/Life photographer; Kent Potter of UPI [United Press International]; and Henri Huet of AP. That was the worst of all. I think that one operation turned me around all the way. I could see there wasn't any hope after that. I knew that we were, as I say, spitting into the wind.

"To my own credit, and I don't mean to make this sound self-serving, I did try to maintain a posture of objectivity. I'm not sure I did. I'd have to go back and see what I reported. But Lam Son 719 was a frustrating operation. The press corps was kept in this one compound, I think probably for control purposes. The Americans had a briefing every morning and afternoon. And they'd bring over the Vietnamese to brief us on their part of the operation. The Americans were strictly in support, supplying the helicopters and the logistical support for the operation.

"I remember one day, Steve Bell and I were making a dash for the border by land, the only way we could get there. We had a hell of a time. We finally got to the border of Laos and Vietnam, and that's where the road stopped. It was just impenetrable jungle from that point on. There wasn't any way of getting in. So we were really at the mercy of the chopper pilots if we wanted to get in. I think that's what happened to Larry Burrows and Kent Potter. Potter was my bunkmate, had the bunk next to me—a nice young kid, always hungry. A lot of us brought our own food, and he was always after me for something to eat. He was a growing boy, I guess, only about 22. He and Henri and Burrows stayed by the helicopter pad for days, waiting to get a ride in. When they finally did, they were shot down. I think that loss got to the rest of us. I made a lot of helicopter flights over the border and even got on the ground one time. But boy, I'll tell you, I didn't stay on the ground, no sir. I came right back out on that same helicopter. The South Vietnamese were bailing out as fast as they could, and anything that landed they were jumping on. Our American pilot—thank God I hadn't gone with a Vietnamese—said we had to go. Dozens of ARVN soldiers, hundreds of them, were barreling toward anything that landed and grabbing the runners to the extent that many helicopters couldn't even take off. One thing I think that kept me alive through all of Vietnam was I could recognize a dicey situation and get the hell out of it."

Bennett also did some reporting from Cambodia. That story was, he recalled "the blackest mark on America's record. What we did to those people! They were tossed into the maw of the war without even knowing what the hell was happening to them—all for the sole purpose of trying to protect Vietnam, no other purpose whatsoever. The whole Cambodian episode was perpetrated with an eye toward trying to pull the war in Vietnam out of the bag for political reasons. The Cambodian people were sacrificed for Vietnam, and to this day we still won't recognize it or admit it.

"Here was a nation of 7 million people that probably will never be a nation again. And I believe the U.S. was largely responsible for that. I could see it happening day by day. When American newsmen were first in Vietnam, and Prince Norodon Sihanouk was in power in Cambodia, we were restricted from going in. After the overthrow of Sihanouk, we all piled over there. By that time I had left NBC and joined ABC, and my assignment with ABC was Cambodia. That was in 1971, and while I still worked in Vietnam a lot, I actually moved my family over to Phnom Penh. They lived there for well over a year. But I would go back to Vietnam periodically. They'd reassign me back there for special events and stories and if they needed to beef up the bureau.

"I watched the tragedy of Cambodia unfold every day, and it *was* a tragedy. The Cambodians didn't understand what had happened. They thought the war was a great event. They didn't have any military establishment as such, only an 18,000-man palace guard. It was really nothing more than a palace guard for Sihanouk, ceremonial troops that would function around the country. They weren't fighters. They had no military equipment, and the U.S. wasn't giving them a hell of a lot. I remember watching them go off to war on Pepsi Cola trucks, which Richard Nixon had introduced when he was between gigs after he made his abortive attempt for the presidency and Kennedy beat him. He went around the world selling Pepsi Cola plants, and he had set up the one in Cambodia. When the war spread to Cambodia, the only troop vehicles they had were Pepsi Cola trucks.

"Then, of course, some of the vehicles, the military equipment, did start to filter in, but in very limited quantities. They were hardly given anything—and didn't know how to fight a war. They were up against the crack troops of North Vietnam who had developed this magnificent machine, the Khmer Rouge. I watched these people turn from this beautiful race of gentle, sweet-natured people into savages. They literally were. At the end they were beheading each other. On any given day, if you dared venture out of Phnom Penh you could film a horrible scene. They used to cut each other's liver out because they felt that the spirits of war lived in the liver, and if you ate the man's liver it would make you a braver person. I used to have shots of them carrying human heads by the hair down the roads. That's what this race of people had degenerated into as the war progressed.

"In Vietnam, a lot of other things had happened, too. I lost a cameraman named Terry Khoo who was killed. And the other young fellow that was with him that day—that was during the Easter Offensive in I Corps—was Sam Kai Faye. It was a strange set of circumstances. Both were Chinese. Both from Singapore.

"I had been up in Hue. The whole press corps had moved out of Da Nang and up to Hue, and we were operating out of there, going north for all of the fighting every day. Terry Khoo was one of the top cameramen in Vietnam, in the world for that matter. He had been with ABC News for years, to the extent that he was finally being transferred to Rome to get him out of Vietnam. He had done enough, and this was his last day. We had been in Hue for two weeks, and we were being replaced by another crew. There was a new correspondent, Arnie Collins, who'd just arrived in Vietnam. He'd just walked in the front door, and they put him on an airplane and slapped him up there to me in Hue. Arnie didn't have any equipment at all. He had come off the plane wearing sandals.

"The night before that, Terry and I had had a big fight. He wanted to take Sam up to the fighting next day. I said no, he was supposed to leave, to fly back to Saigon and leave the country, and I didn't want him to go. 'We're going to make this transition as easy as possible,' I told him, 'and you're going to get back to Saigon. They [the ABC brass] don't want you doing anything more.'

"Well, there was some stuff going on up north, and the following morning there was poor Arnie. I said, 'Let's go over to the black market and get you some boots. You can't walk around in shower shoes, for Christ's sake.' While I was gone, Terry and Sam and the sound man, T.H. Lee, geared up and went off. When Arnie and I finally came back, I found out they had left, but I didn't know where they had gone. A couple hours later, T.H. Lee came bursting through the door at the hotel—he said that he, Terry and Sam had gotten into a firefight, right off Highway One, north of Hue about 10 miles or so. They'd come across this gun battle and Terry, Sam and T.H. had cut across a field. Apparently, Terry thought they were going around and coming in from behind to join up with the South Vietnamese troops. The trio was walking across this terrain when out of the clear blue sky they were ambushed. T.H. said he saw Sam go down and then Terry; he hit the deck. He wasn't wounded, and he lay there for a while. T.H. said he could hear Terry moaning, but nothing from Sam. Finally T.H. described how he got up and ran and got away. That's when he came back to get me.

"We went out there, but we couldn't get to them. There was a very serious battle going on. The worst part was that the ARVN was calling in an airstrike. If there had been any opportunity to get to Terry and Sam, it ended when they called in an airstrike and blew up the whole terrain. If they had still been alive, they weren't alive after that. We didn't get to them until the following day.

"Just a few weeks before, I had gotten kind of close to Sam. I was close to Terry, too, but when Sam had first come into country, which was about six months before, I had kind of taken him under my wing. He and I had been up in Hue together before. We did a marvelous story that I believed more or less typified what was happening during that particular offensive, which was a losing proposition. On this one particular day, we were coming back, having been up to the front, so to speak, and we came across this long funeral procession. An ARVN honor guard was carrying two or three caskets, with the wailing families trailing behind. They were walking down the road and started to cut across an open field. It was a very dismal, dim, drizzly day, cold and dank, and death was in the air. It turned out these were three ARVN soldiers who had been killed in one of the recent battles. It was a Catholic ceremony, with the priest and the altar boys trailing behind in this procession. And I said: 'Let's shoot this, Sam. I think this story tells a hell of a lot.'

"Sam grabbed the hand camera, with the three lenses on the front, Bell & Howell, and I was going to wild track it with a tape recorder. I wasn't going to do any interview, so we didn't need the big sound camera. It was great sound, with the wailing and so forth going on. We followed the procession and they were going through the liturgy there at the grave site. It was a very moving scene. When they started to lower the caskets into the ground, I was standing on the opposite side from where Sam was filming. I looked up at Sam and, my God, he had his lens cap on. And, Jesus, I just came apart and began screaming at him, jerked him around and really landed on him terribly. He felt so bad.

"Well, he managed to recoup. He got his lens cap off. There was enough of the ceremony left that we did make a marvelous story. It typified what I believed was happening in Vietnam—the lost cause, the look of despair and suffering on these survivors' faces, an atmosphere so symbolic of what was happening in Vietnam in those days. It was an excellent story, one of my best.

"Sam felt so bad about it, and I just couldn't get over the fact he had his lens cap on. And then, when he went like that, I never had a chance to even say I was sorry.

"So I quit my job. I quit and moved my family to the island of Penang, off the coast of Malaysia. I put my kids in an American missionary school there. I stayed down for about three months. I just had to have time off, I guess. But I literally had quit.

"One day David Jayne, who was ABC's Far Eastern bureau chief in Hong Kong and a good friend, the one who had really gotten me over to ABC when I came to the parting of the ways with NBC, called me and asked me if I'd go back. I had managed to stay on the beach for nearly four months, but then when David called I had to go. I still hadn't seen it through.

"The Paris peace talks had just ended, and David said, 'All these years that you've covered the war, don't you want a piece of the peace, don't you want to see what it's going to be?' That did kind of attract me, I guess. American troops were leaving. The war was grinding down. It looked like maybe peace was going to come, at least the peace treaty was about to be signed after all that Paris bull that went on there. So I said I'd go back.

But you know, the peace was worse than the war. There was no peace.

"I think everyone was amazed that we were giving up on our commitment in Vietnam in 1973. As I say, the peace was really worse than the war. But in any event, they finally decided to close the Saigon bureau down entirely. Frank Mariano was moved over to Hong Kong, becoming senior correspondent. Frank was very unhappy. He wanted very badly to either be in Vietnam, which he dearly loved, or back in the States. He didn't take to the Hong Kong assignment at all. He'd had enough of the Far East unless he could be in Vietnam. They weren't about to do that, so Frank was reassigned back to the States.

"Then came 1975, and we could see that the end of the war was approaching. I was sent into Saigon to reopen the Vietnam bureau right after the ARVN collapse in the Central Highlands in March 1975. Getting in and out of Phnom Penh was getting hairier all the time. But that was the assignment I wanted the most. I wanted to spend more of my time there because I could see that the end was coming rapidly, and I knew there wasn't any hope for those people. Cambodia did something to me. I felt very acutely for those people and what we had done to them.

"I had been sent over from Phnom Penh to Saigon, and I was there when the plane carrying orphans went down. I was called from New York and told to fly to Hong Kong to do a live report with Peter Jennings by satellite. The only facility for live broadcasting was in Hong Kong. I flew out that day, on the flight just preceding the orphan flight. I didn't know about it until I got into Hong Kong.

"I couldn't get back into Vietnam, so I watched the fall of Saigon from Hong Kong. Oh God, I wanted to get back to Saigon, but they sent me from Hong Kong to Bangkok, because the fall of Cambodia had come about. I cruised along the Thai-Cambodia border to see what was happening. There was a lot of fear there would be an invasion of Thailand. Everyone was thinking, now the domino effect is real, they're not going to stop. It isn't going to stop with just the fall of Cambodia. Now the domino theory is really going to take effect.

"It didn't happen, of course, so I went back to Hong Kong and interviewed Americans and refugees coming out of Vietnam. I was acutely aware that this was an important moment in history. But I think also my feeling was one of relief. My story had come to an end, and I had seen it through. By that time I realized fully the end was going to come, and it was going to be an American defeat. I referred to it as 'the fall.' You can talk to other people who refer to it as the 'liberation.' But I guess it will always be in my mind as the fall of Vietnam, because our participation was so heavy, and it was such a heavy commitment that came a cropper. There wasn't going to be any victory for us. And I was bitter. Bitter.

"There was a real feeling of bitterness, I think, toward the politicians. Who could I really blame for not having prosecuted the war successfully? Johnson? Nixon? I remember especially my feeling of utter frustration when that last congressional delegation came over with Congresswoman Bella Abzug and Representative Pete McCloskey. President Ford was seeking an additional appropriation of something like 300 or 500 million dollars, and this delegation was a fact-finding committee that was coming through to determine whether or not any more funds should be spent in Vietnam. And so here was Abzug—this ridiculous woman, for Christ's sake—in her silly hat, and some other politicians who went around talking to God knows who, trying to make a determination on the future of this country. Of course, I will have to admit, the infusion of 300 million more dollars was not going to make the difference. Probably 300 *billion* more dollars would not have made a difference at that time. The cause was lost. But these were the representatives of the United States who had made the determination that the cause would be lost all along. Those were the people that I was bitter against.

"I remember my stand-up closer on that particular story because it was one time when I had purposely let my objectivity slip away from me. I said something to the effect that this committee had come all the way to Vietnam to find the courage of their convictions. They had obviously made up their minds even before they left Washington. Their coming there was just a sham, a show, and they had traveled all the way to Vietnam to find the courage of their convictions for not releasing any more funds to Vietnam. My report made the air. Either nobody caught it or somebody must have agreed with it.

"And my bitterness was directed at Jane Fonda. My bitterness was at Senator J. William Fulbright. My bitterness was at Bella Abzug, maybe because she was the closest target. Who the hell was she to be deciding these momentous things? What did she know about the sacrifices that had been made there? What did she know about Sam Kai Faye? What did she know about all of the people, how we had perverted and subverted a nation like Cambodia? My bitterness, I think, was really directed that way. Probably because there wasn't anybody else I could hate or be bitter against."

Operation Menu's Secret Bombing of Cambodia

By Henry B. Crawford

In the spring of 1969, President Richard M. Nixon authorized a bombing campaign against Communist-held territories in the supposedly neutral country of Cambodia. Because of sensitive diplomatic and political considerations, the administration decided that the bombings were to remain secret. Important military and civilian officials as well as the full body of Congress were not informed about the bombings and were given false reports and doctored data to avoid arousing suspicion.

Cambodia had a very delicate position during the decades preceding and during American combat involvement in Vietnam. Moreover, Cambodia was on relatively good terms with China and North Vietnam. During this period, Cambodia's leader, Prince Norodom Sihanouk, made some very important friends in Communist China and in Hanoi.

By the early 1960s the United States was increasing aid to South Vietnam, causing Prince Sihanouk to fear that war could spill over into his country and threaten its neutrality. In response to the situation, Sihanouk suspended diplomatic relations with the United States. He then looked to China, France and North Vietnam as allies who could help him maintain his country's existence. He allowed the North Vietnamese leaders to expand their supply routes through Cambodia, forcing out indigenous Cambodian populations in some areas. Sihanouk also allowed the Communists to establish bases and staging areas in his country near the South Vietnamese border.

By 1967 the Communists had fully established their supply depots and staging areas, which the Americans called sanctuaries, on the Cambodia–South Vietnamese border. These enemy sanctuaries played an important role in the Communists' Tet Offensive of January 1968, as well as in routine hit-and-run raids across the border.

The inauguration of President Nixon on January 20, 1969, opened a new chapter in the Cambodia story. Nixon had campaigned on a peace platform, with the goal of bringing an honorable end to American involvement in the unpopular war. As president, he would be expected to carry out his promise. The two-pronged plan he devised was an important component of what was to become known as the Nixon Doctrine. The first objective was called "Vietnamization." The aim was to sufficiently train and equip the South Vietnamese army so that it could sustain itself after the Americans left the country. The second objective was to take steps to protect American lives during the crucial period of disengagement. It was the second part of Nixon's withdrawal plan that led to the bombing campaign.

Communist sanctuaries straddling the border between Cambodia and South Vietnam were perceived as the greatest threat to the withdrawing American troops. General Creighton Abrams, commander of American forces in Vietnam since 1968, recommended "Arc Light" strikes—the code name for B-52 bombing missions—against the sanctuaries while the troops withdrew, a kind of aerial rear-guard action.

The sanctuaries were apparently viewed early on by American military officials as a threat to an allied victory in Vietnam. The proposal to bomb the Cambodian sanctuaries had twice been to President Lyndon B. Johnson, who rejected it each time. But it was routine for the military to submit previously rejected proposals to a new president or secretary of defense. In 1969 the proposal was offered once again to the White House, through Secretary of Defense Melvin Laird. President Nixon, who was planning a trip to Europe, gave instructions to postpone official discussions on bombing until he returned, but while in Europe he sent instructions through a top-secret communication "back channel" to Laird and the Joint Chiefs of Staff to continue preliminary planning sessions.

The bombing was related to the Vietnam theater of the war in three important ways. First, the target areas were indeed vital to the logistical support network for enemy operations in the South. Second, North Vietnam had refused to use restraint in shipping troops and supplies through Laos and into their bases inside Cambodia. The assumption was that when President Johnson curtailed American bombing activities, Hanoi would reciprocate by decreasing its activity along the supply routes. North Vietnam, however, did no such thing, and in fact it increased the flow of support into the South. Third, as mentioned before, the bombing was tied directly to Nixon's overall strategy of disengagement.

Upon his return from Europe, the president held several meetings with the National Security Council and the Joint Chiefs of Staff. The last meeting, held on March 16, 1969, involved the president, Laird, National Security Adviser Henry A. Kissinger, Secretary of State William P. Rogers, and General Earle Wheeler, chairman of the Joint Chiefs. According to Morton Halperin, a planning assistant on Kissinger's National Security staff, intelligence reports indicated large concentrations of North Vietnamese–Viet Cong (NVA/VC) troops in Cambodia. Military Intelligence had further concluded that the sanctuaries held the headquarters for the Communist central office for South Vietnam, or COSVN, the Communist "bamboo pentagon." When interviewed for a television documentary on Vietnam, Brigadier General Douglas Kinnard, who worked on the planning of the land incursion into Cambodia a year later, remarked on the seeming overemphasis the administration placed on the COSVN headquarters. He further stated that as far as he was concerned, the bamboo pentagon was nothing more than "a foxhole and a couple of radios."

As far as justifying the bombing, the group discussed such things as the high rate of American casualties, particularly during the weeks immediately prior to that meeting. The figures for the period averaged around 420 per week. Also it was noted that the bombing operations from 1965 to 1968 (Operation Rolling Thunder) seemed to have had no appreciable effect on the steady flow of Communist troops and supplies into the South. Systematic airstrikes against the NVA/VC staging areas and headquarters in Cambodia, however, offered a more effective approach. One consideration that caused much discussion, according to Halperin, was the political status of the still officially neutral Cambodia. Prince Sihanouk's government had allowed the Communists to establish bases along the border early on. Although the Communists had begun to assert a degree of authority in the border territories they had occupied and had forced out most native Cambodians, the Nixon administration would still be in an awkward position if it approved the bombing of territory that was officially labeled as neutral.

The Joint Chiefs of Staff argued that since the Communists were using the border areas, these areas were within the military theater of operations and could justifiably be bombed. Secretaries Laird and Rogers opposed the plan. They feared that since the president had been elected on a peace platform, the press and the public would not accept the rationale for widening the war through more bombings. Nixon agreed with both the military solution and the political objections. He therefore proposed a third option: bomb, but keep it secret. Rogers and Laird agreed, and the decision to bomb became unanimous. The president ordered the decision to be passed on to the Pentagon along with a request for special security precautions. He wanted the bombing to begin the next day if the weather conditions were favorable.

The secret bombings of Cambodia were not officially acknowledged until July 16, 1973, but unofficial press reports appeared early in the campaign. On March 26, 1969, just a week after the bombings began, *The New York Times* reported that certain high officials in the State Department were "strongly opposed to any military proposals for air or ground raids against [Communist] bases in Cambodia." The report also stated that General Abrams had requested permission to order B-52 strikes against sanctuaries just inside the Cambodian border.

Much of what is known about the bombings is based on official Pentagon, State Department and White House documents and public testimony of those involved. One individual who was close to the operation was Major Hal Knight, a 16-year Air Force veteran who supervised the bomber control radar-guidance station at Bien Hoa Air Base in South Vietnam. Major Knight was among those persons summoned to testify before the Senate Armed Services Committee in the summer of 1973. According to his testimony, the secret bombing missions over Cambodia began on the night of March 17-18, 1969, and all subsequent missions were also flown at night to avoid detection.

The missions and their corresponding target areas were assigned code names. The target areas, six in all, were called "Breakfast," "Lunch," "Snack," "Dinner," "Supper" and "Dessert." The whole bombing campaign was referred to as Menu. The first mission was against the target area Breakfast, a logistical storage network officially designated as target area 353, some 75 miles east of the Mekong River and three miles inside the Cambodian border.

The airstrikes, carried out by Boeing B-52D Stratofortresses, were designed to take out the target areas completely. The B-52Ds, formerly nuclear strike aircraft, had been outfitted to carry conventional 750-pound bombs since the American buildup began in 1965. Each plane could carry 30 tons of bombs, and General Abrams could specify as many as 60 sorties each night to hit a designated target.

When the order to bomb came through, the crews were briefed as usual, with one exception. The pilots and navigators were told to expect changes in their coordinates. The new directions would guide them into Cambodia. These men had instructions not to disclose their true destination to the rest of their crews. One cannot help but think, however, that after a few missions the crews would begin to recognize headings and coordinates, and come to realize that they were indeed hitting Cambodia without actually being told. Pretty soon the rumor mill would begin turning, and the "secret" would no longer be a secret among air and ground crews.

The bombers were guided to their target areas by bomber control radar sites, called Combat Skyspot stations. The Combat Skyspot target information was delivered secretly by a courier each afternoon before that night's raid. These instructions were then fed into computers and transmitted to the bombers en route to their targets. The airborne radar crews received information on a Menu target area from Combat Skyspot and prepared charts, forms and other data necessary to carry out the mission. The information was then fed into an onboard-computer that guided the bombers by radar to the predesignated target area and signaled the on-board computer precisely when to release its big load of 750-pound iron bombs.

The special security procedures needed to keep the missions secret involved an elaborate system of dual bookkeeping, which made it appear that the bombs were falling east of the Cambodian border instead of west. Colonel Ray Sitton, formerly of the Strategic Air Command, worked out the special security measures. According to the plan, General Abrams would request two strikes: one would be against a target in South Vietnam, the other against a corresponding target in Cambodia within a few miles of the Vietnam target location or along a similar heading. Since all of the targets in Cambodia were right along the border, this would not be very difficult.

On May 9, 1969, *The New York Times*, citing Nixon administration sources, said that American B-52 bombers had raided several enemy supply dumps and bases inside Cambodia "for the first time." The story went on to say that the raids had coincided with bombing missions on the Vietnamese side of the border. The source probably identified the "raids" on the Vietnam side with certain false mission reports that had been filed to hide the Cambodian attacks.

When *The New York Times* story came out in May, Nixon suggested to Kissinger that the informant could have been someone on the National Security Council staff. Kissinger replied, "I will destroy them!" Nixon's reaction was less dramatic, yet nonetheless severe. On May 10, he ordered 17 wiretaps placed on the telephones of National Security Council staff officials and members of the news media, which remained in place until 1971. It was not until 1972 that the Supreme Court ruled such domestic spying to be illegal unless there was evidence of foreign intelligence activity.

Requests to bomb targets in Cambodia went from General Abrams in Saigon through secret, back-channel communications directly to the Pentagon. Once approved, the briefings would be scheduled and the crews would take to the air. The missions were flown so that the aircraft would pass over or near the "dummy" target in South Vietnam and hit the real objective in Cambodia. When the crews returned to the base, routine (but false) reports were filed that told of a mission over South Vietnam instead of Cambodia. According to Major Hal Knight's testimony, the radar crews prepared false reports to be sent back to the Pentagon. (It is interesting to note that General Earle Wheeler, chairman of the Joint Chiefs of Staff, stated during his testimony that he did not think there was false reporting and that "no one was ordered to make a false report.")

On the morning after each raid, Knight took the original secret bombing orders and the computer tape containing the secret data out to a garbage barrel and burned them. He did this in the morning to prevent losing one of the documents in the dark, fearing that it might be found by someone unauthorized to know its contents. After burning the orders, he then phoned a special secure number in Saigon and said "The ballgame is over." This coded phrase was an indication to personnel at the other end that the day's mission had been completed.

Major Knight was one of several civilian and military officials who were selected to conduct the special security procedures in connection with the bombing. The chain of command in the affair was so narrow that Dr. Robert C. Seamans, secretary of the Air Force, and General John Ryan, vice chief of staff of the Air Force, were not informed about the secret missions. Military personnel with a "need to know" were the Joint Chiefs of Staff, the bomber pilots and navigators, the radar crews, and the individuals in Washington and Saigon directly connected with the operation. Several key members of Congress were informed, as well. Among them were Senators Richard Russell of Georgia, Everett Dirksen of Illinois, John Stennis of Mississippi, and Barry Goldwater of Arizona. All except Dirksen, who sat on the powerful Senate Judiciary and Finance committees, were members of the Senate Armed Services Committee. On the House side, those informed were Representatives L. Mendel Rivers and Leslie Arends of the House Armed Services Committee, and future president Gerald R. Ford, then House minority leader. Throughout the 14-month bombing campaign, the American public was regularly being reassured that the neutrality of Cambodia was being respected by the U.S. military, and that the North Vietnamese Army and the Viet Cong were the only violators of Cambodian neutrality.

The U.S. Senate became concerned about the bombings after Knight wrote to Senator William Proxmire in January 1973 for clarification of a policy on border operations. As a principal operative in the bombing campaign, the major had problems. On the one hand he was obligated to obey orders from superiors in accordance with Article 92 of the Uniform Code of Military Justice. But according to Article 107 of that same code, he was forbidden to falsify records. Obviously he had a dilemma, because to carry out his orders he was disobeying Article 107, and to refrain from falsifying records he would be in violation of Article 92. When Knight wrote to Senator Proxmire for advice, the senator referred the matter to the Senate Armed Services Committee. The committee wanted to know more about the bombing operations and asked Knight to testify on what he knew.

The U.S. House of Representatives also became interested in the secret bombings of Operation Menu. On July 30, 1974, after a lengthy investigation and debate, the House Judiciary Committee voted on the following article: "In his conduct of the office of President of the United States, Richard M. Nixon, in violation of his constitutional oath, authorized, ordered, and ratified the concealment from the Congress of the facts, and the submission to the Congress of false and misleading statements concerning the existence, scope, and nature of American bombing operations in Cambodia, in derogation of the power of the Congress to declare war; and by such conduct warrants impeachment, and trial, and removal from office."

It is obvious that the concern of the Judiciary Committee was not the bombing raids on neutral Cambodia per se, but that Congress itself was not informed of the raids. The significance of this article is paramount, as it was the first call for the impeachment of President Nixon by a congressional committee.

The resolution passed the Judiciary Committee, but not unanimously. Illinois Representative Thomas F. Railsback, a member of the committee, voted against the article and later suggested that the reason it failed in the full House was that Congress could not realistically prosecute the president for actions in the war that other presidents since Dwight D. Eisenhower had gotten away with. A direct result of the congressional hearings, however, was a repeal of the Gulf of Tonkin Resolution, removing substantial war-making powers from the president and placing them back into the hands of Congress. Several additional articles concerning alleged improprieties of the Nixon administration were voted upon and reported to the full body of the House of Representatives. When the smoke cleared, it became evident that Nixon's only option was to resign, lest he become the first president to suffer impeachment.

As to the overall effectiveness of the bombing campaign, General Wheeler, as chairman of the Joint Chiefs of Staff, appeared before the Senate Armed Services Committee and testified that "the enemy was forced to shift his forces and disperse his supplies over a greater area, imposing increased hardships on him. Extensive loss of personnel and material inflicted on the enemy saved American lives." After the Senate hearings in 1973, the Nixon administration produced figures showing a drop in casualties among troops stationed along the border. One might theorize, however, that the figures do not reflect the effect of the bombing entirely—that another factor may have been the withdrawal of troops from the border areas during the same period. On the other hand, Pentagon tallies showed that monthly casualties increased during the first six months of the bombing, perhaps because of losses among the aircrews themselves.

Statistics on tonnage are more conclusive than the casualty figures. In 3,695 sorties from March 18, 1969, to May 1, 1970, the Air Force dropped 108,837 tons of bombs on Cambodia. By May 26, 1970, the last day of Operation Menu, 4,308 B-52 sorties had been flown, and a grand total of 120,578 tons of bombs had been dropped on Cambodia's border regions. According to a former B-52 pilot, the tonnage figures are not excessive when one considers that the average payload of a B-52D, the model used in Vietnam from 1966 until 1972, was around 60,000 pounds. Each bomber could carry 42 750-pound bombs internally and an additional 24 on external wing racks added to the aircraft's underwing pylons. Senator Harold Hughes of Iowa estimated the total cost of the secret bombing campaign to be around $158 million.

Mission costs and bomb tonnages are important, but even more significant is the central issue—the question of Cambodia's neutrality. It is known that there were Communist sanctuaries along the Cambodian border, sanctuaries, in fact, that straddled the boundary between that country and South Vietnam. Sihanouk himself had allowed some border areas to be occupied by Vietnamese Communists. According to statements made by Henry Kissinger in a television interview, the president did not have the right to attack a neutral country. But, Kissinger added, the primary question was whether or not the president had "the right to react against concentrations of enemy troops that have already occupied neutral territory for a number of years, having established themselves there, having expelled the local populations there, and were launching raids from that territory against American positions." This was the diplomatic dilemma the Nixon administration had been facing.

Furthermore, there was the political position of Prince Sihanouk, who walked a fine line between entities much more powerful than himself. There seemed to be little Sihanouk could do about the sanctuaries, even if he wanted to. What he did was simply to make the best of a bad situation by allowing the Vietnamese to use Cambodian border areas, while secretly allowing the Americans to bomb them.

Still another factor was that the Cambodian border was not as well-defined as one may think. Vietnam air power analyst Earl Tilford wrote that those involved could never be absolutely sure where the border was located, and, as a result of the confusion, each country tended to claim territory that was a kilometer or two on either side of the line. Whether or not the American bombs were hitting Cambodia or Vietnam was merely an academic question in most cases. Prior to the commencement of the secret bombings, American tactical aircraft routinely pursued the enemy across the Cambodian "border" and delivered ordnance upon enemy positions. But all the B-52 Arc Light strikes over Cambodia during Operation Menu were conceived as clandestine operations from the beginning, where the Air Force "made a definite effort to conceal the true nature of the missions" from the Congress and other government officials who perhaps should have been informed.

The practice of pursuing an enemy across international borders, just as the U.S. Army had done a century earlier in its campaigns against Comanche and Apache Indians, has often been viewed as a necessary evil. One can only sympathize with those who bear the heavy responsibility and frustration involved in conducting military operations in close proximity to international boundaries. The hope is that the fundamental principles of the U.S. Constitution are observed whenever such military action is deemed vitally necessary to maintaining our national security.

Keep 'Em Flying

By Colonel Karl J. Eschmann,
U.S. Air Force (ret.)

With the wide assortment of literature and movies portraying the "typical" Vietnam-era GI, one might be led to believe that most Americans involved in that war were either bloodthirsty warmongers or soldiers tripped out on drugs. For the majority of the personnel who served their country in Southeast Asia (SEA), the truth was exactly the opposite. This was certainly the case with the F-4 maintenance troops of the 388th Tactical Fighter Wing (TFW) at Korat Royal Thai Air Force Base, Thailand, during the 1972 Linebacker II air offensive.

Most of the maintenance personnel assigned to the F-4 section were young airmen in their late teens or early 20s. Considering the fact that F-4E Phantoms were designed to be maintained by an experienced crew chief with a "technical sergeant" skill rating, it was quite a responsibility for a young airman to be assigned as a crew chief on this multimillion-dollar weapon system. The reason for the shortage of experienced personnel was that, in late October 1972, President Nixon had halted all bombings north of the 20th parallel in North Vietnam in anticipation of a negotiated cease-fire. For the next several weeks, most of the Americans stationed in SEA felt that an end to the war was imminent. Apparently, the manpower planning staffs also felt that way because the flow of replacement personnel was reduced to a trickle.

Throughout the months of October and November, maintenance and other support organizations lost experienced personnel at a far higher rate than normal due to a large number of expired DEROS (Dates of Expected Return from Overseas) for completed one-year tours, as well as the end of many TDY (Temporary Duty) cycles. Since many U.S. Air Force personnel had deployed directly to SEA during the April-May period following the North Vietnamese (NVA) Eastertide invasion into the South, they had finished their 180-day TDY cycles and were therefore due for a return to their home stations. In light of the bombing halt situation, there appeared to be no reason to retain the TDY people. But by the end of November, the realization finally struck a number of commanders that unless the personnel pipeline was reopened, the flying units would be in a situation of trying to maintain an in-place force without adequate manpower to do so.

Finally, during the first part of December, relief in the form of new TDY personnel arrived from a number of Stateside bases and from areas in the Pacific. Some of the more experienced men who were due to rotate just before Christmas were also involuntarily extended to January or February 1973 dates. This was a highly unpopular action as most of the extended troops had families expecting them home for the holidays, but as things later turned out, it proved to be a very fortuitous decision. Since many of the new TDY people were somewhat unfamiliar with working on F-4 aircraft, it was up to those extended crew chiefs to provide them with quick on-the-job training.

Although most units were still sitting far short of their normal manning requirements, the maintenance officers were reasonably confident they could handle the kind of flying schedule

*that the squadron wing had supported during Linebacker I opera-
tions from March to October 1972 in response to the NVA Eastertide Offensive. That effort had been characterized as a "standard"
schedule whereby missions were flown by day, and night shift was
used as a time for the maintenance system to correct all discovered major discrepancies to get the aircraft ready for the next
day's schedule. The demands of concurrent aircraft launch and
recovery operations required greater manpower loadings during
the day shift. The men on night shift could usually perform their
jobs with a less than full complement since their main role was to
act as a coordinator for specialists doing the actual troubleshoot-
ing or repair actions on the aircraft. Under these kinds of conditions, the maintenance officers and senior NCOs felt that even
with shortages the troops could "hack the program."*

In the meantime, the North Vietnamese were using the respite
from the post-Linebacker I bombing halt to rebuild their military
strength. On December 13, 1972, the North Vietnamese delegates
walked out of the Paris peace talks, and two days later, the president ordered the execution of Linebacker II—the resumption of
airstrikes against North Vietnam. The majority of U.S. Air Force
people stationed in Thailand were completely surprised by the
new air offensive.

The first hint that something unusual was going on was on
December 16, when the author, then the most junior F-4E maintenance officer, was told by his flight line maintenance supervisor to go to his quarters to get some rest in preparation for a
return to the night shift beginning the next evening. A new second lieutenant with only four months of experience, the author
was in temporary command of the wing's fighter section because
all of the more senior maintenance officers had departed for
Christmas leave.

But before he left for his quarters, he was tasked to supervise a quick detail to transport dozens of empty, center-line fuel tanks from the tank storage area to the aircraft revetments. The men on night shift were given the duty of loading the tanks and to begin putting together all friendly aircraft undergoing routine, scheduled maintenance. The flight-line personnel were also informed by the supervisor of the Thai work crews, who were assembling new fuel tanks, that they would be working overtime to build up a large reserve of operational tanks (which arrived in kit form from the Stateside stocks). This activity seemed to point toward an expected large expenditure of external tanks and spawned numerous rumors that U.S. forces were possibly going to be involved in a new bombing effort above the 20th parallel. During Linebacker I, it had been standard procedure for F-4 aircrews to punch off their external fuel tanks prior to entering North Vietnamese airspace, thereby lessening drag.

These rumors became fact when the maintenance officer in charge reported back to work on the evening of December 17. He was told to report directly to the Wing Maintenance Control Room for an important briefing prior to his shift-change muster and roll call. He noted immediately that every single aircraft status board was covered over by curtains. The F-4 board controller, an experienced master sergeant, lifted up the curtain covering the status board for the F-4 section and, amazingly, almost all of the aircraft appeared as either operationally ready (OR) or well on the way to being so.

On a normal basis, the section maintained an OR rate of about 80 to 85 percent, but the board was showing an OR status of 92 percent, with 23 out of 25 F-4s available for service. Every aircraft was loaded for either an air-to-air configuration (AIM-7 Sparrow and AIM-9 Sidewinder missiles) or a hunter-killer configuration (cluster bomb units, or CBUs) with fully fueled center-line and wing tanks. This had to mean only one thing—the 388th aircrews were definitely headed back to North Vietnam!

Although no one would even then provide an official word as to exactly when, where and how the aircraft were to be used, the air in the control room was filled with excitement for what was sure to come. These feelings were mixed with a sense of apprehension as well, since it was known that the North Vietnamese had all but replaced their air defense network, which had been seriously damaged during Linebacker I.

The maintenance status boards for other types of aircraft provided even more proof of a large-scale restrike effort against targets deep into North Vietnamese territory. The EB-66s were getting new installations of ECM packages (electronic countermeasures). All of the Wild Weasel F-105Gs were fully armed and loaded with AGM-45 Shrike radar-seeking missiles and AGM-78 Standard ARMs (antiradiation missiles, used to home in on enemy acquisition radars). Almost everyone who had leave, passes, or rest-and-recreation trips scheduled was getting a cancellation and being told to remain on base. The cover story was simply that a new offensive was being planned against new supply bases in southern Laos. Hardly anyone on the base believed this story, but then again, no one believed that they would be going back to Route Package Six (i.e., the Hanoi area in North Vietnam) either.

In the meantime, the F-4 section was informed that it would be tasked to support a schedule to sustain both a day and a night effort until further notice. The successful outcome for such a flying schedule usually relied upon a maximum effort even when units were manned at full strength—and the 388th's section was still suffering from a shortage in manpower.

The only thing that had prevented the problem from reaching a critical state was the fact that some of the experienced troops had been involuntarily extended for several weeks pending the arrival of new permanent party replacements. This action enabled the wing to perform the assigned mission. But even so, there were still barely enough certified crew chiefs to handle launching, recovery, and maintenance for the 25 Phantom aircraft within each 12-hour shift.

The real shock of having to support a 24-hour flying schedule was based upon the previous Linebacker I experience when everyone *knew* that it routinely required an entire 12-hour night shift to generate enough F-4 airframes to support each day's flying commitments. That was the situation when the unit had the luxury of having a permanent crew chief assigned to almost every aircraft. Now the troops were being told that they would launch and recover twice as many missions with half as many crew chiefs and without any appreciable maintenance stand-down time. It seemed impossible.

A strange thing happened as the word was relayed to the troops by the maintenance officer. They acted relieved. Prior to this, many of the extended people had been angered at having to remain in SEA over the holidays for no more apparent reason than "babysitting" their aircraft without any "real" mission in mind. But now, these same individuals were making statements about almost missing out on the action.

On the afternoon of December 18, the unit commanders finally got the straight word on what the preparations were all about. Very few believed it when it was finally disclosed that B-52 bombers would be attacking targets within the dense Hanoi-Haiphong defense zones. There were a lot of discussions taking place throughout the base over whether or not the huge Strategic Air Command (SAC) bombers would be sitting ducks against the expected concentrated enemy defenses. As of yet, it had not been revealed as to how many B-52 bombers were involved in the new offensive, nor the tactics they would be using during their night attacks.

The mission plan was explained to the flight-line people by the aircrews during their preflight inspections of the aircraft as they prepared for the first launches. The main intent of Line-backer II was to take the war to the major cities and complexes in North Vietnam. The operation differed from previous air offensives in that it provided for continuous around-the-clock air attacks against the North Vietnamese homeland. The primary aim was to strangle the Communist war effort by shutting down the sources of the massive pipeline of equipment and supplies that gave Hanoi its capability to sustain a major ground offensive within South Vietnam.

It was also meant to show America's serious "get-tough" attitude to convince the North Vietnamese that it would be in their own best interests to return to the negotiating table. In earlier air offensives against North Vietnam, our fighterbombers had limited capability in attacking pinpoint targets during night or poor-visibility periods. Thus, the Communists had been able to adjust to American bombing schedules by hiding and storing their valuable supplies during U.S. daylight attack periods and moving them at night when U.S. air operations were not nearly as effective.

Therefore, the plan for Linebacker II was to maintain constant pressure on the North Vietnamese by an intensive bombing campaign against specific key targets by U.S. Air Force B-52s and F-111s and Navy A-6s at night, with continuing bombing strikes against the same areas conducted by Air Force and Navy fighterbombers during the day. This kind of offensive had never been experienced by the North Vietnamese before, and they would now understand America's true abilities to wreak destruction upon their homeland.

Throughout the afternoon and night of December 18-19, aircraft were being launched from every base in Thailand to support the B-52 night strike force. The first night, more than 120 B-52s attacked in three separate waves against targets in the Hanoi area. The 388th's F-4E Phantoms were assigned two primary missions throughout the operation: to provide a "MiG CAP" aerial protection for the B52s against MiG fighters; and to serve as a component of the hunter-killer teams with the F-105G Wild Weasels to attack threatening surface-to-air missile (SAM) sites surrounding the Hanoi-Haiphong complexes.

The main purpose of the hunter-killer team mission was to "troll" the enemy skies looking for ground-launched defensive threats. The Weasel F-105G crew would be alert for any signals indicating a tracking radar for SAMs, and then would fire one or more of their anti-radiation missiles into the radiated signal. The missile would then home onto the signal source and ride right down into the radar antenna site. Once the site was marked, the accompanying F-4s carrying cluster bombs would destroy the remainder of the site, including the actual SAMs and support personnel. Additionally, the F-4s carried two AIM-7 Sparrow air-to-air missiles in their aft fuselage launchers to protect the Wild Weasel team from MiG attacks.

Every night of the offensive, Air Force and Navy fighters preceded the B-52 entry routes with attacks on such threats as MiG airfields, gun batteries and known or suspected SAM sites. The missions that U.S. aircrews flew over North Vietnam during those days in 1972 were in the highest threat areas of the world at that time. The North Vietnamese air defense network was composed of 2,000-plus surface-to-air missiles, 4,000-plus heavy anti-aircraft gun batteries, and a couple of hundred MiG fighters.

The Wild Weasel teams were constantly operating along the planned ingress/egress routes to maintain a vigilance for the SAMs. Although relatively few Weasels were available (six F-4Cs on TDY from Okinawa and two Korat-based F-105G squadrons), it became apparent that dozens of B-52 crew members probably would owe their lives to the umbrellalike cover provided by the Weasels. The Weasel motto was "First in, last out," and these aircraft made their presence known.

The NVA's SAM-site personnel had long since learned to respect the capabilities of the Weasels, and for the U.S. B-52 attack force, a turned off radar to avoid a Weasel attack was nearly as good as an actual kill of a SAM site. This forced the North Vietnamese to employ a tactic of firing their SAMs like skyrockets without the benefit of acquiring good lock-ons with their acquisition radars. Thus, they often had to rely on aiming at a point in space toward the B-52 bomber streams in hope of scoring hits with the missile's proximity fuzing system.

Enemy MiGs also flew parallel courses with U.S. bombers and would radio information to the SAM battery crews concerning B-52 altitudes and headings to assist them with their aims. Although some 15 B-52 bombers were lost due to the SAM defenses, the high expenditure rates associated with the salvo tactics rapidly depleted the available SAM assets to the point where the North Vietnamese ability to defend themselves was seriously affected.

Maintenance personnel fully understood and appreciated the implications of keeping available the needed mission-capable fighter aircraft to protect the B-52 attack force. Even though the crew-chief shortage was such that each primary crew chief was maintaining and supporting up to three aircraft per shift, the men consistently volunteered to work longer than their normal 12-hour shifts almost every day of the offensive. Many of the crew chiefs even slept in their aircraft's parking revetment areas.

Additionally, many airmen and NCOs assigned to other areas of maintenance, such as the Phase Docks, the Nonpowered Aerospace Ground Equipment Sections or the Specialist Maintenance Squadrons, aided in the effort by volunteering to work as crew-chief assistants. Although inexperienced in performing crew-chief functions, these volunteers quickly learned to accomplish tasks such as conducting end-of-runway quick-check inspections, depaneling aircraft to remove and replace defective equipment, towing, fuel servicing, uploading fuel tanks, and assisting with aircraft launches and recoveries.

As it turned out, the inexperienced volunteers did quite well because they learned their new roles fast and, more important, because *they wanted to.* Everyone sensed that they were involved in a historic event, and they all wanted to have an active part in it. Most of these volunteers performed the flight-line functions in addition to their normal shift duties within their own respective primary work areas.

Toward the end of the first week of the offensive, the aircraft systems were already straining local supply-support capabilities due to the compressed requirements of a day-and-night flying schedule. This was especially true for the F-4 Phantoms, since so many F-4 units were assigned in Thailand, and each was competing for many of the essential parts that were in short supply worldwide.

As it was, the entire Tactical Air Command was sacrificing mission readiness in other parts of the world to keep the flow of critical parts maximized to the SEA theater of operations. These part shortages caused some of the aircraft to be ineffective for a number of missions. A number of the on-board F-4 avionics used for performing important functions in the areas of radar, fire control, navigation and communications were quite vulnerable to the extreme climatic conditions of Southeast Asia. Very rare was the aircraft that returned from a mission without a problem in a least one of its avionic areas.

In the initial days of Linebacker II, U.S. forces had to make do with what was already on hand within the American local supply warehouses. This meant that, in some cases, certain individual aircraft awaiting parts on order could not fly specific missions due to inoperative subsystems with deficiencies in either air-to-air or air-to-ground modes. These problems led to restricted flexibility in assigning primary or spare airframes for specific mission configurations. Throughout the offensive, units had to continuously tailor individual aircraft for specific mission blocks by cannibalizing parts during the turnaround periods.

As aircraft returned from completing a mission and were being reserviced, the maintenance troops would have to "borrow" the aircrafts' parts or avionics equipment and put them on F-4s getting ready to launch out on the next immediate sortie blocks. This was not a preferred approach since it required double the effort to turn an aircraft in preparation for subsequent missions. But it was necessary where there were only a limited number of reliably calibrated or fully operational avionic units, and the aircrews simply could not afford to fly up North with anything less than fully operable weapon systems. The stakes were just too high.

At first the wing tried to support a planned, formalized flying schedule as worked up by the Plans and Scheduling Staff. They had printed up a series of "frag sheets," or flight schedules, where specific tail-numbered aircraft were assigned to time blocks for specific types of missions. But, because of the "real-time" turnaround problems and constant changes in aircraft readiness factors, it became difficult for schedulers to assess which tail numbers would possess some reasonable capability to perform specific functions for the next day's missions.

Changes to the published schedules became too numerous after Day 2, and the flight-line section chiefs were finally just given blank schedule forms with printed mission times which were filled in with tail numbers as airframes became available. Often, this would happen just minutes prior to the scheduled launch times, and aircrews patiently waited in the revetments for the word to climb aboard in a last-minute assignment. More times than not, they had very little time to conduct a proper preflight of their aircraft, since the other aircraft within their mission block had already started engines.

The aircrew's trust in their maintenance troop's judgments strengthened the resolve to provide the aircrew with the best possible airframes within the abilities to do so. Any mistakes on a crew chief's part could very well mean the loss of another aircrew over North Vietnam. This could occur either by a failure of a critical aircraft system or by enemy defensive actions if the weapon systems weren't operating at optimum performance with equipment such as the ECM, which was needed to counter the enemy SAM radars.

The pilots and backseaters paid back the efforts by continually keeping their support folks informed on the progress of the offensive. The troops were invited to intelligence briefings and combat film shows which gave them an idea as to what effect Linebacker was having on the North Vietnamese. The value these informative briefings had on morale cannot be emphasized enough. They continued to spark the efforts of the tired and weary maintenance personnel to press on.

The real break came when President Richard Nixon halted the bombing during Christmas. This happened just at a point when it seemed that the U.S. forces would run out of enough mission-capable aircraft to fully support the next day's missions. The stand-down period gave the tired support personnel a breathing spell and allowed them to perform some catch-up maintenance on the also tired birds.

In many cases, replacement parts had arrived for some of the more critical discrepancies, but the crew chiefs were forced to leave the problems open as temporary "hold-fly" write-ups, due to the lack of available time to correct them. Each hold-fly write-up on its own was not sufficient to ground an aircraft, but a combination of several of them could easily cause a degradation of weapon-system performance. During the bombing break, however, the maintenance personnel were able to work on some of the more serious discrepancies and again bring the F-4s up to some measure of their full capabilities.

Although it was a sure thing that the North Vietnamese were using the temporary halt as a means to rebuild some of their damaged areas and defensive sites as well, the break was far more beneficial to the American side since the effectiveness and ability to restrike the North in force was largely restored.

After the 24-hour halt on Christmas Day, the bombing resumed with a vengeance. As the official history relates: "By 28 December, American airmen had swept away virtually all the enemy's defenses, and the B-52s were free to roam the skies of North Vietnam. . . . On 30 December Hanoi agreed to resume the peace talks which culminated in the 27 January [1973] agreement."

The "can-do" spirit of the ground maintenance personnel had paid enormous dividends. During Linebacker II, the 388th Tactical Fighter Wing flew several hundred sorties over North Vietnam with only two countable aborts. The F-4E Phantoms at Korat did not suffer a single loss during this 11-day campaign due to either accidents or enemy action.

Battle of the Bulge vs. Eastertide Offensive: Lessons Unlearned

By Bob Baker

It is difficult to understand how the U.S. military could have been surprised by the North Vietnamese Army's 1972 Eastertide Offensive. The Americans had already been taken by surprise four years earlier during the enemy's 1968 Tet Offensive. Furthermore, surprise is one of the nine classic principles of war, and the 1962 U.S. Army field manual on combat operations cautioned against surprise attacks. The text warned, "Factors contributing to surprise include . . . effective intelligence, and counterintelligence, including communications and electronic security."

Unfortunately, it was the U.S. military's hubris over its success in communications and electronic warfare, the so-called "Ultra syndrome" (after the interception and deciphering of secret German radio traffic in World War II), that led to the U.S. susceptibility to deception. The Americans assumed that because the intercepts they had obtained were so authentic and so eloquent, those intercepts must tell everything.

U.S. intelligence analysts in 1972 should have known better. Even though valuable information had been intercepted from the Germans during World War II, the Ultra syndrome had also caused a near disaster in the Ardennes, when an unexpected German offensive almost changed the course of the conflict. But those lessons from the Battle of the Bulge, as the resultant engagement came to be called, were ignored. Vietnam was seen as a "counterinsurgency," not a war in which the old rules still applied. Unfortunately the enemy, in the words of British strategist Correlli Barnett, was "terribly old-fashioned." George Santayana's famous 1906 observation that "those who cannot remember the past are condemned to repeat it" was once again validated.

The other common thread running through both of these military surprises was complacency, the most dangerous of military vulnerabilities. By December 1944 it appeared that the German army was in full retreat and that the war would be over by spring. In only six months of combat, Allied lines had been extended from Holland in the north across all of eastern France. Likewise, by the spring of 1972 it looked as if the war in Vietnam was nearing an end, at least as far as the Americans were concerned. "Vietnamization" was proceeding apace, and the U.S. troop withdrawal begun in July 1969 had reached the point where all seven of the U.S. Army infantry divisions and the two Marine combat divisions had been withdrawn. The only U.S. ground combat troops left in-country were the 1st Brigade of the 1st Cavalry Division (Airmobile) and two battalions of the 196th Light Infantry Brigade—and these units were scheduled to be withdrawn before the Eastertide Offensive drew to a close.

In Europe in World War II, the American leadership's false assumptions regarding the Nazis' morale and combat effectiveness fed the complacency of the U.S. troops. Most of the Allied commanders at the Bulge did not consider the Germans capable of launching an attack until the Allies had crossed Germany's Roer River. Even then only a spoiling attack was anticipated. As General Dwight Eisenhower, the SHAEF (Supreme Headquarters

Allied Expeditionary Forces) commander, wrote: "When [the German Sixth Panzer Army] arrived on our front it was originally stationed opposite the left of the [Allied] Twelfth Army Group, apparently to operate against any crossing of the Roer. . . . Previously [the Germans] had, like ourselves, been using that portion of the front in which to rest tired divisions. . . . None of us . . . was thinking in terms of a major strategic counterattack."

The British commander, Field Marshal Bernard Montgomery, "agreed with our thinking [that the Germans] cannot stage a major offensive operation," wrote Lieutenant General Courtney Hodges, the First U.S. Army commander. "He also agreed with us that [German Field Marshal Karl] von Rundstedt was 'unlikely' to commit his panzer reserves 'until the Allies advance over the Roer to present a threat.'" Only Lieutenant General George Patton, the Third U.S. Army commander, disagreed, saying, "The First Army is making a terrible mistake in leaving [its] VIII Corps static, as it is highly probable that the Germans are building up east of them."

Since no enemy attack was expected, VIII Corps was left to defend a 75-mile front manned by the understrength 4th and 28th Infantry divisions—both still recovering from recent hard fighting in the Huertgen Forest—the headquarters and combat command reserve of the 9th Armored Division and the green 106th Infantry Division, only recently arrived overseas. On these fragile units the sledgehammer of the main assault of the German counterattack would descend, sending the VIII Corps reeling back and forcing the surrender of the 106th Infantry Division's 422nd and 423nd Infantry regiments.

Twenty-eight years later and half a world away, the U.S. and ARVN commanders were equally complacent on the eve of the NVA's Eastertide Offensive. Although there had been some forecasts of enemy action during the 1972 Tet holiday period, no combat had materialized. While the NVA's 324B Division was known to be headed for its usual area of operations in the A Shau Valley, only a slight buildup north of the DMZ had been detected. Asked if the NVA was liable to launch an attack across the DMZ, the ARVN I Corps commander, Lieutenant General Hoang Xuan Lam, said bluntly, "They cannot."

The U.S. XXIV Corps, which had succeeded the III Marine Amphibious Force as the principal U.S. adviser to the ARVN Corps, was being deactivated and replaced by the First Regional Assistance Command (FRAC). FRAC's commander, Major General Frederick J. Kroesen (who would later rise to four-star rank and serve as Army vice chief of staff), agreed with his ARVN counterpart and said that Lam's "appraisal appears reasonable and well-founded." As a result, a green division, the newly formed 3rd ARVN Division, was committed to the DMZ defenses. Its 2nd Infantry Regiment, detached from the veteran 1st ARVN Division to form the core of this new unit, was solid. The 56th and 57th Infantry regiments, however, were composed of draftees, deserters and Popular Force irregulars. Lieutenant Colonel Phan Van Dinh would surrender his 1,800-man 56th Infantry Regiment to the enemy at Camp Carroll on Easter Sunday 1972. His was the only ARVN unit to surrender en masse during the course of the war. The issue in this article is not the battles per se but the uses and misuses of intelligence in determining the outcome of the Easter fight.

A preliminary to that analysis is an evaluation of METT: mission, enemy, terrain and weather, time and troops available. That standard military template can highlight the lessons that should have been learned from the 1944 Battle of the Bulge and that could have been applied to the 1972 Eastertide Offensive.

As far as mission is concerned, in both cases the enemy's driving force was desperation, which should always be a major warning indicator, since desperate times call for desperate and unexpected measures. But this indicator was overlooked in both the Battle of the Bulge and the Eastertide Offensive.

In the late fall of 1944, Germany was being pushed against the wall. Allied armies were on its very border, and in order to keep the ground war away from the German homeland, Adolf Hitler ordered three German panzer armies to attack through the Ardennes, hoping this desperate gamble would split the boundary between the U.S. Twelfth Army Group (composed of the U.S. First, Third and Ninth armies) and the British 21st Army Group (consisting of the Canadian First Army and the British Second Army) and capture the port of Antwerp. If these attacks were successful, Hitler hoped they might lead to a negotiated settlement of the war.

Although it was not as obvious, in the spring of 1972 North Vietnam was also in a desperate situation. Militarily their guerrilla war in the South had collapsed in the wake of the 1968 Tet Offensive, and any hopes of a great general uprising in the South had been dashed. North Vietnamese Regular forces now made up 90 percent of the fighting forces in the South. Politically the situation was also grim. Richard Nixon had been elected president of the United States and was working successfully to drive a wedge between North Vietnam and its Soviet and Chinese allies. Negotiations in Paris to end the war, underway since May 1968, were reaching a critical stage.

During the Eastertide Offensive, North Vietnam committed all of its Regular forces in an all-out attempt to reverse its desperate situation. It would put direct pressure on Saigon with an attack on An Loc in III Corps. It would attempt to once again cut South Vietnam in two, an effort first frustrated by the American intervention in the Ia Drang Valley in 1965, with an attack on Kontum in II Corps. Its main attack, however, would be on Quang Tri in I Corps, with the objective of seizing South Vietnam's two northern provinces to use as bargaining chips at the negotiating table in Paris. This attempt had previously been thwarted during the 1968 Tet Offensive.

Allied analysis of the enemy had concluded that offensive action was possible, but in both cases the Allied leaders did not perceive that the enemy would launch such widespread attacks. Therefore, they seriously underestimated the severity of the assaults that ensued.

In World War II, General Eisenhower admitted that SHAEF was surprised by the "strength of the attack" in the Ardennes after the previous American successes. Loath to admit that he had been taken unaware, he argued that the German attack had been anticipated: "[General Omar] Bradley and I were sufficiently convinced that a major attack was developing against the center of [Bradley's] Twelfth Army Group to agree to begin shifting some strength from both flanks toward the Ardennes sector. This was a preliminary move—rather a precaution—made in order to support the seventy-five-mile length of the VIII Corps front, providing our calculations as to German intentions should prove correct." In fact, only on December 16, 1944, after the German offensive had begun earlier that day, were the 10th Armored Division from General Patton's Third Army and the 7th Armored Division from Lieutenant General William Simpson's Ninth Army detached to hit the flanks of the German spearhead. The haste with which this was accomplished is also evidenced by the fact that Eisenhower's strategic reserves, the 82nd and 101st Airborne divisions, were not instructed to deploy to the area until December 17—the day after the start of the offensive.

Eisenhower had felt secure enough regarding an imminent major German attack that he gave British Field Marshal Montgomery, his Twenty-first Army Group commander, permission to return to England for Christmas. SHAEF—though loath to admit it—had been surprised by the German attack in the Ardennes.

Twenty-eight years later, MACV and the ARVN Joint General Staff (JGS) were just as surprised by the NVA's Eastertide Offensive in Vietnam. When the expected enemy Tet Offensive never materialized in early 1972, JGS was lulled into a false sense of security. When movement of the NVA 324B Division in the A Shau Valley was detected in February 1972, the assessment of a JGS Intelligence officer was that "the enemy's apparent objective is to occupy Hue, the ancient capital, and threaten the harbor and airfield at Da Nang, 60 miles to the south."

Haunted by memories of Hue's capture by the NVA during the 1968 Tet Offensive, the U.S. and ARVN commands became fixated on the idea that the city was the enemy's primary objective to the exclusion of all other possibilities. By presenting the obvious—the movement of their 324B Division into the A Shau Valley, the NVA managed to persuade the Allies to see what they wanted—and expected—to see.

The A Shau Valley "was the base from which the NVA always attacked Hue," said General Kroesen, the FRAC commander. So deeply was this idea ingrained that even after the NVA divisions crossed the DMZ, immediate attention still centered on the defense of Hue, as if the assaults across the DMZ were mere feints. "The NVA had never attacked openly through the DMZ," wrote Kroesen in retrospect. "In the face of friendly air power, armor, and armored cavalry, an attack across the open coastal plain by NVA infantry, even with armor support, seemed illogical. Furthermore, the old pattern of movement into western Quang Tri . . . strengthened the conclusion that the attack would come from the west, possibly as early as May, but more likely in June."

The third element of METT, terrain and weather, was also a factor in both the Battle of the Bulge and the Eastertide Offensive. The terrain and weather were favorable to the Germans in their '44 offensive. The Ardennes is laced with hills and forests that shielded the German advance. German forces also concentrated behind the Siegfried Line, a series of fortified positions just inside the German border that obscured the massing Nazi legions. The snowy weather was also beneficial to the German attack, and they considered it a necessary element in launching a successful campaign, for such atmospheric conditions precluded a major Allied ground assault and also grounded Allied air operations.

Patton was known for believing that "fixed fortifications are a monument to the stupidity of man," and in Vietnam the fixed allied defensive firebases and fire support bases along the DMZ allowed the enemy to maneuver his forces almost at will. The weather in Vietnam also favored the enemy Easter attack; low clouds and rain covered the DMZ region and kept most allied close-air-support aircraft from assisting ground operations.

Time and troops available were also major factors in both the German and NVA decisions to attack. Time was running out for the Germans in 1944, and for the North Vietnamese in 1972. In 1944, the awesome power of U.S. mobilization for war continued to be felt as new weaponry flooded the battlefield and fresh combat divisions, such as the newly arrived 106th Infantry Division in the Ardennes, continued to be deployed. While the Allied buildup showed no signs of slowing, German strength continued to be eroded by its combat operations on the Eastern and Western fronts and by the devastation of the Allied bombing. The clock was ticking. Realizing that his only alternatives were either attack or surrender, the Führer chose to risk everything on one final massive assault.

Time was also running out for the North Vietnamese at the strategic level in 1972, as their Chinese and Soviet allies began to falter and the Paris peace talks became more serious. But at the tactical and operational levels, time appeared to favor an immediate NVA attack. Almost all U.S. ground combat forces had been withdrawn, and it appeared that the anti-war movement in the United States and growing opposition to the war in Congress would preclude President Nixon's reintervening in the war. South Vietnam's defenses were manned entirely by ARVN forces that had been easily outfought by the NVA during their Lam Son 719 incursion into Laos a year earlier.

As far as the issue of troops available was concerned, the RVNAF defenders in the northern provinces were outgunned and outmanned by the NVA attackers. The NVA massed five division-equivalents, including three tank regiments, against the 1st ARVN Division headquartered at Hue, the 3rd ARVN Division with its attached 20th Tank Battalion at Quang Tri, and the 147th and 258th VNMC (South Vietnamese Marine Corps) brigades.

The NVA 324B Division, supplemented by the 5th and 6th NVA regiments, would move from the A Shau Valley to engage the 1st ARVN Division at Hue. Meanwhile, the field army–level NVA B-5 Front, which was the headquarters responsible for NVA operations in South Vietnam's northernmost provinces, would swoop down from the north. From the western DMZ would come the 302nd NVA Division with its attached 204th Tank Battalion, while from the eastern DMZ would come a division-sized task force composed of the 27th and 31st Infantry regiments and 126th Sapper Regiment with the attached 201st Tank Regiment. The 304th NVA Division with its attached 203rd Tank Regiment would infiltrate from Laos.

To negate the Allied advantage in air support, as many as 16 SA-2 surface-to-air missile emplacements were positioned in and to the north of the DMZ, and a full range of 23mm to 100mm AAA guns were located throughout Quang Tri province. But the main NVA advantage was in field artillery. As many as six NVA artillery regiments, including the 38th, 68th and 84th, operating as a corps artillery group, were carefully positioned above Dong Ha. Their 122mm guns and especially their Soviet-supplied M-46 130mm guns outranged every U.S. and ARVN artillery piece except the few 175mm guns that remained in-country.

With the background provided by the METT evaluation in mind, the reasons for the surprise of the 1944 German Ardennes offensive and the 1972 NVA Eastertide Offensive can be brought into focus. Stated succinctly, the Americans and their allies had become complacent because of their successes.

That was evident in the aftermath of the Battle of the Bulge. "One major fault on our side," said one analyst, "was that the intelligence community had come to rely far too heavily on Ultra to the exclusion of other intelligence sources. Ultra had become virtually infallible. But Ultra depended on radio intercepts. Now that we had advanced almost to the German border, the German Army had less need for radio communications and more and more often used secure and uninterceptable land lines. Moreover, it apparently did not occur to our intelligence community that the Germans could—or might—plan and launch an operation with complete radio and telephone silence imposed." In fact, Hitler forbade, under pain of death, communications about the offensive to all but a select few prior to the battle. Thus there was little Ultra traffic related to the upcoming Ardennes offensive.

"The fallacy that crept into our thinking was that since Ultra had not specifically forecast or suggested a major strategic counterattack, there was no possibility of one," said Field Marshal Montgomery's G-2 (division intelligence officer). The Twelfth Army Group G-2, Colonel Eddie Sibert, was even more specific: "As for general intelligence operations . . . it occurs to me that we may have put too much reliance on certain technical types of intelligence, such as signal intelligence [SIGINT], upon which we had come to rely too much."

But those lessons gained at so high a price during the Battle of the Bulge went unheeded during the Eastertide Offensive in Vietnam 28 years later. There has been little written on SIGINT reporting during the Eastertide Offensive, but it can be presumed, from the actions not taken, that there were few intercepts warning that such an attack was likely. General Creighton Abrams, the MACV commander, would not have been on R&R with his family in Thailand if an enemy attack had been expected. In addition, a country-wide alert would have been issued if an attack were deemed imminent. Although an ARVN JGS account would later claim such an alert was issued, it was never received by MACV, the ARVN I Corps or by FRAC.

The attack had been anticipated, however, by the 1st Battalion, 525th Military Intelligence Group. They had accurately published the NVA's grand design (to include preliminary objectives and commanding officers) at the inception of hostilities, only to have this bevy of information fall on deaf ears because their information was HUMINT (human intelligence) versus SIGINT.

Unfortunately, it was some time after the NVA launched their initial cross-border attack on Good Friday, March 30, 1972, before the true intent of the NVA offensive was recognized throughout the American command structure. So intent was the focus on the defense of Hue that it was not until April 27, 28 days after the offensive had started, that General Kroesen wrote to General Abrams: "Reports are fragmentary at this time but intelligence indicates that the [enemy] objectives are ... to establish a blocking force on the Quang Tri/Thua Thien [provincial] border. Other NVA forces will then assume offensive operations to capture Quang Tri City"—the same information that 1/525 Military Intelligence Group had come up with three weeks earlier.

As in the Battle of the Bulge, the enemy had succeeded in sufficiently cloaking his aggressive intentions. The main lesson in both cases is that SIGINT is not the sole form of intelligence but should be treated as just one of many elements in an all-source intelligence analysis. SIGINT cannot (and should not) be the crux, or final, determining factor in assessing enemy intentions or capabilities. In fact, the absence of SIGINT in the Eastertide Offensive, just as in the Bulge, could have been an indication that the enemy was planning something big. Americans and their allies lacked SIGINT and mistrusted HUMINT.

"It was not intelligence that failed," said one of Patton's sub-ordinates in the wake of the Battle of the Bulge. "The failure was the commanders and certain G2s, who did not act on the intelligence they had." Those words could just as easily have been written about the 1972 Eastertide Offensive.

Trapped in Saigon

By Dan Feltham

In April 1975, Saigon fell to an NVA multidivision, cross-border invasion. Among those trapped in the city were some 130 Vietnamese employees of IBM-Vietnam and their families. Part of the IBM World Trade Corporations, IBM-Vietnam did not sell or service IBM products used by the U.S. armed forces (that was done by a separate IBM organization), but rather worked with the South Vietnamese army, navy and air force, as well as with Saigon's downtown commercial data processing users. Nevertheless, it was part of the IBM family.

In 1975, I was an IBM employee working on Saipan, in the northern Mariana Islands, helping to install a computer system for the trust territory's government. I was awakened one day by an early-morning call from a vice president in New York. "Go to Guam," he said, "and help set up a task force to receive and care for 130 Vietnamese IBMers and their families. Saigon is about to fall, and our people will be airlifted to Guam refugee camps in the next few days. You'll be joined by other IBMers flying in to help, but I want you to set up a war room environment at the Agana Hilton and get things started." It was April 25, 1975—seven days before Saigon would actually fall.

I was on the first morning plane to Agana—a 20-minute

flight—and at the IBM Guam office by 9:30. A meeting was called of all local office personnel. Our mission was explained, and we started making arrangements for the days ahead. We needed such things as radios, signs, rental cars, money, secretarial help and hotel reservations. Everyone would pitch in as necessary. The permanent population of Guam in 1975 was around 100,000 persons; but with refugees pouring in, the population would double almost overnight.

I asked an IBM friend, George Winter, to join me, and we began driving to the refugee camps that were suddenly sprouting up at or near various military bases around the island. Our first stop was the new camp at Asan Annex, and there we got lucky. We found an IBM-Vietnam employee, Mr. Chang, and his family. We told him we would be back to him soon with the things he needed. At that point, George and I naively thought this was going to be an easy assignment. We drove to Barrigada Camp, then to Andersen Air Force Base and North West Field, past rows of awesome B-52 bombers now in menacing repose. We left IBM signs, made announcements on public address systems and gathered evacuation information, but did not find any other IBM employees. Chang had somehow been the first and, so far, only employee to reach Guam.

That afternoon, IBM executives began to arrive and take charge of our rescue operation. They were IBM World Trade employees who had direct personnel responsibilities for the Vietnamese IBMers headed our way. Charlie Swift, of IBM Far East in Tokyo, the ranking executive, was joined by Frank O'Keefe, Matt Ash, Ted Robinson and Jack Ewen from Tokyo and Hong Kong. Ewen had been the IBM Saigon country manager up until the previous month, when he had been told by upper management to get out of Vietnam until conditions returned to normal.

George and I briefed the newcomers on the current situation

and then returned to the arrival area at the naval air station (NAS), where overloaded transports were arriving with Vietnamese refugees. I remained at the NAS until 2:15 Saturday morning, holding a large IBM sign and watching transports come and go. I reflected on my own experiences in South Vietnam, the good IBM friends I had made there just four years before, and the tragedy that must be unfolding in the streets, homes and offices of Saigon.

The Guam IBMers had been most helpful throughout that day. We made some progress by developing a search-and-communications strategy, learned some basic refugee camp procedures, displayed our signs and found one more family. The incoming Vietnamese were quiet and seemed dreadfully tired. They stood patiently in lines to complete necessary paperwork. They accepted food and drink and queued up for bus rides to the new camps. Some appeared worried, and others worked hard to help other refugees when help was needed. The reception and processing centers were well-organized; there were a great many American military and civilians helping the new arrivals. What a day!

The newly arrived executives had called a 9 A.M. organizational meeting for the next day. Charlie Swift laid out responsibilities for those of us who were there to help. During that initial meeting, concern was expressed that certain critical Vietnamese IBMers might not be allowed to leave Saigon because of necessary maintenance on computer systems belonging to the South Vietnamese government. Sadly, this would prove to be the case.

At 11 A.M., Swift and I drove to Asan to talk with Chang and to learn how he had escaped Saigon so quickly when other IBMers had been unable to do so. He told us that he had a sister who had married an American journalist, and that the journalist had sponsored the whole family's departure several days earlier. Obviously, we needed more information. We talked to several military officers and a chaplain.

That afternoon, I drove out to Andersen again and checked with the folks at Military Airlift Command, gave an IBM sign to an Air Force colonel and received a quick briefing. Flights from Saigon had become less frequent by that time, and Andersen refugees were being transported to other camps around Guam. I made a public address broadcast to the refugees in "Tin City," which went something like: "I am an IBM Corporation employee and am looking for any IBM World Trade Vietnamese who might be listening. If you hear and understand me, please come to the main office so that I can help you." There was no response, so I drove to the NAS again and learned that flights into Guam were being purposely delayed because of space restrictions on any more refugees. However, flights were continuing past Guam to the individual islands of Wake, Midway and Saipan. After making another broadcast, I went to Barrigada and the Black Construction Company camps. I talked to anyone who would stop and listen.

The Vietnamese families were huddled in small groups, clutching their meager belongings. Many had small black suitcases, which contained a few personal effects plus any gold, jewels or other valuables they had been able to bring with them in their hurried departure from Saigon.

Back at the Hilton, each team member presented a status report at a 6 P.M. meeting. IBM developed a plan that would selectively place our Vietnamese refugees in different countries and provide them with homes and jobs once they were free to migrate. (Some countries had specifically stated that they did not want to have anything to do with the refugees.) IBM intended to sponsor each employee to a country like the United States, France, the Philippines, Thailand or Indonesia. It was even rumored that IBM headquarters was considering setting up a rehabilitation center at San Jose, California, which would handle follow-on relocations. But first we had to find our people! Time seemed to be running out.

At 9 P.M. that evening, we received a call from Bruce Tomson, IBM Thailand's general manager in Bangkok. Tomson had new information that indicated our IBMers were behind 10,000 other Vietnamese in the "staging queue." He said there was a high likelihood that they would not escape Saigon at all. Tomson had worked with IBM in South Vietnam for three years in the late 1960s. He knew what he was talking about. He said he was in direct contact with Jim Oshida at the U.S. Defense Attaché Office (DAO) in the American Embassy office in Saigon. They were evaluating alternative evacuation plans—such as sending in a chartered TWA Boeing 747 with people who knew Saigon, with enough money to buy our Vietnamese out.

Permission to send a 747 to Vietnam was requested from DAO and IBM Far East headquarters in New York. Tomson also told us that 15 IBMers wanted to remain in Saigon and that the acting Vietnamese manager, Quan Trang Nguyen (not his real name) had re-established priorities for the departing employees. It seemed that 315 of them, divided into three groups, would be allowed to leave over the next few days. Our people were classified with Saigon's general business population. Those of us in that small, faraway Hilton hotel room began to agonize over what to do and what to recommend to IBM in New York. We began to understand more about the tragedy that was taking place—and we realized that the number of people trying to escape from Vietnam had increased drastically.

At 9:25 P.M., Charlie Swift called Ralph Pfieffer, president of IBM's Asia Pacific Corporation, who was in Tarrytown, N.Y. We then heard that the four-day cease-fire might end Monday night, and that the embassy was "suggesting that we send in a 747 to rescue our 315 people and others. It is not known whether permission and arrangements to charter the 747 can be made." Swift provided what details he had been given and explained that the maintenance of Saigon's IBM computers was considered a "critical industry" and that our IBMers might not get out at all.

He said that Air Vietnam, China Airlines, Air France and Singapore Airlines were still scheduling flights into Tan Son Nhut, but that Pan American was not. Buses were still running in Saigon, and it was assumed that Oshida could arrange transportation out to the Tan Son Nhut airport. At 11 P.M., we received another call from Bangkok. It was Bruce Tomson again, saying that there might not be a 747 rescue attempt, since our people had been classified as a "critical industry" providing essential services to the South Vietnamese government—along with the telephone, water and electric companies, Honeywell at USAID and a few commercial banks. Tomson had talked with Oshida again, and Oshida said he was going to bring our problem to Denny Ellerman at the U.S. Embassy's commercial attaché office.

During the night, I received several calls from American IBMers in the United States who had worked in Saigon in the '60s and who still had extended families in Saigon. They gave me names and asked that I try to locate their Vietnamese relations in the refugee camps. I said I would try, and I did. But I sure didn't know what would happen.

The morning papers of Sunday, April 27, were filled with refugee stories. I had another call from Tomson in Bangkok, who told me: 1. Aircraft were still flying into Tan Son Nhut (TSN) and TSN base operations would assist with a quick turnaround if the Pan American 747 standing by in Manila was committed to the mission; 2. The IBM-Vietnam manager, Nguyen, had notified 100 IBMers that they might be able to leave that day, but the fate of the remaining 215 was dependent on our ability to convince the

U.S. Embassy that a few customer engineers could maintain the essential computers (someone would have to make a presentation at the embassy); and 3. Nguyen had lists of nonessential and essential personnel.

Tomson also told us: "There are two types of evacuation notices being issued by the embassy: A., first alert, which means departure in 48 hours; and B., second alert, which means go to location X in two hours and presumably you will be picked up by buses and somehow evacuated." He also said that the consensus was that Ambassador Graham Martin was calling the shots in Saigon and not our U.S. authorities in Washington, D.C. It was becoming evident that, without an on-site American IBM representative dealing with the embassy "eyeball to eyeball," an evacuation plan for our employees had little chance for success. Tomson closed the call by telling Swift that he should leave Guam and come to Bangkok.

What we didn't know at the time was that a frustrated but determined Bruce Tomson was also trying to arrange a backup plan. He definitely knew the territory, and he was also resourceful. He had contacted a quasimilitary source and arranged for an Air America DC-4 to fly into TSN, pick up the IBMers and fly them to Bangkok. The second half of their flight to freedom would be provided by an Air Siam Airbus, which would ignore Thailand immigration requirements and take the refugees to Guam. Tomson even called an IBM liaison office in Washington to obtain permission for the Airbus to fly through Philippine airspace and refuel at Clark if necessary.

There was one catch: Tomson was probably going to have to fly into Saigon himself and buy a bus for an exorbitant sum. He also knew he would need additional contingency money for various payoffs along the way through the chaotic streets between the IBM office and TSN—not an easy task! There was a high probability that the bus would be demolished while crashing through the TSN gates. He called Chase Manhattan Bank in Bangkok, and they filled a large bag with small denomination U.S. currency worth $75,000, which Tomson would carry with him.

Another alternate plan was developed by Wil Derango, then general manager of IBM Malaysia (and a former IBM-FSD manager in Saigon). He had offered the Thai government five IBM System/360 Model 50 computers (a huge amount of computing power) in exchange for any Thai aircraft that would fly into TSN on a rescue mission. The Thai government was indeed interested, but could not obtain the proper approvals in time. It is probably a good thing, too, since Derango hadn't the slightest idea of how he was going to provide the five large processors.

At 10 A.M., Pfieffer called Swift to tell him that yet another alternate plan was being considered—to evacuate our Vietnamese to Manila. The State Department in Washington had said that all 315 IBMers would be going to Clark Air Base. On Guam, we had grave doubts that such a plan had any real chance for success. It seemed to us that Washington, D.C., and New York were definitely out of touch with reality.

Sometime that same morning, we learned that another IBMer, with her nine dependents, had arrived at Clark. The Red Cross there had sent a wire to the Red Cross office in White Plains, New York, which notified IBM HQ in Armonk. The IBMer's father had worked for USAID, and the family had departed Saigon via a USAID evacuation plan. Additionally, someone told us that a cable had been sent to the U.S. Embassy in Saigon from Washington, D.C., telling the staff to send the 300-plus IBMers to Clark. We felt that there was a strong possibility that the embassy could not or would not comply with that directive. However, several of our executives thought they should go to the Philippines on the basis of this news.

We then received a call from IBM Hong Kong with new information. Several IBM Vietnamese had volunteered to remain in Saigon. Nguyen had briefed the embassy. He was talking about the possibility of evacuation for his people by the end of the following week, and he needed funds with which to pay those who would stay behind. And we learned that we could not obtain a 747 to actually fly into TSN, but we could charter one elsewhere when we needed it, for the peaceful air space between Clark and Guam.

An IBM executive called from Hong Kong (he was in contact with IBM Saigon) and said that the embassy's Denny Ellerman had told Nguyen that he did not know when the IBMers would be going. Great! Then Tomson called again and talked with Swift for one full hour. I thought that Tomson was probably trying to put together a plan that might have some chance of success (I did not find out about the DC-4 plan until much later). Out of that conversation came the following plan of action: A few of us would maintain our Guam watch; one man would go to Manila; Charlie Swift and Jack Ewen would go to Bangkok and set up a command post there; and, finally, Tomson and probably Ewen would go into Saigon to negotiate the evacuation for most of the Vietnamese employees, minus a few technical men who would volunteer to remain.

At 10:30 P.M. on the 27th, we called Ralph Pfieffer in New York and passed along as much information as we had, including the fact that the meeting between Nuygen and the embassy had produced no results—the U.S. Consulate had not bought our withdrawal plan, and no IBMers could leave. The embassy told Nuygen that there was no cable from Washington, D.C. The telegrams had evidently either been lost in the shuffle or were ignored.

The only conclusion to draw was that our Vietnamese IBMers were hostages of the U.S. Embassy. Apparently, the embassy believed that if some of the employees and families were to be evacuated, the others would quit their computer maintenance responsibilities and also try to leave. The embassy rejected

Nguyen's presentation and said, "No IBMer may leave." Pfieffer was also told that Ambassador Martin was in charge—and he was firmly backing the retention of essential services.

(Editor's note: Ambassador Martin felt there was a possibility of a negotiated settlement with North Vietnam, and it was therefore necessary for all the essential services to be maintained, including those provided by IBM-Vietnam. Even the embassy personnel planned to remain in Vietnam after the fall, but they were ordered out by Washington.)

Since that time, with the help of some correspondence with various IBMers, I have been able to reconstruct what was actually happening in Saigon. On April 10, 1975 Nguyen hand delivered a list of all IBM Vietnam employees and their dependents to the U.S. Embassy's reception desk; it was addressed to Mr. Wolfgang Lehman, Deputy Chief of Mission, U.S. Embassy, Saigon. This list was to have formed the basis of an embassy-sponsored evacuation. The political and military situation was deteriorating fast, so Nguyen went to see Jim Oshida, the commercial attaché, a week later (April 17). He learned that Oshida had not seen the list and also that Oshida needed a sponsorship letter from IBM outside of Vietnam, which would state that IBM would take full responsibility for every person on Nguyen's list.

Nguyen returned to his IBM office, sent a duplicate list to Oshida and called Ewen in Hong Kong. He outlined the need for the sponsorship letter. A letter and another complete list was sent to the U.S. Embassy in Saigon via diplomatic pouch direct from the U.S. Consulate in Hong Kong. Nguyen received a copy of this same set of documents via friends at Air Vietnam, and called Oshida for an appointment. At their next meeting, on April 24, Nguyen was able to show Oshida exactly what had been sent, and Oshida stated that he had not received such a diplomatic pouch. Oshida then told Nguyen to have his 315 people ready to leave on a two-hour notice and that he would be informed as to the pickup place and time. At this point, every-thing looked organized; all the IBMers had to do was wait for instructions from the embassy.

On April 26, Nguyen called Oshida and asked for an update on their evacuation. Oshida told him that all the paperwork had been completed and he was waiting for approval from his boss, Denny Ellerman. Oshida also told Nguyen that it looked like all 315 might go together, since IBM was planning to send a Boeing 747, and that the people from the Bank of America and 3M Cor-poration might join them. The next day, April 27, Oshida asked Nguyen to come to the embassy and meet with Ellerman. Eller-man told Nguyen that he could not let IBM personnel go because the highly trained IBM technicians were essential to Vietnam's future government. He said something to the effect that, if he allowed Nguyen's people to leave, it would jeopardize the back-bone of the structure that would support the new government's efforts to reconstruct the country.

Nguyen tried to explain about those IBMers who had volun-teered to remain and suggested that the others should be permit-ted to go immediately. By the end of the conversation, Ellerman had eased up and promised to reconsider IBM's case. On the morning of April 29, Nguyen heard the firing that signaled that the attack at Tan Son Nhut had begun and was told that the air-port was closed to all fixed-wing aircraft. His air evacuation route was cut off. Nguyen tried to call the embassy but couldn't get through. He also tried to walk the few blocks from IBM to the embassy but could not approach it because of the mobs trying to storm the embassy walls. He had to sit and wait.

Meanwhile, our little group's new plan had been finalized. Swift and Ewen would go to Bangkok as soon as possible. Our embassy in Thailand had contacted the Thai military and said that embassy personnel would help if needed. It seemed that one, two or maybe three American IBMers would have to go to Saigon to rescue our people. Whoever went would have to know the streets and back alleys, and they would have to convince the embassy that we had an acceptable plan. My notes of April 27 actually say that the embassy would arrange for a military aircraft! Just before departing for Bangkok, our executives stated: "I think the embassy is trying to help and that Ambassador Martin is sincere. The general feeling is that if we don't cooperate, the embassy will forget us, but if we do cooperate, we will have their support."

History has, of course, proved that the situation was much different. TSN was useless to fixed-wing aircraft as of the 27th. Meanwhile, Tomson in Bangkok had hired a TSN-based twin Beechcraft that was to be available after its crew took video clips of new President Big Minh's swearing-in ceremony. The Beechcraft was to return to Bangkok with the film and then be available to take Tomson, his bag of money, and one other person to Saigon. Departure for Tomson's charter was scheduled for 9 A.M. on the 29th. No one knew that the 29th would be too late, and that there were only two days remaining to help our people.

Back to the story on Guam—the next day was Monday the 28th, and things were relatively quiet. I continued to visit refugee camps, still looking for any of our people who might have escaped. I did find several family members for the Stateside IBMers who had called me for help, and I notified those concerned. Tomson later told me that sometime on the 28th, he called Ellerman's office to update him on his plan to fly into Saigon. Ellerman's secretary answered the phone in a trembling voice and said to Tomson, "Don't come!" and hung up. He then found out that the Beechcraft had never left TSN for Thailand because the runways were inoperable. Moreover, the Air America Douglas DC-4 that Tomson had planned to use for the evacuation of the IBMers suddenly became unavailable. It was one of two

DC-4s that had been used to fly ex-President Thieu and his entourage out of Vietnam, and the plane had been detained in the Philippines. Tomson called Ellerman that night with the hope that he could still help. Ellerman was upset. He confirmed that TSN was not usable and that Tomson should definitely not come to Saigon. Things were clearly falling apart fast.

At 7 A.M. on the 29th, I called my office in Honolulu and said that things didn't look good for the IBMers trapped in Saigon. I didn't know that this was to be the last day of freedom in South Vietnam for many years to come. That morning, Saigon's U.S. Armed Forces FM radio station played "White Christmas" to signal the final massive helicopter evacuation. Nguyen told me later that when he heard the song he thought to himself, "How strange to play such a song at the hottest time of the year; then again, with Americans you can expect anything, even the craziest." He didn't know it was the evacuation signal.

I continued to search the camps, make speeches on public address systems, check arrival lists, post signs, talk with new arrivals, ask questions and watch the hundreds of C-141s and other overloaded aircraft land as the last refugees continued to arrive. Somehow I knew our people would not be among those arrivals. Sometime during the 29th I talked with Tomson in Bangkok. He told me TSN was a shambles and that he wouldn't be going to Saigon. He was tired and dejected but wasn't giving up. He had been on the phone to Saigon and was trying to persuade the stranded IBMers to use the helipad within the walls of the Alliance Francé compound, next door to their office, as a means of escape. He was told that it wasn't available, even though some rescue helicopters had already taken off from there. Tomson also called Frank Cary, IBM Chief Executive Officer in New York, to ask what Cary could do, but there seemed to be little hope for success.

At 10:11 P.M. on April 29, according to David Butler's account, *The Fall of Saigon*, a telegram was received by the U.S. Embassy that read: "For Martin from Brown [former Ambassador Dean Brown, who had been brought out of retirement to head up a task force for the evacuation and resettlement of Vietnamese refugees]. IBM Headquarters reports its personnel still in Saigon and is most disturbed. Do what you can." And at 11:06 P.M., a message came into the embassy from President Gerald Ford's chief of staff: "To Martin from [Don] Rumsfeld. I understand that 154 IBM employees, including their families, are still awaiting removal from Saigon. I further understand that they are standing in front of the IBM building awaiting instructions where they should go for evacuation. I ask that you do your utmost to see they are evacuated with the current helicopter lift." These messages were, of course, way too late.

Late that night, I had a call from Nguyen. He said that the IBM families, comprising a couple of hundred men, women and children, had all packed and gone to the nearby Ben Bach Dang navy docks. A last-minute effort to get them successfully evacuated by barge down the Saigon River had been arranged by the embassy. Hopes were high that freedom was yet possible.

The large group was quickly organized and arrived at 5 P.M. The barge was there, but it was deserted and unmotorized. They waited nearby in the dark for directions and hoped for a tow boat or another barge. Nearby boats were already overfilled. Two IBMers tried to climb up the side of a large Navy vessel but were repelled by gunfire.

At dawn they returned to their IBM office, four blocks from the embassy. Nguyen went on to say that the families had again waited in the street, but no one from the embassy or with any authority to guide them ever showed up. After a couple more hours they realized there was no hope; they had been left behind.

Some went home, but most remained at the office to await the Communist takeover.

Nguyen had decided to make one last phone call to our small group on Guam to let us know of their fate. He said he would send everyone home, turn off the lights, lock the office door and go himself. He said an emotional "Good-bye," and the line went dead.

Tragic Postlude To "Peace"

By Colonel William E. LeGro, U.S. Army (ret.)

Humorist Will Rogers once quipped that the United States had never lost a war nor won a peace conference. His words were bitterly fulfilled in January 1973, when the United States signed the so-called Paris Peace Accords that supposedly ended the Vietnam War.

Under the terms of that agreement, the North Vietnamese returned some of the prisoners of war they were holding and allowed the United States 60 days to dismantle what remained of its military assistance command, but the North Vietnamese maintained a number of their combat divisions in the South, as well as in Cambodia and Laos. The war was not over; the accords had only caused a temporary armed truce. What the United States and South Vietnam gained was a short-lived period of reduced expenditures of ammunition and shorter casualty lists. The agreement was soon violated by both sides. Instead of marking the beginning of peace, the Paris Peace Accords only marked the beginning of a new phase of the war.

The "Agreement on Ending the War and Restoring Peace in Vietnam" (the official name of the cease-fire agreement) took effect on January 27, 1973, but 1973 was anything but peaceful. In March, the Communists launched a major attack against the town of Hong Ngu, a port on the Mekong River just south of the Cambodian border, employing three regular regiments supported by artillery, striking south from their Cambodian sanctuary.

The United States supported the Army of the Republic of Vietnam (ARVN) defense and counterattack by sending B-52s to pound the Communist base area north of the border in Cambodia. By May, the ARVN had retaken Hong Ngu and cleared the banks of the Mekong to the Cambodian border. Casualties were heavy on both sides.

The summer of 1973 also saw heavy combat in the Central Highlands beginning with the North Vietnamese Army (NVA) attack on the ARVN outposts west of Kontum. The ARVN counterattacked, and what began as minor skirmishes soon developed into a major campaign in Kontum and Pleiku provinces. Another major action occurred in the highlands when the NVA sent a division-sized task force into Quang Duc province to destroy the ARVN outposts controlling the lines of communications. The ARVN counterattack was successful in driving the North Vietnamese from Quang Duc with heavy losses.

Following the Hong Ngu battle, operations in the vast Mekong Delta of Military Region 4 were largely characterized by fierce but short local engagements. The NVA efforts to infiltrate from Cambodia, destroy ARVN outposts and corner the rice crop were challenged in the Seven Mountains close by the Cambodian frontier, resulting in the destruction of the 1st NVA Division by the Rangers of the 44th Special Tactical Zone.

The NVA launched dozens of attacks against ARVN positions in Military Region 3, north of Saigon, in the months following the cease-fire, with the apparent purpose of screening infiltration and protecting the buildup of its forces and installations, but no territory changed hands. The South Vietnamese Air Force (VNAF) responded with an intensive air campaign against NVA bases, but the results were nearly negligible because the bombers were kept at high altitudes by new concentrations of anti-aircraft artillery and Strella ground-to-air missiles introduced by the NVA in violation of the cease-fire.

In early 1974, the Communists issued statements presenting their views on the failure of the cease-fire and the situation in South Vietnam. Hanoi published a "white paper" assailing U.S. and Saigon "provocations." Its charges were accompanied by the rattle and roar of thousands of trucks coursing south across the DMZ (Demilitarized Zone) and through Laos in a mammoth "transportation offensive." Thousands of tons of supplies were accumulating in the southern stockpiles; by the cease-fire anniversary, the NVA had sufficient stocks to support, for more than a year, an offensive comparable to that of their 1972 Eastertide invasion. Meanwhile, NVA engineers extended their fuel pipelines into the A Shau Valley of Thua Thien province, and the Laotian pipeline was passing through the tri-border junction into Kontum province. In the year following the cease-fire, the NVA increased its artillery and tank strength in the south fourfold and added an air defense division and 12 air defense regiments to its force deployed in South Vietnam. Included were SA-2 and SA-7 missiles and radar-controlled guns.

That wasn't all the Communists were doing. Preparations for resuming the offensive were being made north of the DMZ as well. The NVA reconstituted its strategic reserve and organized its I Corps to control three regular divisions garrisoned just north of the DMZ.

Viewed from the South, the warning was clear: although there existed a rough parity of military power deployed in the South, considering the obviously heavier requirements on South Vietnam to protect a dispersed population and long lines of communications, the Republic of Vietnam Armed Forces (RVNAF) could retain not even one division in general reserve. The defense possessed no flexibility whatsoever and adjustments were possible only by giving up terrain and usually population along with it. On the other hand, the NVA not only had considerable flexibility in the choice of objectives and forces to employ but it also had six full-strength infantry divisions in reserve, supported by artillery, tanks and adequate logistics to throw into battle at the decisive moment. Furthermore, improvements in the roads southward, and the absence of air interdiction, reduced NVA deployment times to the point where a surprise appearance of the NVA reserve became a worrisome possibility.

Against this ominous backdrop, it was clear to South Vietnamese political and military leadership, and to the American officials in Saigon as well, that continued U.S. logistical support would be essential to survival.

U.S. support of the South Vietnamese military forces was "service funded." This meant that the money was contained in U.S. Army, Navy and Air Force sections of the defense appropriations bill. A carryover from the days of active U.S. participation in the war, the Military Assistance Service Funded (MASF) program for Vietnam became obsolete with the departure of American forces from Vietnam in January 1973. Months passed, however, before the Defense Department, the services and the Congress could adjust to the changed situation with a new military assistance program.

In the interim, supplies and equipment for the Republic of Vietnam Armed Forces were requisitioned under continuing resolution authority, based on the program developed jointly with South Vietnam's defense ministry and Joint General Staff in early 1973 and in anticipation of adequate funds to be contained in the Defense Appropriation Act for fiscal year 1974. The U.S.-funded portion of the RVNAF fiscal 1974 budget called for expenditures of $1.126 billion, and no problems were foreseen in Saigon, either by the RVNAF staff or the responsible American officials in the Defense Attaché Office (DAO), although all recognized that the unanticipated high levels of combat following the cease-fire would call for adjustments upward of the $1.126 billion budget. Then events in Washington shattered the illusion of confidence that had existed in Saigon.

On December 19, 1973, Major General John E. Murray, the defense attaché and senior U.S. military official in Vietnam, received the disquieting news that the Senate committee had reduced the 1974 funds for Vietnam and Laos to $650 million from the $1.126 billion recommended by the House committee. In conference, the two legislative bodies agreed on $900 million, of which only $813 million would go to Vietnam. Meanwhile, money was being obligated (spent) under the $1.126 billion ceiling set by Congress under the continuing resolution. Concerned that the lowered ceiling would be exceeded before the year was out, the Department of the Army suddenly, and without prior notice to General Murray, cut off all operational and maintenance funds to Vietnam for the balance of the 1974 fiscal year. With a four-month order-to-ship time, the supply line dried up in April 1974 and would never recover. The armed forces of Vietnam, and the Americans in Saigon who were charged with assisting them, were faced with a double-barreled problem: the funds they expected to carry them through the summer of 1974 were cut off, and the support they required to continue the defense of the country through 1974 and 1975 was under severe attack in the U.S. Congress.

The most critical shortage was in ammunition for the South Vietnamese forces. Although the United States was committed to replace expenditures and losses of ammunition on a one-for-one basis after the cease-fire, stocks were at dangerously low levels. At least $221 million would be needed to bring ammunition stocks up to cease-fire levels, but this would require nearly all the funds remaining for the balance of fiscal year 1974, leaving nothing for fuel, spares or any of the other critical requirements.

For the rest of December and throughout January, General Murray was the unhappy recipient of confused and conflicting information on funding from Washington and the U.S. Pacific Command in Honolulu. He wisely did not wait for resolution of the matter, but brought to the RVNAF logistics staff the unpleasant news that U.S. cuts in support would require immediate changes in RVNAF operational practices. Dealing principally with Lieutenant General Dong Van Khuyen, the chief of logistics, and General Cao Van Vien, the chief of the RVNAF Joint General Staff, General Murray impressed upon them the urgency of the need to conserve supplies, particularly ammunition. Without divulging all he knew about the cuts in the fiscal 1974 program, he urged them to apply strict controls against the likelihood of diminished resources. General Vien reacted immediately, ordering new limitations on ammunition usage rates.

In messages to the Commander in Chief Pacific Command (CINCPAC) and to Washington, General Murray explained how the new ceiling imposed overly severe restrictions on the Vietnam program, how the situation had changed in Vietnam since the program's drafting in early 1973 and the impact of these changes on the requirements of the RVNAF. Since the fiscal 1974 program had been agreed upon, significant price increases had occurred in equipment and fuel, and the low level of combat anticipated after the cease-fire had not happened. Increased enemy capabilities created a high-threat environment, and an inflation rate of 65 percent in South Vietnam correspondingly drove up subsistence costs. The imposition of a lowered ceiling after 75 percent of the funds had been obligated left no flexibility for the adjustment of priorities. Also, the inability to identify prior-year funds to be applied to the ceiling had compelled the suspension of all Army requisitions for the past two months; the apparent inclusion of unanticipated costs within the ceiling, such as packing, crating, handling and shipping, further reduced the amounts available for

RVNAF support; and bookkeeping adjustments had imposed considerable fiscal year 1973 costs on fiscal 1974 funds.

While the U.S. Congress was cutting drastically its support of South Vietnam, the North Vietnamese Lao Dong Central Committee and the military committee were preparing the offensive strategy for 1974, a strategy that would severely strain the reduced resources of the South. In October 1973, DAO Saigon assessed the situation and informed Washington that while the Communists were prepared logistically for a major offensive, they would most likely embark on a strategy of widespread attacks on garrisons, outposts and lines of communications, imposing on the RVNAF overwhelming requirements for defense throughout the country. This was not described as a replay of Tet 1968 or the Eastertide Offensive of 1972, but rather a gradual, "phased" offensive. The first major action in this phased offensive occurred when the North Vietnamese 5th Division attempted to infiltrate from Cambodia into the Tri Phap base area in the "Plain of Reeds," northwest of Cay Lai. The ARVN anticipated and skillfully pre-empted this move with an attack into the Tri Phap that killed more than 1,100 enemy and drove the NVA 5th Division back into Svay Rieng, mauling three NVA regiments in the six-week campaign.

Back in Svay Rieng, the NVA 5th Division shifted its attention to the east, to the ARVN outpost at Duc Hue. Its March 27 assault on the base was driven back with heavy losses, but it continued the siege with heavy artillery bombardments and interdiction of the only route into the base.

This was the situation in Vietnam when the Senate Armed Services Committee, responding largely to the leadership of Senator Edward Kennedy, refused on April 3 to raise the ceiling on fiscal year 1974 expenditures. The next day, the House rejected the administration's request to raise the ceiling to $1.6 billion, as well as a compromise increase to $1.4 billion. The issue was dead, but the Defense Department kept trying. It informed the Senate and House committees that it had discovered $266 million in unobligated, prior-year funds and asked to have this amount excluded from the ceiling. The committees agreed that this would be proper, but on May 6, the Senate passed a resolution sponsored by Senator Kennedy to the effect that any expenditures over the fiscal year 1974 ceiling would be illegal.

The dispute between the administration and Congress over the fiscal 1974 program, clearly won by the latter, was only the preliminary to the main event: the fight for the fiscal year 1975 authorization and appropriation.

In Vietnam, the RVNAF conducted its last major offensive operation, an armored sweep into Svay Rieng province, in Cambodia, to relieve the siege of Duc Hue. When the fighting columns returned to their home bases in early May, they were faced with new restrictions. By imposing rigid controls, the RVNAF managed to survive through the difficult summer. Many of its vehicles were on blocks, its aircraft grounded because of parts and fuel shortages, its radios silent for lack of batteries, and its far-flung outposts suffering from inadequate artillery support. The stream of supplies had dwindled to a trickle, and weeks would pass before the pipeline would be flowing again.

Toward the end of May, the House passed the defense authorization bill for fiscal year 1975 with the familiar ceiling of $1.126 billion for MASF, while the Senate committee was recommending only $900 million. Since it was obvious the House ceiling would not survive the House-Senate conference, and that the appropriation would inevitably be passed below the authorization, General Murray sent a 30-page message to CINCPAC and Washington to explain the impact of reduced funding.

He began with a review of Defense Secretary James Schlesinger's comments to the press on May 21: "The most telling argument is the point he [Schlesinger] made so eloquently that it was we who told the South Vietnamese that we would give them the tools and they would have to finish the job. It was we who undertook a commitment to replace their combat losses on a one-for-one basis . . . any further reductions will seriously cripple the South Vietnamese capability to defend themselves and will be a violation of the clear understandings they had from us at the time of the cease-fire."

General Murray told Washington that "cuts and economies have mortgaged the future." The entire program was in trouble. Because stock replenishment had been at a virtual stand-still for over four months, the supply of many common items was below safety levels. In this category were clothing, spare parts, tires, batteries and M-16 rifle barrels. Even if authority to requisition were granted immediately, the lag in order-to-ship time would prevent timely recuperation. The RVNAF staff had imposed strict controls on motor vehicle and marine fuels and estimated that about 70 percent of the vehicle and naval fleets could continue to operate. But this proved to be too optimistic; only 55 percent of the equipment was operating at severely curtailed levels.

The quality and responsiveness of medical service had also suffered. Many lifesaving supplies were seriously depleted, such as blood collection bags, intravenous fluids, antibiotics and surgical dressings. Meanwhile, hospital admissions of wounded increased from 8,750 per month during the first three months of 1974 to more than 10,000 per month by summer, and would continue to rise as the enemy intensified his strategic raids campaign, his "phased offensive." The onset of the wet monsoon would bring with it the scourge of falciparum malaria in the northern provinces, and the supply of insect repellent for the troops was exhausted. In fact, the total supply picture was bleak. Roughly half the items on the stockage list were not there, and shipments to the depots had fallen off from 24,000 metric tons received in March to less than 8,000 metric tons in May.

Because of severe controls placed on ammunition usage, and because ammunition had top priority for available funds, the stockage had remained relatively constant during the last half of the fiscal year. Nevertheless, the NVA's attempt to seize and hold the "Iron Triangle" (the nickname for a Viet Cong guerrilla base area less than 20 miles northwest of Saigon)—a multidivisional effort that lasted six months—had imposed heavy demands on the system. And these demands could only increase. While ammunition constituted a management problem for General Murray and the RVNAF staff, the impact of the restrictions in the field was immediate and often decisive. Experienced infantrymen, accustomed to carrying six grenades into battle but now limited to two, responded with less aggressiveness to orders to advance and were less tenacious in holding threatened positions. Artillery was limited to clearly defined targets and harassing fires were stopped altogether. The consumption of radio batteries was reduced 25 percent by combining nets and operating fewer than 20 days per month. As tactical efficiency suffered, casualties mounted. After noting that 41 percent of the authorized stockage list for tactical communications equipment had been depleted, General Murray reported:

"Equipment in the combat divisions is suffering between 30 and 40 percent deadline rate. The divisions are losing communication flexibility and in MR 2 can no longer provide telephone and teletype communications to attached forces such as ranger units that do not possess VHF TO/E assets. The AN/PRC-25 radio operational readiness has decayed to 67 percent ... ARVN has adjusted to priorities and are reducing tactical divisions to 40 percent of authorized TO/E teletype assets. . . . Continued depletion of communications parts stocks is creating a catastrophic threat to an already seriously degraded tactical communications posture."

One-fifth of the Vietnamese Air Force was grounded for maintenance, a condition bound to worsen before fiscal year 1975 funds would have any effect. The situation for ground combat equipment was similar. In early March, the deadline rate for medium tanks was 25 percent; by mid-May, spare parts shortages had forced the rate to 35 percent. The availability of armored personnel carriers, the main fighting vehicle of the armored cavalry, was sinking to only one-half of organizational strength. In December 1973, RVNAF's mobility, exemplified by the air movement of the ARVN 23rd Division from Kontu, and the rapid shift of the 22nd Division to cover the gaps, had been crucial in rescuing Quang Duc province. This mobility had all but vanished with the decline in funding for maintenance requirements and the skyrocketing costs for all supplies, particularly fuel and ammunition. For example, when ammunition requirements were programmed for fiscal year 1975, the cost was set at $400 million; but when the prices were posted in April 1974, the same tonnages would cost $500 million.

The U.S. commitment to replace RVNAF equipment losses on a basis of one-for-one was ignored. VNAF had lost 281 aircraft since the cease-fire and had received only eight 0-1s as replacements. The navy had lost 58 ships and boats and none had been replaced. The funds could not accommodate the RVNAF's operational requirements, much less replace losses.

General Murray concluded his discussion on RVNAF capabilities under the constraints of a $1.126 billion fiscal 1975 program with an unequivocal, prophetic statement: RVNAF would be capable of defending the country against the current level of enemy activity and of countering countrywide high points, but not capable of defending against a sustained enemy offensive. In his final paragraph of this long message, he summarized the impacts of successively austere levels of support:

"In the final analysis, you can roughly equate cuts in support to loss of real estate. As the cutting edge of the RVNAF is blunted and the enemy continues to improve its combat position and logistical base, what will occur is a retreat to the Saigon-Delta area as a redoubt (precisely what happened in March-April 1975). In a nutshell, we see the decrements as follows: (a.) $1.126 billion level—gradual degradation of equipment base with greatest impact in out-years. Little reserve or flexibility to meet a major enemy offensive in fiscal year 1975. (b.) $900 million level—degradation of equipment base that will have significant impact by third or fourth quarter of fiscal year 1975. No reserve or flexibility to meet major offensive in fiscal year 1975. (c.) $750 million level—equipment losses not supportable. Operations ("O") funds would not support hard-core self-defense requirements. Any chance of having Hanoi see the light and come to the conference table would be sharply diminished. If the enemy continues current level of military activity, RVNAF could defend only selected areas of country. (d.) $600 million level—write off RVN as bad investment and broken promise. GVN would do well to hang on to Saigon and Delta area. The Vietnamese are a determined people, capable of defending themselves and progressing economically, provided they are given the tools we promised them when we decided to end our own military participation. $1.450 billion will provide the essential elements of a viable defense."

President Ford signed the authorization bill on August 5 that fixed the ceiling of support for Vietnam at $1 billion. The ceiling became irrelevant on September 24 when the Congress passed the Defense Appropriation Bill for fiscal year 1975, including only $700 million for Vietnam. The bill provided that all shipping expenses, certain undelivered fiscal years 1973-74 items and commitments, and the operating costs of the Defense Attaché Office as well, were included in the $700 million. This left less than $500 million to be applied to the operational requirements of the RVNAF. The army share was about $410 million, while army ammunition requirements alone were $500 million at 1974 prices. The VNAF would receive about $160 million, less than 30 percent of its requirement.

Draconian measures were applied. Only 55 percent of available transportation could be fueled, and tactical movement required the approval of the corps commander. Bandages and surgical dressings were washed and reused, as were other disposable surgical supplies such as hypodermic syringes and needles, intravenous sets and rubber gloves. Replacement criteria for combat boots were changed from three to two pairs per year. Squadrons in the VNAF were reduced from 66 to 56, flying hours and contractor support were reduced further, and 224 aircraft were placed in storage, including all 61 remaining A-1 bombers, all 52 C-7 cargo ships, 34 C-47 and C-119 gunships, and all O-2 observation planes. Among other operational reductions, the navy inactivated 21 of its 44 riverine units. This was hardly the posture for an armed force on the eve of its final battle for survival. Disaster was predicted and disaster ensued.

PART FOUR

FORGETTING
AND
REMEMBERING

Post Traumatic Stress Disorder

By Margaret Benshoof-Holler

Like an Irish band whistling through the air—Whe-e-e-o-o-o-o-o!—rockets are on you quick. If you are lucky, there is still time to jump for cover before they hit.

One of the most profound memories of the Vietnam War for combat veteran Edward "Robbie" Robinson is his leaning over a 19-year-old kid with a chest wound received in combat near the Demilitarized Zone (DMZ). "Don't let me die! I want my mom!" the young man cried. Robinson, of the 3rd Division, 9th Marines, knew there was nothing he could do. So he cradled him in his arms, gently murmuring: "It's okay. Mommy's here." When the boy died, "the best part of me died with him," Robinson said. "To this day, I tell my wife, and she understands it, that I can never be close to her in an act of love the way I was holding that kid in my arms!"

It is war's tender moments that bring tears to Robinson's eyes. Recalling the brutalities—a buddy blown to pieces by a booby trap—can stir up "flashbacks so real that you can smell the gunpowder, the death, the decaying bodies, the jungle." For him, the war is not over. Posttraumatic stress disorder (PTSD) helps it linger on.

According to Dr. Clifford Levin, a clinical psychologist at the

Mental Research Institute (MRI) in Palo Alto, Calif., the trauma that produces PTSD, such as that experienced in combat, holds the memory in an excitatory fashion, and the natural mechanisms that occur during sleep to reduce that excitement do not work. Stimuli in the environment trigger the trauma, and with it come old thoughts like, "Maybe I'm to blame for my buddy getting shot," says Levin. The PTSD sufferer relives traumatic events and often has recurring dreams and exaggerated startle responses.

It was Robinson's 18th birthday on July 7, 1968, the day he boarded *John J. Pope* in Oceanside, Calif., to go to Vietnam. He had just finished advanced infantry training at Paris Island, where he trained on rifles—the M-14 and the M-16.

Seventeen days later he hit the beach at Da Nang and headed for Dong Ha in Quang Tri province, just below the DMZ, in what was known as "Leatherneck Square." He was a "grunt" and soon got in the thick of the terror and bloodshed.

Being in combat means "growing up real quick," Robinson said. "But you don't grow up, believe me. You're dealing with some very tender psyches, very fragile, vulnerable young men— 18, 19, 20 years old. And you're exposing them to the kind of brutality that only exists in somebody's worst dream." Fresh out of high school, with values still being worked on, most who fought in the Vietnam War had never been away from home before.

The average age of those who went to Vietnam was 19.2 years. "It was the youngest U.S. war ever fought," said Dr. Francis Abueg, a research clinical psychologist at the National Center for Posttraumatic Stress Disorder in Menlo Park. The average age for World War II soldiers was 26.

During World War II, men went and returned as a unit, with time on the way home on a slow-moving troop ship to readjust. In Vietnam, "You go over alone, you overload, and you come back alone," said Robinson. "One day you're shooting a machine gun, the next day you're back home." Vietnam produced more victims of PTSD than any other U.S. war.

Without a moment's notice, Robinson digressed to January 1969. He's back in the war. "Artillery—you can hear it way up in the mountains. B-o-o-o-m! B-o-o-m! B-o-o-o-m! Then you start looking because you have got maybe three, four seconds to run before it lands."

Next he's out on a reconnaissance mission, walking through the jungle in the steamy heat; suddenly, the guy 50 or 60 yards ahead steps on a booby trap. "You get his brains and his body matter sprayed onto your shirt. You spend a half-hour making out a casualty report and trying to put what's left of his pieces of flesh into a sandwich bag."

In 30 minutes the chopper is going to come. The troop is going to move out again. "Maybe next time, you will walk into an ambush," Robinson said. "You just never know. All these things are going through your head, but the consistent thought is, 'I've got to stay alive because I'm no good to myself dead, and I'm certainly no use to my friends if I crack under pressure."

At 18 years old, you build a wall with each casualty. Robinson explained: "People get blown away, they get blown up, they get smoked, they get waxed, they get dinged, they get danged. Nobody ever died in Vietnam. That's how we coped."

Full-blown PTSD affected 15 percent of the 3.1 million men and women who were involved in combat in Vietnam, according to a National Vietnam Veterans Readjustment Study (NVRS) done in 1990. One hundred and seven thousand of those live in the western United States. The numbers include only those who are receiving treatment. Only a small portion of those who have full-blown PTSD are getting help. Another 50 percent have partial PTSD.

PTSD's core symptoms—emotional numbing and reduced

capability for intimacy, reliving the experience through flashbacks or dreams, difficulty in sleeping and exaggerated startle
responses—are the same across all traumas, such as combat, prisoner of war experiences, rape, abuse, natural disasters, incest,
homelessness. Symptoms have not changed since the original
descriptions of PTSD in Homer's time, says Dr. Charles Marmar of
the University of California San Francisco PTSD Program. They
have been exhibited with every war since.

The psyche is not set up for war, said Robinson. Response to
combat has no consistency. Some cope better than others. A guy
could be a hero one day and break down the next.

During the Civil War, the most destructive war in American
history, according to Richard Gabriel in his book *No More Heroes*,
6,000 soldiers were discharged from the Union Army alone for a
psychiatric condition known as "nostalgia." Other men exhibiting
psychiatric ailments were escorted to the outskirts of a military
camp and turned loose to wander the countryside and die. They
were considered to be cowards or weak.

During World War I, the term used to describe psychiatric
reactions to war was "shell shock." The military treated men with
it as close to the front as possible, then sent them back out to
fight, says Gabriel. This procedure, called forward treatment, was
developed by the Russians in the 1905-6 Russo-Japanese War.
Psychiatric casualties during World War I were considered to be
those with a weaker character.

To reduce psychiatric casualties in World War II, draftees
were screened to weed out the "weak," said Gabriel. Still, psychiatric casualties were the single largest category of disability discharges.

In the Vietnam War, most psychiatric casualties on the field
were due to "nostalgia." The rate of psychiatric discharges was
12.6 percent. The military practiced "forward treatment" on a
large scale. Vietnam was a different kind of war, according to

Rose Sandecki, nurse clinician at the Veterans Administration Hospital in San Francisco. Because of the camaraderie, or esprit de corps, in Vietnam, many of the men with physical or psychiatric injuries would get treated at a medical facility and then go back to the war. They felt they had to take care of their buddies.

Effectiveness in combat, according to Gabriel's book, has nothing to do with heroics. The reason soldiers are motivated is because they don't want to let the men in their unit down.

"Being exposed to the unconditional loyalty of the men you're fighting with," is what Robinson remembered most about the war. He said that when looking for friends even now, he looks "for that kind of loyalty. If somebody rolls a grenade into the room, are they going to jump on it? Do they measure up?" He is often let down.

It was allegiance to his buddies that prompted Vietnam veteran Jack McCloskey to form Vietnam veteran support groups in the early 1970s to help men deal with the psychiatric repercussions of the Vietnam War.

McCloskey, an ex-Marine medic, was involved in Vietnam Veterans Against the War in the late 1960s when he began to see a pattern among many Vietnam vets. With so many of them using alcohol and drugs, abusing themselves and their spouses, he knew something was wrong. He began holding rap groups in 1971. The vets involved were called "Twice Born Men" after Philip Berrigan's description of those who came out of prison or war and began to work through their fears.

As those in McCloskey's groups started talking about what they were going through, they realized that the things they had to do to survive in Vietnam were common to all. "A whole range of emotions were opened up to a generation of men, raised on John Wayne, who were told the only feelings they could have were angry or horny," McCloskey said.

The men, as well as the women—many of whom had served as combat nurses in Vietnam—who came to the groups, found they were not alone. Some of the women were exhibiting more extreme symptoms, since they had had no break in the war. PTSD, then called "the Vietnam syndrome," began to make itself known. These groups, which McCloskey later integrated into "Swords to Plowshares" when he started it in 1974, became the model for the Veterans Administration (VA) rap groups in "Operation Outreach" to treat veterans with PTSD.

The large number of men and women in the groups was what gave PTSD the credibility it has today, said Sandecki. The numbers prompted studies by the medical profession, and in 1980, PTSD became a part of the psychiatric "bible," the Manual of Mental Disorders (DSM-R-III).

McCloskey, now a mental health counselor at the Progress Foundation after working with Vietnam veterans for 23 years, saw a distinct difference between those who have experienced "a one-shot trauma," such as an accident or rape, and those who have been exposed to trauma over a period of time. What combat veterans go through is more akin to the "battered women's syndrome," he said.

"Brutality comes in different forms," said Robinson, who works as a clinical counselor and has a broad-based clientele. In the most extreme cases of spousal or child abuse, he added, "I see the real ugliness I've been exposed to in combat."

More than 80 percent of those seen at La Casa de Las Madres, a San Francisco center for abused women, exhibit PTSD symptoms, according to community education director Edie Resto. "What they've been through is a combat zone, only the war is at home."

PTSD symptoms show up in abused women who go to sleep and wake up in sweats, said Resto. Some can't concentrate, and they sleep too much. Some are antisocial, get into fights, forget appointments. When the stress is extreme and they can't cope or react, some women turn to drugs or alcohol to escape the stress.

Many Vietnam combat vets exhibit similar behavior patterns. Inability to become intimate is the most pronounced symptom McCloskey has seen in vets. "For a lot of these guys, Vietnam was the first time they were ever intimate with someone, and later those people were hurt or killed," he said. Years later, they are having problems with relationships.

Two percent of the U.S. population, not including veterans of war, now have PTSD, according to a Center for Disease Control study done in Atlanta, Ga.

Most people with PTSD have experienced loss, said Robinson's wife, Elizabeth Robinson Anello, a practicing psychotherapist and social work director at the Tom Waddell Clinic in San Francisco. It is related to the loss of life, of a job, or of a home. For seven years Anello has worked with the city's homeless who "in the streets experience every day as a combat zone."

For the homeless as well as the veterans suffering from PTSD, angry verbal outbursts and physical aggression are not uncommon. Often, it's an endless cycle that some of the sufferers try to "end" with heavy drinking, drugs or suicide. One-third of Anello's present caseload in San Francisco is exhibiting PTSD. Living in shelters and on the street, "homeless people develop a paranoia," Anello said. "Many are not sleeping well. They become very vigilant at night so they don't get hurt." Carrying belongings everywhere they go "represents their personal space in the world." Wearing lots of layers is practical, but it's also protective—"The more I can layer myself, the more I'm protected against the outside world," underlies how they feel, Anello said. "It reminds me of the Vietnam combat vets who 20 years later still walk around wearing uniforms and military paraphernalia, hiding behind dark glasses and gear."

War really is hell, said Robinson. "No one comes out of it 100 percent." Some wounds are worse than others, but the psychological wounds go deep; they're harder to get over than the physical ones. Still, Robinson volunteered to go back to Vietnam after he was discharged and returned to the States in 1969.

It's like a woman who has been abused by her husband, said Robinson. She goes back to him again because she loves him. "My buddies couldn't make it without me. I had to go back to help them out," he said. When he broke his femur in five places in an automobile accident caused by drinking just before he was scheduled to return to Vietnam, he was laid up for nine months. He never returned to Vietnam.

Cocaine, metamphetamines, valium, morphine and alcohol kept him from facing his PTSD symptoms for 15 of the past 25 years. It was his way of coping with his horrible dreams. "When you stay loaded, it's difficult for those things to break through," he explained. As his PTSD became more acute, "being medicated just wasn't enough."

According to the NVRS study, 25 percent of those who have PTSD from the Vietnam War suffer from alcohol dependence. Seven to 8 percent are into drug abuse.

Robinson didn't talk about Vietnam for 15 years. When he first came home from Vietnam, he turned to alcohol and drugs instead. His startle responses were chronic. There were many sleepless nights. He never got rated for PTSD. The VA would not rate him because of his drug abuse, "despite the fact that it started in Vietnam when the military gave me a quarter grain of morphine every four hours when I was hospitalized."

A song, a word, or even "Rascals' music from the '60s" can bring flashbacks for Robinson. "Even now, when I go on a picnic down in the woods," he says, "I'm looking, because when you're in the jungle, you never fixate on an object because it will move on you." He feels particularly violated as a Vietnam veteran. "I can never trust Washington, D.C., again," he said.

When Vietnam veterans returned to the States from Vietnam, the older generation told them they had lost the war. Their peers called them baby killers. Robinson was spit on when he stepped off the plane in San Francisco. The woman sitting next to him on the plane home to Philadelphia would not talk to him after she found out he had been in Vietnam. His family knew he was coming, but when he got home the lights were out.

For McCloskey, "it was easier for me to love Vietnam vets than for me to love my wife." After 23 years of working with veterans, he finally went into therapy himself. "My PTSD symptom is still being a medic. My therapist told me I was still trying to save the guys in Vietnam."

PTSD doesn't go away, said McCloskey. He realized that "it's going to be with us the rest of our lives." Whenever he gets depressed, he has a recurring nightmare where he reaches into his medical bag to get a bandage. "When I open it up, it turns into a body bag."

Robinson got most of his early help through Operation Outreach groups and therapy. He goes to 12-step groups to deal with drug and alcohol abuse. Being involved in the theater arts also helps him deal with PTSD. Group therapy is widely used as PTSD treatment. Abused women helping women and veterans helping vets develop community and support for those with PTSD.

The VA uses groups as an essential part of treatment for combat-related PTSD, according to Dr. Howard Lipke, chief psychologist at the North Chicago VA Medical Center. They also use conventional psychotherapy for some patients.

The use of eye movement and desensitization and reprocessing (EMDR), developed in 1987 at the MRI in Palo Alto, is rapidly increasing in the VA, according to Lipke. "We're using EMDR with at least 100 PTSD patients at the North Chicago VA Center. And it's quite effective," he added.

With EMDR, a therapist has a person hold a traumatic thought in mind—what they saw, heard, smelled, any physical sensations or emotions. By focusing on the thought, "they light up that part of the brain that holds old memory," Levin says. A therapist then has them add eye movements and track out fingers in front of the eyes so they have saccadic eye movements (rapid jumps from one fixed point to another, as in reading). "Some of those walls that have walled off old memory come down and the brain starts to process memory again in a natural, healing way."

McCloskey says that Vietnam veterans have as great a potential for violence as anyone in this country, but he adds that they also have the most potential for bringing about positive social change. If they work through their feelings, they are often more nurturing than individuals who have never been through the trauma of war. It is related to the tenderness they found they could feel for those dying in Vietnam.

"If I was lifting a body, it was always done in the most gentle fashion because this bag represents somebody's son," said Robinson. "If there were some way we could transfer that deep nurturing you feel for your buddies dying on the field of battle and point it to those on the street, what a better world it would be.

"I buried those feelings for so long, those female instincts," he recalled. The tears come long and hard. Then he added, amid the tears, that now, "I can turn to a woman and say, 'I know what it's like to be somebody's mom!' "

Never Forgotten:
Accounting for American MIAs

By Colonel John B. Haseman, U.S. Army (ret.)

T he endless line of soil-filled buckets is passed from hand to hand in the energy-sapping 105-degree heat, then dumped onto thin-meshed screens. From time to time the screens turn up a bone chip, a boot eyelet or some fragmental clue about what happened to fellow servicemen in a war now over 30 years in the past. No other nation in history has ever made such an effort to repatriate the remains of men lost in war.

The scenario is repeated nearly a dozen times each year in Laos, Vietnam and Cambodia. The Americans involved, military and civilian personnel from several commands, are under the operational control of Joint Task Force–Full Accounting (JTF-FA), the organization created in 1992 and assigned responsibility for determining the fate of nearly 2,000 American military personnel still listed as unaccounted for from the Vietnam War.

JTF-FA itself is the analytical, investigative and negotiating arm of the mission. Its personnel compile dossiers on each person missing in action. They then work with host country governments to schedule investigation and recovery operations, locate and interview witnesses, and provide in-country logistical support to all field operations. JTF-FA operates three subordinate detachments in Southeast Asia. Detachment 1 in Bangkok conducts operations in Cambodia and also provides logistical support for all regional operations. Detachment 2 is in Hanoi and Detachment 3 is in Vientiane, Laos.

Bob Gahagan is one of many men and women participating in JTF-FA's efforts who have suffered from the Laotian heat. More formally, he is Colonel Robert Gahagan, who served as the commander of JTF-FA Detachment 3 from 1998 to May 2000. After his two years in Laos, Gahagan, an armor officer and former battalion commander, became a department director at the U.S. Army Armor School at Fort Knox. Looking back on his time with JTF-FA, he said, "If I had to single out one thing that makes me proud of this effort, it's the people I work with."

JTF-FA's partner in this important mission is the U.S. Army Central Identification Laboratory, Hawaii (CILHI), the operations and identification arm of the team. The CILHI has the scientific expertise to locate the crash sites and supervise field search and recovery operations. After repatriation of remains, the CILHI conducts the delicate, time-consuming work of identifying them at its state-of-the-art laboratory in Hawaii. The CILHI is actively involved in cases from World War II, the Korean War and other conflicts and contingencies—but most of its effort is spent on Vietnam War cases. Once remains are recovered, the CILHI is charged with their formal identification. Only then can a missing soldier, sailor, airman or Marine be removed from the MIA roster.

When the Vietnam War ended in 1975, there were 2,583 Americans unaccounted for in Southeast Asia. Since then, recovery and identification efforts have reduced that number to 1,991, as of January 11, 2001. Of those, 642 may never be resolved— notably the several hundred American airmen whose aircraft went down at sea in water too deep for recovery operations.

JTF-FA Detachment 3 in Vientiane is the smallest of the three field detachments. It consists of a lieutenant-colonel commander, a senior civilian who acts as second-in-command, one logistics NCO and two NCOs who look after administration and operations. The detachment is augmented on a rotational basis by a Lao linguist who works on archival research. Also on hand are several Laotian foreign service nationals.

Detachment 3 was formed in 1992. Its personnel have their hands full. The detachment plans and coordinates all joint Lao–U.S. investigations and excavation operations, also coordinating closely with the Lao government on Laotian unilateral investigations. It strives to facilitate trilateral investigations in which U.S., Laotian and Vietnamese representatives work together to solve cases that cross national borders. Like its counterparts in Vietnam and Bangkok, the detachment investigates reports of live sightings, interviews walk-in witnesses, conducts an oral history program jointly with its host country officials and conducts joint archival research with military and civilian government offices.

The February-March 2000 joint field activity (JFA) in Savannakhet province was an attempt to bring to closure a poignant story. In 1969 a McDonnell RF-4 reconnaissance aircraft was shot down near Xepone. The reconnaissance officer ejected safely and was rescued, but the pilot was never found. He was last seen attached to his ejection seat. Thus the key to resolving this case was to find either human remains or physical evidence—such as pieces of an ejection seat—that would pinpoint the crash site. In addition to bone fragments, search crews look for dog tags, personal and life-support items (life vest, parachute, boots, etc.), clothing and flight gear (flight suit, buckles). Even the smallest piece of debris may be the key to finding human remains.

Each Southeast Asian country has its own policy for JTF-FA operations. Time and personnel strength for the Savannakhet recovery operation were limited by strict rules worked out jointly by U.S. and Laotian officials. In Laos each joint field activity operation is limited to a maximum of 30 days, and no more than 40 Americans are permitted in any one JFA iteration.

JFA excavation operations in Laos must be conducted in geographic order from north to south, with the entire country covered before resuming operations elsewhere. In contrast, research investigations, which involve the search for witnesses and efforts to pinpoint the location where a missing American was last seen, can take place in any geographical area. Despite these constraints, Detachment 3 has been able to operate effectively. In 1973 there were 565 Americans missing in action in Laos. As of January 2001 that total was down to 420.

"There are going to be some cases that will never be resolved because of various factors," Colonel Gahagan said, "but we are making steady progress." The small detachment averages five 30-day recovery operations each year. The advance research effort, coordination, planning and preparation for each operation are formidable tasks for such a small group. And the mission has become more difficult as the years pass.

"We are in a real race for time," Gahagan explained. "Family members of our missing servicemen are aging. Witnesses on the ground are aging, too, and that may be even more critical to our success. And here in Laos, because of the soil conditions, human remains and physical evidence deteriorate very rapidly."

The Savannakhet operation is a good example of U.S.–Laos cooperation. Laotian officials assisted in locating witnesses and in pinpointing the best possible search site. The entire American-Laotian team is deployed by Lao air force helicopters—Russian Mil Mi-17s. Detachment 3 also has one full-time dedicated Lao helicopter, and the operation is augmented by a New Zealand charter company that provides additional helicopter transportation support.

Virtually all JFA operations in Laos are conducted from remote base camps. The country's infrastructure is rudimentary, and there are no facilities in the countryside for Lao and American personnel that make up a JFA. For the Savannakhet operation, the team's base camp at Ban Alang provided reasonably comfortable facilities. Tents on concrete pads, hot showers, good food and sports equipment made life as pleasant as possible during the arduous 30-day window for operations. "We go first class as much as possible," Colonel Gahagan noted, "and we never put the field teams in hotels. We live right on the site with our Lao counterparts and work there until the task is completed."

From the base camp, each of three 10-man recovery teams is assigned to work a separate excavation site. A typical recovery team is headed by a captain from the CILHI and includes CILHI scientists, mortuary affairs personnel, life-support equipment specialists, explosive ordnance disposal technicians, medics and other technical personnel. Also on each recovery team are an anthropologist and an archaeologist from the CILHI, and several team members from the U.S. Pacific Command (PACOM), including an explosive ordnance disposal technician, a life-support technician, a medic/doctor and a linguist. Completing the team is a photographer from either the CILHI or PACOM. Teams deployed to Vietnam are slightly larger, usually including an additional mortuary affairs NCO and a communications technician.

A simultaneous work plan allows three or more sites to be covered during the 30-day duration of any JFA deployment. If circumstances warrant, two or three teams can converge on a single site, particularly when time or weather constraints might limit success. Fifty to 100 local workers augment each of the recovery teams at the excavation site. The objective is to complete work at each site within the 30-day period. Major problems result if an excavation is not completed within the time available—among them the loss of potential evidence because of scavenging and the effects of weather. The work of the archeologists is particularly important, since their thorough knowledge of soil condi-

tions and excavation techniques enables them to pinpoint distur-
bances in the ground caused by the impact of an aircraft, an
explosion or a field burial. Their skills are key to site discovery,
since time has erased virtually all surface indicators such as aircraft debris. While much of the heavy earthmoving labor is done
by local people employed for that purpose, the site archeologist
supervises digging and screening of earth down to "sterile soil,"
that is, ground no longer affected by the impact of an aircraft
crash.

Because of the remote location of field deployments and the
rudimentary medical infrastructure in rural Laos, Cambodia and
Vietnam, the doctors and medics who accompany the teams often
are the only health professionals available in the area. Virtually
every field deployment has needed medical support for illness,
broken bones and other medical emergencies. JTF-FA doctors and
medics also treat an average of 1,000 to 2,000 Laotian villagers
during each JFA. Over the years they have saved 11 or 12 lives.

Field deployments are risky operations due to the large amount
of unexploded ordnance in most of the areas where JTF-FA teams
are working. Hundreds of Laotian, Cambodian and Vietnamese
civilians are killed or maimed each year from unexploded ordnance. Explosive demolitions specialists scour and clear every
operational area before any work begins.

Laos is the most bombed country in history. "More ordnance
was dropped on this little country than in all of World War II,"
Gahagan noted. "Our men and women risk their lives every day
they walk around out there."

Disease is another threat to teams in all three countries.
Malaria and dengue fever are endemic throughout the region.
There are also poisonous snakes and centipedes to contend with,
as well as the constant concern about heat casualties among
workers.

JTF-FA Detachment 1 in Bangkok, Thailand, is responsible for all operations in Cambodia. Compared to the large efforts in Vietnam and Laos, the scope of Cambodian operations is smaller because there were only 65 Americans missing in Cambodia. Detachment 1 conducts one JFA in Cambodia per year. The one held in January 2000 consisted of an investigation and two recovery operations. As in Laos and Vietnam, the Cambodian armed forces provide extensive helicopter support and also have allowed American aircraft to visit excavation operations on a case-by-case basis, a privilege not available in either Laos or Vietnam.

Air Force Lt. Col. Jeff Smith, who commands Detachment 1, volunteered for the assignment after hearing a JTF-FA briefing while he was a student at the Naval War College. His detachment consists of six other U.S. military personnel, one American civilian and four Thai civilians. The Cambodian government, he said, has been "extremely easy to work with. There are far fewer restrictions and conditions imposed on our operations, as compared to the situation in Laos or Vietnam."

In addition to its investigative and recovery responsibilities in Cambodia, Detachment 1 also provides logistic support for all three of JTF-FA's field detachments. Bangkok was selected for the region-wide logistical support mission for a number of reasons. It is a regional hub for many U.S. government offices and also offers easy access to manpower and resources. The Thai government provides great assistance to the mission by providing access to U-Tapao Royal Thai Air Base, which serves as the hub for deployments of all JTF-FA and CILHI teams to Southeast Asia. "We stay pretty busy," Colonel Smith noted.

The largest of the JTF-FA elements is Detachment 2 in Hanoi. The challenges faced in the search for closure on Americans missing in Vietnam are much the same as in Laos and Cambodia, but the numbers are larger. Army Lt. Col. Mike Peppers heads an office of six permanently assigned personnel, augmented full-time by two American linguists fluent in Vietnamese.

In May 2000, Colonel Peppers was in the mountains of central Vietnam, accompanying the 60th JFA team to work in Vietnam. That mission, conducted between April 25 and May 24, 2000, was staged mostly from Da Nang. The team of 96 personnel included six recovery elements, plus two investigative elements and a research and investigation team. Like Detachment 3 in Laos, Detachment 2 conducts five JFAs in Vietnam each calendar year, but they are larger than those in Laos.

"We average around 100 men per JFA," explained Detachment 2's operations officer and deputy commander, Air Force Major John Fisher. "We don't have the same restrictions on team size and geographical constraints as Laos does."

The areas that were covered in May 2000 illustrate the broad scope of the recovery operations in Vietnam. Investigation elements worked on leads in 13 provinces scattered all over the country. Recovery teams worked at six excavation sites in five different provinces. Quang Ninh, the northeasternmost province in Vietnam, posed unusual weather challenges. "We can only get in there about two or three months a year because of the weather," Major Fisher said. "So our Vietnamese counterparts suggested this would be the best time to get in there and get busy now, while we could."

The Quang Ninh crash site was very difficult to reach—a steep mountainside covered with bamboo and thick jungle foliage. Temperatures rose above 100 degrees, and poisonous snakes, centipedes and the steepness of the terrain posed health and safety hazards to the American and Vietnamese workers. Most sites also had the hazard of unexploded ordnance. Another team assigned to a crash site in Thua Thien province required technical rock climbing skills to gain access to the crash site.

One of the most significant advances achieved by JTF-FA has been the resolution of cases involving missing persons who, either through debriefings from returned prisoners of war or photographs and other documentary evidence, were last known to have been alive after being shot down or captured. These so-called discrepancy cases have been among the most contentious issues of the postwar accountability effort, and resolving them is the highest priority for JTF-FA detachments. At the end of American involvement in the war in 1973, there were 196 individuals who were listed as "last known alive" in Vietnam but not accounted for by the Vietnamese. By January 2001 only 41 individuals remained on that list. In Laos, the number of those last known alive has been reduced from 81 to 63, and in Cambodia, from 19 to 15.

Another controversial area of JTF-FA's accountability is the investigation of so-called live-sighting reports of Americans held in the region against their will. There have been 119 live-sighting reports to date, and every one of them received immediate and intensive investigation. Not one single report was found to be a valid instance of a missing American serviceman.

Both the CILHI and JTF-FA personnel are highly qualified in their specialties. JTF-FA detachment commanders go through a particularly rigorous selection process. Prerequisites include successful battalion- or squadron-level command. Candidates are scrutinized to determine whether they can operate in a remote environment and deal effectively with senior officials of the host country.

Although most CILHI and JTF-FA personnel are too young to have fought in Vietnam, they are singularly dedicated to resolving the fate of their fellow servicemen. Every person involved in the process says his or her biggest disappointment is when an arduous search turns up physical evidence of a crash site or incident, but no remains are recovered. "We never want to give up on a single person," one team member said. "We just owe it to them and their families to do everything we can to resolve each and every case."

Slowly but surely, that resolution effort proceeds. Recovery of remains is just the first step in final resolution of a case. The remains are treated with honor during every step of the long journey from Southeast Asia to Hawaii for continuation of the identification process. Solemn ceremonies are conducted at the airport of the country of departure, with traditional military protocol and honors rendered to each returning serviceman's remains.

Detachment 2 personnel were privileged to participate in a ceremony on April 25, 2000, marking the repatriation of six sets of remains. The ceremony at Hanoi's Noi Bai Airport included U.S. Ambassador Douglass B. Peterson and Senator John McCain, both of whom had been prisoners of war. Peterson's words on that occasion sum up the sense of honor and dedication of the men and women working to reach that "best possible accounting" of Americans still missing in Southeast Asia: "Never before in the history of mankind has any nation done what we are doing." We can only hope that history will not require us to do it again.

Editor's note: On April 7, 2001, a chartered helicopter carrying 16 members of an MIA search team crashed into a mountainside in Quang Binh province, about 280 miles south of Hanoi, in heavy fog. The search team members, none of whom survived, included seven Americans and nine Vietnamese who had been preparing for the excavation of several crash sites for JTF-FA on a mission that was to begin in May.

Among the seven Americans killed in the crash were both the current commander of the task force, Army Lt. Col. Rennie M. Cory, Jr., and Lt. Col. George D. "Marty" Martin III, who was scheduled to take over command in July. The other Americans lost were Air Force Major Charles E. Lewis, Master Sgt. Steven L. Moser, Tech. Sgt. Robert M. Flynn, Navy Hospital Corpsman Pedro J. Gonzales and Army Sgt. 1st Class Tommy J. Murphy. The nine Vietnamese search team members included eight military officers as well as Nguyen Thanh Ha, deputy director of the Vietnamese Office for Seeking Missing Persons, Vietnam's own MIA search group.

According to the U.S. Department of Defense, this was the first fatality of American servicemen on active duty in Vietnam since the Vietnam War, and also the first loss of life in any joint recovery operation.

Names on the Wall

By Bill Abbott

T he 58,152 names of those who died in Vietnam are etched onto the two rising black marble slabs of the Vietnam Veterans Memorial in Washington, D.C. The slabs meet at a vertex of 125 degrees 10 feet above ground level to form "the Wall." The shining surface is intended to reflect the sun, the ground and those who stand before the memorial. The names are listed chronologically by date of death—the first to last—and as one walks the Wall slowly, examining the ineffably American names, one is struck by the same recurring surnames. How many Smiths can there possibly be who died in Vietnam? There were 667. How many Andersons? 178. Garcias? 102. Murphys? 82. Jenkins? 66. One wants to know more about these Americans. Who were they?

A new Department of Defense (DOD) database computer tape released through the National Archives allows researchers for the first time to take a much closer look at our 58,152 Vietnam casualties. From 1964 to 1973, 2,100,000 men and women served in Vietnam. That was exactly 24 percent of the 8,444,000 who were in the active armed forces during those years, but only 8 percent of the 26,000,000 Americans who were eligible for military service.

The vast majority of Americans who were eligible by age but did not serve in the armed forces were exempted by reason of physical, mental, psychiatric, or moral failure; or they were given status deferments because they were college students, fathers, teachers, engineers or conscientious objectors. Others, later in the war, were simply ineligible because of high lottery number. Still others joined the reserves or National Guard, which were not mobilized in appreciable numbers during the war. A relatively small number refused to register for the draft. Some went to Canada or Sweden. Few of those who evaded the draft were actually prosecuted, and most were eventually pardoned by President Jimmy Carter in 1977.

The DOD database shows that of the 2,100,000 men and women who served in Vietnam, 58,152 were killed. The Army suffered the most total casualties, 38,179 or 2.7 percent of its force. As a branch, however, the Marine Corps lost 14,836, or 5 percent of its own men.

Eight women were killed in Vietnam—five Army lieutenants, one Army captain, one Army lieutenant colonel and one Air Force captain. All were nurses, all were single and all but one were in their 20s. An estimated 11,000 women served in Vietnam.

In this article we will refer to casualties as the 58,152 who died in Vietnam, but it should be emphasized that there were 153,303 who were wounded seriously enough to be hospitalized. Thus, there were 211,455 killed and wounded, or one in every 10 Americans who served in Vietnam. The Army as a branch had 134,982 killed or wounded (9.5 percent), but the Marines suffered 66,227 killed or wounded (22.5 percent) or almost one of every four Marines who served.

Since the days of Alexander the Great and the Roman Legions, it has always been the young, inexperienced, low-ranking enlisted man who has taken the brunt of combat casualties. Vietnam was no different, and the DOD percentages reveal that nearly 75 percent of Army enlisted casualties were privates or corporals. The Marine Corps losses were skewed even more to the lower ranks: 91 percent were privates or corporals. If the two branches are combined, then 80 percent of the Army and Marine enlisted casualties were privates or corporals—grades E-1 to E-4.

Although it is a truism that the young die in war, one is still unprepared for the fact that 40 percent of Marine enlisted casualties in Vietnam were teenagers; that more than 16 percent of Army enlisted casualties were also teenagers; and that nearly a quarter of all enlisted casualties in Vietnam were in the same 17- to 19-year age group. If the demographic is expanded to 17-to-21, then we find that 83 percent of Marine enlisted casualties, 65 percent of Army enlisted casualties, and nearly 70 percent of all enlisted casualties were 21 or under. Only the Navy, with 50 percent of its enlisted casualties over 21, and the Air Force, with 75 percent over 21, showed an older, more experienced age demographic.

No other American war has presented such a young profile in combat. These young men were trained quickly, shipped to Vietnam quickly and died quickly—many within a few weeks or months of arriving in Vietnam.

Given the draft policies, the hard-sell recruitment, the severe escalations from month to month, the refusal by President Lyndon Johnson to call up the older reserves or National Guard, it could not have been otherwise. The burden of combat fell on the very available non-college-bound young. The civilian and military men who formed the policy did not see it necessarily as a disadvantage. The very young are considered by many to be preferred combat material. Despite their inexperience, they are thought to accept discipline readily. They do not, in most cases, carry the burdens of wife or children. They are at their peak physically. Perhaps more important, many of them probably do not yet fully understand their own mortality and are therefore less likely to be timid in combat. And, as in all American wars, it is the very young who are the most willing to volunteer.

It may come as a surprise to some that 63.3 percent of all Vietnam enlisted casualties were not draftees but volunteers. If officers are added, then almost 70 percent of those who died were volunteers. Of course, the Marine, Navy and Air Corps enlisted personnel were, with the exception of a small number of Marines, all volunteers, but as it turned out, almost 50 percent of Army enlisted casualties were also volunteers. It should be noted, however, that the draft was specifically designed to "trigger" volunteer enlistments. The draft policy at the time of the Vietnam War was called the Universal Military Training and Service Act. Since its adoption in 1951 at the time of the Korean War, it had been renewed by Congress every four years. It called for the registration of all 18- to 26-year-old males, with induction to take place at 18 1/2 if so ordered by the local draft board. The draftee, if found mentally and physically fit, would be inducted for a period of two years, to be followed by another two-year period in the active reserves and a subsequent two years in the inactive reserves. But recruiters could point out that the volunteer could enlist as early as age 17 (with parental consent); that he was allowed to select his branch of service; that he would receive specialized training if he qualified; that he could request a specific overseas assignment; and that his three year enlistment satisfied his military obligation immediately, to be followed by another three years in the inactive reserves. Sad to say, many of these recruitment promises were fudged in one way or another, and many of these young men found themselves shipped directly to Vietnam after basic training.

One additional factor, often overlooked, that influenced volunteer enlistment was military tradition—the influence of fathers, grandfathers, brothers, uncles and others who had served in previous 20th-century wars. In these families, no matter what was thought of the legitimacy of the Vietnam War itself, it was considered unpatriotic and indeed reprehensible to avoid active duty by requesting a status deferment, enlisting in the reserves or National Guard, or seeking out a "draft counselor" for advice on how to avoid the draft. This, of course, was one of the great and abiding agonies of the Vietnam War, causing repercussions within families that have lasted to this day.

The training for American officers is thought by many foreign military authorities to be the best in the world. With few exceptions, almost all of the 6,600 commissioned officers who died in Vietnam were graduates of the service academies, college Reserve Officers' Training Corps (ROTC) or the Officer Candidate School (OCS) programs. The major service academies and other military colleges provided close to 900 of the Vietnam officer casualties: the U.S. Military Academy 278, the U.S. Air Force Academy 205, the U.S. Naval Academy 130, Texas A&M 112, The Citadel 66, Virginia Military Institute 43, Virginia Polytechnic Institute 26 and Norwich University 19.

Officer casualties in Vietnam, including warrant officers, numbered 7,874, or 13.5 percent of all casualties. The Army lost the greatest number of officers—4,635, or 59 percent of all officer casualties. Ninety-one percent of these Army officers were either warrant officers, second lieutenants, first lieutenants or captains. This was a reflection of the role of warrant officers as helicopter pilots (of the 1,277 warrant officer casualties, 95 percent were Army helicopter pilots), and of the young lieutenants and captains as combat platoon leaders or company commanders.

The same profile holds true for the Marine Corps, where 87 percent of all officer casualties (821 of 938) were either warrant officers, lieutenants or captains. Army and Marine officer fatalities in Vietnam were also quite young. Fully 50 percent were in the 17-to 24-year age group, and astonishingly, there were 764 Army officer casualties (16 percent) who were 21 or younger.

Quite a different profile emerges among the Navy and Air Force officer corps. The Air Force lost the highest percentage of officers. Of 2,590 Air Force casualties—officers and enlisted personnel—1,674, or 65 percent, were officers. Many of them, as experienced pilots, were older (two-thirds were 30 or older), and many were high-ranking: almost 50 percent were majors, lieutenant colonels and colonels, and three were generals. The Navy had a similar profile—55 percent of its 622 officer casualties were 30 years of age or older, and 45 percent were ranked at lieutenant commander or above when they died. It should be emphasized that 55 percent of all Navy and Air Force officer casualties came as a result of reconnaissance and bombing sorties into North Vietnam, Laos, Thailand and Cambodia. As a result, it was mainly the families of Navy and Air Force pilots who suffered the great agony of the POW (prisoner of war) and MIA (missing in action) experience that came out of the Vietnam War.

The makeup of U.S. combat forces in Vietnam has long been the subject of controversy among social scientists. The feeling is that the poor, the undereducated and the minorities made up the vast majority of the combat arms during that war. This makeup, they say, was the very antithesis of what we stand for as a democracy—a shameful corruption of our values and our historical sense of fairness and social justice. There is some truth to this, but it is instructive to look at what the DOD database reveals in terms of race, ethnicity, national origin, religious preference and casualties by U.S. geographic areas.

Of all enlisted men who died in Vietnam, blacks made up 14.1 percent of the total. This came at a time when blacks made up 11 percent of the young male population nationwide. However, if we add officer casualties to the total, then this overrepresentation is reduced to 12.5 percent of all casualties. Of the 7,262 blacks who died, 6,955 or 96 percent were Army and Marine enlisted men.

The combination of the selective service policies with the skills and aptitude testing of both volunteers and draftees (in which blacks scored noticeably lower) conspired to assign blacks in greater numbers to the combat units of the Army and Marine Corps.

Early in the war (1965 and 1966), when blacks made up about 11 percent of our Vietnam force, black casualties soared to more than 20 percent of the total. Black leaders, including Martin Luther King, protested, and President Johnson ordered black participation in combat units cut back. As a result, the black casualty rate was reduced to 11.5 percent by 1969.

During the Vietnam War, the Navy and Air Force became substantially white enclaves. Of the 4,953 Navy and Air Force casualties, including officers and enlisted personnel, 4,736 or 96 percent were white. Officer casualties of all branches were overwhelmingly white. Of the 7,877 officer casualties, 7,595 or 96.4 percent were white, 147 or 1.8 percent were black, 24 or .3 percent were Asian, 7 or .08 percent were Native American, and 104 or 1.3 percent were unidentified by race.

Hispanics can be of any race, but the 1980 census revealed that only 2.6 percent of Hispanics regard themselves as black. In a massive sampling of the database it was established that between 5 and 6 percent had identifiable Hispanic surnames. These were Mexican, Puerto Rican, Cuban and other Latino-Americans with ancestries based in Central and South America. They came largely from California and Texas, with lesser numbers from Colorado, New Mexico, Arizona, Florida and New York, and a few from many other states across the country. The 1970 census that is being used as our Vietnam-era population base estimated Hispanic-Americans at 4.5 percent of the U.S. population. Thus it is safe to say that Hispanic-Americans were overrepresented among Vietnam casualties—an estimated 5.5 percent of the dead against 4.5 percent of the 1970 population.

In terms of national origin/ancestries, an extensive sampling of the database reveals that Americans of French Canadian, Polish, Italian and other Southern and Eastern European surnames made up about 10 percent of the Vietnam casualties. These casualties came largely from the Northeast and North Central regions of the United States, many from the traditionally patriotic, Catholic working-class neighborhoods.

The remaining 70 percent of our Vietnam enlisted casualties were of English/Scottish/Welsh, German, Irish, and Scandinavian ancestries, more from the South and Midwest than the other regions, many from small towns with a family military tradition. The officer corps has always drawn heavily on English, German, Irish and Scandinavian-American ancestries from lower-middle and middle-class white collar homes, with other large percentages from ambitious blue collar and, of course, career military families. Officer casualties came more from the South and West regions—4.1 deaths per 100,000 in contrast to 3.5 from the Northeast and North Central (Midwest).

The DOD database listed precise religious preferences for the Vietnam casualties. Protestants were 64.4 percent (37,483), Catholics were 28.9 percent (16,806). Less than one percent (.8 percent) were Jewish, Hindu, Thai, Buddhist or Muslim, and 5.7 percent listed no religious preference or it was unknown. Blacks were exactly 85 percent Protestant. Officers of all services, by tradition largely Protestant, remained so during the Vietnam War, sustaining casualties over their Catholic brethren on a 5-2 ratio.

As a region, the South experienced the greatest numbers of dead—nearly 34 percent of the total and 31.0 deaths per 100,000 of population. This compared strikingly with the Northeast region—23.5—while the West was 29.9 and the North Central (Midwest) region stood at 28.4 deaths per 100,000 of population. This uneven impact was caused by a number of factors: (1) While the South was home to some 53 percent of all blacks in the 1970 census, almost 60 percent of black casualties came from the South; (2) Although we cannot be as precise, we do know that a considerable majority of Hispanic-American casualties came from the West (California, New Mexico, Arizona, Colorado) and the South (Texas); (3) Better employment opportunities in the Northeast reduced the number of volunteers; (4) Greater college matriculation in the Northeast increased the number of status deferments for the region's 17- to 24-year-olds; (5) More anti-war sentiment in the media and on college campuses in the Northeast and a correspondingly greater tradition of military service in the other regions had its effect. It is not surprising, for instance, that West Virginia, Montana and Oklahoma had a casualty rate almost twice that of New York, New Jersey and Connecticut.

Another factor was "channeling." World War II had been, for the most part, "a perfect war," clear of purpose, the forces of democracy and freedom lined up against the forces of fascism and tyranny. Our combat arms were thought to be completely classless. They drew on every segment of American society. We were one giant Hollywood B-17 bomber crew, one perfect socioeconomic platoon storming Omaha Beach or Okinawa. All classes were drafted or volunteered and all served and died equally—although it must be noted that most blacks died separately. But with the beginning of the Cold War, that perfect paradigm of purpose broke down. One of the features of that breakdown was the withdrawal of the educated classes from the spectrum of military service.

A kind of educational apartheid had settled over the United States after World War II. Where previously a high school diploma had been an acceptable goal, now it was college and all the benefits it would bring. Early on, it had been evident to President Johnson, his advisers and the Congress that the Vietnam

War could not be conducted beyond its first year if the draft were truly equitable and included combat assignments for the sons of educationally advantaged and influential Americans from the professional and managerial classes.

Congress and the Johnson administration, therefore, sought to protect our college-bound and educated young men. The "Channeling Memo" of July 1965 instructed local draft boards to defer the college bound, undergraduates and postgraduates: "The Selective Service System," it said, "has the responsibility to deliver manpower to the armed forces in such a manner as to reduce to a minimum any adverse effect upon the national health, safety, interest and progress."

Forgotten now is that in the beginning Congress and the American people were almost all behind our containment effort in Vietnam. The young enlisted volunteer or draftee had not had much time to form any complicated theories about our Vietnam commitment. He accepted the tradition of military service passed on to him by the popular culture and by President John F. Kennedy's ringing words: "Let every nation know, whether it wishes us well or ill, that we shall pay any price, bear any burden, meet any hardship, support any friend, oppose any foe, to assure the survival and success of liberty."

Eventually, of course, as the war dragged on and the casualties mounted, our commitment was re-examined, and for all the well-known reasons we were forced to conclude that the courageous wheel of Communist containment that we had fashioned after World War II had finally developed a badly broken spoke. Thus college deferments took on a new significance.

Most of the young American enlisted men who served in Vietnam were not college prospects at the time they entered the service. Those who could have qualified for college probably did not have the funds or motivation. Many of the 17- and 18-year-olds were simply late in maturing; they were struggling through or dropping out of high school or—if high school graduates—they had tested poorly for college entrance. Yet, as it turned out, the percentage of Vietnam veterans who subsequently applied for the GI Bill was higher than after either World War II or Korea.

The DOD database provides no civilian or military educational levels for Vietnam casualties. However, the DOD does provide general levels for all enlisted men across all the services during the Vietnam era. The figures show that on average 65 percent of white enlisted men and 60 percent of black enlisted men were high school graduates. Only 5 to 10 percent of enlisted men in the combat units were estimated to have had some college, and less than 1 percent were college graduates.

The Armed Forces Qualification Test (AFQT) was given to all enlisted men. The resulting aptitude scores were used to classify entrants into four categories and determine their subsequent assignments. On average, 43 percent of white enlisted entrants placed in categories I and II (scored 65-100) and 57 percent in categories III and IV (scored 10-64). For blacks, however, only 7 percent placed in categories I and II and 93 percent placed in categories III and IV. In civilian life, poor aptitude testing can have a tremendous negative impact—whether for college placement or for simple job advancement. In the military it can be somewhat more deadly. John Kennedy said that life is unfair. True enough, but many of the surviving Vietnam casualty families would reply that the ultimate unfairness is death at an early age, in a land far from home, for reasons not clearly defined.

Adding to the problem was "Project 100,000." Lower end category IVs (those who scored below 20 on the AFQT test) were usually rejected for service. But in 1966 President Johnson and Secretary of Defense McNamara decided to institute Project 100,000, which would allow category IV personnel to enter the military. This, they felt, would offer these men the opportunity to get remedial training in the service and then be able to compete successfully when they returned to civilian life. Many high-ranking military men (including General William C. Westmoreland, the U.S. commander in Vietnam) opposed this program, feeling that the effectiveness of some units was reduced and that fellow soldiers were sometimes put in greater jeopardy by these less mentally capable personnel. Of the 336,111 men who were phased into the service (mostly the Army) under Project 100,000, 2,072 were killed. This amounted to 4.1 percent of all enlisted casualties in Vietnam.

Thus we can see that the "channeling" philosophy continued within the armed forces. Through the AFQT process the men scoring in the higher categories were more likely to be "channeled" into further specialized training and eventually assigned to non-combat technical and administrative units.

Having said that, however, the widely held notion that the poor served and died in Vietnam while the rich stayed home is simply not true. A more precise equation would be that the college bound stayed home while the non-college bound served and died. The idea that American enlisted dead were made up largely of society's poverty-stricken misfits is a terrible slander to their memory and to the solid middle-class and working-class families of this country who provided the vast majority of our casualties. Certainly some who died came from poor and broken families in the urban ghettos and barrios, or were from dirt-poor farm homes in the South and Midwest. And more's the pity, because many of them were trying to escape and didn't make it.

Indeed, recent studies tend to refute what had been the perceived wisdom of social scientists and other commentators that our Vietnam dead came overwhelmingly from the poor communities. A Massachusetts Institute of Technology (MIT) study released in October of 1992 found that our Vietnam casualties were only marginally greater from the economically lowest 50 percent of our communities (31 Vietnam deaths per 100,000 of population) when compared with the economically highest 50 percent (26 deaths per 100,000 of population). The class aspects of Vietnam service had to do more with the obvious unfairness of sending very young non-college candidates to serve and die while the college bound stayed home. It became particularly reprehensible when the stay-at-homes sometimes became the most visible protesters against the war.

It is instructive to read the literature of the war—the letters home from those who died, the novels and narrative accounts of those who served in combat and returned. They often reveal a typically warm American family atmosphere. They refer to older or younger siblings who are either in or on their way to college. And they often show a heartbreakingly wry sense of humor with the same sensibilities as their college-bound peers.

It forces us to the conclusion that many of the names on the Wall were kids who just couldn't quite get it together in high school, who perhaps were a little late in maturing intellectually and, even had they wanted to, didn't have the resources or the guile to get into college and out of the way when the war came.

What will be the evolving historical judgment for those names on the Wall? With the end of the Cold War, many now believe that at its outset the Vietnam War was a quite honorable extension of our ultimately successful policy of Communist containment; that our effort in Vietnam became flawed because of political and strategic failures having nothing to do with those who served there; and that these young Americans were asked by three presidents and six Congresses to give up their lives so that freedom would have a better chance everywhere in the world. As one stands before the Wall, one feels that no other judgment is acceptable to their living memory. As Maya Ling Lin, the architect of the Wall, has said: "It was as if the black-brown earth were polished and made into an interface between the sunny world and the quiet dark world beyond that we cannot enter. . . . The names would become the memorial. There was no need to embellish."

Her Parents' Legacy

By Wendy Loughlin

It was the Saturday after Veteran's Day in Washington, D.C., and at least 200 people had gathered near the edge of the Mall to file past the polished granite wall of the Vietnam Veterans Memorial. The black expanse was morbidly beautiful in the afternoon sun, reflecting the faces of the visitors who stood before it. I walked the length of the monument, part of a crowd as silent as the stone.

Mementos adorned the Wall all along its base: poems, flowers, American flags. A little girl skipped forward to look at an Army shirt that lay folded on the ground. "Mom, what's this all about?" she asked. Her mother was crying too hard to respond.

The Wall slopes upward toward the middle to represent the steady increase of deaths that marked the progression of the Vietnam War. At the place where the slab reaches its highest level, I saw a piece of white cardboard propped against the stone. A photograph of a young man in fatigues, and that man's obituary, were pasted to the bottom of the sign. Written above, a message: "After 22 years, I'm going to finally say good-bye."

Twenty-two years spans almost the entire length of my life. I cannot remember this war that ended when I was a child. The body bags, the evening news, the protests, the grief—it is all remote to me, all a piece of history, like the Great Depression or the New Frontier.

And yet, as I looked at the 58,000 names etched on that wall, as I witnessed the tears and the emotions of the people who gathered there, I felt a kind of link to this war that I do not feel for any other element of history that precedes my birth. There are pictures of my mother, as young as I am today, with peace symbols painted on her cheeks; there are my father's dog tags, hidden in his dresser drawer. I do not know the man and the woman they were back then, but somehow, that man and that woman are a part of me. And if their generation was shaped and changed by the Vietnam War, my generation continues to feel the effects of that war, some 25 years after its finish.

For my generation, Vietnam touches us in fragments of emotion rather than overwhelming us with one intense feeling. It comes to us through songs, pictures, film footage. And, as we look back at it through our parents' eyes, it comes to us as a memory that, although we never owned it, is nonetheless striking and vivid. So, like our parents, we regard that time with confusion. We see our fathers, sent to fight in a war they did not understand; we see the loss of young lives, which in retrospect seem squandered. But we also see a movement that rocked administrations and made people listen. And we realize that our parents were players in a process that brought about change and gave power to the young.

Still, the legacy of that war is often difficult for my generation to decipher, and difficult to accept. Laurie Liddell, a 23-year-old student in public policy, said that, thinking about Vietnam, she feels a sense of bitterness. "I think our parents, because of their experience with that war, instilled in us a great feeling of distrust and corruption," she said. "We look at our government with suspicious eyes. We even look at each other that way."

Liddell also believes that much of the so-called apathy of the younger generation stems in part from the memory of Vietnam. Many children of the baby boomers react to their parents' past with indecisiveness. "We are a bunch of moderates," she said of her generation. "We are afraid to be left-wing, but unwilling to be conservative. That's why we are the generation X. The Vietnam era left us confused."

But not all young people feel that way. Elizabeth Madigan, a 24-year-old paralegal in New York City, said she thinks the Vietnam legacy has a lot to do with freedom. "Our parents felt they had the right to stand up to their government, to question the way things were," she said. "I think that has, in turn, given us a lot more freedom in our time, despite some of the pessimism and negativity we may have to face."

Still, my generation, born and raised in post-Vietnam America, has always known that pessimism. It is hard for us to comprehend the hope and optimism of the "American Dream" idea that surrounded our parents' childhood—a notion that was later contradicted by the war in Vietnam. My father told me of growing up in the idyllic 1950s, a time marked by a nationalistic adoration of the United States that had been fostered and nourished in the afterglow of World War II. "I just can't explain to you what it was like then," he told me, knowing that, to my generation, such unquestioning faith in country and government is an archaic idea.

Still, it was partly the serenity of the Eisenhower years that made the coming turbulence so hard to bear. "We grew up believing we were the best, we took it for granted," my father said. "All that changed with Vietnam." In retrospect, the war appears as the starting point for a slow disputation of those ideals set forth at the end of World War II. And the whole period leading up to Vietnam seems like a steady flow into the turbulent 1960s. As my father observed, "1945 kicked us into the future—into the brick wall of Vietnam."

Part of the betrayal of Vietnam lay in a discrepancy, for the baby boomers, between the things they had been taught and believed in as children and the horrible, often unbelievable things that came with the war. My father said that, despite his initial doubts about Vietnam, he still wanted to serve. "I loved my country, and it was the right thing to do," he said. "I was patriotic, I believed in America. It was just so hard to accept that what we were doing over there might be wrong. So I did my duty."

I do not think the Vietnam War shattered the American Dream, but I do believe it did a lot to alter that concept, and to change the self-image of America. Now, more than 35 years after the war began, I can only imagine the kind of patriotism that made many young men willing to go to Vietnam. The notion of fighting a hard and fearful war for duty and honor seems almost dated and strange, though I know that part of me mourns those lost convictions. Maybe it's because our parents paid such a high price for those beliefs that my generation has strayed from them. We do not want that kind of betrayal, that kind of mental injury, to infest our youth the way it did theirs. We are unwilling. That unwillingness is one of the things our parents taught us.

My mother remembered the war as it looked to her then. She was a teenager, listening to the chants of protesters and watching the death toll mount on her television screen. "I was terrified," she remembered. "So much was out of our control. But at the same time, we had power. We were going to make a change. It was a revolution." I understand her meaning now, though I don't believe the movements of the 1960s truly brought a revolution. And I know that she must not believe that, either.

I think there is a certain sadness among the baby boomers today when they realize that the ideals of their "Woodstock Nation" have not come to pass. My generation senses that. Referring to the Janis Joplin song "Me and Bobby McGee," Elizabeth Madigan said, "That line: 'Freedom's just another word for nothing left to lose'—well, I think that came back to slap them in the face." And Laurie Liddell noted that the boomers' authority status within the system they once hated must be hard for them to accept. "They thought it was a revolution, but where did it take them? They said, 'Don't trust anyone over 30.' Well, 30 has come and gone for them, and I don't think they know what to do now."

Still, my mother thinks a lot that is good can be attributed to the era of the counterculture. "I think we gave our children the power to ask why, to look before they leap," she said. "We want informed choices for our children. We don't want them to have to take everything for granted, like we did, and then watch it backfire."

So we take nothing for granted, and perhaps we are grateful for the heightened awareness brought about by our parents' coming of age in a deeply divided nation. But today, when negative journalism is the cornerstone of society and the president's sexual behavior warrants more coverage than his legislative activities, we may long for some of the lost innocence and hope of our parents' youth. My generation knows no John Kennedys.

The war itself remains the sticking point for most Americans today, regardless of generation. And although I cannot personally remember the feeling of that time—I did not experience the draft, or the loss of a brother, husband, father or son—still, I have come to understand how that war changed our society and, as a result, our lives. If analysis of the war is full of guesses, confusion and half-truths, this fact remains clearly intact.

While it was happening, Americans debated whether the war was right or wrong. I grew up believing the debate was over, but I have realized how it still rages within. Robert McNamara sheds crocodile tears in a New Yorker drawing that accompanied an article on his book about Vietnam. He says now that the war was wrong. But what does that really mean? And how much vindication can anyone afford, even today? I read that some Vietnam veterans were suing McNamara, claiming that his book had caused many veterans "a lot of anguish." I don't suppose he anticipated that anguish; he may have hoped all those vets would forgive him. But sometimes, thinking about this, I can't shake the feeling that perhaps it's my job to forgive him; that, in the end, forgiveness for the war is the obligation of my generation.

Liddell believes our generation takes on the responsibility of avoidance. "There's that old notion that if you don't learn from your mistakes, you are bound to repeat them," she said. "And if you don't learn from history's mistakes, history will, in fact, repeat itself. We have to stop that repetition." If Vietnam was a mistake, whose was it? Maybe there is no one to blame, no way to know, no one there. But my generation knows that we don't ever want to let it happen again.

So many questions remain unanswered. As young now as our parents were then, there are those in my generation who are no less desperate to find the answers. It's hard to say why Vietnam remains such a forceful presence in our lives. But I think we know that, good or bad, obvious or subtle, we learn something from that time, and we carry it with us.

This is one of the reasons why so many young Americans today visit the Wall. Standing before the memorial, we face 58,000 names—lives cut short, possibilities ended, senselessness etched in stone. But the polished granite wall presents us with another image as well—that of our own faces, reflected across the names. We know the Vietnam era left our nation with a void of hope. Perhaps we need to fill that void with ourselves.

In the end, the emotional connection between my generation and the Vietnam War, like the Wall itself, represents a memorial to the trials of that time. We cannot, on our own, remember the war. But we have been raised, taught and influenced by a generation for whom that war was the single most defining element of their coming of age. Our parents give us many things, not the least of which are their memories.

A Trip to Vietnam

By Colonel David H. Hackworth, U.S. Army (ret.)

All of us—nearly 3 million American veterans—are scarred in some way by the Vietnam War. It altered our lives and our country forever. Two decades have passed since our forces pulled out of that war-ravaged land, yet hundreds of thousands of men and women who went there in their youth still cannot deep-six their emotional baggage in middle age.

Despite presidential proclamations such as George Bush's post–Desert Storm comment, "By God, we've kicked the Vietnam syndrome once and for all," Vietnam just won't go away. Shrinks and scholars can explain it but can't cure it. As with a head-throbbing hangover, sometimes the hair-of-the-dog treatment is the only way to stop the pain.

I drank a long, cool glass of Vietnam's hair-of-the-dog brew in July 1993 when I flew into Saigon from Bangkok on a rattling and wheezing 30-year-old Russian-made passenger plane that to my amazement landed safely at Tan Son Nhut airport. (Northwest flies direct; it's easier on the wallet and blood pressure.) I had that helicopter-combat-assault-into-a-hot-LZ feeling as the plane landed: adrenaline wildly pumping, gut white-knuckle tight, head LSD high and body ready for "fight or flight."

Communist dudes in uniform, wearing green pith helmets

with little red stars, and faces that used to be on the mean end of AK-47s didn't make things much better. My hands acted as if they had palsy; my mouth was desert dry and my heart was going far faster than its 63-year-old speed limit. Two things happened just before I self-imploded that let the air out of my fear like a burst of M-16 slugs into a jeep tire. The Vietnamese-American woman in front of me was officiously told by the immigration officer that her Yankee passport was not in order. She slipped a $20 bill into it and passed it back. He smiled, gave it a stamp of approval, and she moved out. And an aircraft bunker near the runway (formerly the foxhole for a U.S. Northrop F-5 fighter) had a 10-foot-by-6-foot peace sign. Its yellow-on-black paint is faded now, but its meaning was "Good morning, Vietnam" clear.

Like an incoming rocket, I got the event's message: nothing had changed in Saigon, aka Ho Chi Minh City, except the color of the new ruler's flag and that our war was a bad war and, in the end, few of us wanted to fight it.

The terminal is hospital clean now and blissfully air-conditioned. As I stepped outside, the midafternoon monsoon rains bucketed down. Again, no change. It rained the July day I left. I thought, "I wonder if it has been raining nonstop for the past 22 years?" For many of the older citizens of that jaded, inscrutable city, the rain has not stopped since the Communists won the war. But the population has doubled since the war's end, and the majority of the people don't remember the war, our good and bad deeds, or the Saigon regime. For them, Communists are the new guys on the block and are to be tolerated, at least for now.

The free-jazz-concertlike crowd at the airport's entrance was made up of mostly young people. "You American, I love Americans," I heard again and again from teeny-boppers with ear-to-ear smiles who seemingly got off, as their parents did a generation before, by rubbing the hair on my arms. Farther out in the bush, where the white man's visit is rare, many kids looked at me as if I were a spaceman fresh out of a UFO. But everyone, from city dwellers to rice paddy people, displayed a genuinely warm welcome, love and good feeling. They were not hung up on the past. For the next three weeks I got this glad-to-see-you reception, from the Mekong Delta to Hanoi. I found no bitterness, rancor or hatred even from former Viet Cong fighters who used to hunt me and whom I did my best to kill during my five-year Vietnam hunting expedition. Most of the people of Vietnam hold no grudges. To them, the war is over, even though our politicians haven't worked this out.

When I left Vietnam, the North and the South were under arms and pummeling each other with every killing device and machine their Soviet and American big daddies could give them. Now the cannons are quiet and the skies are empty except for the occasional passenger jet. Tan Son Nhut, once the busiest airport in the world, with a fighter or bomber taking off every minute, gets about the same traffic as big, blue-sky Kalispell, Montana.

For me, the end of the fighting and dying was the most striking contrast between the two Vietnams—the one at war and the one today that's at peace. It's unified now, reasonably self-sufficient and, after 100 years of struggle, free of foreign influence. It's no longer under the gun. It's under the plow, the hoe and the wheel, and it looks like it's about to explode into the 21st century.

Saigon's streets are still a sea of people, bikes, motorbikes and litter. Soviet-style Communist bungling sank the Vietnamese economy, which is now at the bottom of the developing world's trash heap. Sadly, the Tu Du Street ticky-tacky bars with their "I-love-you-too-much" tea girls are gone. They've been replaced with little shops that sell everything from "old" Zippo lighters made in the 1990s to fake G.I. dog tags and real helicopter clocks. Beautiful girls in graceful *ao dais* still ride their bikes with their long black hair blowing in the wind.

Corruption survived big time. Pickpockets and pimps, beggars and bandits still work the streets. I couldn't go three steps without hearing: "You want young girl or young boy? Fifteen, clean and very sexy." Cycle drivers whispered their pitch: "Steam baths, massage parlors, grass a dollar a bag." The whores ply the streets on motorbikes, working the oldest profession with Honda mobility.

Saigon, like most major cities, is booming. The skies over Saigon and Hanoi are filled with building cranes, and construction workers hustle day and night slapping together tourist hotels and new homes and offices for foreign capitalist businessmen who are spearheading Vietnam's first welcomed invasion. Walking through the city is like being in the center of a beehive. It seems as if all of Saigon's 4 million folks spend all their time in these buzzing bazaars, bargain hunting for the best deal. The energy they put out is on the wild side. The small stores are stacked from floor to ceiling with TVs, sewing machines and other "high-tech" stuff, all from Asia; nothing new made in the U.S.A.

The Yankee dollar is the common street money, and U.S. credit cards are accepted at most of the class act (read expensive) joints. Keep in mind, cash is king, and Saigon's pickpockets are princes. The place is dead cheap as long as you stay out of the clip joints, run mostly by non-Vietnamese. Hotels run from $10 a night to $80 for first-class accommodations like Saigon's Continental Hotel—but bring your own mosquito net for the cheapies.

It was scary at first driving down the roads out of Saigon, which used to be full-pucker streets without joy. The 19 million gallons of defoliant we dumped on Vietnam has mostly washed away, and the countryside is again lush green and botanical garden beautiful. I visited My Tho, Can Tho, Cao Lanh, Cai Be and Cai Lai, places in the delta where I spent several years. The paddies were rich with rice and the trees loaded with fruit. Every inch of ground is now being used. Nothing, but nothing, is wasted, and the people all move at double time, as if they'll be late for pay call.

My old 9th Division firebase, "Danger," which sat near Cai Be on the edge of Highway 4, is now a busy gas station. Mango and banana trees stand where my cannons, machine guns and barbed wire were. I met former Viet Cong Private Nguyen Van At there. He lost his leg to one of my sharpshooters in 1969. He said, "I welcome you in peace; but if Americans come back with guns, we'll go at it again."

I talked to a dozen other former Viet Cong hard-core soldiers while I was near Danger. All welcomed me with open arms and warm hearts. Together we visited the places where we once met in battle. There was much laughter and no hard feelings. Few traces of our desperate struggles are left. Had I not brought military maps, I would never have found those spots. Now the bunkers and booby traps are gone, replaced with trees and plants that produce things for the living; 2,000-pound bomb craters are about the only signs of the war, and they are now filled with fish and ducks.

Throughout my journey in Vietnam, I saw almost no sign of Vietnam's 30-year war unless I was at one of the "War Worlds" such as the "Tunnels of Cu Chi," where a uniformed guide takes the visitor through the tunnels that once hid battalions of Viet Cong. T-shirts sporting the logo of a beautiful black-pajama-clad girl with an AK-47 are available, as is time for target practice at a Fort Benning-like range where an AK-47 can be fired, for a buck a round. The war museums in Saigon and Hanoi are filled with gear we once used, and a tour up the Ho Chi Minh Trail can be arranged with one of the many tour companies that take vets to their old battlefields. The exception to the rule that all damage done during the war is no longer visible is the cemeteries. Each district maintains well-kept mini-Arlingtons. Three million Vietnamese died in the war.

After two days, I didn't have that I'm-walking-through-a-minefield feeling. All fear was gone. My head knew I was in a Communist state where freedom is meted out with an iron hand, yet it didn't seem to be the heavy, repressive hand I've seen in other Red lands before the Iron Curtain disappeared. Authority seems to be low-keyed, as are uniforms and weapons, and the people of the South seem to take their new liberators as they did the Chinese, French, Japanese and Americans—as casual visitors to a land that has a history of absorbing their masters. My impression is that Coca-Cola will eventually win over communism.

I liked Hanoi better than the Southern cities. I saw no beggars, pimps or littered streets. Everything was Saturday morning inspection neat. The people there are dead serious and hard workers. They're more like Connecticut Yankees, while the Southerners are laid back like Florida Keys crackers.

While in Hanoi, I talked to the Americans and their Vietnamese counterparts from the POW recovery teams and confirmed what I have long felt: that it is highly unlikely American POWs are still alive anywhere in Southeast Asia. Also, I saw a photo of Jane Fonda taken during the war in a North Vietnamese Army anti-aircraft gun position. My guide said she was "a national people's hero." Jane, like many of the rest of us, carries her own guilt from that war, when she let the idealism of a 25-year-old override common sense.

Colonel Dang Vet Mai was the commander of the 502nd Viet Cong Main Force Battalion for eight years. He fought almost non-stop from 1950 to 1990, first the French, then the Americans and the Saigon regime. He hung up his AK after whipping the Cambodian Khmer Rouge in 1990. His hardcore bunch of mothers and my 9th Division battalion had a few stiff encounters. They were damn good fighters. Mai and I spent a day going over past battlefields and tactics and talking about war fighting. I asked Mai if his soldiers—many of whom had decades of combat because their

DEROS (date eligible to return from overseas; i.e., return date) didn't happen until the war was over—had stress problems similar to those of American soldiers. He said, "I know of not one case. We have no guilt. Our cause was just. U.S. stress problem is from guilt." Mai is a rawhide-tough former soldier, not a shrink. Allowing for Communist propaganda, Mai no doubt has a point, but I'm sure there are former Vietnamese soldiers who fought for the Red flag and who suffer from combat fatigue, which is what posttraumatic stress disorder was called in other wars.

A trip to Vietnam could bury ghosts, heal wounds that have been hurting since the war, and get rid of a lot of guilt, shame and hang-ups for those who actually did the killing and those who served in supporting roles. In a nonhostile environment, the people aren't gooks but human beings who didn't have the advantage of being born in Carmel, California, and who are trying like hell to claw their way out of the bottom of a Third World hole.

After we'd spent a day together looking at killing fields and refighting the war, former Viet Cong Captain Nam Hoa told me: "The people of America and Vietnam will soon hold hands and get on with their future. Our governments will follow."

Thousands of vets have made the trip, and all those I have interviewed say that returning cleared their heads, purged their souls and slayed a lot of dragons. Your visit will speed that process, help end any guilt you're toting.

Try it soon, before Vietnam becomes another Thailand and the golden arches of McDonald's replace all the century-old soup stands on the sides of the roads.

I'm glad I did. I was able to leave a 747-size load of baggage at Tan Son Nhut's front gate on the way out.

Vietnam War Web Sites

THE HISTORY NET	http://www.thehistorynet.com
The Vietnam Center	http://www.ttu.edu/~vietnam http://www.ttu.edu/~vietnam/ namlinks.htm
Encyclopedia of the Vietnam War	http://www.vietnamwar- reference.com
The Cyberspace Military Cemetery of the Republic of Vietnam	http://www.vietmemorial.org
The Army Historical Foundation	http://www.armyhistoryfnd.org
U.S. Army Center of Military History	http://www.army.mil/cmh-pg

The H-War Net	http://www.h-net.msu.edu/~war/
The Virtual Wall	http://www.thevirtualwall.org
Library of Congress	http://www.loc.gov http://www.americaslibrary.com
Casualties	http://www.emh.everton.com/ vietnam.htm http://www.nara.gov/nara/ electronic/korvnsta.html
Boat People	http://www.boatpeople.com
LBJ Presidential Library	http://www.lbjlib.utexas.edu/ shwv/link-faq.html http://www.lbjlib.utexas.edu/ shwv/shwvhome.html
Vasser College (Includes Hanoi Archive Material)	http://www.vassar.edu/vietnam/ index.html
Clemson University (Prof. Edwin Moise Bibliography)	http://hubcap.clemson.edu/ ~eemoise/bibliography.html
UC Berkeley	http://www.ci.berkeley. ca.us:80/vvm/
Canadian Forces College Information Service	http://www.cfcsc.dnd.ca/links/ milhist/viet.html

Vietnam Veterans
Home Page
http://www.vietvet.org/

Vietnam Veterans
Against the War
http://www.prairienet.org/vvaw/

Vietnam on Line
(Companion to PBS TV
Series)
http://www.pbs.org/wgbh/pages/
amex/vietnam/index.html

Vietnam Electronic
Library
http://members.aol.com/
warlib.vel/vel1.htm

Women Veterans
http://userpages.aug.com/
captbarb/femvetsnam.html

Seton Hall Univ.
(Photo Collection)
http://icarus.shu.edu/
gallery/V_Portfolio/

U.S. Army Vietnam
Combat Art
http://members.aol.com/
jimm844224/vietart1.html

Spartacus Educational
http://www.spartacus.schoolnet.
co.uk/vietintro.htm

Staples High School
http://204.249.212.251/shsira/
Vietnam.html

Books
http://www.tavbooks.com/
vietnam.shtml

OTHER VIETNAM WEB SITES

The Vietnam War Resource Guide
http://members.aol.com/veterans/warlib6v.htm

Vietnam War History Research Files
http://members.aol.com/warlibrary/vwhrf.htm

University of Victoria Vietnam War History
http://web.uvic.ca/hrd/history.learn-teach/VietnamPage.htm

http://kalital.polisci.yale.edu/

http://www.panix.com/~tegtmeie/shwv/archlink.html

http://wwwgeog.ssn.flinders.edu.au/Indochina/Vietnam/History/shwvhome.html

http://members.aol.com/jimm844224/vietart1.html

http://www.oakton.edu/~wittman/

http://drn.zippo.com/news-bin/wwwnews?soc.history.war.vietnam

This list has been compiled with the gracious assistance of:

Mr. Mike Unsworth, University of Michigan Libraries

Lt. Col. Jay Carafano, Editor, *Joint Forces Quarterly*